Monstrous Women in Comics

Monstrous Women in Comics

Edited by
Samantha Langsdale
and Elizabeth Rae Coody

University Press of Mississippi / Jackson

The University Press of Mississippi is the scholarly publishing agency of
the Mississippi Institutions of Higher Learning: Alcorn State University,
Delta State University, Jackson State University, Mississippi State University,
Mississippi University for Women, Mississippi Valley State University,
University of Mississippi, and University of Southern Mississippi.

www.upress.state.ms.us

The University Press of Mississippi is a member
of the Association of University Presses.

Copyright © 2020 by University Press of Mississippi
All rights reserved

First printing 2020
∞

Library of Congress Cataloging-in-Publication Data

Names: Langsdale, Samantha, editor. | Coody, Elizabeth Rae, editor.
Title: Monstrous women in comics / edited by Samantha Langsdale and
Elizabeth Rae Coody.
Other titles: Horror and monstrosity studies series.
Description: Jackson: University Press of Mississippi, 2020. | Series:
Horror and monstrosity studies series | Includes bibliographical
references and index.
Identifiers: LCCN 2019052202 (print) | LCCN 2019052203 (ebook) | ISBN
9781496827623 (hardback) | ISBN 9781496827630 (trade paperback) | ISBN
9781496827647 (epub) | ISBN 9781496827654 (epub) | ISBN 9781496827661
(pdf) | ISBN 9781496827678 (pdf)
Subjects: LCSH: Comic books, strips, etc.—History and criticism. | Comic
books, strips, etc.—Social aspects. | BISAC: LITERARY CRITICISM /
Comics & Graphic Novels | LCGFT: Essays. | Literary criticism.
Classification: LCC PN6714 .M66 2020 (print) | LCC PN6714 (ebook) | DDC
741.5/3522—dc23
LC record available at https://lccn.loc.gov/2019052202
LC ebook record available at https://lccn.loc.gov/2019052203

British Library Cataloging-in-Publication Data available

Contents

Acknowledgments.. ix

Introduction.. 3
Samantha Langsdale and Elizabeth Rae Coody

Part 1: The Origins, Agency, and Paradoxes of Monstrous Women

1   Rewriting to Control: How the Origins of Harley Quinn, Wonder Woman, and Mary Magdalene Matter to Women's Perceived Power 15
Elizabeth Rae Coody

2   Exploring the Monstrous Feminist Frame: Marvel's She-Hulk as Male-Centric Postfeminist Discourse 31
J. Richard Stevens

3   "There Is More to Me Than Just Hunger": Female Monsters and Liminal Spaces in *Monstress* and *Pretty Deadly* 51
Ayanni C. H. Cooper

Part 2: The Body as Monstrous

4   The (Un)Remarkable Fatness of Valiant's *Faith* 69
Stefanie Snider

5   New and Improved? Disability and Monstrosity in Gail Simone's *Batgirl* 84
Charlotte Johanne Fabricius

6   Horrible Victorians: Interrogating Power, Sex, and Gender in *InSEXts* 99
    Keri Crist-Wagner

Part 3: Childbearing as Monstrous

7   Kicking Ass in Flip-Flops: Inappropriate/d Generations
    and Monstrous Pregnancy in Comics Narratives..................... 115
    Jeannie Ludlow

8   The Monstrous Portrayal of the Maternal Bolivian Chola
    in Contemporary Comics 135
    Marcela Murillo

9   The Monstrous "Mother" in Moto Hagio's *Marginal*: The Posthuman,
    the Human, and the Bioengineered Uterus.......................... 152
    Tomoko Kuribayashi

Part 4: Monsters of Childhood

10 SeDUCKtress! Magica De Spell, Scrooge McDuck, and the Avuncular
    Anthropomorphism of Carl Barks's Midcentury Disney Comics 171
    Daniel F. Yezbick

11 On the Edge of 1990s Japan: Kyoko Okazaki
    and the Horror of Adolescence 191
    Novia Shih-Shan Chen and Sho Ogawa

12 Chinese Snake Woman Resurfaces in Comics:
    Considering the Case Study of *Calabash Brothers*................. 207
    Jing Zhang

Part 5: Taking On the Role of Monster

13 Monochromatic Teats, Teeth, and Tentacles:
    Monstrous Visual Rhetoric in Stephen L. Stern
    and Christopher Steininger's *Beowulf: The Graphic Novel* 223
    Justin Wigard

14 Beauty and Her B(r)east(s): Monstrosity and College Women
    in *The Jaguar* 239
    Pauline J. Reynolds and Sara Durazo-DeMoss

15 UFO (Unusual Female Other) Sightings in *Saucer Country/State*:
    Metaphors of Identity and Presidential Politics....................... 257
    Christina M. Knopf

    About the Contributors 275

    Index 281

Acknowledgments

The origin of this book, like that of so many monsters, begins in conversation with the sacred. In May 2016, Ken Koltun-Fromm of Haverford College hosted a two-day symposium that brought together scholars from all disciplines to analyze "the visual registers of religious expression across a broad spectrum of religious traditions." It was here, at the Comics and Sacred Texts symposium, that the two editors of this volume met and where Sam Langsdale first unleashed her fascination with monstrous women in comics. The reception of Sam's presentation from colleagues was so positive and supportive that she took the combination of monstrous women and comics back to her home institution, the University of North Texas, and began to plan an interdisciplinary conference. A year after Comics and Sacred Texts, Sam—with the support of the Philosophy and Religion Department at UNT—hosted Monstrous Women in Comics: An Interdisciplinary Conference on Women in Comics and Graphic Novels. As the event unfolded, it quickly became apparent that it was not only a conference but the beginning of a community of scholars committed to exploring sequential art in new and fascinating ways. By the end of the weekend, Sam, together with Elizabeth Coody, set to work rallying that community to create a little monster of their own—this very book. We are so proud of this project, and even prouder of the monstrous friendships that have been forged in its making.

Sam would like to express her deep gratitude to Ken Koltun-Fromm for his work on Comics and Sacred Texts, without which she would not have made lasting friendships with her coeditor Elizabeth, Jeff Richey, Joshua Plencner, and A. David Lewis. She is also so grateful to Assaf Gamzou for his support, encouragement, editorial guidance, and sound advice. Thanks are owed to Doug Anderson for his willingness to imagine philosophy in monstrous ways such that the Monstrous Women conference was made possible. Sam is also grateful for the amazing women who served on the conference committee, and who are her dear friends—Jacqueline Vickery, Raina Joines, Agatha Beins, and Clarissa Pulley. Many thanks are owed to Michael Thompson and Nancy

Ellis, both of whom provided support and helped the conference run smoothly. Finally, Sam would like to thank her family for tolerating all of her strange scholarly obsessions, and her partner, Adam Benkato, who lends not only his support for all of Sam's monstrous projects but also, quite frequently, his impeccable copyediting skills.

Elizabeth shares Sam's gratitude to everyone who planned and participated in the Comics and Sacred Texts and Monstrous Women conferences. Friendly scholarly gatherings around topics that push us are the future of our fields, and Elizabeth is delighted when someone else sets the table. She thanks Sam for allowing her to tag along in the editing process as a faithful Igor to her crafty Dr. Frankenstein. She would also like to thank her partner, David Scott, who ensures that she watches every horror movie worth a watch and engages her in deep philosophical conversation on each one.

Both editors wish to thank the keynote speaker of the Monstrous Women conference, Carol Tilley, for her insightful scholarship, for her friendship, and for inspiring all of us to continue comics research. We would like to thank Elizabeth LaPensée and Jonathan R. Thunder for allowing us to share their work on *Deer Woman* both at the Monstrous Women conference and on the cover of this volume. We are grateful to the editorial staff at the University Press of Mississippi, particularly Vijay Shah and Lisa McMurtray. And lastly, we are so grateful for all of our contributors, whose intellectual curiosity and sound scholarship have brought this monstrous book roaring into the world.

Monstrous Women in Comics

Introduction

Samantha Langsdale and Elizabeth Rae Coody

Monsters are everywhere these days: they drive the plot in popular TV shows like *Stranger Things* (2016), they fill the pages of award-winning novels like Brian Kirk's *We Are Monsters* (2015), and they are resurrected again and again in Hollywood blockbusters like the *Jurassic Park* franchise. Far from being a novelty, however, monstrosity is one of the most fundamental sites from which cultures make meaning.[1] In creating, identifying, studying, and describing monsters, a society makes apparent its anxieties and fears, as well as its ideals and desires. Monsters are figures that lurk in the margins and so by contrast help to illuminate the center; they are the embodiment of abnormality and so summon the definition of normalcy by virtue of everything they are not. Monsters are receptacles of taboos, and so while they often inspire horror, they also indicate forbidden desires. Monsters are slippery and dangerous because of their ability to transcend boundaries, often acting as unwelcome reminders of how very fragile those boundaries are. "The monster is difference made flesh," whether that flesh is real or imaginary (Cohen 1996, 7). That is, the discursive framing of the monstrous—be it through text or visual culture—almost always relates to material differences such that certain types of people are made to have less livable lives. As *Monster Theory* scholar Jeffrey Jerome Cohen argues, political and ideological difference within a given society can work to transform "an unwilling participant in a science experiment" into a real, marked, aberrant subject (8).

The authors of this volume are specifically interested in patriarchal cultural contexts, wherein men are assumed to be representative of the normative, universal subject such that women frequently become monsters—particularly those women who "overstep the boundaries of [their] gender [roles]" (Cohen 1996, 10). Also of interest is the fact that the coding of woman as monstrous, and the monster as dangerously evocative of women/femininity/the female, is overwhelmingly exacerbated by the intersection of gender with other markers of identity like sexuality, race, nationality, and disability. Cohen describes this process of compounding:

> One kind of difference becomes another as the normative categories of gender, sexuality, national identity, and ethnicity slide together like the imbricated circles of a Venn diagram, abjecting from the center that which becomes the monster. This violent foreclosure erects a self-validating, Hegelian master/slave dialectic that naturalizes the subjugation of one cultural body by another by writing the body excluded from personhood and agency as in every way different, monstrous. (11)

Again, this type of knowledge production matters because even when the outcome is text based, or observable in visual culture, it is necessary to recall "the real violence these debasing representations enact" (11). Thus, to analyze monstrous women is not only to examine discursive constructions, or to solely explore textual terrain, but also to witness how those constructions correspond to women's real material experiences. The cover of this volume, for example, is evocative of how cultural definitions of women as "less than human" can allow and justify monstrous treatment of them. This image, by Jonathan R. Thunder, comes from *Deer Woman*, a vignette by Elizabeth LaPensée (2015). Deer Woman is a character common to several tribes and nations in North America who traditionally appears as a beautiful woman with hooves instead of feet. In LaPensée's vignette, she becomes a means of violent retribution for wrongs done to Native women. Recently, LaPensée collected more stories about the titular character for an edited anthology (2017) that reflect on the varied ways Indigenous women are turned into monsters because of having been treated monstrously. These "myths" are indicative of truth; Indigenous women across North America suffer staggeringly high rates of violence with up to 84 percent reporting that they have experienced some form of violence in their lifetimes (Rosay 2016). But monsters like Deer Woman are not solely figures of victimization—as our cover image suggests, the intersections of gender, ethnicity, and monstrosity may also prove empowering. Deer Woman is a reminder that sharp hooves and antlers may be monstrous, but they can also be useful to the oppressed.

We believe that it is crucial not to collapse a study of monstrous women into nothing more than a survey of degradation and marginalization. As women exist at the intersections of gender, race, sexuality, and disability, and as representations of women become more monstrous as difference compounds, the potential for escape from damaging cultural norms expands. Cohen writes: "A danger resides in this multiplication: as difference, like a Hydra, sprouts two heads where one has been lopped away, the possibilities of escape, resistance, disruption arise with more force" (11). Deer Woman, like so many of her monstrous sisters, appears when violence has been inflicted on Indigenous women, but as the stories in LaPensée's vignette and edited anthology suggest, she does not appear only to haunt the men who inflict violence; she is also a part of the women who have been victimized. She is the materialization of their own power. As such, all of the chapters that follow explore not only the ways monstrous women evoke damaging cultural norms in patriarchal contexts, but also how constructions of woman as monster contain within them the potential to destroy the systems of thought that are productive of such norms.

We have chosen a page from *Deer Woman* to wrap this volume in not only because of the resonances our own work has with its narrative content, but also because it is a comic.[2] While many studies of the monster and monstrosity have focused on women, and most do so (at least in part) in relation to some type of visual culture, few have examined the appearance of monstrous women in comics in particular. Like horror films, sequential art has an abundance of monsters and fantastical beings. Indeed, Scott Bukatman, whose comics scholarship has long included the language of monstrosity, has gone so far as to argue that "comics are little monsters, too"; they "permit the emergence of [. . .] little utopias of disorder" (2016, 19). No less important to this volume than the sheer abundance of monsters within comics is the fact that they are often marked by gender, race, and disability in complex ways. Therefore, we suggest that certain representations of women in comics provide fertile opportunities for further examining the various ways the monster acts as a gendered "meaning machine." In the spirit of monster studies, the collection that follows resists easy categorization. Interdisciplinary studies tend toward the "monstrous" in that they are hybrid by nature. If this anthology is successful in emulating Cohen's monster—"a form suspended between forms that threatens to smash distinctions"—the authors hope it smashes the silos between their fields (1996, 6). Having said that, however, our aim is to show that there is insight to be gained from many fields turned toward the same subject: namely, to understand and critique the representations of women in comics as framed by monstrosity more thoroughly and from multiple disciplinary perspectives.

So, while our approach is indeed transdisciplinary—drawing from fields such as feminism, gender studies, critical race studies, and disability studies—the research presented in this volume can be said to share a methodological starting point: each chapter provides a text-critical analysis of a particular (or perhaps several) comic, manga, or graphic novel in order to ask how the monster makes meaning within the text(s) and what it means for the monster to be coded as a woman. Further, building on the work of monster studies scholars such as Jeffrey Jerome Cohen, Barbara Creed, Margrit Shildrick, and Julia Kristeva, the authors will *also* reflect on the various ways their analysis of the comic, and the meaning made by the monstrous woman therein, connect to the broader cultural context in question. As Cohen argues, "monsters must be examined within the intricate matrix of relations (social, cultural, and literary-historical) that generate them"; they must "be read against contemporary social movements or a specific, determining event" (5). Thus, the chapters in this volume share as their primary aim the analysis of the ways monstrous women make meaning in particular comics, as well as how those texts connect to wider social and cultural discourses of gender. In order to further converse with existing scholarship on monsters and on gender, and to further enable dialogue between chapters, this book is organized along a number of common themes. Drawing out these strands of commonality among the fifteen chapters in this volume—and in relation to existing scholarship—is not an attempt to dim the cacophony of distinct and varied monstrous voices; instead, we endeavor to demonstrate both the complexity and the widespread applicability of "reading cultures from the monsters they engender" (Cohen 1996, 3). To achieve that end, each chapter will combine careful textual analysis with reflections on each of their particular cultural contexts along one of five lines of focus: power, embodiment, childbearing, childhood, and performance.

Part 1: The Origins, Agency, and Paradoxes of Monstrous Women

Much of the fear surrounding monstrous women in comics springs from their paradoxical nature. When female characters actively choose monstrosity and exhibit agency that rejects normative femininity, they often create powerful tensions in books created by or aimed at traditionally male creators and audiences. These types of characters cannot be read as purely liberatory; they might make use of their monstrosity while still being exploited. As Cohen asserts, the monster "breaks apart bifurcating, 'either/or' syllogistic logic with a kind of reasoning closer to 'and/or'" (1996, 5). Monstrous women are neither wholly empowered nor entirely disenfranchised, but often they are both. This section explores the various ways power is generated but, because of the imbrication of gender and monstrosity, is never held in one normative location, thus frequently creating paradox.

In chapter 1, "Rewriting to Control: How the Origins of Harley Quinn, Wonder Woman, and Mary Magdalene Matter to Women's Perceived Power," Elizabeth Rae Coody argues that for each of these women there is a "multivocal" origin story that walks a tenuous line between heroism and monstrosity. Each woman paradoxically becomes monstrous when someone telling her origin story rewrites the story to resolve a tension and ameliorate a discomfort with a particular aspect of her power. Claiming control of a specific narrative or noting the context of changing perceptions around these heroic women's origins can offer power to actual women who wish to reclaim their own life stories. In chapter 2, "Exploring the Monstrous Feminist Frame: Marvel's She-Hulk as Male-Centric Postfeminist Discourse," Rick Stevens shows in the various portrayals of She-Hulk the paradoxes of female agency in a hypermasculine sphere. She-Hulk is nearly always a giant green woman, but her monstrosity varies depending on the space she occupies. Despite their consistently having superhuman powers and a law degree, the varied portrayals of the transformed, incredibly strong She-Hulk and her alter ego Jen Walters reveal the tenuous agency of a woman in hypermasculine public spaces, both in the text and in US culture more broadly. In chapter 3, "'There Is More to Me Than Just Hunger': Female Monsters and Liminal Spaces in *Monstress* and *Pretty Deadly*," Ayanni C. H. Cooper analyzes the power of liminality that forces readers to identify with the transgressive "other." For the important female characters in these two comic books, liminality and the abject are paradoxically sources of their power as revealed through their relationship to profanity, blood, and boundary crossing. While these female characters are undoubtedly situated as monsters because of their liminal, abject natures, they are also the protagonists, and so the reader is compelled to identify with monstrosity. Because the celebrated creators of these comics, Marjorie Liu and Kelly Sue DeConnick, have influential voices in the wider US pop culture context, there is powerful potential in their choices to compel readers to examine their own relationship to the abject and thus challenge assumptions of social normalcy.

Part 2: The Body as Monstrous

The body plays an important role in our thinking through how women are perceived as monsters in comics. As Margrit Shildrick has it:

> Monsters of course show themselves in many different and culturally specific ways, but what is monstrous about them is most often the form of their embodiment. They are, in an important sense, what Donna Haraway [. . .] calls "inappropriate/d others" in that they challenge and resist normative human being, in the first instance by their aberrant corporeality. (Shildrick 2001, 9; Haraway 1992)

Thus, in chapter 4, "The (Un)Remarkable Fatness of Valiant's *Faith*," Stefanie Snider examines the potential, as well as the limits, of making the superhero

Faith Herbert/Zephyr fat. Typically framed as monstrous in Western superhero comics, Faith's fatness is treated narratively and visually as if it is not in any way aberrant. Snider questions whether this representation marks a positive shift in Western popular culture in relation to fatness, or whether, in this case, Faith as a monstrous woman has been "defanged" and denied the potential to be subversive of marginalizing norms. When bodies are disabled, the form of their embodiment resists the norm even further.

In chapter 5, "New and Improved? Disability and Monstrosity in Gail Simone's *Batgirl*," Charlotte Johanne Fabricius examines how the miraculous recovery of the character Barbara Gordon/Batgirl may erase the powerful subversive potential in Barbara's previous, disabled manifestation as Oracle and instead may perpetuate the status quo in superhero comics for compulsory able-bodiedness. Fabricius analyzes how disability and gender intersect in *Batgirl*, and asks critical questions about whether Barbara becomes, in some ways, more monstrous by passing as an able-bodied "girl" and how that representation relates to broader cultural ideals of embodiment and femininity. In chapter 6, "Horrible Victorians: Interrogating Power, Sex, and Gender in *InSEXts*," Keri Crist-Wagner analyzes Marguerite Bennett's *InSEXts* comic via her own systematic "Diamond of Violence" and "Queerness Score" tools to study how violence against queer bodies works. By tracking precisely how these monstrously insectoid women who claim their sexual power are punished or rewarded, she shows how embodied queer identity and pleasure supersede patriarchal violence even in an era with repressive ideals of sexuality and restrictive gender roles. Violence, queerness, and power are all linked in the monstrous bodies of *InSEXts* protagonists.

Part 3: Childbearing as Monstrous

It is not just bodies as they exist that are at the center of monstrosity, though; what female bodies can sometimes do—that is, bear children—is another central point of their monstrosity. As scholars like Julia Kristeva (1980) and Barbara Creed (1993) have shown, representations of women as monstrous are frequently linked to maternity because of the ways maternal figures disturb borders, disrupt patriarchal order, and defy pure identity formation. Childbearing is also associated with bodily phenomena that, for many people, are sources of abjection—bodily fluids like blood or breast milk are framed as polluting and shameful.

In chapter 7, Jeannie Ludlow examines a number of comics to determine whether texts about abortion, motherhood, and birthing exceed normative discourses of maternity (which frequently frame such life events as horrific and monstrous), or if, despite their potential to perform otherwise, certain comics perpetuate the characterization of these topics as abject. "Kicking Ass in Flip-Flops: Inappropriate/d Generations and Monstrous Pregnancy in Comics Narratives" provides an analysis of how particular comics do, or do not, make use of monstrosity in order to imagine im/possibilities relating to birth. In chapter 8, Marcela Murillo reads three contemporary Bolivian comics with the goal of analyzing their representations of indigenous Aymara or Quechua (chola) mothers. In "The Monstrous Portrayal of the Maternal Bolivian Chola in Contemporary Comics," Murillo demonstrates how normative Bolivian discourses of maternity frame cholas as grotesque. However, recent changes in government policies as well as in economic conditions have empowered chola women and have resulted in changes in how they are represented in social arenas such as theater. In light of such shifts, Murillo interrogates whether comics, too, have evolved beyond monstrous representations of chola maternity. And in chapter 9, Tomoko Kuribayashi analyzes monstrous childbearing in a manga text that introduces us to a graphic world where female reproduction is a rarity. Centering on the narrative of a genetically engineered, posthuman character called Kira, *Marginal* examines what it means when the uterus is separated from the female body. In "The Monstrous 'Mother' in Moto Hagio's *Marginal*: The Posthuman, the Human, and the Bioengineered Uterus," Kuribayashi asks whether the erasure of gender from the process of childbearing can indeed shift patriarchal gender matrices in more promising directions, or if childbearing continues to be framed as problematically monstrous because of Kira's "artificial" existence, her connection to the natural environment, and her lack of control over her body/reproductive organs.

Part 4: Monsters of Childhood

Moving from the occasional horrors of childbirth, turning toward the monsters of childhood itself affords us another area for discussion around what makes representations of a woman or girl monstrous. Women are traditionally responsible for and have historically been associated with children; the comics in this section show women refusing this association with monstrous results. As in the work of Marie-Hélène Huet, the children here say more about the women around them than about childhood itself; children are sometimes the "monstrous births" that reveal women's dangerous female imaginations (1993). These are stories that include and even cater to children and adolescents but say more about the perceptions of women in their cultures.

In chapter 10, "SeDUCKtress! Magica De Spell, Scrooge McDuck, and the Avuncular Anthropomorphism of Carl Barks's Midcentury Disney Comics," Daniel F. Yezbick selects a fascinating duck-faced character to highlight the sexual tension. Even as a duck, Magica De Spell defies the traditional connection between women and children and is thus a monstrous threat to the order of Scrooge's empire. Her malevolence and charm demonstrate a power to be reckoned with in Duckburg, and as a part of Disney's influential picture of the wider social world, she exposes midcentury America's most flagrant hypocrisies of gender and class. In chapter 11, "On the Edge of 1990s Japan: Kyoko Okazaki and the Horror of Adolescence," Novia Shih-Shan Chen and Sho Ogawa present a study of the social struggles around female sexuality in the context of the economic struggles of 1990s Japan, as observable in one manga writer's career. Okazaki was critical of the monstrous ways young women were being portrayed during this time. Her unconventional work in cutting-edge *hentai*, ladies' comics, and subcultural fashion magazines presented commodified women's bodies in a nuanced way. She created manga in the midst of moral panic over adolescent women that leveled a subtle critique of structures around her while leading the way toward emergent, nomadic identities for young people in this pivotal decade in Japanese cultural and financial history. In chapter 12, "Chinese Snake Woman Resurfaces in Comics: Considering the Case Study of *Calabash Brothers*," Jing Zhang provides an art historical study of a transgressive female figure from Chinese legend who enjoys lasting popularity but who also has a dubious moral standing when one examines her relationship to the eponymous young brothers. Snake Woman's monstrous qualities are revived alongside the magical brothers as the proper counterpart to their superhuman feats in a Shanghai Animation Film Studio revival from 1986. Zhang shows this to be part of a history that reveals what Chinese culture holds to be both repugnant and appealing about a woman embedded in a children's narrative.

Part 5: Taking On the Role of Monster

This final set of chapters analyzes women's complex relationships with normative, patriarchal social roles and identity categories. Being labeled a monster means playing a part with regularly contested lines. Being labeled a monstrous woman means an even more fraught performance. Each of these chapters provides a nuanced look at comics portraying women in worlds they transgress by existing within. In other words, this section investigates how the roles women perform—mother, hero, politician—simultaneously solidify their status as monster while also enabling them to push back against often harmful social norms.

In chapter 13, "Monochromatic Teats, Teeth, and Tentacles: Monstrous Visual Rhetoric in Stephen L. Stern and Christopher Steininger's *Beowulf: The Graphic Novel*," Justin Wigard turns the analysis of performance of social roles back in time. He studies the way the visual depiction of Grendel's mother changes in the shift from literary epic to comic book. Through a close study of visual rhetoric in her creaturely body, Wigard reveals how the portrayal of the monster perpetuates the desire to see gender performed in traditional ways. What is ancient is run through a modern comics lens to reveal problematic contemporary bias toward normative ideals of gender, even as they are embodied by a monster. In chapter 14, "Beauty and Her B(r)east(s): Monstrosity and College Women in *The Jaguar*," Pauline J. Reynolds and Sara Durazo-DeMoss show how idealized foreign, exotic female characters become monstrous in comics. Specifically, in their reading of *The Jaguar*, Reynolds and Durazo-DeMoss examine the ways ethnicity, female sexuality, and language mark the identity of Maria/the Jaguar as bestial and thus position her as monstrous in ways that undermine her performance as a hero. Further, they also explore how a social role fraught with so much contradiction—both beast and hero—can reveal the lived complexity of navigating college campuses for real-world international students. Finally, in chapter 15, "UFO (Unusual Female Other) Sightings in *Saucer Country/State*: Metaphors of Identity and Presidential Politics," Christina Knopf shows us how a strong female lead might resist monstrosity in the pursuit of political power. As an abused, divorced, Mexican American woman, Arcadia Alvarado is solidly situated in the margins of the fictional US society depicted in *Saucer Country*. Despite being marked as monstrous because of her race and gender, Alvarado finds her strength in resisting the monstrous political norms that dominate her US context. In this science-fictional world (which reveals the real intersectional failings of the American political world), Alvarado transgresses her assigned role as marginalized "other" by powerfully performing as a political leader without becoming a monster.

Women are often called monsters. We exist at intersections and on porous borders. Our potential for escape, disruption, and resistance from damaging cultural norms expands as the representations become more monstrous. With this collection, we use comics to try to figure out what that monstrosity means and what women, scholars, and comics have done and should do about it. Like Deer Woman proclaims, "whatever we have experienced . . . we always return to ourselves" (LaPensée, Vasquez, and Thunder 2015). Women's experiences in patriarchy may involve violence, marginalization, and erasure, but we are never simply victims—we are also always agents. Whether in, behind, or in front of the pages of comics, women may be culturally positioned *as* monstrous, but the monster is also *in* us, and she is powerful.

Notes

1. Portions of this introduction have been previously published in Samantha Langsdale's forthcoming article "Moon Girls and Mythical Beasts: Analyzing Race, Gender, and Monstrosity," to be published in *Signs: Journal of Women in Culture and Society*.

2. This volume contains chapters that engage with a variety of texts wherein one finds "juxtaposing images in a sequence"; these range from superhero comics to Bolivian manga to indie graphic novels and more. It is not our intention to elide the differences in history, process, or distribution between these various forms. However, because the focus of our project is not on the theoretical debates centered on definition, we have chosen to use "comics" to act as an umbrella term for volumes "in which all aspects of the narrative are represented by pictorial and linguistic images encapsulated in a sequence of juxtaposed panels and pages" (Duncan and Smith 2009, 4). It is our hope that this particular use of the word is sufficiently inclusive to do justice to the diverse literature surveyed throughout this book.

Bibliography

Bukatman, Scott. 2016. *Hellboy's World: Comics and Monsters on the Margins*. Oakland: University of California Press.

Cohen, Jeffrey Jerome. 1996. "Monster Culture (Seven Theses)." In *Monster Theory: Reading Culture*, edited by Jeffrey Jerome Cohen, 3–25. Minneapolis: University of Minnesota Press.

Creed, Barbara. 1993. *The Monstrous Feminine: Film, Feminism, Psychoanalysis*. New York: Routledge.

Duffer, Matt and Ross. 2016. *Stranger Things*. Produced by Karl Gajdusek et al. Netflix.

Duncan, Randy, and Matthew J. Smith. 2009. *The Power of Comics: History, Form and Culture*. New York: Continuum.

Haraway, Donna. 1992. "The Promises of Monsters: A Regenerative Politics for Inappropriate/d Others." In *Cultural Studies*, edited by Lawrence Grossberg, Cary Nelson, and Paula Treichler, 295–337. London: Routledge.

Huet, Marie-Hélène. 1993. *Monstrous Imagination*. Cambridge, MA: Harvard University Press.

Kirk, Brian. 2015. *We Are Monsters*. Cincinnati: Samhain Publishing.

Kristeva, Julia. 1980. *Powers of Horror: An Essay on Abjection*. New York: Columbia University Press.

LaPensée, Elizabeth, Weshoyot Alvitre, Patty Stonefish et al., eds. 2017. *Deer Woman: An Anthology*. Albuquerque: Native Realities Press.

LaPensée, Elizabeth, Allie Vasquez, and Jonathan R. Thunder. 2015. *Deer Woman: A Vignette*. Albuquerque: Native Realities Press.

Rosay, André B. 2016. "Violence against American Indian Women and Alaska Native Women and Men: 2010 Findings from the National Intimate Partner and Sexual Violence Survey." National Institute of Justice, US Department of Justice, Washington, DC. Available at https://www.ncjrs.gov/pdffiles1/nij/249736.pdf. Accessed September 1, 2018.

Shildrick, Margrit. 2001. *Embodying the Monster: Encounters with the Vulnerable Self*. Los Angeles: SAGE.

Part 1

The Origins, Agency, and Paradoxes of Monstrous Women

1

Rewriting to Control: How the Origins of Harley Quinn, Wonder Woman, and Mary Magdalene Matter to Women's Perceived Power

Elizabeth Rae Coody

Origin stories are never innocent. When individuals or groups explain to each other how comics characters, nations, or artifacts came to be, they layer their values in their choices. Harley Quinn, Wonder Woman, and Mary Magdalene each have several origins, some of which reflect different writers' discomfort with women's power—power so subversive and border-crossing it ends up portrayed as monstrous. Even comics that ordinarily revel in the transgressive are thrown into a tailspin when women have too much of their own power. Origins are used to explain away or undercut women's agency. This chapter is not for those "wry pleasures of catching patriarchy up to its old tricks once again" (Johnson 2007, 16). Rather, people who are considered "monstrous" because they cross normative, patriarchal borders must insist on owning the power associated with origins. These boundary-crossing monsters include, but are not limited to, women and people outside of gender binaries, queer people, and many of those who disrupt white, largely Christian norms in the United States. Women must own the porous nature of our origin stories; I suggest we must be monstrous about it. This is not only a matter for comics but a larger question of origins that comics can help us understand.

What mainstream comics offer to an extent that other media forms do not is what I call a "multivocal" origin story. That is, North American, especially US, mainstream comics allow for and even encourage multiple origins, especially multiple retellings or "resellings" of an origin story. Both the traditionally ephemeral nature of comics and the direct market that governs comic shops have a pull toward "entry points" that makes it possible and preferable to regularly remind readers of how a character came to be. These are serialized magazine stories told in short episodes. The expectations for entry have historically been low; only the advent of the internet has created a vitriolic "know-everything" culture of high entry points. The point at which a reader jumps on a story track with a "Fabulous New #1" places her in a particular generation, even if these generations have the longevity of fruit flies in the current mainstream reboot strategy; a series that an editorial team sees as having potential might reboot within the calendar year. *The Unbeatable Squirrel Girl*, no. 1 (December 2015) joked that it was "only their second #1 so far this year!" (North and Henderson 2015, cover).

Creators, too, have a stake in the multivocal origin story when they try to add their voice to a character with a history. Long-term comic properties thrive on the judicious "ret-con," or retroactive continuity, which gives authors the chance to give their own spin on an older property. A fresh voice can do wonders for an old character. Older properties in the comics canon are reaching toward the century mark; Wonder Woman has been having adventures since 1941. That does not sound like a long time when compared with ancient New Testament biblical stories, but in terms of the sort of demand placed on modern characters, it is a story that is showing some age. To remain viable, creators need to try new voices with old characters.

Beyond the market and creators, the multivocal origin has to do with the inherent double voice of the form. In comics, there is an active interplay of visuals and text and a flexibility of familiar visuals and reinterpretation possible over time, meaning that every page has the potential to speak with the voice of both what is seen in images and what is read in words nearly simultaneously. The images usually speak first. As Ann Marie Seward Barry says: "The logic of the image is also *associative* and *holistic* rather than linear, so that not only does the image present itself as reality, but it also may speak directly to the emotions, bypassing logic, and works according to alogical principles of reasoning" (1997, 78). When an image is combined with words as in a comic strip, the words become secondary as the language of images becomes primary. What makes this domination or first impression of art important to understanding comics is the way the art opens meanings. The art of comics allows for bundles of information that the reader interprets to his or her context and understanding of the story context.

The medium of comics matters to my interpretation of the function of origin stories here. This chapter will set up a specific pattern around origins that can be applied to other situations. The pattern begins when there are at least two origin stories. At least one origin story is uncomfortable for some specific but often unsaid reason. Changes to these origin stories point to specific cultural discomfort over women's agency (their monstrous will to subvert patriarchal expectations) in nuanced ways. The shift in origins can help us identify the patriarchal discomfort that these women have highlighted more precisely. That is, changes to the origins can show us what is deemed border-crossing or monstrous about these women in the ways they are characterized as unnatural by their respective patriarchal cultures.

In this study, I address three examples of women who cross patriarchal boundaries in their origins: a long-running comics superhero character (Wonder Woman), a recent chaotic comics character (Harley Quinn), and a biblical character (Mary Magdalene). I have chosen women whose stories inspire women in the real world: Wonder Woman has been a feminist icon for decades; Harley Quinn, a wildly popular cosplay model and daring character that often inspires women to play up their chaotic power; and Mary Magdalene, an inspiration for women who seek a position of power in the Christian Church. All three cross the boundaries set around the types of power that are proper to women in a patriarchal society, and then in retellings of their stories, this boundary-crossing is erased, shamed, or otherwise taken in a new direction. This study concentrates on the way that retelling their origins serves to quell their power but also on how alternative retellings offer a chance to reclaim that power. Comparing these women characters across distinct times and inside and outside comics can show the usefulness of analyzing their types of "monstrous" qualities. These are women whose quality of the "monstrous is produced at the border which separates those who take up their proper gender roles from those who do not" (Creed 1993, 11). By using these stories across time, we can reflect on the real-life implications of encouraging women to retell their own stories from multiple angles.

Wonder Woman Magically Arrives

In part because of the many-decades-long view we can take with Wonder Woman, she gives us one of the most transparent instances of this change in origin stories as an indicator of patriarchal culture anxiety. When Gloria Steinem adopted Wonder Woman as the cover image for the first full-size edition of *Ms.* magazine in July 1972, she embraced exactly the most "monstrous" and boundary-crossing of Diana's qualities, even insisting to DC Comics' Dick Giordano that she get "Paradise Island back as her origin story" as part of a play for a revival (Desta 2017). There are far more than two Wonder Woman origin stories to compare, but this chapter concentrates on one aspect of two important versions to show how this pattern works. Although the character first debuted in *All-Star Comics*, no. 8, it is not until *Wonder Woman*, no. 1 (May 31, 1942) that readers learn how Wonder Woman came to be in a set origin story. In this story, she is the product of a doubly virgin birth. First, Hippolyte is the Queen of the Amazons, all of whom Aphrodite (the goddess of love) made to be her ideal women—fierce warriors able to protect themselves from the bloodthirsty and abusive men that populate the globe. Her name switches spellings to "Hippolyta" in later works, but this is a sign of editorial inconsistency that I have used as the authors do. Here, Hippolyte lives with her sisters on Paradise Island, where no man may enter. She is not given much of a motive more than the generally understood need at the time for women to have children, but she seeks the teachings of Athena in order to mold her own daughter out of clay. Aphrodite gives her daughter life and names her Diana. The page in question is a "word-specific" one; the pictures illustrate what the words say. The art squeezes around her words across four crowded panels emphasizing the layers of meaning and allusion packed into this story; the moon goddess Diana ("mistress of the chase"), Pygmalion's worship of Galatea, the strength of Hercules, the thunderbolts of Zeus, all the swiftness of Mercury are all present in Wonder Woman's beginnings.

Perhaps cynically, it is no surprise that the next creator changed the origin story to run from this sort of undisguised advocacy of women's superiority to men. Wonder Woman was too much of a monstrous boundary crosser. Robert Kanigher, who wrote and edited *Wonder Woman* starting in 1946 and for over twenty years, made such changes as giving the title a romantic focus, taking away Etta Candy and the Holiday Girls, and, more to the point of this chapter, changing Diana's origins to be the child of members of the opposite sex and giving the story a tragic rather than triumphant focus.[1]

Wonder Woman's origin is convoluted, even from the beginning; the story's historical complexity invites changes that the compact origins of Batman and Superman do not. Her story is more difficult to follow than those of the other persons of the DC trinity. Bruce Wayne's parents are murdered, and he seeks out justice in varying forms across many different styles of comics, but his core origin story always remains. It is multivocal but unified. Superman's story is so well known that Grant Morrison and Frank Quitely could create a four-panel introduction for *All-Star Superman* that compressed his entire origin into an elegant series of images and the words: "Doomed Planet / Desperate Scientists / Last Hope / Kindly Couple" (Morrison, Quitely, and Grant 2007, 11). Wonder Woman has not shared this elegance since her very first origin story. Arguably the fact that she is a woman is already a complication that Batman and Superman do not share—that is, by being a woman, she is from the beginning not the normative superhero type. Changes to her origins are an attempt to bring "man"-centric logic of later publishers to a story designed originally to be woman-centric. They are all multivocal stories, but only Wonder Woman's story does not hold a center. That is, Wonder Woman's origin story invites change because it does not align comfortably with a patriarchal world view. The number of changes both subtle and major to her story run from Kanigher's 1940s "tragic genesis" version of events to even her most recent incarnations (Hanley 2014, 99).

The focus in this chapter, though, is on a more recent change to Wonder Woman's origin from "The New 52" reboot. In 2011, DC cancelled *all* of its ongoing comics titles (not just *Wonder Woman*) and started them over at #1 in a campaign called "The New 52." Pursuant to an emphasis on "realism" by the DC team, "The New 52" version of Wonder Woman could no longer be the creation of women using mystical means without male involvement. In issue no. 3 of the new *Wonder Woman* series, we find the Brian Azzarello version of the story with Cliff Chiang's art. Hippolyta has told Wonder Woman that she was made of clay to be the perfect Amazon—that is, "no male seed" created her (2012). But, in issue no. 3, Wonder Woman and readers learn that Hippolyta has lied about Diana's origins. Instead, Hippolyta had a consensual and erotic affair with Zeus that left her pregnant. The page that reveals Zeus in this context strategically places a huge sword blade to block a view of his crotch (i.e., the necessary equipment for the act) while Hippolyta's narration emphasizes "There was a *man*" (Azzarello and Chiang 2012, 9; emphasis in the original) (fig. 1.1).

Hippolyta is happy to have a child and happy to be left alone by the father. She knows that Zeus's wife, Hera, has a reputation for murdering the illicit offspring of her husband's many romances, and his partners, too. She fabricates the story about making Diana out of clay. People are convinced, but Hippolyta is still beset by Hera. Diana is resented by the bitter residents of Paradise Island. Rather than being her loyal sisters, these women bully and sneer at her. They call her "clay" as an insult, even before the story is debunked. The magic is gone from her origin. Yes, there is still an affair with a god to be addressed, but asexual reproduction is removed. It is Hippolyta's unusual maternity that crosses the line into the "monstrous-feminine" (Creed 1993). What made the original Hippolyte shocking was her ability to make a child without a phallus, as a "phallic woman" (Creed 1993, 156–58). That is, Hippolyta has the abilities of the phallus without consulting a man; her phallic qualities are replaced with a vengeance in "The New 52" story. The story eliminates the elements that the patriarchal culture deems outside of the ordinary imagination. Hardest of all to imagine seems to be harmony between women. There is no feminist utopia of any shape here.

Figure 1.1. Hippolyta narrates her meeting with Zeus that leads to Wonder Woman's conception. Note the strategically placed sword. *Wonder Woman* (2011–2015), no. 3, p. 8, by Brian Azzarello and Cliff Chiang. Copyright 2012, DC Comics.

What is the source of cultural discomfort here? First, taking away women's power to create life alone means that reproduction without a male contributor makes the culture uncomfortable even today. It also changes the nature of *conflict* in Wonder Woman; Azzarello's Diana is not set against a "Man's World" that threatens her sisters, as William Moulton Marston's was. The conflicts here are in-group: between women, most of whom are related to one another. No longer is Wonder Woman a product of a loving paradise, full of brilliant and supportive women; she's an outcast even before her birth is questioned. However, this is not a matter of recovering a story for 2017 from 1942. I want to say clearly that the first-wave feminist paradise that Marston created was, if I am the most charitable I can be, misguided. He based his claims about women's potential to lead on perceived *biological* differences between the sexes. Paradise Island was full of white women of a certain sort of perceived perfect shape—it is not innocent in terms of its racial ideals around white superiority, a single "correct" voluptuous body type for women, and strict biological gender identity. Despite the entertaining, even beguiling naïveté of the 1942 story, it is not innocent of biases from its culture and time. Origins never are.

Despite these obvious imperfections in the 1942 story, in the 2012 story, there is hardly an allowance for women to even get along in the search for what DC senior vice-president of sales Bob Wayne calls "real world," "accessible," "modern" stories in "The New 52" (Doran 2011). The source of Wonder Woman's strength is no longer her relationship to other women—her mother, her sister Amazons, even aspects of a number of gods and goddesses. In the first story, she is a magical clay vessel filled with the first-wave feminist picture of perfect womanhood. In the latest story, she inherited her warrior instincts biologically from her mother and father. In the oldest story, she is nurtured and loved. In the latest, she is outcast and bullied. Azzarello's story cuttingly reflects an accurate picture of the United States' discomfort with women who have too much power over their bodies or in general. Women with power must be monsters in this case. The cultural discomfort with the power that women have over the reproduction of the species is paired with discomfort over women getting along without men.

The two Wonder Woman origins fit into the specific pattern here around multivocal stories. That is, in both Marston's first origin story and "The New 52," Wonder Woman comes to be; these are both origin stories that are a part of the larger mythos. Because Wonder Woman's origin is multivocal, both stories are real parts of her character. Neither story can be dismissed, but both together sound discordant. The Marston story showed Hippolyta to be able to produce a child without a man; Wonder Woman herself thrives in a gynocentric Paradise Island. In "The New 52," showing Zeus to be her biological father and subverting the established female love and friendship on the island (their monstrous will to subvert patriarchal expectations) shows the parts of the story that will not hold up as "true" for the culture. The shift in origins shows that Wonder Woman has highlighted discomfort with both the phallic woman and positive female relationships. The change to the origin shows these to be "monstrous" in the sense of "unnatural to the patriarchal culture." Being multivocal means that both origins are still part of what makes this character a whole character; she is both monstrous and tamed at the same time.

Harley Quinn Explodes into Being

The multivocal origins of Harley Quinn are similarly complex in that she too has several different origins stories, though over a much shorter, not quite quarter-century timeline. In this section, I will focus on her first origin story, her entry into the main DC Universe (DCU), and another origin story from a DC line-wide relaunch. Despite the shorter timeline, it is not a clean move from her first origin story in 1994 to her "Rebirth" story in 2016.[2] Her agency shifts wildly—sometimes she plays a victim of monstrous circumstances, sometimes she is a monstrous psychopath, sometimes she is the gleefully naughty "lil' monster." Her performance as a loose cannon may or may not be a tightly controlled act. Her character debut was outside of comics, in *Batman: The Animated Series*, in 1992 (Kirkland 1992); her first print appearance was in *Batman Adventures*, no. 12, the next year (Puckett, Parobeck, and Burchett 1993). Despite the mixed media of her early appearances, her first origin story came in print in the prestigious Eisner Award–winning self-contained story, *The Batman Adventures: Mad Love*, by Paul Dini and Bruce Timm (1994). This book is part of the larger "Adventures" line that takes place outside of the main interconnected set of DC stories or the DCU. Here, Dini and Timm set Harley Quinn up as a young grad student willing to sleep her way to real success—by which she means pop psychologist stardom. At Arkham Asylum, she is in control. She is attracted to the Joker from the first moment she lays eyes on him, because he is a patient who can make her reputation. But after weeks of the Joker sharing his hard-luck stories, she genuinely falls for him. But, these stories are a precarious connection. Later in the narrative, when Harley alone has Batman all tied up and absolutely helpless over a tank of piranhas, he reveals that the stories are suspect: "What did he tell you Harley? Was it the line about the abusive father, or the alcoholic mom? Of course, the runaway orphan story is particularly moving, too." Harley resists: "Stop it! You're making me confused!" But, whether the stories are true or not, her move to follow the Joker in the original story is a result of her own agency and choice. Yes, he gave her the idea and was psychotically manipulative, but she executed her own transformation to villainy (fig. 1.2).

The Joker's abuse is uncomfortably playful in *Mad Love*. It carries few consequences for him, but Harley suffers. Furious and unhinged by the fact that she has Batman tied up in a way that he never could, the Joker throws her out of a high window. When the police find her in the alley in a pool of her own shining blood, she's muttering in a wavy speech balloon in shaky letters: "My fault . . . I didn't . . . get the joke . . ." (Dini and Timm 1994, 53). She immediately blames herself rather than her abuser. In the grim climax played for a laugh, Harley is bandaged and hospitalized. On the penultimate page of the story, she swears off the Joker after seeing "the slime for what he is," but on the last page the Joker has left her a single rose on the nightstand (62). She brightens and says to herself that the abusive experience "felt like a kiss" (63). This scene is presented with a cartoony playfulness; despite the blood and the bandages, Harley is chipper. It is chilling to see her return to her abuser, but it is played for laughs in the art; there is a Looney Tunes quality to the final panel, with its angled "Finis." Readers see that she will stay with him because she is in love, whether they agree with her choice or not.

In her 1999 entry into the main DCU, *Batman: Harley Quinn*, she finds the Joker's "charms irresistible"—"What can I tell ya? The guy just did it for me." But by the time the issue concludes, she is done with him. He shoots her off in a cartoony rocket before she swears off him, but she ultimately does. It is in this 1999 version, already distancing her from the abusive relationship in the first versions, that the addition of chemicals into her system gives her superpowers. This is the turn to "realism" for the character that she needs when she enters the DCU. That is, this is the moment that explains the comic book logic of how she can keep up with the Joker and Batman. When the rocket the Joker forced her into comes down, she has extensive injuries. The literally toxic supervillain Poison Ivy, scientist and poison expert, gives her a dose of power-up juice out of a concern for her that runs from sisterly to romantic to erotic in subsequent retellings. Harley looks the same, but we get a comics-appropriate explanation for her supernatural acrobatic prowess. Both stories are part of her origins, but they do not contradict each other. They are not yet multivocal; here, two different stories simply tell two different parts of the same ongoing story. Although it took five years though the 1990s, these "compound" origin stories explain together how Harley regularly returns to her abuser, makes her own choices about being a chaotic villain, and gets the supernatural aspect of her powers via the loving act of a woman.

The multivocal aspect comes when comparing the compound 1990s origins to her origin in "The New 52" (from 2011), which is *mostly* shared

Figure 1.2: In this dramatic splash page, Harley Quinn bursts into the Joker's room in Arkham Asylum in her brand-new, self-created persona. *Batman Adventures: Mad Love*, p. 36, by Paul Dini and Bruce Timm. Copyright 1994, DC Comics.

by the "Rebirth" series (from 2016). Specifically, her *Secret Origins* (no. 4, July 2014) informs the reader that her violent tendencies are much more a part of her character than in the 1990s origin stories (Palmiotti, Conner, and Roux 2014). She goes undercover as a patient in Arkham Asylum to start her relationship with the Joker; she insists on disguising herself as a patient out in the prison yard without any protection rather than remaining in the clinical setting. She makes herself vulnerable and immediately gives up her control. Instead of a power-up from Poison Ivy as a loving act, the Joker throws her into a vat of chemicals that permanently bleach her skin and give her vaguely defined powers. Interestingly, after this violent act, the New 52 Harley Quinn is distanced from the abusive relationship with the Joker almost entirely. The vat-of-chemicals incident is shown in flashback; in the timeline of the series, she does not return to her abuser. In issue no. 25 of the series, she violently confronts the Joker and leaves with her self-respect and his blood on her knuckles (Conner and Palmiotti 2016). She does team up with Poison Ivy several times; their relationship is a meaningful one in the series. This version is told without sympathy for the Joker; the multivocal stories both sound at the same time. That is, Harley and Poison Ivy forge a real partnership, but Poison Ivy is not the source of her powers.

Alongside the change to Harley, it is important to note the change to the Joker that is going on around the same time. The Joker has one of the most multivocal and traditionally monstrous origin stories in all of comics. Despite some fan theories and even the 2016 film adaptation blunting the original ambivalence, Alan Moore and Brian Bolland's *The Killing Joke* (1988) did not actually answer the question of the Joker's origins. The reality of the story is pointedly ambiguous in the text. The Joker has been maniacal since his first appearance in 1940 (Finger and Kane), but the tone of the Joker in the main continuity has followed the early 2000s gritty pattern to the extreme. Far from a joke, especially through the *Batman: Death of the Family* story arc, the Joker has become so irredeemable that it is simply hard to imagine someone falling for him. It might be reasonable to ask a reader to identify with a gangster's moll—attracted to power in a fringe form—or a person staying in an abusive relationship for longer than they feel safe. Such stories *might* even be helpful. But it is much harder to suspend disbelief (or still understand Harley) when she falls for a deranged psychopath who removes his own face, or sympathize with Harley when she steals the Joker's face and uses it in her own talk therapy in an issue of *Suicide Squad* (Glass, Henry, and Guara 2012). The art style has gone from a 1990s cartoon-animated style to a gritty, more painterly style, too. In the *Death of the Family* story arc, Harley has to be too sad to be much fun. That is, she is tragic in a way that works well for this sort of serious story that does not allow her to serve as comic relief. Her harlequin makeup drips down her face in tearful streaks—recalling the wretched clowns of French expressionist painter Georges Rouault (1871–1958). In the "Funny Bones" issue in that arc, Harley even longs for the old days before the Joker changed (Snyder and Capullo 2013). Of course, the reader of those older stories knows that he has always been abusive, but the tone has shifted from cartoon violence to painful drama. When explaining where Harley came from, it makes sense to give her an origin that meshes with her zany, fun character. The Joker's abuse is serious in this version, and it takes *distancing* her from him to make her fun again. Cultural discomforts here need to be written out to continue the character. The monstrosity of the patriarchy rather than of its boundary crossers is too obvious.

There are at least three main points of cultural discomfort in the original origin: (1) making *light* of an abusive relationship; (2) not having Harley be violent and monstrous *enough* without the Joker; and (3) giving her a chemical makeover from a kindly female source that gives her power without making a physical change. In order to make Harley understandable in light of the Joker's change, her origin has to account for her violence, her relationship to the Joker, and her powers. It is important that Harley be appealing. While acting as one of DC's copublishers, Jim Lee called her the "fourth pillar" of their sales behind Wonder Woman, Superman, and Batman; the publishers found her valuable as comic relief and are excited about her ongoing potential as a screen presence (Riesman 2016). They want her to appeal broadly, and a return to her abuser is a risk to her appeal. This origin is designed to appeal with a lighter tone, an account of the monstrous elements of her personality, and a physical manifestation of her boundary-crossing monstrosity. The multivocal origins sound together to course-correct the character—both pulling her toward a visual representation of her difference and giving her a more violent representation of her powers. Here, she is both less connected to the Joker in regular stories and more dependent on the Joker in her origins. Harley's control is contested but present; multivocal origins allow it to be both ways.

Mary Magdalene's Canonical Origins

Women's multivocal origins can allow them to hold conflicting story roles at the same time. Rather than a comic book superhero, I take the next inspiring woman with a boundary-crossing origin from the ancient Christian New Testament to show how this lesson from comics works in another context. In the world of biblical interpretation, the multivocality of characters often enables them to mean different things at the same time across different tellings in the four Gospel portrayals (Matthew, Mark, Luke, and John) or in different interpretations. Interpreters for centuries to various degrees have tried to discredit Mary Magdalene, the original preacher of Jesus's resurrection, by giving her a past of sexual deviancy. Mary Magdalene does have an origin story in the canonical New Testament. She is named twelve times in the Gospels, more than most of the apostles. Jesus cast out seven demons from her, but there is no indication of what these demons were like or what behavior they caused for her (Luke 8:2; Mark 16:9). She also was a witness at the crucifixion (Matthew 27:56; Mark 15:40; John 19:25) and the burial of Jesus (Matthew 27:61; Matthew 28:1; Mark 16:1). Crucially, she was the first person to see Jesus raised from the dead and to "preach" that fact to others (Matthew 28:1; Mark 16:9; Luke 24; John 20:1). That is, she is the first witness to the central and defining moment of the Christian tradition. In this analysis, I count the canonical story as her first origin. Her later interpreters (any of those working within or after Roman imperial Christianity from around the early 300s CE) were uncomfortable that she was so important and powerful in this first origin story. They needed her to fit into a patriarchal Church hierarchy, so they explained her power as part of a reform from prostitution. In other, more provocative words, some of the earliest traditional and sympathetic Christian interpreters of the Bible slut-shamed one of the most important figures in their own religious tradition. In order to remain in the tradition in this important position, she needed to be seen as an undesirable model to women—monstrous, even. Women were in fact important to the early spread of Christianity, but once the Church hierarchy was controlled by men, the patriarchal order tried desperately to distance itself from the woman-financed house churches that made up the first three hundred or so years of Christianity. These women had established what the Church fathers now wanted to claim as their own. In order to make this claim, they needed to show that these women were somehow monstrous. When Christianity moved from these woman-led private spaces to public spaces, there was an effort to downplay or discredit the work of women that had expanded the movement from provincial preaching to an empire-wide phenomenon (Torjesen 1995). Mary Magdalene was an important figure of inspiration to the early, powerful women in the Christian movement.

Mary Magdalene's name simply means that she was a woman from Magdala, which was the ancient name of at least two places in the region of Galilee. The place-name means something like "tower," but the word "magdalene" now literally means a reformed prostitute. The "composite Mary" inspired the word. The "composite" of several Marys into one character comes from the simple fact that Mary is a common name in the stories recounted in the New Testament. Jesus has other encounters with women that are often combined into Mary Magdalene's story—including a woman caught in adultery (John 7:53–8:11) and a Mary who anoints Jesus's feet (e.g., Luke 7:36–42, 10:38–42). Both are indicted in some sort of sexual deviancy, and the tradition of combining them stems at least as far back as a sermon by Pope Gregory the Great around 591 CE (Wallace 2014). There is resistance to this composite view from more than just textual sticklers. The Junia Group, a

California-based group with an egalitarian theology, reminds preachers every Easter *not* to preach that Mary Magdalene was a reformed prostitute. They are deeply invested in making sure the story is told this way to help them in their mission of including more women in ministry and leadership in the Wesleyan-Holiness Christian tradition (Wallace 2014). They seek to eliminate prostitution as one of the voices in her multivocal story, and they find more power in the story when this aspect is not included.

However, here is where my work with comics makes this issue more complicated than simply correcting a textual mistake. The Junia Group is concerned over whether or not the story is told accurately and represents history, but this gets complicated. For example, one of the criteria often used to determine whether something in the Bible is a historical record is the "criteria of embarrassment" (Rodríguez n.d.). That is, scribes would not add in something that might be embarrassing to them, but they may have kept something embarrassing in out of a sense of obligation to the text. In this case, it is embarrassing for later scribes that Mary Magdalene was the first to see and proclaim the risen Christ. However, it is also an ironic sort of reversal (another common trope in the New Testament) to have not just a woman, but a forgiven prostitute, perform this act. Both criteria mean that it is quite probable that Mary Magdalene's act of proclamation is historical. Her historicity is based on how uncomfortable she makes interpreters.

Applying the pattern I noticed in comics to this story indicates that the source of cultural discomfort here is what changed in subsequent changes to Mary Magdalene's origin story. It was not ironic enough for this preacher to just be a woman. The reversal had to go further. Also, as much as I want to be with the Junia Project in their campaign to help women gain power in the Church, I wonder if it is not better to have a woman moving out of a prior life of prostitution at such a pivotal place in the story. Even though she is a historical figure, she can have a multivocal origin story to put to use as a source of power for women. For example, Lutheran pastor and best-selling author Rev. Nadia Bolz-Weber sees Mary Magdalene's origins as a prostitute who preached the first good news as a source of continued strength: "Here's this flawed woman who was delivered of much in her life, and she was chosen to tell the resurrection," she says. "I don't know what more authority I need to be a preacher" (Chitwood 2013). Bolz-Weber connects her own struggles to the different stories of Mary Magdalene—both as prostitute and preacher—in a way that allows her to accept her own flaws and yet take control and preach her own messages. Mary Magdalene's boundary crossing and her very "monstrous" qualities and multivocal origin help Bolz-Weber and other women who preach claim power.

Multivocal origins have impressed upon me that women can change their power based on the stories that are told about where they come from. What I want to highlight here is not the "true" story versus the "false" story, but the fact that all origin stories *are* multivocal. In comics, these stories exist alongside each other in a convoluted but acceptable sort of continuity. Both Wonder Woman and Harley Quinn have troubling origins that are changed in ways that reveal which of these multiple voices are acceptable to their cultures and which are not. Mary Magdalene's story was changed for similar reasons but with different, religious stakes. Comics' narrative flexibility can teach people about the places where women's power breaks boundaries and gives them a monstrous reputation; applying this pattern to other multivocal stories in the real world can allow us to identify the source of cultural discomfort and recover stolen power.

Notes

1. Kanigher edited *Wonder Woman* from issue no. 17 (May–June 1946) to issue no. 176 (May–June 1968) (Grand Comics Database n.d.). Tim Hanley offers a deep dive into Kanigher's rather sloppy changes to Wonder Woman's origin and mission (2014, 99–106).

2. Testifying to the perceived discontinuity between these two incarnations of Harley, a DC "Black Label" tale (and therefore noncanonical and outside of the main DCU continuity) posits that they are actually two different women (Murphy 2017).

Bibliography

Azzarello, Brian, and Cliff Chiang. 2012. "Clay." *Wonder Woman* 4, no. 3 (January). New York: DC Comics.
Barry, Ann Marie Seward. 1997. *Visual Intelligence: Perception, Image, and Manipulation in Visual Communication*. Albany: State University of New York Press.
Bastién, Angelica Jade. 2016. "Vulnerability and the Strong Black Female Archetype." In *Bitch Planet*, no. 7. Portland, OR: Image Comics.
Chitwood, Ken. 2013. "Tattooed Traditionalist: Nadia Bolz-Weber." *Publishers Weekly*, July 25. Available at http://www.publishersweekly.com/pw/by-topic/industry-news/religion/article/58497-tattooed-traditionalist-nadia-bolz-weber.html.
Clanton, Dan W., Jr., ed. 2012. *The End Will Be Graphic: Apocalyptic in Comic Books and Graphic Novels*. Sheffield, England: Sheffield Phoenix Press.
Conner, Amanda, and Jimmy Palmiotti. 2016. "Twenny Five Big Ones." *Harley Quinn* 2, no. 25 (April). Burbank, CA: DC Comics.
Creed, Barbara. 1993. *The Monstrous-Feminine: Film, Feminism, Psychoanalysis*. New York: Routledge.
Desta, Yohana. 2017. "How Gloria Steinem Saved Wonder Woman." *Vanity Fair*, October 10. Available at https://www.vanityfair.com/hollywood/2017/10/gloria-steinem-wonder-woman.

Dini, Paul, Yvel Guichet, and Aaron Sowd. 1999. *Batman: Harley Quinn*. New York: DC Comics.
Dini, Paul, and Bruce Timm. 1994. *The Batman Adventures: Mad Love*, no. 1 (February). New York: DC Comics.
Doran, Michael. 2011. "DC Releases New 'The New 52' Info and Answers to Retailers." *Newsarama*, July 1. Available at https://www.newsarama.com/7920-dc-releases-new-the-new-52-info-answers-to-retailers.html.
Finger, Bill, and Bob Kane. 1940. "The Legend of Batman: Who He Is and How He Came to Be." *Batman* 1, no. 1 (June). New York: DC Comics.
Glass, Adam, Clayton Henry, and Ig Guara. 2012. "The Hunt for Harley Quinn (part 2); The Origin of Harley Quinn." *Suicide Squad* 4, no. 7 (May). New York: DC Comics.
Grand Comics Database. n.d. "Robert Kanigher (editor)." Available at https://www.comics.org/editor/name/Robert%20Kanigher/sort/chrono/.
Hanley, Tim. 2014. *Wonder Woman Unbound: The Curious History of the World's Most Famous Heroine*. Chicago: Chicago Review Press.
Johnson, Merri Lisa. 2007. "Ladies Love Your Box: The Rhetoric of Pleasure and Danger in Feminist Television Studies." In *Third Wave Feminism and Television: Jane Puts It in a Box*, edited by Merri Lisa Johnson, 1–27. London: I. B. Tauris.
Kirkland, Boyd, dir. 1992. "Joker's Favor." *Batman: The Animated Series*, episode 22, September 11. Written by Paul Dini. Burbank, CA: Warner Brothers Animation.
Marston, Christie. 2017. "My Grandmother Was the Real-Life Wonder Woman." *Hollywood Reporter*, June 2. Available at https://www.hollywoodreporter.com/heat-vision/wonder-woman-my-grandmother-inspired-dc-superhero-1009032.
Marston, William Moulton, and Harry G. Peter. 1942. "The Origin of Wonder Woman." *Wonder Woman*, no. 1 (May). New York: DC Comics.
Moore, Alan, and Brian Bolland. 1988. *The Killing Joke*. New York: DC Comics.
Morrison, Grant, Frank Quitely, and Jamie Grant. 2007. *All Star-Superman*, vol. 1. New York: DC Comics.
Murphy, Sean. 2017. *Batman: White Knight*. DC Black Label. Burbank, CA: DC Comics.
North, Ryan, and Erica Henderson. 2015. *The Unbeatable Squirrel Girl* 2, no. 1 (December). New York: Marvel.
Palmiotti, Jimmy, Amanda Conner, and Stéphane Roux. 2014. "Harley Quinn." *Secret Origins* 3, no. 4 (September). New York: DC Comics.
Puckett, Kelley, Mike Parobeck, and Richard Burchett. 1993. "Batgirl: Day One." *The Batman Adventures*, no. 12 (September). New York: DC Comics.
Riesman, Abraham. 2016. "The Harley Quinn Boom Is Just Getting Started." *Vulture*, August 10. Available at http://www.vulture.com/2016/08/harley-quinn-boom-suicide-squad.html.
Rodríguez, Rafael. n.d. "Criterion of Embarrassment." *Passages* (blog), Bible Odyssey. Available at http://www.bibleodyssey.org/passages/related-articles/criterion-of-embarrassment.
Snyder, Scott, and Greg Capullo. 2013. "Funny Bones." *Batman* 2, no. 14 (January). New York: DC Comics.
Torjesen, Karen Jo. 1995. *When Women Were Priests: Women's Leadership in the Early Church and the Scandal of Their Subordination in the Rise of Christianity*. San Francisco: HarperSanFrancisco.
Wallace, Gail. 2014. "Mary Magdalene: 5 Things You Should Know." Junia Project, November 21, 2014; rev. April 16, 2017. Available at https://juniaproject.com/mary-magdalene-5-things-should-know.

2
Exploring the Monstrous Feminist Frame: Marvel's She-Hulk as Male-Centric Postfeminist Discourse

J. Richard Stevens

Although the *Incredible Hulk* narrative drew from classic monster stories like *Frankenstein* (Coogan 2009, 82) and *Dr. Jekyll and Mr. Hyde* (Howe 2012, 39), creators Stan Lee and Jack Kirby had sought to make a "hero out of a monster" (Lee 1974, 75) and encapsulated anxieties about masculinity in the atomic age (Genter 2007). Lee's clearly derivative She-Hulk extends that conversation into questions of femininity, including a second-wave feminist critique of the struggles to balance male relationships against physical markers of female public success. Classic understandings of the monstrous present readers with dichotomies of naturalness contrasted with unnaturalness that privilege the human form (Boon 2007, 33). In this manner, the monstrous teaches us about our own humanity by holding up a distorted mirror of the unnatural.

Early portrayals of She-Hulk wrestled with femaleness as a monstrosity; women gain unnatural privileges at the expense of social acceptance and community. But She-Hulk's monstrous proportions would eventually transcend her human condition, becoming an iconic site of feminine struggle and celebration. Over the course of her publication history, She-Hulk's portrayals varied greatly in form (superhero, lawyer, celebrity, sexual object) until evolving in 2008 as a character much more closely aligned with a feminist ideal. Her narrative articulates the paradoxes and challenges of female agency in a hypermasculine public sphere.

"One benefit of analyzing gender through comics is the ability to track attitudes over time" (Blanch 2013), and long-standing characters such as She-Hulk provide opportunities to consider the evolution of portrayed gender frames over time. This chapter considers the She-Hulk character, tracing portrayals of feminist discourse and female representation across different eras and through the lenses of particular (mostly male) creators.

Feminism in Male-Centric Comics

Comic books serve as a unique reflection of American culture. Comics' extremes become representations of how common stereotypes become archetypes and inform scholars about elements of American social structure. This is particularly clear in studying gender roles.

She-Hulk first appeared in 1980 within the pages of *The Savage She-Hulk*, where Jennifer Walters struggled with the gains from second-wave feminism, balancing her law career (battling blatant sexism from her peers) against the empowered escapism of her giant jade form. However, these explorations would cease with the end of the first series, yielding to more symbolic and personal struggles with identity politics. Her comic narratives throughout the late 1980s and 1990s abandoned most concerns consistent with second-wave feminism, instead reflecting that era's observed media trends of embodied neoliberal postfeminism frames and their emphasis on sexual freedom, materialism, self-empowerment, and the use of sexual objectification for personal gain (Tasker and Negra 2007, 8). John Byrne's *Sensational She-Hulk* series continued and expanded the postfeminism discourse into a self-reflective conversation about gender roles in comics, defining the character as a location for conversations and controversies about gender for a generation of Marvel readers.

As Mike Madrid (2009) writes in his book *The Supergirls*, "It's always been difficult for the comic book industry to find an audience for a title starring a female superhero" (304). *Ms. Marvel* (1977) presented a female hero clothed and conversant in superficial symbols of feminism, but the series was canceled in 1979 for poor sales. *Spider-Woman* (1978) and *The Savage She-Hulk* (1980) were Marvel's next attempts at female-led titles, and each series experienced moderate success. After She-Hulk's initial solo series, the character was featured in the pages of the 1980s' *The Avengers* and *Fantastic Four*, was the feature of a solo graphic novel in 1985, received a second solo series that ran from 1989 to 1994, and would later be featured in four additional solo series. With relatively few exceptions, She-Hulk's narratives have been written exclusively by male comics creators.

The Origin of Marvel's She-Hulk

Stan Lee claimed to have consistently argued for more female comics characters with productive roles (1977, 57), and his 1960s creations have been considered "an unprecedented world of gender equality" for their time (Housel 2009, 85).

She-Hulk's creation represents both a literal and a structural derivative text of the Incredible Hulk. Through merchandising, animated cartoons, and 1970s live-action television programming, Spider-Man and the Incredible Hulk were two of Marvel's most popular icons, and Stan Lee worried that Universal would create female versions of the characters (Howe 2012, 220). As Lee explained in 1978:

> I suddenly realized that some other company may quickly put out a book like that and claim they have the right to use the name, and I thought we'd better do it real fast to copyright the name. So we just batted one quickly, and that's exactly what happened. (Dawson and Groth 1978)

To protect against possible spin-offs, Marvel rushed comic book titles for *Spider-Woman* (1978) and *The Savage She-Hulk* (1980) into production to secure the copyrights to those characters (Raphael and Spurgeon 2003, 205). *The Savage She-Hulk* was an unexpected hit, selling 250,000 copies of its first issue (Howe 2012, 236).

Lee wrote the first issue, and David Kraft wrote the next twenty-four issues. The first issue established Jennifer Walters as the previously unmentioned cousin of Bruce Banner (the Hulk). Walters serves as a Los Angeles defense attorney, and her aggressive litigation style attracts the ire of mobsters. She is shot, and the visiting Banner gives her an emergency blood transfusion to save her life (Lee and Buscema 1980). Thus, Walters literally derives her power from the Hulk, as the gamma-irradiated blood engenders her abilities, which manifest in the hospital when a second murder attempt causes her first physical transformation. Her 5'10" frame grows to 6'7" and turns green, prompting one of her assailants to exclaim: "It's like—she's some kind of She-Hulk" (19). She-Hulk was created and written by males and receives her powers from her male cousin, and a male even provides her new, derivative name.

Unlike her cousin, whose transformation places him in a mindless state, Walters instead experiences "a perpetual state of PMS" (Madrid 2009, 255), highly agitated yet rational. In the first series, Walters constantly struggles to control her temper despite constant misogynistic antagonization. Her male colleagues frequently worry aloud that Walters cannot handle the stress of a "high-pressure man's world" (Kraft and Vosburg 1980c, 6) and bombard her with verbal slights: District Attorney Buck Bukowski remarks that perceived mistakes on her part indicate "how flighty you females are!" (Kraft, Vosburg, and Springer 1980, 8). Walters takes such comments in stride.

As She-Hulk, Walters enjoys the status of monstrous female empowerment, in terms of becoming free from threats of male domination; or, as one commentator observes:

> From the very start, She-Hulk was recognizable as a manifestation of a particularly female dilemma that persists today. She is an expression of how terrific it would be not to have to censor yourself, to be allowed to be angry without some man declaring you unladylike. (Rosenberg 2014)

Upon her initial transformation, She-Hulk exclaims: "I never felt like this way before! I can do anything! I'm throbbing with power!" (Lee and Buscema 1980, 26). Later, she would claim that her transformation "[h]urts more ... every time I become ... the She-Hulk! But with the pain—comes the power! Power! That means no one can push me around! No one!" (Kraft and Vosburg 1980c, 7).

And yet, She-Hulk's early success largely depends on maintaining her rational faculties during physical confrontations. For example, when she encounters a destructive device called the Silver Serpent (a giant phallus), she tries bringing conservation of momentum to bear: "Instead of pounding away at it mindlessly with her naked fists—the She-Hulk has used her awesome strength in an even more effective way—to bring the stupendous mass, weight and size of the silver serpent to a breaking point!" (Kraft and Vosburg 1980b, 19–20).

Walters has access to a traditionally male-dominated profession marked by constant patriarchal pressures and misogyny, even as her alter ego struggles to put a feminine touch on the hypermasculine world of superheroes. In one sense, Kraft's stories show a world in which occupational access merely reveals the cultural sexism of a patriarchal society and implies the importance of a continued feminist critique of those power structures. But male writers created She-Hulk to serve a mostly male audience, so the narrative's sense of feminism remains largely superficial. Lillian Robinson argues that She-Hulk cannot be a feminist icon because she does not share her strength with a female community (2004, 104), and it is certainly true that in her original series, Walters never bonds with female characters in any significant way. Her mother being long deceased, Walters's only real female companionship comes from her friend Jill, who dies in a car accident resulting from another attempted mob hit (Kraft and Vosburg 1980a, 26).

Through the 1980s series, Walters strives to define herself against the judgments of her male colleagues and her desire for male companionship. She frequently observes that her goals are contrary to her personal autonomy, that she is "trying to convince [her]self that [she] don't need anyone" (Kraft and Vosburg 1981, 4), but privately Walters longs for male acceptance. A romantic triangle emerges between two suitors, Danny "Zapper" Ridge, whom She-Hulk prefers, and Richard Rory, whom the non-monster-form Walters prefers (Kraft, Vosburg, and Bulanadi 1981). Walters struggles to maintain both relationships, which serves to illustrate her own empowerment crisis. As She-Hulk, Walters reacts more impulsively and retains strength of voice and agency while destroying property and complicating situations. Meanwhile, Walters longs for her father's acceptance and quietly endures Morris Walters's sexism and disdain.

In the final issue, the story concludes with Walters repairing her relationship with her father and choosing Zapper as her love interest (thereby choosing her She-Hulk identity's preference and denying herself the desires of her Jen Walters identity). The final splash page displays visual and textual articulations of the achievement of a pseudo-family status (Kraft and Vosburg 1982, 40).

For all of the second-wave feminist symbolism in *The Savage She-Hulk*, Walters ultimately succeeds only in her aspirations of the approval of her father and a boyfriend. The themes of social justice and opposition to patriarchal structures safely banished, She-Hulk's initial narrative journey concludes with mere personal emotional fulfillment from the men in her life.

From Monstrous Feminist to Amazon Postfeminist

Banishing She-Hulk's superficial feminism to domestic concerns would only be the beginning of her gendered contradictions. The latter 1980s would see the character mirror the postfeminist trends aimed at female magazine readers (Tasker and Negra 2007, 8). Postfeminism repositions female empowerment into stylized (and commercialized) aesthetics divorced from metrics of progress, relegating the struggles of equality as exclusively a question for legal domains and ignoring the cultural barriers that continue to be reproduced in society daily.

Avengers, vol. 1, no. 221 (Shooter, Michelinie, and Hall 1982) featured a membership drive to replace departed heroes; both Wasp (Janet van Dyne) and Iron Man (Tony Stark) privately muse that adding "more girls" to the roster would be desirable. She-Hulk is selected as a new member, and by the next issue, van Dyne offers Walters a new designer wardrobe, about which she thinks, "I hate to admit this to myself, but . . . it MIGHT be fun!" (Shooter, Grant, and LaRocque 1982, 3). Thus begins Walter's seduction into materialism as replacement female empowerment fantasies (Lazar 2006). Her designer outfit draws compliments from most of the male heroes, but when a fight with the Masters of Evil breaks out, Wasp insists that She-Hulk remove the clothes, and she engages her first fight alongside the Avengers in her lingerie.

The letter columns in *Avengers* nos. 225, 226, and 227 contain reader letters addressing the new lineup, with overwhelming praise for She-Hulk's membership. Her initial tenure on the Avengers was brief but notable, as she became the first character to actively challenge sexual mores. In *Avengers* no. 234, She-Hulk asks teammate Starfox out on a date, and a few pages later, the two are shown the next morning in She-Hulk's room in postcoital preparations for the day (Stern and Milgrom 1983, 7).

Through *Avengers* and *Fantastic Four* comics, Walters would find some semblance of female community, but those experiences largely revolved around consumeristic consumption and were framed as oppositional to her second-wave feminist roots:

> She-Hulk: And what better opportunity for girl-talk than a trip to the beauty parlor? I wonder if they have the latest issue of "Modern Movie Star"?
> Janet van Dyne: Ha ha! Careful now, Jen. Much more of that kind of talk and you'll have to surrender your N.O.W. membership! (Byrne 1986, 4)

At the conclusion of the 1984 *Marvel Super Heroes Secret Wars* miniseries, She-Hulk leaves the Avengers to replace the Thing on the Fantastic Four, a move that she privately thinks should give her legitimacy as a superhero (Byrne 1984, 2). John Byrne, writer of *Fantastic Four*, would have a significant hand in She-Hulk's development. Perhaps the most significant postfeminist discourse would initially revolve around the character's ongoing struggles with exploitations of her sexuality.

In *The Sensational She-Hulk* graphic novel, corrupt factions within the antiterrorism group S.H.I.E.L.D. arrest She-Hulk and strip-search her in front of leering male agents. The nudity occurs off-panel, but the reader experiences it through the male gaze reflected by the ogling reactions of the witnessing agents (Byrne 1985a, 26–27). Later, She-Hulk is hit by gunfire, which doesn't harm her but leaves her torso and breasts exposed (though again her nakedness is strategically shielded from the reader). This phenomenon would become a recurring convention for writers as She-Hulk would often struggle to keep clothed during battles.

She-Hulk is caught on film sunbathing topless on the roof of the Baxter Building by a tabloid publisher in *Fantastic Four*, vol. 1, no. 274 (Byrne 1985b). Byrne would later report that the inspiration for this plot came from seeing a provocative pinup drawing of She-Hulk in *Marvel Fanfare*, vol. 1, no. 18. Such portrayals signal the growing fascination with She-Hulk as a sex object, a theme that would pervade her second solo series.

Byrne's 1989 *The Sensational She-Hulk* series offered an unusually reflective narrative for superhero comics, one in which the character demonstrates awareness that she is in a comic book and often breaks the fourth wall to converse with the reader. In the premiere issue, She-Hulk pauses in the narrative to discuss the plot with the reader (Byrne 1989a, 21), and in the second issue, she complains to Byrne himself about an undesired twist in her story (Byrne 1989b, 13). This form of metadialogue allows She-Hulk to gaze directly at the reader, which is important, for "[e]ven a cursory survey of contemporary comic book covers reveals women's faces drawn facing away from the camera, suggesting their passivity in relations to the male protagonist—whose gaze strongly faces the reader" (Stuller 2012, 237).

This metanarrative allows She-Hulk to critique how certain conventions of comic books function in her stories (Palumbo 1997), particularly matters related to her sexual mores. *The Sensational She-Hulk* would present the "first major female superhero to be openly, and explicitly sexual and engage in sex with men in comics" (Beerman 2012, 204). This sexuality would take many postfeminist forms, in sharp contrast to *The Savage She-Hulk*'s second-wave feminism.

This shift fits both contemporary understandings of postfeminism, that "popular perceptions of gender relations often suggest that feminism can now safely be relegated to the past" (Budgeon 2011, 281), and the notion that feminism is something women should be liberated from in order to focus on consumption and sexuality (Whelehan 2000). The increased narrative emphasis on clothing, consumer culture, and sexuality are hallmarks of postfeminist discourse (Kinser 2004, 134–35), normally functioning within that discourse to provide superficial symbols of empowerment disconnected from feminist critique. In this way, "feminism itself is no longer needed—it has become a spent force" (Sarikakis and Tsaliki 2001, 112).

During the run of *The Sensational She-Hulk*, the letters columns regularly reported the presence of female readers (Witterstaetter 1991), yet it was often noted that male readers greatly outnumbered their female counterparts. As She-Hulk explored her sexual empowerment, she did so squarely within the boundaries of the male gaze (and explicitly articulated, as when addressing the readers directly). She-Hulk would sometimes appear in the comic completely naked,[1] although, as she explained in *The Sensational She-Hulk*, no. 4, the Comics Code (manifested as censor tape and logos) would cover her genitals and prevent indecency (Byrne 1989c, 27). As the series' sales declined, the emphasis on She-Hulk's sexuality increased, particularly to present her body for the male reader's gaze. For example, on the cover of *The Sensational She-Hulk*, no. 39, Walters sprawls in a vulnerable pose wearing a bikini, saying: "Don't get the wrong idea . . . I'm only doing this because it makes a good cover!!" (Byrne 1992a). In the following issue, She-Hulk stands awkwardly on the cover, trying to cover her apparent nakedness with a Comics Code seal as her writer hands her a jump rope from off-panel (Byrne 1992b), a reference to an earlier letter-column joke suggestion to readers to boost sales (Witterstaetter 1992).

These portrayals and behaviors were largely celebrated by the readership as "cheesecake," the use of "[i]magery that prizes sexualization above all else—especially when that doesn't make sense for the story" (Brothers 2012); this closely resembles contemporary definitions of hypersexualization, which emphasizes

> the exaggerated portrayal of a woman's body, focusing on her breasts, hips, or backside to the detriment of the storytelling. This does not advance the story, and is done solely to titillate the reader. (Jorgensen and Lechan 2013, 282

In the 1990s narratives, She-Hulk not only consistently lost clothing and posed for the male gaze but also commented on the role her sexual image plays in enticing male attention to the comic book, with the goal of increasing sales. For example, In *The Sensational She-Hulk*, no. 41, as She-Hulk recaps the events of the previous issues' events, the panels show her striking provocative poses and flaunting her physical attributes (Byrne 1992c, 7). When partner Louise Mason inquires about the poses, She-Hulk responds:

> Hey, get with the program, Weez! You know Byrne-boy loves doing cheesecake shots of me—mostly because the readers don't mind so much if he scrimps on the backgrounds . . . as long as I'm doing something interesting in the foreground. (Byrne 1992c, 8)

Exchanges like these illustrate how the Byrne series embraces the tenets of postfeminism instead of third-wave feminism. Although feminist Elizabeth Evans explains that "confusion surrounding what constitutes third-wave feminism is in some respects its defining feature" (2015, 22), one consistent element across discourses is the interrogation of the male gaze and male power structures. *The Sensational She-Hulk* instead engages the male gaze and male readers explicitly on the tropes and terms of male stereotypes and values.

Not only are the progressive social causes from the original *Savage She-Hulk* series replaced by more postfeminist considerations of style and sexual politics, but even when She-Hulk is confronted with classic concerns and positions from second-wave feminism, her responses mirror postfeminist logic, such as when she confronts a man who has just blown up an abortion clinic:

Figure 2.1: She-Hulk appears to jump rope naked in order to draw more male readers. *The Sensational She-Hulk*, no. 40, p. 1, by John Byrne. Copyright 1992, Marvel Comics.

> Bomber: I don't understand. How can you be in favor of abortion?
> She-Hulk: Actually, Craig, the subject of abortion poses a real moral quandary for me . . . I am pretty sure where I stand on bombers, though. (McDuffie, Chaplik, and Brigman 1989, 13)

Instead, She-Hulk's concerns revolve around identity issues, her biological clock, and how her superhero career could be balanced against her desires for family, performing the pursuit of "successfully balanced femininity" indicative of the postfeminist struggle that replaced second-wave feminism concerns (Adamson 2017; Sørensen 2017). This postfeminist frame is particularly well articulated in issue no. 10 of *The Sensational She-Hulk*, in which Lexington Loopner (a character parody of DC Comics' Lex Luthor) describes She-Hulk's market profile:

> You're probably aware, then, that you profile out as a nearly impeccable role model for the woman of the Nineties. You're perceived as intelligent, independent, strong but non-threatening to men, emotionally vulnerable—yet professional enough to manage dual careers, as an attorney and an Avenger, no less—and deeply concerned about environmental issues. (Gerber and Hitch 1990, 21)

Deconstructing Postfeminism

Contemporary She-Hulk comics, such as the 2004 Dan Slott series *She-Hulk*, have offered critiques that deconstruct some of the appropriated feminist themes in postfeminist frames. In stark contrast to her 1990s comics, She-Hulk finds that she must wrestle with the uncomfortable "morning after" consequences of waking up with a stranger in Avengers Mansion (Slott and Bubillo 2004, 4–5), and is ejected from Avengers Mansion by Captain America and the Wasp because of the security risks posed by her frequent overnight guests (15).

Behavior previously framed as sexual liberation soon nets She-Hulk a reputation for promiscuity. Soon, She-Hulk's dual personalities begin quarreling, signaling an identity crisis for the character:

> I'm Jen Walters and I'm She-Hulk. Only Jen wouldn't have done that. When I'm She-Hulk I do what I want, when I want. And with who I want. I have fun. I have adventures. I've got it all. So tell me . . . why don't I feel grounded anymore? (Slott and Burchett 2007a, 22)

This internal conflict between personalities allows She-Hulk to explore different components of her feminine empowerment. Both sides of her identity inform this dichotomy, as she struggles to reconcile the power of her heroic stature against the intellectual and professional accomplishments of her meeker alter ego. Approaching the conflict as Walters, she makes a list of the strengths of each personality, deciding that Jen Walters is "smart, resourceful, accomplished, dresses well for work, considerate, polite," and She-Hulk "outgoing, brave, determined, dresses well for clubbing, funny, confident" (Slott, Templeton, and Burchett 2007).

These lists serve to illuminate the struggles of female success. In Walters's human form, Slott frames her as an effective professional woman (if less concerned with social issues than her original incarnation), but She-Hulk represents a monstrous freedom from patriarchal constraint, without critiquing that constraint. The original *Savage She-Hulk* series featured She-Hulk verbally chaffing against males "pushing her around," but the contemporary She-Hulk often protects the masculinity of her friends, such as when she throws an arm-wrestling contest with Hercules to avoid damaging his ego (Slott and Pelletier 2005, 24).

She-Hulk's negative sexual reputation would continue to serve as a defining story component. After a rumor circulates that She-Hulk has bedded the supervillain Juggernaut, She-Hulk witnesses her advances toward Wolverine rebuked in *She-Hulk*, vol. 2, no. 16, because he doesn't want "Juggernaut's sloppy seconds" (Slott and Burchett 2007b, 23). The slut-shaming outrages She-Hulk, and she begins to internally question the double standards concerning how sexual activity affects men and women differently. She articulates the question with Tony Stark (Iron Man) after spending the night with him. The discussion revolves around why Stark's male sexual prowess earns him the celebrated status as a "player," while hers earns her the reputation of being a "skank" (Slott and Burchett 2007c, 9). She-Hulk appears to be overly concerned with how others consider her actions and would soon profess her tiredness at "being a sexual pinball" (David and Moll 2008, 14), but then would soon thereafter bed Hercules again (David and Cucca 2008a) and struggle to reconcile that choice against her new convictions (19). She-Hulk would not resolve this internal conflict, at least not until she would stop measuring herself against the males in her life and begin to look for validation and support from females.

Liberating Feminism

Peter David took over the *She-Hulk* series in 2008, and She-Hulk experienced a shift more consistent with a fourth-wave feminist ideal. The fourth wave, focusing on intersectionality, the complex layering of oppressions, champions the empowerment of marginalized groups (Munro 2013). She-Hulk would not only take up this cause but do so by forming a female community for advocacy and action.

After a new antagonist Red Hulk character assaults She-Hulk from behind, knocking her unconscious (Loeb and McGuinness 2008, 2–5), She-Hulk assembles a group of her closest female hero friends for help (Loeb and Cho 2008). The combined might of nine female heroes as the "Lady Liberators" incapacitates the Red Hulk (Loeb and Cho 2009).

The Lady Liberators gather again to consider a mission of mercy; She-Hulk becomes frustrated by the plight of the citizens of Marinmar, a fictitious Middle Eastern country in which the government has blocked NGO aid for a famine affecting regions with antigovernment sentiments. She-Hulk bristles as the international community deliberates, held in check by Russia's strategic interests in the country. With the Valkyrie, Thundra, the Invisible Woman, and Jazinda assembled, She-Hulk discusses the situation (David and Cucca 2008b, 12–13).

The women acknowledge that typical masculine intervention would not result in permanent outcomes, and so they seek to use their collective reputations to garner international public opinion. Such exchanges pass the Bechdel Test (two or more women who talk to each other, and not about men or relationships) as the women discuss the political ramifications of their mission as well as the implications for various individuals and groups involved.

In *She-Hulk*, vol. 2, no. 35, the group enters the country to transport supplies to the affected areas. After a brief skirmish, those efforts are joined by the Winter Guard, a team of Russian heroes, in an act of international collaboration (David and Qualano 2009a).

She-Hulk's experiences with the Lady Liberators reinvigorates her spirit and restores her faith in both the system and her heroic mission:

> I love these women. I love the whole hero thing. But because of the events of Civil War, and finding out what Tony and his pals did to Bruce . . . I turned my back on it all. I hated it and all it stood for. But I couldn't sustain the hatred. Instead I'm re-embracing the life I thought I'd left behind . . . because I can't get enough of it. (David and Qualano 2009b, 23)

The Lady Liberators exemplify the ideals of feminist community: all possess and share agency, they reason with one another to solve common problems, and each respects her teammates. During this particular story arc, She-Hulk is not once portrayed without her clothing, not even during a threatened rape by the dictator President Darqon Par. Instead of presenting her body for male sexual fantasy, She-Hulk on comics covers during this era emphasized the

Figure 2.2: She-Hulk and members of the Lady Liberators discuss a humanitarian crisis and plan to use their status and community influence to resolve it. *She-Hulk*, vol. 2, no. 34, p. 1, by Peter David and Vincenzo Cucca. Copyright 2007, Marvel Comics.

muscularity and strength of her monstrous form. However, in the narrative pages, She-Hulk's monstrosity reverses the monstrous paradigm; instead of providing contrast to privilege the human form (Boon 2007, 33), She-Hulk's monstrosity provides a contrast to critique the masculine failures of "normal" ways of superhero tropes like "justice."

For example, although it is common for female heroes to act like male heroes in terms of aggression and violence (Reynolds 1992, 79–80), the Lady Liberators mostly refrain from violence to achieve their goals. Yet, this restraint stands in stark opposition to the artwork that positions the female heroes in classic frames of masculine empowerment. As a result, both the Lady Liberators and She-Hulk appear unusually consistent with fourth-wave feminist forms by opposing the systems of oppression without reenacting the tools and forces that encouraged their development.

This burgeoning feminist framing of female heroes would continue in the pages of Marvel's 2015 *A-Force*. Written by G. Willow Wilson, the series not only presented explorations of superheroic feminism but was also the first time a She-Hulk-led series was consistently written by a female writer. Previously, Louise Simonson had written a two-issue arc of *The Sensational She-Hulk* (Simonson and Morgan 1991a, 1991b). Set within the continuity-realigning Secret Wars event, A-Force presented a realm where female heroes led their society, and among those representatives, She-Hulk was ultimately the leader (Bennett, Wilson, and Molina 2015). The series focused on the struggles of the female heroes to deliberate within their community while She-Hulk found ways to compromise with the patriarchy (represented by a god-like Doctor Doom). The narrative continued past the end of the Secret Wars event in a second volume (Wilson and Molina 2016), although declining sales resulted in the second series' cancellation after ten issues.

Prior to *A-Force*, the 2014 third volume of *She-Hulk* appeared, written by Charles Soule. The opening line of the comic, "No one is only one thing" (Soule and Pulido 2014, 1), is an allusion to the narrative's attempt to present an intersectional view of the challenges to balance a career, duty to one's community, personal relationships, and a devotion to equality. Before joining Marvel, Soule practiced immigration law, transactional law, and corporate law. In the series, She-Hulk has a legal showdown with Matt Murdock, but she also maintains ongoing female relationships with characters like Hellcat (Patsy Walker).

The art style of the book, drawn by Javier Pulido and Ron Wimberly, deviates strongly from the Marvel house style. Characters are drawn with rounder edges, softening the character forms to reduce gender contrast. Soule explains how the art style fits into the theme of his series:

Sure, I'm a lawyer, and I wanted to write what I know, but I also wanted to create a project about a woman who didn't have to read as a "woman" or a "man" or a "superhero"—but instead, just as a person dealing with life, using her expertise and confidence as weapons even more potent than her fists (although she can use those too—like any actual person, Jen Walters has more than one side to her). (Soule 2014)

Monstrous bodies typically appear as "disturbing hybrids whose externally incoherent bodies resist attempts to include them in any systematic structuration. And so the monster is dangerous, a form suspended between forms that threatens to smash distinctions" (Cohen 1996, 6). Interestingly, Pulido's art style reduces the contrast between monstrous and nonmonstrous forms, bringing the forms visually closer together, which reduces distinction, serving the intersectionality theme of the comic series.

The theme of intersectionality permeates the narrative of the series as well, as both heroes and villains alike are presented in frames that challenge their historical roles. The courtroom scenes pit Matt Murdock and Walters into unusual roles for them, both in the sense of the differences between their loyalties and their function and also how they perform their duties in a manner contrary to their instincts and roles. Although her monstrous form still presents an imposing physical presence, She-Hulk's actions and decisions are usually to talk other heroes (like Hellcat) out of resorting to exclusively physical solutions to problems.

Soule's She-Hulk achieves her goals by assembling communities from the supporting cast of characters, each of which maintains a different element of "monstrous" form, one of many forms fraught with paradoxes related to the "no one is only one thing" theme of the comic series. In particular, her paralegal Angie Huang looks nondescriptly normal but exhibits strange psychic and supernatural abilities, Huang's monkey Hei Hei is revealed to have mystical powers, and the series' villain turns out to be Nightwatch, a 1990s hero whom the series positions as having only appeared to have been a hero through his publication history because of false memories implanted in all the characters. In short, the heroes are often secretly monsters, the beings that appear to be monsters act heroically, and heroes like Hellcat wrestle with their own inner demons. Physical forms may signal identities of oppression or empowerment, but the narrative increasingly employs intersectionality as a challenge to such identities.

As for Walters herself, Soule explains that his approach to She-Hulk's form involves as much her attitude about her form as much as the form itself:

> One of my favorite things about Jen is that she sees the fun side to being a superhero. She doesn't look at her bright green skin and consider herself a freak—she thinks it's something that makes her special, unique. (Richards 2013)

Where the 1989 *Sensational She-Hulk* positioned Walters as a character who flaunted the sexuality of her monstrous form (embracing the empowerment of postfeminist command of the male gaze), Pulido's She-Hulk exemplified her expressiveness of facial expressions while allowing her empowered physicality to reside in more relatable shapes. Gone are the supermodel lines and poses, allowing characters to interact without the explicit visual commentary that emphasizes the monstrous form as exclusively a site of sexual power. These competing tensions continue to frame the female experience in American professional life and signal She-Hulk's likely continued status as a unique location for exploring intersectional feminism.

Conclusion

This chapter has considered more than eight hundred She-Hulk appearances, demonstrating the continued popularity of the character. Created with superficial representations of feminist critiques, explorations of empowered femininity have been a fixture, as has her male authorship. Other than the fifteen *A-Force* issues, the fifteen comics written by Mariko Tamaki in 2017–2018, and the two Louise Simonson stories, men have written She-Hulk, making She-Hulk a site of male-centered feminist discourse, from a male authorship, often explicitly for a male readership.

As such, it is not surprising that it took nearly three decades for She-Hulk to build female communities. The feminisms expressed through her texts represent male explorations of monstrous tensions rather than accountings of female voices. And yet, She-Hulk's long-standing popularity with male readers positions her to be a particularly accessible site for further gender explorations.

Beyond representation of gender forms and cultural conflict, the evolution of She-Hulk's monstrous form provides a useful frame for setting apart questions of identity from their embedded cultural states. During an era in which the Hulk's form served post-9/11 audiences well because his abilities and strength are derived from anger (Pollard 2015, 82), She-Hulk's form continued to represent a diversification of roles and identities, to represent more cultural complexity than her cousin's hypermasculine form.

Notes

1. For examples, see Gerber, Dixon, and Artis 1991, 19–20; Furman and Hitch 1991, 26; and Byrne 1991, 2.

Bibliography

Adamson, Maria. 2017. "Postfeminism, Neoliberalism and a 'Successfully' Balanced Femininity in Celebrity CEO Autobiographies." *Gender, Work and Organization* 24, no. 3 (May): 314–27.

Beerman, Ruth J. 2012. "The Body Unbound: *Empowered*, Heroism and Body Image." *Journal of Graphic Novels and Comics* 3, no. 2: 201–13.

Bennett, Marguerite, G. Willow Wilson, and Jorge Molina. 2015. *A-Force* 1, no. 1 (July).

Blanch, Christina. 2013. "What Do Comic Books Teach Us about Gender Attitudes?" *Forbes*, January 23. Available at http://www.forbes.com/sites/forbeswomanfiles/2013/01/23/what-do-comic-books-teach-us-about-gender-attitudes/#4538f76a16ac.

Boon, Kevin Alexander. 2007. "Ontological Anxiety Made Flesh: The Zombie in Literature, Film and Culture." In *Monsters and the Monstrous: Myths and Metaphors of Enduring Evil*, edited by Niall Scott, 33–43. Amsterdam: Rodopi.

Brothers, David. 2012. "Art and Superheroines: When Over-Sexualization Kills the Story [Sex]." Comics Alliance, February 16. Available at http://comicsalliance.com/superheroine-sex-art-story/.

Budgeon, Shelley. 2011. "The Contradictions of Successful Femininity: Third-Wave Feminism, Postfeminism and 'New' Femininities." In *New Femininities: Postfeminism, Neoliberalism and Subjectivity*, edited by Rosalind Gill and Christina Scharff, 279–92. New York: Palgrave Macmillan.

Byrne, John. 1984. "A Small Loss." *Fantastic Four* 1, no. 267 (June).

Byrne, John. 1985a. "The Sensational She-Hulk." *Marvel Graphic Novel: The Sensational She-Hulk* 1, no. 18 (January).

Byrne, John. 1985b. "The Naked Truth." *Fantastic Four* 1, no. 275 (February).

Byrne, John. 1986. "Prisoner of the Flesh." *Fantastic Four* 1, no. 287 (February).

Byrne, John. 1989a. "Second Chance." *The Sensational She-Hulk* 1, no. 1 (May).

Byrne, John. 1989b. "Attack of the Terrible Toad Men (or Froggy Came Cavortin')." *The Sensational She-Hulk* 1, no. 2 (June).

Byrne, John. 1989c. "Tall Dis-Order." *The Sensational She-Hulk* 1, no. 4 (August).

Byrne, John. 1991. "Interrupted Melody." *The Sensational She-Hulk* 1, no. 31 (September).

Byrne, John. 1992a. "Date Worse Than Death." *The Sensational She-Hulk* 1, no. 39 (May).

Byrne, John. 1992b. "Can You Believe This . . . ??" *The Sensational She-Hulk* 1, no. 40 (June).

Byrne, John. 1992c. "Battle? Why?" *The Sensational She-Hulk* 1, no. 43 (September).

Cohen, Jeffrey Jerome. 1996. "Monster Culture (Seven Theses)." In *Monster Theory: Reading Culture*, edited by Jeffrey Jerome Cohen, 3–25. Minneapolis: University of Minnesota Press.

Coogan, Peter. 2009. "The Definition of the Superhero." In *A Comics Studies Reader*, edited by Jeet Heer and Kent Worcester, 77–93. Jackson: University Press of Mississippi.

David, Peter, and Vincenzo Cucca. 2008a. "He Loves You, part 2." *She-Hulk* 2, no. 31 (September).

David, Peter, and Vincenzo Cucca. 2008b. "Lady Liberators, part 1." *She-Hulk* 2, no. 34 (December).
David, Peter, and Shawn Moll. 2008. "Jaded: Episode 3." *She-Hulk* 2, no. 24 (February).
David, Peter, and Pasquale Qualano. 2009a. "Lady Liberators, part 2." *She-Hulk* 2, no. 35 (January).
David, Peter, and Pasquale Qualano. 2009b. "Lady Liberators, part 3." *She-Hulk* 2, no. 36 (February).
Dawson, Jim, and Gary Groth. 1978. "Hello, Culture Lovers: Stan the Man Raps with Marvel Maniacs at James Madison University." *Comics Journal* 42, no. 55 (October): 45–55.
Evans, Elizabeth. 2015. *The Politics of Third Wave Feminisms: Neoliberalism, Intersectionality, and the State in Britain and the US.* London: Palgrave Macmillan.
Furman, Simon, and Bryan Hitch. 1991. "Game, Set and Match." *The Sensational She-Hulk* 1, no. 27 (April).
Genter, Robert. 2007. "'With Great Power Comes Great Responsibility': Cold War Culture and the Birth of Marvel Comics." *Journal of Popular Culture* 40, no. 6 (December): 953–78.
Gerber, Steve, Buzz Dixon, and Tom Artis. 1991. "Las Vegas Mon Amour." *The Sensational She-Hulk* 1, no. 23 (January).
Gerber, Steve, and Bryan Hitch. 1990. "Mass-Market Menace." *The Sensational She-Hulk* 1, no. 10 (January).
Housel, Rebecca. 2009. "X-Women and X-istence." In *X-Men and Philosophy: Astonishing Insight and Uncanny Argument in the Mutant X-Verse*, edited by Rebecca Housel and J. Jeremy Wisnewski, 85–98. Hoboken, NJ: Wiley.
Howe, Sean. 2012. *Marvel Comics: The Untold Story.* New York: HarperCollins.
Jorgensen, Anna, and Arianna Lechan. 2013. "Not Your Mom's Graphic Novels: Giving Girls a Choice beyond Wonder Woman." *Technical Services Quarterly* 30, no. 3: 266–84.
Kinser, Amber E. 2004. "Negotiating Spaces for/through Third-Wave Feminism." *NWSA Journal* 16, no. 3 (Autumn): 124–53.
Kraft, David, and Mike Vosburg. 1980a. "Deathrace!" *The Savage She-Hulk* 1, no. 2 (March).
Kraft, David, and Mike Vosburg. 1980b. "Breaking Point!" *The Savage She-Hulk* 1, no. 5 (June).
Kraft, David, and Mike Vosburg. 1980c. "Enter: The Invincible Iron Man." *The Savage She-Hulk* 1, no. 6 (July).
Kraft, David, and Mike Vosburg. 1981. "The She-Hulk War!" *The Savage She-Hulk* 1, no. 23 (December).
Kraft, David, and Mike Vosburg. 1982. "Transmutations." *The Savage She-Hulk* 1, no. 25 (February).
Kraft, David, Mike Vosburg, and Danny Bulanadi. 1981. "Delusions." *The Savage She-Hulk* 1, no. 15 (April).
Kraft, David, Mike Vosburg, and Frank Springer. 1980. "The Power of the Word." *The Savage She-Hulk* 1, no. 9 (October).
Lazar, Michelle M. 2006. "'Discover the Power of Femininity!' Analyzing Global 'Power Femininity' in Local Advertising." *Feminist Media Studies* 6, no. 4: 505–17.
Lee, Stan. 1974. *Origins of Marvel Comics.* New York: Simon and Schuster.
Lee, Stan. 1977. *The Superhero Women.* New York: Simon and Schuster.
Lee, Stan, and John Buscema. 1980. "The She-Hulk Lives." *The Savage She-Hulk* 1, no. 1 (February).
Loeb, Jeph, and Frank Cho. 2008. "Hell Hath No Fury . . ." *Hulk* 1, no. 8 (December).

Loeb, Jeph, and Frank Cho. 2009. "The Revenge of the Lady Liberators!" *Hulk* 1, no. 9 (February).

Loeb, Jeph, and Ed McGuinness. 2008. "Who Is the Red Hulk? Part 2." *Hulk* 1, no. 2 (April).

Madrid, Mike. 2009. *The Supergirls: Fashion, Feminism, Fantasy, and the History of Comic Book Heroines.* Minneapolis: Exterminating Angel Press.

McDuffie, Dwayne, Robin D. Chaplik, and June Brigman. 1989. "Part 1." *The Sensational She-Hulk in Ceremony* 1, no. 1 (October).

Munro, Ealasaid. 2013. "Feminism: A Fourth Wave?" Political Studies Association, November 12. Available at https://www.psa.ac.uk/insight-plus/feminism-fourth-wave.

Palumbo, Donald E. 1997. "Metafiction in the Comics: *The Sensational She-Hulk*." *Journal of the Fantastic in the Arts* 8, no. 3: 310–30.

Pollard, Tom. 2015. *Hollywood 9/11: Superheroes, Supervillains, and Super Disasters*. New York: Routledge.

Raphael, Jordan, and Tom Spurgeon. 2003. *Stan Lee and the Rise and Fall of the American Comic Book*. Chicago: Chicago Review Press.

Reynolds, Richard. 1992. *Super Heroes: A Modern Mythology*. Jackson: University Press of Mississippi.

Richards, Dave. 2013. "Soule Combines Superheroics and Legal Justice in 'She-Hulk.'" Comic Book Resources, October 23. Available at https://www.cbr.com/soule-combines-superheroics-and-legal-justice-in-she-hulk/.

Robinson, Lillian S. 2004. *Wonder Women: Feminisms and Superheroes*. New York: Routledge.

Rosenberg, Alyssa. 2014. "She-Hulk Is a Feminist Hero, Not a Male Fantasy." *Washington Post*, May 21. Available at https://www.washingtonpost.com/news/act-four/wp/2014/05/21/she-hulk-is-a-feminist-hero-not-a-male-fantasy/.

Sarikakis, Katharine, and Liza Tsaliki. 2011. "Post/Feminism and the Politics of Mediated Sex." *International Journal of Media and Cultural Politics* 7, no. 2 (August): 109–19.

Shooter, Jim, Steven Grant, and Greg LaRocque. 1982. "A Gathering of Evil!" *Avengers* 1, no. 222 (August).

Shooter, Jim, David Michelinie, and Bob Hall. 1982. "New Blood!" *Avengers* 1, no. 221 (July).

Simonson, Louise, and Tom Morgan. 1991a. "The Fourth Wall . . . and Beyond." *The Sensational She-Hulk* 1, no. 29 (July).

Simonson, Louise, and Tom Morgan. 1991b. "A Change of State." *The Sensational She-Hulk* 1, no. 30 (August).

Slott, Dan, and Joan Bubillo. 2004. "The Girl from Gamma Gamma Gamma." *She-Hulk* 1, no. 1 (May).

Slott, Dan, and Rick Burchett. 2007a. "Part One: She-Hulk; Agents of S.H.I.E.L.D." *She-Hulk* 2, no. 15 (March).

Slott, Dan, and Rick Burchett. 2007b. "Planet without a Hulk, part 2: Gamma Flight." *She-Hulk* 2, no. 16 (April).

Slott, Dan, and Rick Burchett. 2007c. "Planet without a Hulk, part 3: Shock after Shock." *She-Hulk* 2, no. 17 (May).

Slott, Dan, and Paul Pelletier. 2005. "Strong Enough." *She-Hulk* 1, no. 9 (January).

Slott, Dan, Ty Templeton, and Rick Burchett. 2007. "The Gamma Defense." *She-Hulk* 2, no. 19 (July).

Sørensen, Siri Øyslebø. 2017. "The Performativity of Choice: Postfeminist Perspectives on Work-Life Balance." *Gender, Work and Organization* 24, no. 3 (May): 297–313.

Soule, Charles. 2014. "Case Closed . . . (on the End of She-Hulk)." *The Land of 10,000 Things*, October 24. Available at https://charlessoule.wordpress.com/2014/10/24/case-closed-on-the-end-of-she-hulk/.
Soule, Charles, and Javier Pulido. 2014. "The Motion." *She-Hulk* 3, no. 1 (April).
Stern, Roger, and Al Milgrom. 1983. "The Witch's Tale!" *Avengers* 1, no. 234 (August).
Stuller, Jennifer K. 2012. "Feminism: Second-Wave Feminism in the Pages of *Lois Lane*." In *Critical Approaches to Comics: Theories and Methods*, edited by Matthew J. Smith and Randy Duncan, 235–51. New York: Routledge.
Tasker, Yvonne, and Diane Negra. 2007. "Introduction: Feminist Politics and Postfeminist Culture." In *Interrogating Postfeminism: Gender and the Politics of Popular Culture*, edited by Yvonne Tasker and Diane Negra, 1–25. Durham, NC: Duke University Press.
Whelehan, Imelda. 2000. *Overloaded: Popular Culture and the Future of Feminism*. London: Women's Press.
Wilson, G. Willow, and Jorge Molina. 2016. *A-Force* 1, no. 1 (March).
Witterstaetter, Renée. 1991. "She-Mail." *The Sensational She-Hulk* 1, no. 29 (July): 31.
Witterstaetter, Renée. 1992. "She-Mail." *The Sensational She-Hulk* 1, no. 36 (February): 31.

3

"There Is More to Me Than Just Hunger": Female Monsters and Liminal Spaces in *Monstress* and *Pretty Deadly*

Ayanni C. H. Cooper

Monstress (2015–), by Marjorie Liu and Sana Takeda, and *Pretty Deadly* (2013–), by Kelly Sue DeConnick and Emma Ríos, are exquisitely crafted series that do not shy away from graphic violence. These creator-owned titles are both published by Image Comics, helmed by two of the most celebrated comics writers in the industry, and revel in a level of gore often reserved for "slasher" or "splatter" horror films. Generally speaking, horror films are said to indulge not only the desire for the "perverse pleasure" of "confronting sickening, horrific images/being filled with terror," but also the desire to reject and expel said perverseness "from the safety of the spectator seat" (Creed 1993, 10). However, Takeda and Ríos render wounds, amputation, and decapitation with such startling beauty that the works become simultaneously alluring and repellant. While the comics may be "gut-wrenchingly violent" (Landsbaum 2016), both exist at an intersection of the beautiful and the grotesque due in part to the painterly quality of the art—readers are "confronted" by "horrific images" but are also invited to consider the exquisiteness with which they were rendered, delaying, if not denying, a complete rejection.

This intersection becomes more intriguing when considering the fact that both comics are populated by female monsters, even if they operate in vastly different universes—one a "steampunk [. . .] fantasy epic for mature readers" (Liu and Takeda 2015, no. 1) and the other marrying "magical realism" with "western brutality" (Image Comics n.d.[b]). I use "monster" here as a catch-all term for a variety of partially human, humanesque, and nonhuman creatures: from adorable fox and cyclops children to grim reapers and formless abominations. Yet, it is also useful to look toward a broader definition of the monstrous featured in *The Monstrous-Feminine* (1993) by Barbara Creed: "In some horror films the monstrous is produced at the border between human and inhuman, man and beast, [. . .] in others the border is between the normal and the supernatural, good and evil [. . .] or the monstrous is produced at the border which separates those who take up their proper gender roles from those who do not" (11). Combining these two definitions, Liu and DeConnick feature female monsters as protagonists, antagonists, and general cast members. They present readers with characters who exist on the boundaries and borders of their worlds, both physically and more abstractly; are inexplicably tethered to the abject; or are the "radically excluded," whose gender expression becomes important "in the construction of [their] monstrosity" (Creed 1993, 9, 3). Moreover, what makes *Monstress* and *Pretty Deadly* particularly engaging is how their monsters are empowered by their liminal positionality and their complex connection to abject activities and substances, through their speech and actions, and by virtue of their very existence. They are not passively beautiful creatures who suffer for their transgressions. Rather, readers are asked to identify with these monstrous women as they struggle, make mistakes, fail, and become heroes *because* of their abjection.

As defined by Julia Kristeva in *Powers of Horror* and focused upon by Creed, abjection embodies "that which does not 'respect borders, positions, rules,' that which 'disturbs identity, system order,'" that which is "'radically excluded' from the place of the living [. . .] propelled away from the body and deposited on the other side of [. . .] [what] separates the self from that which threatens the self" (Kristeva, quoted in Creed 1993, 8–9). Reading *Pretty Deadly* and *Monstress* in conversation with *The Monstrous-Feminine* can illuminate the more violent aspects of the narratives—along with the characters committing the violence—as more than simply "forced," unnecessary gore (Lehoczky 2016). I make this argument through a three-pronged approach: first, focusing on blood and how it coats the work, both artistically and figuratively; second, analyzing obscene objects, symbols, and language; and third, discussing a few specific boundaries our monstresses transgress and what they gain for bypassing traditional norms and rules.

Although I am suggesting a tandem reading of these two comics with Creed, there are aspects of Creed's text that will not be useful for analysis when applied to these works. For example, the way Creed links classifications of female monsters to the abject proves infinitely valuable, specifically in relation to "'abominations' [such as]: sexual immorality and perversion; [. . .] decay and death; human sacrifice; murder; the corpse; bodily waste; [and, of course,] the feminine body" (Creed 1993, 9). Conversely, Creed spends a great deal of time considering "male fears" and a variety of other psychoanalytic tropes that will not factor in this discussion (106). Liu has commented that *Monstress* has "nothing to do with men or their institutions [i.e., patriarchy]. Because there are almost no men in *Monstress*, we're focused completely on women" (Landsbaum 2016). To say that men, or relationships with men, have no bearing on the plots of *Monstress* and *Pretty Deadly* is incorrect, though not disingenuous. However, in the case of this analysis and to Liu's point, exploring the abject in these works bears more fruit when not wholly centered around patriarchal concerns or stereotypes. "The feminine body," and the female monster body specifically, are ultimately more important to this discussion of liminality. A major focus on, or contrast to, a metaphorical "masculine body" would detract from the overall argument.

Monstress is "set in an alternate matriarchal 1900s Asia" populated by five races: humans, Arcanics, ancients, cats, and the old gods[1] (Image Comics n.d.[a]). The protagonist, Maika Halfwolf, is a young Arcanic woman "struggling to survive the trauma of war, and who shares a mysterious psychic link with a monster of tremendous power" (Image Comics n.d.[a]). Stubborn, hardened, and violent, Maika is traveling to learn all she can about the life and death of her mother, while searching for a way to separate herself from the primordial monstrum, Zinn. Called the "Mother of all Monsters," Zinn is one of the old gods who hungers for their memories as much as they do for intelligent prey (Liu and Takeda 2016, no. 5, 17).[2] The two are bound together, both their physical bodies and the inner sanctum of their minds, through a magical bargain Zinn made with one of Maika's ancestors. The duo, along with their companions, are pursued by Arcanics, humans, cats, and ancients alike, although the Cumaea are their most dogged hunters. The Cumaea, or "witch-nuns," perform macabre experiments on Arcanics, pulling a substance known as lilium from their bones. The entire organization is secretly orchestrated by old gods in human clothing, who have their own machinations involving Zinn and Maika's capture. Although the story is ongoing, this study concerns the first fifteen single issues of the monthly comic.

Pretty Deadly is a dark, historical fantasy following an ensemble cast of grim reapers, ghosts, and people who can see both (Romano 2015). In a work marketed as "magical realism," DeConnick and Ríos pull heavily from Westerns, surrealism, and samurai films in cultivating the comic's aesthetic (Romano 2015). While the ensemble cast is sizable, the narrative largely focuses on two characters: Death Face Ginny, the Reaper of Vengeance and daughter of the personification of Death; and Sissy, a young beggar girl in a vulture cloak who takes over the role of Death after Ginny's father is killed. The first arc, consisting of issues 1–5, takes place in the "wild west" and follows Sissy as she learns of her history and takes up the mantel of Death. This arc also spends significant page time with Ginny, introducing readers to her character and her various conflicts. The second arc, issues 6–10, is set during World War I after a considerable time-skip. The ensemble cast grows in these chapters, but Ginny becomes the main focus, driving many of the major plot beats.

Blood

In both these series, the characters regularly encounter blood in literal and figurative forms. According to Creed, "blood, as a bodily emission, is itself an abject substance" (1993, 62). Blood runs in torrents through *Pretty Deadly* and *Monstress*: in dialogue, imagery, and even the metanarratives. Both comics' settings lend themselves to depictions of violence and, as stated above, both Ríos and Takeda are unafraid of aesthetically portraying gruesome moments. Discretion shots are rare even when characters are viciously wounded. Building on this, "woman's blood has been represented in patriarchal discourses as more abject than a man's," due to the connection with menstruation and the birthing process (Creed 1993, 62). Although the first arc of *Pretty Deadly* is about "death," DeConnick highlights two births that associate natal blood with blood spilled in violence (Romano 2015). In issue no. 1, during a story-in-a-story narrated by Sissy, readers learn about Ginny's birth. Four sepia-toned panels on page 8 depict Ginny's mother, "Beauty," biting her wrists, in a panel labeled "The Summoning"; the pool of blood that forms; an upside-down close-up of Beauty's face with blood spilling from her mouth, called "Death Fell in Love"; and an infant curled on the floor, hiding her face and covered in afterbirth, dubbed "The Babe" (DeConnick, Ríos, and Bellaire 2014, 11). Ginny's birth is directly correlated to violent blood, "human sacrifice," "the corpse," "and death"—all compounding the abjection (Creed 1993, 9). This idea of compounded abjection is incredibly important when looking at the power Ginny receives as a reaper from her linage and boundary-crossing. Although her birth is discussed in issue no. 1, her father is not confirmed until issue no. 3, page 19; this makes the bloody circumstances of her birth the initial focus, then makes her bloodline a supplemental reveal.

Sissy is the second important birth shown in the first arc. Born from a river of blood, she is "the spawn of a thousand violent deaths"; "her father was violence and her mother was grief" (DeConnick, Ríos, and Bellaire 2014, 74, 99). The blood of death is literally, simultaneously, the blood of birth in Sissy's case. Her emergence from the river is relayed through another story-in-a-story, this time shared by Fox, who is revealed to be Beauty's husband. The entire page—a series of six long/thin panels and two small boxes—is steeped in the lapping waves of the blood river. Toward the middle of the page, baby Sissy is upheld tenderly by more than fifteen disembodied arms emerging from the gore. Baby Sissy, like baby Ginny, is covered in what looks like afterbirth, visually different from the blood of the river.

The text on the page is minimal; however, the comic has already primed readers to think that a "beast" will "rise" from the river, based on earlier narration (DeConnick, Ríos, and Bellaire 2014, 74). "Beast" is repeated with the actual birth, creating a direct juxtaposition, and seeming dissonance, between what readers expect and what appears (77). But it is this dissonance—this boundary breaking—that saves Sissy's life. Fox "could not raise his sword" to kill the "beast" (77).

Men play important roles in Ginny's and Sissy's births, but not so much in the violence of *Monstress*: "*Monstress* responds to violence committed against women by giving them agency [. . .] in violent situations [. . .] in a context that makes it impossible for the violence to be based in misogyny" (Landsbaum 2016). It may seem odd that the focus is on untangling the violence from misogyny rather than forgoing it altogether. However, Liu does not believe that removing men from the equation would suddenly fix society's ills and create a utopia: "[If] men disappeared tomorrow, we'd still have war, poverty—the exact same problems we have now [. . .] women aren't a superior kind of life form [. . .] we're human. Just like men" (McMillan 2015). Thus, bloodshed is intentionally not glossed over and serves a greater purpose in the work. Here, violence in the comics challenges ideas of "acceptable femininity"—Western, hegemonic feminine ideals that exemplify "socially accepted standards," such as softness and gentleness (Fahs 2017, 184; Krane 2001). This makes the series' aestheticization of violence essential to DeConnick and Liu's construction of female monstrosity while simultaneously fortifying a relationship with the abject. Considering Maika, for instance: as she continues to kill and be wounded, her connection to Zinn and their power grows stronger. Throughout the first issue, Maika struggles (in the present time and in flashbacks) to use the power of the old gods. Only after she is beaten in a Cumaean dungeon does she tap directly into Zinn's power to kill her captor. However, this power is complicated. Old gods recharge by feeding on humans and Arcanics, appearing to suck the life-force from people and leaving behind dry husks. Although she fights against it, Maika's connection with Zinn makes her an accomplice to this vampiric, somewhat cannibalistic behavior. On one hand, this vampirism deepens Maika's tie to the abject, as she calls on Zinn's power even though she's aware of the consequences. She participates in this "unacceptable" behavior as a matter of survival. On the other, Zinn often feeds against Maika's will or while

Figure 3.1: Sissy held aloft by arms emerging from the blood river. *Pretty Deadly* (2013–), no. 5, p. 23, by Kelly Sue DeConnick, Emma Ríos, and Jordie Bellaire. Copyright 2014, Image Comics, Inc.

she is unconscious. In issue no. 12, Zinn devours a ship's entire crew. Maika is livid, tears in her eyes and blood spattered on her face:

> Maika: You killed them all. Every last one.
> Zinn: . . . No . . . it is *we* . . . it is *us* . . . who fed . . .
> Maika: Doesn't it matter to you? Is every life but yours so fucking worthless?
> Zinn: . . . survival . . . is not . . . gentle . . . mercy . . . is for the . . . weak . . .
> Maika: Is that why you murdered your friend? Is that what you whispered to the Shaman-Empress? You said you weren't her slave . . . but maybe she was yours. How long did it take you to turn *her* into a murderer? (Liu and Takeda 2017, no. 12, 19)

Zinn consciously associates Maika with the carnage, making her morally accountable. They together push beyond acceptable femininity, acceptable humanity even, into a liminal space few creatures occupy. There are even instances during these feedings when Takeda draws Maika's face differently, signaling perhaps a deeper relation to her monstrosity. This art-shift appears consistently, starting with issue no. 1, but an excellent example is in issue no. 7 on page 4. In contrast to her usual appearance, Maika's irises and pupils are drawn solid black, with heavy black around her outer eye. Her skin is colored a greenish hue and is covered with deliberate cross-hatching; her teeth are yellow and purposely drawn individually. While it is not completely certain what is physically happening to Maika in these moments, Takeda's intentional art-shifts further separate her from the comfortable boundaries of humanness and draw her into the liminal uncanny valley of the monstrous. Moreover, as the story continues and additional information is revealed about the monstrum and the Shaman-Empress, Maika is pulled deeper into the realm of the repulsive and the obscene.

Obscenity

Obscenity is notoriously difficult to define, although it functions as an important literary tool. Here I understand the "obscene" to be: "offensively or grossly indecent, lewd [. . .] tending to deprave and corrupt those who are likely to read, see, or hear the contents [. . .] offending against moral principles, repugnant; repulsive, foul, loathsome."[3] Looking mainly at *Monstress*, this operates on two levels, the first of which is the use of obscenities or coarse language. The narrative in and of itself is not "grossly indecent," but it does perhaps "offend against a moral principal," an effect DeConnick achieves in another of her series, *Bitch Planet*. That series directly addresses notions of social compliance—what is acceptable and what is not within the bounds of society. I would argue that *Monstress* (and, by extension, *Pretty Deadly*) further challenges tepid ideas of what a woman is supposed to be, both within comics and on a larger scale, through dialogue. In an interview with Claire Landsbaum of *Vulture*, Liu states: "We're not accustomed to giving women the space to express the full range of emotions and flaws that men are permitted. Anger and aggressiveness aren't part of the scale of what is acceptable behavior in women," echoing my earlier consideration of acceptable femininity (Landsbaum 2016). DeConnick and Liu deliberately craft female characters who are aggressive, do not "take up their proper gender roles" as part of their monstrousness, and are noticeably not reprimanded for this behavior (Creed 1993, 11). Although DeConnick's monstresses are often brusque or crass—Ginny especially—Liu amplifies her characters' range of expression through obscenities. Expletives are peppered throughout Liu's dialogue, with Maika being one of the top users of this language. Although the "poverty-of-vocabulary" theory argues that "swearing is the 'result of a lack of education, laziness or impulsiveness,'" here it is used as an unbridled acknowledgment of rage, fear, and ire, circumventing the limitations of acceptable feminine language to express the inexpressible (Valdesolo 2016). Her language provides a strong sense of who Maika is and how she views those around her. She hurls expletives at an enemy, or even at Zinn. When the monstrum "returns" from a flashback, muttering to themselves, Maika grumbles, "Oh Goddess . . . what the fuck are you mumbling about?" (Liu and Takeda 2016, no. 9, 9). This instance, among many others, shows that Maika has no time for idle pleasantry and does not respect the "rules" of polite language.

In addition to obscenities, Maika is also in possession of two obscene objects: the Mark of the Eclipsing Eye and a portion of the Mask of the Shaman-Empress. The first time readers see the mark is on the first page of issue no. 1, emblazoned on Maika's chest as a slave handler begins her auction to a group of aristocrats and Cumaea.

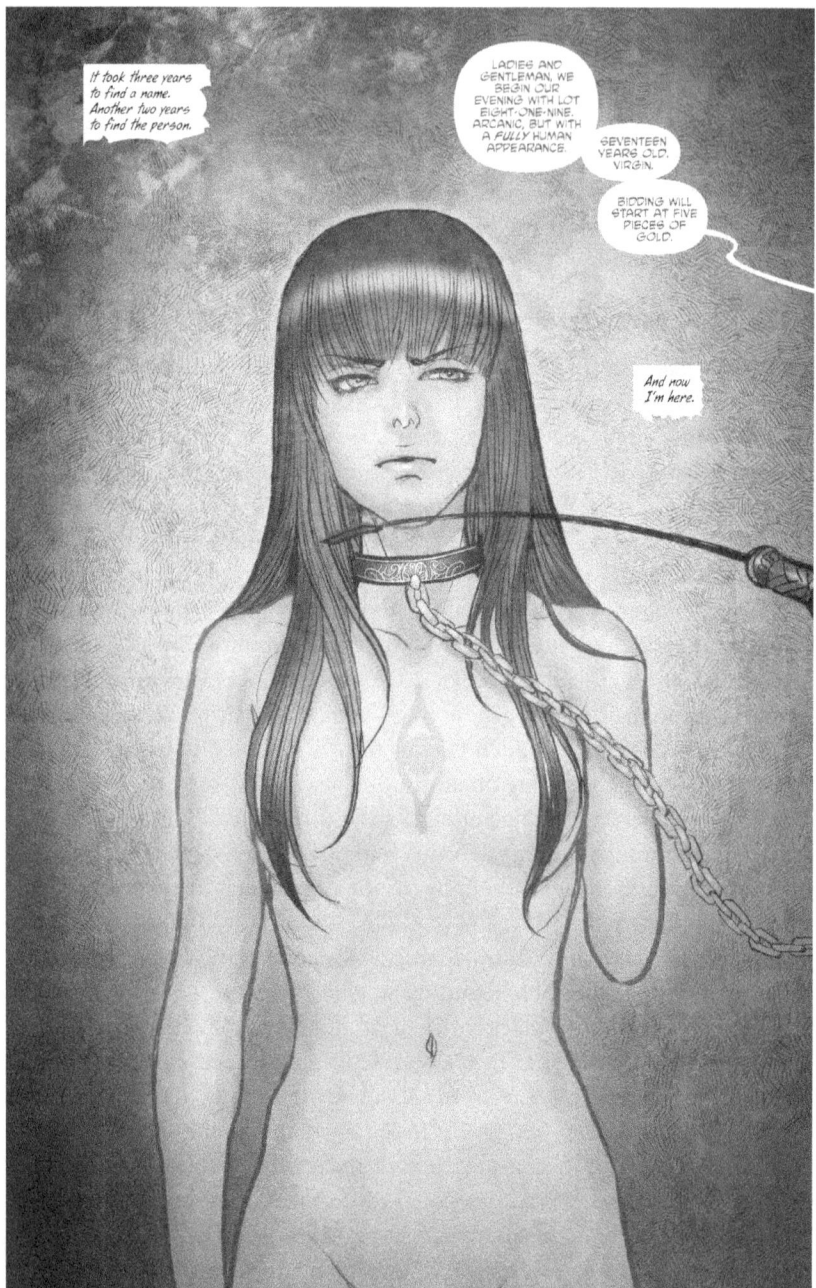

Figure 3.2: Maika stands naked while being auctioned off to an unseen audience of humans and Cumaea. *Monstress* (2015–), no. 1, p. 1, by Marjorie Liu and Sana Takeda. Copyright 2015, Image Comics, Inc.

Although she is naked, the image is far from sensual and rather makes readers uncomfortable as they move from her clearly perturbed expression, to the collar and her amputated arm, to the marking. This brand shows that she is a descendant of the Shaman-Empress, the woman who made the initial bonding bargain with Zinn. For many Arcanics, this mark is a curse. After the Shaman-Empress died, "all who showed the mark of the eye were imprisoned . . . experimented on . . . bred" in an attempt to rouse the old god (Liu and Takeda 2017, no. 11, 13). Having this mark near the center of the first image of the comic places the obscene in a position of prominence once readers understand its significance. From the moment *Monstress* begins, readers have a hint that something unsettling is inside of Maika. However, this focus on the mysterious obscene is not to play into hackneyed tropes of "the lethal, cannibalistic, non-human monster" lurking "behind the apparently beautiful face of the woman of color," as explored by Jane Caputi and Lauri Sagle (2004, 100). Caputi and Sagle concentrate primarily on the "the white hero's perspective," which is a nonfactor in *Monstress* (108). Maika's abjection becomes, instead of a "[warning] about the inherent danger of liaisons with the 'other,'" a site of immense, coveted power and a link to her ancestry (96).

The mask, on the other hand, falls more in line with that which would "deprave and corrupt those who are likely to read, see, or hear the contents."[4] Described as an "artifact from the lost age, wrought of blasphemous materials poisonous to all living creatures," pieces of the mask sting almost anyone who touches them—a violent rejection of the self (Liu and Takeda 2015, no. 2, 14). In issue no. 11, Maika learns that the Shaman-Empress created the mask to draw Zinn into her own body, but, before she died, she "broke the mask and hid it from the world . . . for at last she came to realize the peril of her creation" (Liu and Takeda 2017, no. 11, 13). However, it is also revealed that bringing the mask pieces together is imperative for Maika's survival—if she does not collect all the shattered remains, Zinn will devour her slowly, a piece at a time. Maika literally loses a piece of her body every time she draws heavily on Zinn's power. For example, during the climax of *Monstress*'s first arc, Maika sacrifices what remains of her left arm to defeat another monstrum. These losses serve as a constant reminder of the cost of the old gods' power. Her survival is dependent on her connection to the abject.

Conversely, her deep connection to this abject object also imbues her with increased power. At the end of issue no. 12, Maika puts a shard of the mask against her face and "set[s] off a ripple effect of mystical activation" that is felt by the ancients and the old gods (Liu and Takeda 2018, no. 13, 2). (Funnily, she comments that "nothing much happened" [24].) A handful of old gods who felt this ripple are introduced in issue no. 14, disguised as human leaders of the Cumaea. Although readers have come to understand the monstra as terrifyingly formidable creatures, issue no. 14, page 25, shows that the corrupt power of the mask is even more than they can bear. A character, so far only known as Commander, is tempted by the voices and sad songs of their "sisterbrothers from the other side" to bring the mask close to their face (Liu and Takeda 2018, no. 14, 24). However, the mask seems to have a will of its own. Although Commander struggles, pulling down their hand holding the mask and stating, "This . . . this is my . . . flesh . . . you cannot . . . make me," the fragment affixes itself to them (25). Commander screams as steam rises from the mask and red cracks appear upon their visage. Based on the mass of red tentacles swirling behind them, it seems that the old god may be losing control of their human form. Although the old gods are also, arguably, aligned with the abject, it is Maika's connection to the obscene—the mask, her mark, and ultimately her bloodline—that give her a distinct advantage over those who pursue her.

Bloodlines and Boundaries

Lineage is significant in *Pretty Deadly* and *Monstress*, be it Ginny's, Maika's, or that of all Arcanics. As I mentioned earlier, Ginny's compounded abjection and the liminality created are vital parts of what make her so formidable. This is highlighted in two pages during the culminating battle of the first arc, when Ginny and company wage war on her father, Death. Page 19 of issue no. 5 is dominated by muted grays, browns, and black, giving the panels a cold, still feeling. Here, Ginny is directly asked if she is "reaper, god, or mortal" (DeConnick, Ríos, and Bellaire 2014, 121). A Molotov cocktail tossed in the window disrupts the stillness with an explosion of active oranges. The subsequent page mirrors these oranges throughout its four panels, along with splashes of red blood. The third panel, which dominates the page, depicts Ginny emerging from the burning building in what TV Tropes refers to as an "Out of the Inferno"–style shot, guns blazing and with a caption reading: "I'm all three" (122).[5] This definitive statement places her at the crossroads "between the normal and the supernatural," highlighting her monstrousness and her might simultaneously (Creed 1993, 11). In this vein, the panel radiates strength: Ginny's silhouette is outlined by the roaring, uncontained fire. Her figure is bathed in warm but disquieting colors, and she appears like the Terminator—unflinching, even as she is shot twice. Coupling the image with the text overlay explicitly creates a connection between her power and the fact that she disrupts the boundaries between reapers, gods, and mortals.

Ginny also transgresses mortal boundaries in her role as a reaper. Reapers can travel in both the lands of the living and the realm of the dead without hesitation. When Ginny is among mortals, she is not a ghostly apparition or intangible being; she can easily interact with the living world around her, though she often passes by unseen. The first arc largely shows her interacting with characters who have the ability to see ghosts and reapers, but the second places her in the midst of a World War I battlefield. In her pursuit of the Reaper of War, Ginny pushes a soldier who is unaware of her presence but reacts to her touch (DeConnick, Ríos, and Bellaire 2016, 71). Taking this a step further, reapers can make themselves visible to humans and can interfere with their lives when advantageous. Ginny is the Reaper of Vengeance, "a hunter of men who have sinned" (DeConnick, Ríos, and Bellaire 2014, 12). Humans who know of her can call for her in song—"If you done been wronged, say her name, sing her song . . . Ginny rides for you on the wind, my child . . . death rides on the wind!" (12). Because of her position as the Reaper of Vengeance and her human mother, Ginny is empowered by her relationship with the living and uses the power provided by her liminal status and connection to the abject to serve as protector.

Turning to *Monstress*, crossing boundaries is undoubtedly tied to the bloodlines of the five races, especially when considering Arcanics. The species exists because ancients could not "deny themselves the pleasure of human company" (Liu and Takeda 2016, no. 5, 25). These relations produced no children for thousands of years, but the first Arcanic was eventually born—the Shaman-Empress. Described as "powerful," with a mind "unlike any that came before—profound and far-seeing," she had abilities that rivaled those of the ancients, gaining strength through her liminality, similar to Ginny (Liu and Takeda 2017, no. 11, 11). Other Arcanics were born in the Shaman-Empress's wake, quickly spreading. Three hundred years before *Monstress* begins, "the witch-nuns had begun to preach that Arcanics were *unclean* creatures," setting them as the other and aligning them with the defiled, the abject (Liu and Takeda 2016, no. 3, 27).[6] By the time Maika is born, "[the] world of *Monstress* is one that has been torn apart by racism, slavery, by the commodification of mixed race bodies. [. . .] Even if you look human, you might not be safe" (McMillan 2015). Maika is not marked by any animal features and is, in a way, passing as human. Propaganda from the Cumaea warns onlookers to "[beware] the DECEIVERS, half-spawn who can pass as human" (Liu and Takeda 2016, no. 8, 25). One could imagine this sort of language emanating from South Africa under apartheid or in America under Jim Crow, Liu even noting that the pervasive sense of unease surrounding identity in the narrative is "a familiar story to people of color in this country" (McMillan 2015).[7] Unlike in many passing narratives, such as Nella Larsen's *Passing*, Maika is not purposely hiding the fact that she is Arcanic. However, she is able to use her position as a "deceiver" to her advantage, making use of her liminal appearance. She references this during a tense sequence in issue no. 8, ironically when an octopus-Arcanic sailor boorishly insists that Maika is "gonna need more than a *drop* of true blood" before she can claim she is Arcanic, an inverse of the "one-drop rule" (Liu and Takeda 2016, no. 8, 5). Liu commented in her interview with the *Hollywood Reporter* that, in *Monstress*, she has "wrestled with [. . .] what it means to be of mixed race, what it means to straddle the borderlands of two cultures," and that is especially apparent in moments like this (McMillan 2015). The sailor physically menaces Maika and threatens one of her companions, to which Maika responds with violence—lifting the sailor by the throat and tearing off a tentacle-like limb. The narration is what makes this scene especially engaging. Maika speaks to her dead mother, saying:

> They don't trust people who look like me anymore . . . Changelings, they call us. Traitors. Do you remember when I was small? How I wanted to have Goddess-marks like the other Arcanic children? I wanted a wolf tail. I wanted wolf claws and wolf teeth. Do you remember what you said? "Little wolf, you have all those things. But they are safe within you where no one can take them. Sometimes, my darling . . . it's better to hide your teeth." (Liu and Takeda 2016, no. 8, 6–7)

The focus on Maika's transgressive appearance, as well as the emphasis on blood in the dialogue and the art, reaffirm her connection to the abject. This scene also places a focus on Maika's relationship with her mother, Moriko Halfwolf. By this point in the narrative, readers are already aware that Maika was an efficient warrior and killer long before her symbiotic relationship with Zinn, due largely to her mother's training and guidance. However, it has become apparent in the most recent chapters of *Monstress* that Moriko is the ultimate catalyst for Maika's journey and her current predicament.

In her chapter covering "Woman as Monstrous Womb," Creed briefly addresses female scientists who use their own bodies to create monsters, noting that "the theme of woman giving birth to (physical) monsters from her own body has been explored by a number of [. . .] horror films" (1993, 56). Moriko could easily fall under this category, if focusing on her deliberate conception of Maika. Similar to the Shaman-Empress, Moriko is described as "powerful of mind, impossible to fool, and a ruthless strategist" (Liu and Takeda 2018, no. 13, 32). She appeared human like her daughter, even though she was the child of an ancient, the Queen of Wolves. She was also chosen to "command the Arcanic armies" of her own mother's court but was captivated by the Shaman-Empress and her power, choosing to abdicate her position to "obsessively search for the old ruins of the Shaman-Empress" (32). Readers know through flashbacks that Moriko found these ruins when Maika was a little girl and that whatever transpired there led to Zinn inhabiting Maika's body. However, later in the story, Liu reveals that Moriko intentionally became pregnant to access the Shaman-Empress's bloodline: "Your mother wanted what all others have desired. Control over the blood. And Moriko did what all mothers do when they want control—she had a daughter" (Liu and Takeda 2017, no. 11, 14). Creed argues that the womb and birthing process are already abject, noting: "The womb represents the utmost abjection for it contains a new life from which will pass from inside to outside bringing with it traces of its contamination—blood, afterbirth, faeces" (1993, 49). While, in this chapter, I am looking to establish ways these characters take abjection a step beyond the normal, it can be helpful to understand the baseline abjection of biological functions typically associated with the reproductive body. Although the particulars of Maika's birth are not provided by a completely reliable source, there is no indication that the facts are, at least on the surface, false. Similar to the women scientists discussed in *The Monstrous-Feminine*, Moriko used her body to "tamper with nature" (Creed 1993, 56) in an attempt to access great power, making Maika's birth even more monstrous, more abject.

Maika is devastated when she learns of her mother's machinations, having desperately wanted to know that she mattered to her mother (Liu and Takeda 2016, no. 9, 22). She angrily asks if she was everything her mother desired, or if she was just a pawn in Moriko's game (Liu and Takeda 2017, no. 12, 12). "Control" over the monster is mentioned by Sharon Russell in "The Witch in Film: Myth and Reality" (quoted in Creed 1993, 56). Russell claims that women rarely control monsters, except through mother/son relationships and through their pregnancy (Creed 1993, 56). While Creed disagrees with this assertion, I think it is worth looking into when thinking about Maika and Moriko. Readers may initially assume that Moriko aims to maintain control of the Shaman-Empress's bloodline, even after she dies. However, during the flashback caused by the mask, Maika sees a vision of her childhood in which she and her mother share a quiet moment after a vicious battle:

> Moriko: No matter that happens, you belong to *no one*. You will be controlled by *no one*. Swear it to me, Maika. I will kill anyone who tells you otherwise.
> Maika: *You* control me, though. I'm *yours*.
> Moriko: I gave up that dream a long time ago. You have a life to conquer. An entire *world* to wake . . . What that world becomes . . . will depend entirely

on the strength of your heart. And your heart, my little wolf, is very strong. (Liu and Takeda 2017, no. 12, 24–25)

Moriko's initial intentions may have been to control the monster she created, setting the entire story in motion to get close to the Shaman-Empress's power. Yet, she ultimately decides to place her trust in the future Maika will create and the woman she will grow into.

Conclusion

Using blood, obscenity, and boundary-crossing, DeConnick and Liu present readers with interesting, relatable, monstrous women. This chapter has focused heavily on the ways the abject is used to both the creators' and the characters' benefit, but these works highlight other issues concerning race and class, disability, and the larger influence of folklore: Chinese, Japanese, American, and otherwise. The chapter is purposely focused on women, but there is more here to unpack about paternity, from Maika's absent—but soon to be revealed—father, to Ginny's intended patricide, and Fox's surrogate-father relationship with Sissy. All these aspects intertwine to create the worlds of *Monstress* and *Pretty Deadly*—complex, violent, and captivating. Unlike most horror films, which allow viewers to delve into the abject and reject it safely, these comics offer an opportunity to ponder the abject, to stare into the monstrous not only to be "filled with terror" but to find a reflection (Creed 1993, 10). Through their monstresses, Liu and DeConnick offer readers a chance to embrace the power of their own liminality, to transgress "the ordinary" or "the normal," and to find courage in the monstrosity that, at its core, makes us human.

Notes

1. Further information about the *Monstress* races is as follows:

    - Ancients: Seemingly immortal animal-like humanoids who have an opulent culture. So far, it has not been revealed where ancients come from.
    - Arcanics: A hybrid species between human and ancients, although they can and do mate with other Arcanics and humans. "Able to breed as quickly as humans, and possessing some of the powers of their ancient forbearers, they carry the best and worst of both parents" (Liu and Takeda 2016, no. 5, 25).
    - Cats: Talking cats that can grow multiple tails, depending on how much wisdom they amass. Have a society that is both separate and integrates into the overall society of *Monstress*. Both adorable and potentially vicious, just like real cats.

- Old Gods: Giant, monstrous creatures, most with a loose animal motif. The majority appear ghost-like in the background, as it seems they've been trapped in a sort of temporal prison.
- Humans: *Monstress*'s humans are ultimately the same as real-life humans, coming in a variety of sizes, shapes, and colors. Some human women join the powerful, perhaps corrupt Cumaea and become "witch-nuns."

2. I am using a gender-neutral pronoun for Zinn because, in issue no. 10, we learn that other old gods refer to Zinn as "SisterBrother." While there is evidence in the comic that other monstra are gendered female, I will use gender-neutral pronouns for the sake of consistency.

3. *Oxford English Dictionary*, online edition, s.v. "obscene, adj."

4. *Oxford English Dictionary*, online edition, s.v. "obscene, adj."

5. "Everything around someone explodes and catches on fire. No One Could Survive That! [. . .] Yes, yes they could, and they're slowly walking out, an Unflinching Walk, because the fire doesn't bother them. [. . .] A very old trope, to the point that 'passing through the flames' and being unharmed/transformed is a classic metaphor" (TV Tropes n.d.).

6. Even though they are called "nuns," the Cumaea are not expected to remain virgins. They are not the focus of this chapter, but it is reasonable to claim that the Cumaea gain their powers from the abject as well, especially since they use the lilium extracted from dead Arcanic bodies.

7. *Monstress* engages in a nuanced conversation around race, othering, and prejudice that I only skim the surface of here, as a thorough analysis could fill a chapter of its own. For further discussion of hybridity and race in *Monstress*, see Rebecca Jones's "My Body Isn't My Own" (2018).

Bibliography

Caputi, Jane, and Lauri Sagle. 2004. "Femme Noire: Dangerous Women of Color in Popular Film and Television." *Race, Gender and Class* 11, no. 2: 90–111. Available at http://www.jstor.org/stable/41675126.

Creed, Barbara. 1993. *The Monstrous-Feminine: Film, Feminism, Psychoanalysis*. Abingdon, Oxon, England: Routledge.

DeConnick, Kelly Sue, Emma Ríos, and Jordie Bellaire. 2014. *Pretty Deadly*, vol. 1: *The Strike*, nos. 1–5. Berkeley, CA: Image Comics.

DeConnick, Kelly Sue, Emma Ríos, and Jordie Bellaire. 2016. *Pretty Deadly*, vol. 2: *The Bear*, nos. 6–10. Berkeley, CA: Image Comics.

Fahs, Breanne. 2017. "The Dreaded Body: Disgust and the Production of 'Appropriate' Femininity." *Journal of Gender Studies* 26, no. 2: 184–96.

Image Comics. n.d.(a). "*Monstress*, vol. 1 TP." Available at https://imagecomics.com/comics/releases/monstress-vol-1-tp.

Image Comics. n.d.(b). "*Pretty Deadly*." Available at https://imagecomics.com/comics/series/pretty-deadly.

Jones, Rebecca. 2018. "'My Body Isn't My Own': War, Monsters, and Matriarchy in *Monstress* (2015–)." *MAI: Feminism and Visual Culture*, no. 1 (Spring). Available at https://maifeminism.com/my-body-isnt-my-own-war-monsters-and-matriarchy-in-monstress-2015/.

Krane, Vikki. 2001. "We Can Be Athletic and Feminine, But Do We Want To? Challenging Hegemonic Femininity in Women's Sport." *Quest* 53, no. 1: 115–33.

Landsbaum, Claire. 2016. "The Bloody Comic *Monstress* Is a Response to *Game of Thrones*, *Ex Machina*, and *The Smurfs*." *Vulture*, July 22. Available at http://www.vulture.com/2016/07/why-the-bloody-comic-monstress-forgoes-men.html.

Lehoczky, Etelka. 2016. "Good, Evil and Long Black Tentacles Make a 'Monstress.'" NPR Book Reviews, August 2. Available at https://www.npr.org/2016/08/02/487633169/good-evil-and-long-black-tentacles-make-a-monstress.

Liu, Marjorie, and Sana Takeda. 2015–2018. *Monstress*, nos. 1–15 (November 2015–March 2018). Berkeley, CA: Image Comics.

McMillan, Graeme. 2015. "'Monstress': Inside the Fantasy Comic about Race, Feminism and the Monster Within." *Hollywood Reporter*, November 3. Available at https://www.hollywoodreporter.com/heat-vision/monstress-inside-fantasy-comic-race-836391.

Romano, Aja. 2015. "*Pretty Deadly*'s Emma Ríos and Kelly Sue DeConnick Talk Myth and Musical Theater." *Daily Dot*, November 29. Available at https://www.dailydot.com/parsec/emma-rios-kelly-sue-de-connick-pretty-deadly-interview/.

TV Tropes. n.d. "Out of the Inferno." Available at http://tvtropes.org/pmwiki/pmwiki.php/Main/OutOfTheInferno.

Valdesolo, Piercarlo. 2016. "Is Swearing a Sign of a Limited Vocabulary?" *Scientific American*, April 5. Available at https://www.scientificamerican.com/article/is-swearing-a-sign-of-a-limited-vocabulary/.

Part 2

The Body as Monstrous

4

The (Un)Remarkable Fatness of Valiant's *Faith*

Stefanie Snider

In 2016, Valiant Comics released a new comic book series focused on a single female superhero, Zephyr. More commonly known as Faith Herbert, Zephyr had originally been part of a group of superheroes called the Harbingers, who came to life nearly twenty-five years earlier, in 1992. *Harbinger* was published for three years (1992–1995) and then later revived in 2012 as part of an ongoing series (Dysart, Evans, and Hannin 2012).[1] In 1992, the Harbingers were teenagers dealing with the development of their psychically activated superpowers as "psiots"[2] in a typical coming-of-age story line about the trials and tribulations of simultaneous adolescent maturation and super-ability growth (Valiant Entertainment 2018). When Valiant began its solo series on Faith in 2016,[3] the lead character was no longer a teenager (as she had been in the 2012 rebooted series), but neither was she in her forties, as she would have been had she aged in real time starting from the 1992 original series. Instead, Faith/Zephyr was now in her early thirties, living in Los Angeles, and experiencing superheroism for the first time on her own—without being a part of a team. Faith's powers consist of telekinesis (allowing her to fly and move objects around at will), superstrength, and the power to create force fields and shields around herself and the people/objects she carries with her.

As a youthful, white, able-bodied, cis-heterosexual heroine with long, flowing hair, Faith/Zephyr[4] is not especially unusual among her contemporaries in pop culture comic representations. Unlike previous and current superheroes of the same race, gender identity, and gender expression, however, Faith is fat. The most remarkable aspect of Faith's size in the first four collected volumes of the comics is that it is *unremarkable*; Faith's fat body goes largely unremarked upon throughout the 2016–2017 run of the series. Visually, we see Faith take part in numerous activities—flying, fighting, rescuing, sleeping, eating, and writing on her computer—in a form-fitting, full-length white-and-blue costume that simultaneously hides her flesh while clearly outlining her curves.[5] As a result, sartorially and otherwise, Faith is both covered and exposed; explicitly fat and never referred to as such. Is this the superhero fat activists have been waiting for? The character who might help advocate for fat acceptance in pop culture? Or is this another variation of fat-oppressive culture that typically portrays fat women as both hypervisible and invisible (Gailey 2014)? This chapter will explore the ways in which Faith is visually and textually constructed based on her corporeality as well as her superhero status in the first sixteen issues of the *Faith* comic book series. The general silence on Faith's fatness in the texts themselves can be read as the normalization of the fat, white, conventionally feminine cis-female body. I will examine whether this is a positive step toward fat acceptance within popular culture or if this normativity obfuscates the potential productivity of Faith's monstrousness as a superpowerful fat woman. Unpacking how monstrosity, ugliness, and awkwardness can be used as anti-oppressive modes of rendering fatness visible builds upon work by scholars and activists in the fat studies, queer studies, and disability studies fields who have looked at nonpathologizing ways of discussing the banality, the awkwardness, and the ugliness of fat, LGBTQIA, and/or disabled bodies and their representations.[6]

In recent Western cultural history, fat people have come to be perceived as monstrous, excessive, and dangerous, to themselves and others, because their physical and discursive identities violate the boundaries of cultural taste. In the decades since the 1960s, fat activists have alternatingly embraced and distanced themselves from such readings of fat and fatness in order to challenge fatphobia and fat oppression. We could argue, however, that one way to disempower dominant cultural ideology dictating that fat and fatness are representative of physical, moral, and visual failings would be to renegotiate how Western culture defines monstrousness, excessiveness, and dangerousness in negative ways. If we were to see these accusations as neutral, or even empowering, in much the same way "queer," "dyke," and "crip" have been reclaimed by LGBTQIA and disabled activists and academics in recent years,[7] we can circumvent the force of hate these terms and ideas initially represented. Indeed, fat as a substance and fat people as embodiments of that substance and all its attached metaphorical meanings have not always been seen negatively in Western culture.

Prior to the last thirty years of the nineteenth century, fat was regarded positively in both Europe and the United States; being able to afford to be fat was a sign of wealth and upper-class social status, and could even be regarded as a virtue in these cultural structures (Stearns 2002). Within the contexts of increasing urbanization, mass production, and emerging late-stage capitalism in the West, fatness was not simply tolerated but celebrated as a sign of physical and intellectual prowess and economic superiority in business as well as family spheres. This appreciation, even celebration, of fat and fatness, however, changed quickly in the 1870s–1880s, to a denigration of fat and fatness as signs of surplus, waste, and likely corruption. It is during this period in the West that capitalist tycoons frequently came to be labeled "fat cats" and rendered as figures of mockery in widely circulated public imagery such as newspaper political cartoons. These figures, whether shown as expressly feline or not, typically were drawn with large, round bodies taking up more than their "fair share" of allotted space and were characterized as excessive figures with no morals to guide their financial or physical gains (Farrell 2011).

Using fatness as a sign of capitalist greed at the turn of the twentieth century directly informs its later use as a sign of villainy in twentieth- and twenty-first-century comic books and pop culture. From Kingpin and the Blob in the *Spiderman* and *X-Men* comics (Scole 2016), respectively, to Jabba the Hutt in *Star Wars* and Ursula in *The Little Mermaid*, fatness is frequently coded as evil. At the same time, however, these villains are also typically characterized as strong, clever, and nearly unstoppable, demonstrating that the monstrousness of fatness need not be automatically coded as a detriment to fat characters. Indeed, fatness can be a core strength that sets fat figures apart from smaller bodies and that renders them powerful in terms of physiology as well as intellect. How might a superhero benefit by appropriating these powers of fatness typically held by monstrous villains? How might a representation of a fat comic book character who uses her monstrousness to defeat enemies while also neutralizing the more typically degrading notions of the limits of fat become a superhero embodying social justice?

The Contradiction of Faith's Fatness

The appearance of Faith in her own comic book series was highly anticipated. Media outlets from the typically "highbrow" *New York Times* and National Public Radio, to the popular market of *The Today Show* and *People*, to the feminist publications *Bustle* and *Women Write about Comics* covered the news that Faith would become a solo superhero—and *the* solo *fat* superhero—in late 2015 and early 2016 (Gustines 2016; Lehoczky 2016; Ospina 2015; Tanski 2016; Mazziotta 2015; Schindler 2016). These stories ranged in focus, with some looking at Faith as an example of the reinvention of Valiant's catalog and others exploring the new collaborative artwork to be included in the series, but nearly all the media responses to the new *Faith* comics mentioned the character's body size. That Faith was fat, and especially that Faith would be, at least initially, portrayed as fat in a way that was taken for granted and inconsequential to her superhero status, seemed to be first and foremost on reviewers' minds. This appears to be the case for several reasons. One is that in Faith's previous incarnations as part of the Harbingers team her fatness was not at all neutral. Instead, it was portrayed more typically for fat characters across media—as the butt of numerous jokes, especially ones that contrasted her ability to fly with her weight. While all of the Harbinger superheroes of the 1990s were suffering through awkward stages of adolescence, Faith was the only character who was mocked because of her weight, size, and shape. Even in the revived series that began in 2012, Faith was often the subject of fatphobic attitudes and actions (Tanski 2016).[8] So, to have the promise of a fat female superhero whose atypical superhero body would be treated neutrally was a significant revelation. Additionally, the individualized Faith came into the world at a time when many other female superheroes were being introduced in additional media formats, including Agent Carter (ABC, 2015–2016) and Supergirl (The CW, 2015–present), as well as Jessica Jones (Netflix, 2015–2019) and Wonder Woman (Warner Brothers, 2017), all protagonists of film, television, and internet shows. This was also a moment when new personas of superheroes that brought to prominence racially marginalized identities were being introduced in the comic book world, including Pakistani American Muslim teenager Ms. Marvel (aka Kamala Khan) and African American Puerto Rican Spiderman (aka Miles Morales). This context for the advent of Faith as a solo superhero both normalizes and highlights her white, fat, cis-female persona, as she is one of many newly powerful marginalized heroes, but different in her most prominent marginalizing characteristic—her size.

Taking these contexts into consideration, why might we question this seemingly new normalization of fat when so many fat activists and academics have been advocating for something like it for decades? Like Faith's other phenotypical characteristics—her whiteness and her conventional femininity—when fatness is normalized to the extent that it is unremarkable, it becomes invisible. As scholars of critical race theory and whiteness have shown, unmarked identity categories can become sites of privilege because they are unnamed and taken as the status quo.[9] When, in Western culture, and especially US culture, we describe some populations as "people" and some as "Black people," or contrast "African American superheroes" with "superheroes," whom we assume are white, we reinforce the notion that some groups' racialization is noticeable while that of others is not. We normalize whiteness and thus do not look critically at how it is constructed to the benefit of white people and to the detriment of people of color. In parallel, living in a world that is fundamentally fatphobic, the normalizing of fatness so that it is unremarkable certainly could have its benefits, especially if actual fat people's living conditions improved by not having to be subjected to taunts, sneers, slurs, and terrible treatment in all aspects of public culture. But while Faith is unremarkably fat within her limited comic book sphere, in our world she is constantly—and will continue to be constantly—marked as *the* fat superhero. I caution against the celebration of the normalization of Faith's fatness not because I think it an unworthy goal, but because I worry that it becomes the exception that proves the rule; it might be mind boggling to some that as a fat woman Faith can fly with agility and grace, but Faith is a fictional character, in particular a superpowerful fictional character, and thus can be made to do nearly anything a writer or artist would like. When we have one single figure representing a large, diverse, and complicated population, we need to be careful of what we expect of her as a representation and carefully consider the labels we place upon her, even if for some she is "the thing of dreams" (Ospina 2015).

Furthermore, when we normalize Faith's fatness, we ignore or downplay her potentiality as a monstrous woman. As a superhero with the psychically linked powers to fly and move objects around at will, Faith is by definition monstrous. She, like her fellow superheroes no matter their gender, embodies an unruliness that is inherent in the very figure of the superhero. That she is a woman adds a deeper layer to this, as women have historically been constructed as those humans whose bodies defy boundaries and norms within a masculinist paradigm (Kristeva 1980; Shildrick 2002). That she is fat could, and I would argue should, add even further to her monstrousness. The monstrosity of women in comics is not something to run and hide from but something that can, and should, be embraced. Monsters and monstrousness offer departures from oppressive modes of classification and constraint, challenge stable and singular identities, and upset the coherence and boundaries of the individual body and its communal biopolitical counterpart. As Margrit Shildrick writes, monsters have an aberrant corporeality, one that is very much useful and productive for exposing norms and, as the Hulk might say, for smashing them (2002). Faith also has an *abhorrent* corporeality—her fatness is not simply different from other superheroes but is actively fought against and constructed as obscene, abnormal, and defective in Western culture; we see just one example of this in the fat jokes Faith's fellow Harbingers make in the earlier comic series. But it is these very qualities of Faith's monstrous body structure and size that can give her such awesome power in her world and ours.

Multiplicities of Faith's Visual Imagery

The variety of ways in which Faith is visualized in the first sixteen issues of the series points to ways in which monstrousness can be empowering. The choices she and her artists make in terms of clothing, body positions, and actions underline the argument that the efficacy of the rhetoric of the monstrous lies, in large part, in its multiplicious possibilities. Rather than perpetuating an exclusive practice and discourse, as conventions of bodily ideals and beauty do, monstrousness—in both its vast range of variety and its inherently excessive productivity—is much more open in whom and what it can liberate. The following analysis will help demonstrate this.

The artwork on the cover of *Faith*, volume 1, called *Hollywood and Vine*, was created by Jelena Kevic-Djurdjevic and shows Faith in her typical superhero costume, the full-length white-and-blue button-up jacket-cape and pantsuit. She perches on electrical lines, gazing happily at the glowing laptop screen in her lap, hands poised for or in the process of typing. On either side are pigeons on the same wires, looking up at her and at us, indicating their confusion at her presence. Looking at this image, it seems an ideal visual metaphor for Faith's newly established solo super career. Faith historically is a nerd and fangirl—that she has her laptop in her lap while she is fully dressed in her superhero costume seems none out of the ordinary.[10] That she is perched on electrical wires with birds seems plausible as well for a character who flies. But Kate Tanski, in a review for *Women Write about Comics*, thinks otherwise. Tanski clearly seems to be coming from a fat activist point of view—her article is entitled "Fat Positivity in Comics: What I Need from Faith"—and she sees this image as a joke being made at Faith's expense. She writes: "While [the artist's] work is incredibly beautiful, Faith's weight is still a punchline. Isn't it funny, the cover tells us, to see a fat woman on a telephone line next to these tiny birds? Isn't it laughable, or ironic, or maybe even precious in that sad way, that this enormous woman can fly?" (2016). But I don't see this same punchline here. Even as I call to embrace monstrosity, the grotesque, and the ugly in fat visual representations of Faith, this image seems as far from those qualities as possible. Indeed, I might argue that the way Faith is depicted here is actually all *too* normative in terms of a conventionally attractive femininity and an idealized fatness. In other words, this representation is of an entirely covered, smoothed-over, and contained fat female hourglass-shaped body. She sits on wires that barely seem to bend under her weight, and she floats contentedly with a smile on her face.

Tanski's critique of this image stands out in part because she seems to be saying two things here about Faith's fatness: one, that Faith is being mocked in this image, and two, that the image is too sanitized and normalized to be effective. Here Faith seems to have been "cleaned up" to appear as "the good fatty"—a fat person who embraces normative body and beauty standards that construct a sense of moral superiority over other fat people who can't or choose not to reify fatphobic and patriarchal corporeal and health norms.[11] Tanski writes: "The grotesque nature of the way the other artist presented her body has been removed, [. . .] and she's drawn beautifully, but that's because she's now *the right kind* of fat, where it's evenly distributed. Faith has gotten to retain her giant stomach and general largeness, but she now has zero fat rolls and her double chin is missing" (2016; emphasis in the original). Tanski argues that Faith's idealization here takes away from her power and meaning, especially as it relates to an audience of fat readers searching for representations that reflect their lived reality. In her conclusion, Tanski continues this argument, writing: "I need her to be the wrong kind of fat, with a double chin, enormous stomach, and fat rolls. Faith could be remarkable" (2016). Tanski's argument points to the complexity of fat visual representation, especially in a fairly accessible pop culture media form like comic books. She is right to call out the tendency toward a sanitized and beautified fatness, when—or more precisely *if*—fat people are visualized in contemporary media in nonpathologized ways.[12] At the same time, however, it seems that Tanski literally was judging the book by its cover, because if we look inside the comic books instead of focusing on the cover imagery, we see a much more dynamically visualized Faith that does deliver on Tanski's, and my, desires for a more remarkable fatness of the superhero.

Several pages and panels from the *Faith* series demonstrate that none of Faith's three personas—Zephyr, the well-covered superhero; Summer Smith, the online tabloid writer; and Faith herself—are consistently pictured as smooth and sanitized fat women. These various personas wear different kinds of clothing and enact different kinds of personalities that we might expect of anyone in terms of their professional and personal lives. For example, we tend to see Faith as Summer dressed in semiprofessional clothing for her day job as a writer for an online entertainment tabloid. She is usually well covered in these garments, typically composed of long-sleeved and layered shirts, sweaters, and pants, sitting at her desk in front of her desktop computer and/or talking with coworkers in their cubicles or the break room. Faith at home, whether alone, with friends, and/or with her boyfriend, is decidedly more casual, often in sweat pants, shorts, T-shirts, or pajamas. Both she and her apartment furnishings are lovingly tousled, imperfectly tossed together primarily for comfort and use value. When Faith goes out into the world as "herself" (neither superhero nor alias Summer), she tends to dress casually and less covered. She often wears short skirts, close-fitting pants, tank tops, and/or other cleavage-bearing shirts. These images, in turn, contrast strongly with Zephyr's superhero garments: the fully covered white-and-blue pantsuit with long, blue-and-white, semidetached jacket-cape.[13] Sometimes sleek, sometimes bulging with fat and muscle, and entirely covered except her head, hands, and feet, Zephyr's body is frequently shown from "distorted" angles as she flies through the landscape to and from her adventures and as she battles supervillains in a wide variety of movements.

Faith's different worlds are also heightened by the fact that she is drawn by multiple artists; this happens across issues as well as in different scenes within the same issue. As a result, Faith's personality and her body are never consistent over the course of each individual comic book, let alone the collected anthologies.[14] These variations in Faith's depictions are not expressly explained or analyzed in the comics themselves, and, as a result, they add a visual sense of multidimensionality and complexity to her character. Just as we all look different in different subject positions (and from different visual angles)—as professional, as partner, as caregiver, as nerd, and so on—so too does Faith in the pages of the comic books.

Moreover, when Faith is depicted in her various activities by her range of artists, her physical positionality is diverse as well. Yes, there are sometimes idealized versions of Faith in her smooth, tight, full-body spandex costume, but just as frequently, if not more so, she is shown with double chin, bulging breasts and belly, disproportionate hips, and thick neck. In fact, the cover imagery of the comic books and collections tends to feature those images that are the most idealized versions of Faith's face and figure, but when we get past those more conventionally heroic fat images into the pages within, we find a more complicated and interesting visual story. For example, in an early panel in *Faith*, no. 1, before Faith has exposed her secret superhero identity to her coworkers, Summer, in her red shoulder-length wig, is pictured from above (fig. 4.1). As we look down on her, she is leaning back in her desk chair wearing a light blue long-sleeve T-shirt and blue pants. The angle at which we see Summer here is not in any way a typically "flattering" pose; her face, neck, chest, and belly are drawn in wide angles, emphasizing her girth. Summer's face is in a three-quarter view, and its round softness, shown in part by drawing and coloring Summer's face, chin, and neck as a single beige shape instead of distinct areas, is emphasized in contrast to Summer's Black coworker's thinner, more angular and bony figure. There is a plain sense that this is a candid moment in Summer's world, a visual and verbal snippet in her conversation with her coworker that is meant to represent any average work interaction. There is nothing out of the ordinary, conventionally beautiful, or glamorous about this moment.

The (Un)Remarkable Fatness of Valiant's *Faith*

Figure 4.1: Faith, at work, conversing with her colleague Paige while leaning back in her chair in an "unflattering" angle. *Faith*, no. 1, n.p., by Jody Houser, Pere Pérez, Marguerite Sauvage, and Colleen Doran. Copyright 2016, Valiant Comics.

We find a similar aerial vantage point in another single image from the second issue of *Faith* as she relaxes at home, sitting on her couch. Faith perches on one end of her L-shaped sectional couch, legs splayed from the knees out. Her light-blue T-shirt, shorts, and flip-flops contrast with the brown sofa fabric. Faith is looking at her phone, in her hands, and is surrounded by the rest of her living room and kitchen. Based on the windows on two sides, it looks like she lives in an apartment building. The decorations are minimal; her space looks more practical than well adorned. The text of this panel reads: "Just because you know who you are doesn't mean the world sees you the same way. I guess I never really fit the mold. The things I like, the way I look." The image clearly is meant to represent Faith's investment in and appreciation of her fat and geeky life. She is literally and figuratively at home, and her body and clothing match the casual sprawl of the scene: fat, bulging, and round. Faith's commentary here hints at a past unease with her fatness but does seem to promote a sense of current self-acceptance and the banality of her physical state.

There is a single, significant, and remarkable image of Faith in one of the first sixteen issues of the comics, however. It comes late in the story line in issue no. 11 (fig. 4.2). In this fourth volume of the series (issue nos. 9–12), Faith battles a group of supervillains who name themselves "the Faithless" because they specifically choose to target Faith and her friends for annihilation, ostensibly to provide the opportunity to rule and ruin the world. In order to advance their

Figure 4.2: Faith imagined as a multitudinous blob by a crowd under the control of Dark Star. *Faith*, no. 11, n.p., by Jody Houser, Joe Eisma, Marguerite Sauvage, and Andrew Dalhouse. Copyright 2017, Valiant Comics.

goals, the four faithless villains work together to make the public fear and hate Faith. Dark Star, a psiot who has mind-control abilities, feeds off the souls of humans; trapped in the body of a black cat, he psychically tricks a large mob of people to envision Faith as an enormous, melting blob giving them chase. In a full-page image, Faith's pink-yellow, fleshy, sphere-shaped body takes up two-thirds of the drawing. She hovers above the red-tinged crowd in an impossible mountainous form with multiple heads, arms, legs, and bodies oozing into one another. The largest drawing of Faith's face in the rippling mass of her body, in the upper center of the image, features a wide-open mouth with white spittle strung between her upper and lower jaws. Her eyes are a demonic pink and roll upward, under her heavy and creased brow. From her left cheek emerges a miniscule hand and forearm, as if trying desperately to escape its terrible fate. This image calls upon the Western cultural assumption that fatness is a horror, meant to be feared and avoided at all costs (Braziel and LeBesco 2001). The image also plays upon the fear of the excessive and boundary-breaking female body and the material debasement of the "formless" as described by feminist scholars Julia Kristeva (1980) and Margrit Shildrick (2002), and art theorist Georges Bataille (1985), respectively. This is the first and only time that Faith appears to be truly monstrous by plan in the series. It further indicates that the artists/writers of this issue remain(ed) aware of the potential terror invoked by fat, both as a substance and as a bodily state. It appears, then, that the creators and other artists also remained conscious not to depict Faith as horrifically or "remarkably" fat in the rest of the comics. What might this mean for our perspective on Faith's fat and incipiently monstrous superhero body? Is this image regressive or progressive, fat-bashing or fat-positive? Is it possible for it to be both at once? And if the answer to this latter question is yes, where does that leave us?

It seems most accurate to see this remarkable representation of the fatness of Faith as indicative of the contestation of fat's current meanings in contemporary mass culture. In relying on the time-honored tropes of the unrestrainable fat woman, the fantasy-horror blob, and the mindless consuming monster, this image conveys just how powerful fat and its visual representations are in Western culture. I would suggest that we attempt to exploit this power, to embrace the monstrousness of the fat Faith, in order to claim it for its potential to aid in the struggle for social justice for marginalized people. The monstrous represents multiplicity instead of singularity; valuing monstrosity means valuing a plurality of narratives, points of view, and embodiments. There is no single "ideal" within monstrousness, providing the possibility for numerous representations to matter rather than only one that is perfected and perpetuated by dominant cultural norms. We can embrace the grotesque, the ugly, and the excessive as key productive strengths of the monstrous for many representations working outside social norms, including Faith. Mia Mingus, a disabled queer writer and activist of color, speaks to this approach, noting:

> As the (generational) effects of global capitalism, genocide, violence, oppression and trauma settle into our bodies, we must build new understandings of bodies and gender that can reflect our histories and our resiliency, not our oppressor or our self-shame and loathing. We must shift from a politic of desirability and beauty to a politic of ugly and magnificence. That moves us closer to bodies and movements that disrupt, dismantle, disturb. Bodies and movements ready to throw down and create a different way *for all of us, not just some of us*. (Mingus 2011; emphasis in the original)

Instead of reclaiming or expanding beauty, Mingus advocates for a politics that embraces the ugly and "the magnificent" that stems from the often painful and violent history of racism, ableism, homophobia, and sexism so that we might dismantle the impossible standard that is conventional beauty. Mingus calls for a revolution based in lived, bodily experiences wherein the power of ugliness in all its corporeal variations is embraced rather than reviled. In doing this, we can revalue the narratives of oppressed people; instead of being seen as individual, different, or out of the ordinary, our visual and other stories can create communal bonds and allegiances and foster interdependence. Such a valuation confronts dominant Western culture's neoliberal falsehoods about individual achievement and brings recognition to people and stories of resistance that have been frequently overlooked, neglected, or actively absented from history. Mingus argues that we need to implement the power of resistance in the ugly: "Seeing its power and magic, seeing the reasons it has been feared. Seeing it for what it is: some of our greatest strength" (2011). Following this call, and embracing monstrousness, gives us a chance to see Faith as a three-dimensional character with whom we can identify in all her, and our, complicated, boundary-breaking, nonnormativity. She can be a representation of resistance for the many.

While Faith's fatness is not typically remarked upon within the story lines of her solo career as superhero, the visual representations within the pages of these comics can provide a different perspective and make Faith as a fat superhero remarkable. To take Faith's fatness for granted, while tempting, can induce a normalization that makes invisible the power of representation and resistance that comes from her body size and shape. To make Faith and her fat remarkable would be to embrace the ugly and the awkward, to celebrate her monstrousness as a woman, as a superhero, and as a fat character, in order to pave a path toward greater justice for fat people in pop culture and everywhere.

Notes

1. The *Harbinger* story line begins anew in the rebooted series starting in 2012.

2. Psiots are a group of humans who have developed psychically activated (what Valiant Entertainment calls "psionically charged") superpowers. In the *Harbinger* and *Faith* series, the term "psiot" is often used interchangeably with "harbinger" because these superpowered humans are constructed as representations of a newly evolved human species—as "harbingers" of the future in human evolution.

3. There are sixteen published issues featuring Faith as a solo superhero during 2016–2017. They are, slightly confusingly, called and numbered *Faith Begins* (nos. 1–4) and *Faith* (nos. 1–12). These are the issues collected in the first four volumes of the series.

4. In the *Faith* comic series, Faith ostensibly goes by three different names: Summer Smith, her "real-world" alias that protects her identity as Faith Herbert; Faith Herbert, her actual name; and Zephyr, the superhero. Throughout the current publication, however, Faith usually goes by Summer when in disguise at work and Faith the rest of the time, whether acting as a typical human or a superhero. Because the name "Faith" is used most consistently in the comics, this is the name I will use in the balance of this chapter.

5. Faith consistently comments that she has chosen this garment for its practicality in terms of coverage and flexibility. During the first sixteen issues of the series, there is only one instance when Faith wears a different garment while on a rescue mission. Early in issue no. 9, Zephyr helps to combat a bank robbery in progress; arriving at the scene, she is wearing a white one-piece garment with long sleeves, short pants (ending at the top of the thigh), and a scoop neck that shows off her cleavage. The garment is adorned with a blue cape, a blue Z on the chest, and a wide gold belt. This is the first and last time in the 2016–2017 run of *Faith* that the superhero wears something this revealing in public. Faith, as Zephyr's alter ego, much more frequently wears garments that bare her cleavage and/or show her legs.

6. For example, see Mingus 2011, discussed later in this chapter, as well as Meleo-Erwin 2012 and Snider 2018.

7. For example, see McRuer 2006 and Wood 2014.

8. For example, Faith might be depicted as oblivious to her fat body, or as stupidly assuming that she was beautiful or worthy of the male heterosexual gaze. In one scene in *Harbingers*, no. 4, Faith is shown wearing a short strapless body-conscious red dress meant to appeal to a male crush while at a mall, and other (thin) teenagers are shown mocking her, calling her "a fire truck."

9. For just a small taste of this literature, see Fanon 1967 and Dyer 1997.

10. There are several moments in the full run of the comics series when Faith happily proclaims her geek/nerd status and shows off her Star Trek, Doctor Who, Star Wars, Buffy the Vampire Slayer, and other sci-fi/fantasy collections.

11. The term "good fatty" has been circulated among fat activists and academics in the field of fat studies for several years, making it difficult to determine who originated the phrase. Two significant bloggers, however, have defined the term in complementary ways: Tori of Anytime Yoga (see "The Temptation to Play 'Good Fatty,'" 2011) and Ragen Chastain of Dances with Fat (see "Good Fatty Conundrum," 2011).

12. For more on the problematic interplay between beauty and fatness in fat imagery and activism, see Snider 2018.

13. Faith comments on her superhero outfit several times in the comics. In issue no. 7, Faith consults with her friend, and fashion designer, Klara, who has provided her with five alternative blue-and-white superhero outfits, none of which seem to fit her needs or personality. In the

end, Faith seems to choose her original costume by default and, across the span of the first sixteen issues, is nearly always depicted as Zephyr wearing the full body garment.

14. The supervising artist for each issue is Jody Houser, but several other artists, including Jelena Kevic-Djurdjevic, Marguerite Sauvage, Francis Portela, Kevin Wada, Joe Eisma, and Kate Niemczyk, have drawn Faith. In addition, Sauvage tends to portray Faith's daydreams and nightmares, which occur with regular frequency in the story line.

Bibliography

Abrecht, Kristi. 2017. Review of *Faith: Hollywood and Vine*, by Jody Houser, Francis Portela, and Marguerite Sauvage. *Fat Studies* 6, no. 2: 233–37.

Bataille, Georges. 1985. "Formless (1929)." In *Visions of Excess: Selected Writings, 1927–1939*, edited by Allan Stoekl. Minneapolis: University of Minnesota Press.

Braziel, Jana Evans, and Kathleen LeBesco, eds. 2001. *Bodies out of Bounds: Fatness and Transgression*. Berkeley: University of California Press.

Chastain, Ragen. 2011. "Good Fatty Conundrum." Dances with Fat, May 5. Available at https://danceswithfat.wordpress.com/2011/05/17/good-fatty-conundrum/.

Dodson, P. Claire. 2016. "How Comic Fans Got Their Faith Back." *Atlantic*, April 15. Available at https://www.theatlantic.com/entertainment/archive/2016/04/faith/478386/.

Dyer, Richard. 1997. *White: Essays on Race and Culture*. London: Routledge.

Dysart, Joshua, Khari Evans, and Ian Hannin. 2012. *Harbinger*, no. 1 (June). New York: Valiant Entertainment.

Fanon, Frantz. 1967. *Black Skin, White Masks*. New York: Grove.

Farrell, Amy Erdman. 2011. *Fat Shame: Stigma and the Fat Body in American Culture*. New York: New York University Press.

Gailey, Jeannine A. 2014. *The Hyper(in)visible Fat Woman: Weight and Gender Discourse in Contemporary Society*. London: Palgrave Macmillan.

Gustines, George Gene. 2016. "Plus-Size Superhero Gets Her Own Series." *New York Times ArtsBeat*, April 4. Available at https://artsbeat.blogs.nytimes.com/2016/04/04/plus-size-superhero-gets-her-own-series/?_r=0.

Kristeva, Julia. 1980. *Powers of Horror: An Essay on Abjection*. New York: Columbia University Press.

Lehoczky, Etelka. 2016. "'Faith' Makes Fat a Force to Reckon With." NPR Book Reviews, July 6. Available at http://www.npr.org/2016/07/06/484012379/faith-makes-fat-a-force-to-reckon-with.

Mazziotta, Julie. 2015. "Meet Faith, the Plus-Size Superhero We Can All Admire." *People*, November 16. Available at http://people.com/books/meet-faith-the-plus-size-superhero-we-can-all-admire/.

McRuer, Robert. 2006. *Crip Theory: Cultural Signs of Queerness and Disability*. New York: New York University Press.

Meleo-Erwin, Zoë. 2012. "Disrupting Normal: Toward the 'Ordinary and Familiar' in Fat Politics." *Feminism and Psychology* 22, no. 3: 388–402.

Mingus, Mia. 2011. "Moving toward the Ugly: A Politic beyond Desirability." Keynote speech, Femmes of Color symposium, Oakland, August 21. *Leaving Evidence* (blog), August 22. Available at https://leavingevidence.wordpress.com/2011/08/22/moving-toward-the-ugly-a-politic-beyond-desirability/.

Ospina, Marie Southard. 2015. "Why Plus Size Superhero Faith Is the Thing of Dreams for the Chubby Nerd in Me." *Bustle*, November 18. Available at https://www.bustle.com/articles/124707-why-plus-size-superhero-faith-is-the-thing-of-dreams-for-the-chubby-nerd-in-me.

Schindler, Rick. 2016. "First Plus-Size Female Superhero Soars into Her Own Comic Book, 'Faith.'" *Today*, January 29. Available at http://www.today.com/health/first-plus-size-superheroine-soars-her-own-comic-book-t69776.

Scole. 2016. "Overweight Superheroes and Supervillains." The Artifice, May 16. Available at https://the-artifice.com/overweight-superheroes-and-supervillains/.

Shildrick, Margrit. 2002. *Embodying the Monster: Encounters of the Vulnerable Self*. London: SAGE.

Snider, Stefanie. 2018. "On the Limitations of the Rhetoric of Beauty: Embracing Ugliness in Contemporary Fat Visual Representations." In *On the Politics of Ugliness*, edited by Sara Rodrigues and Ela Przybylo. London: Palgrave Macmillan.

Stearns, Peter R. 2002. *Fat History: Bodies and Beauty in the Modern West*. New York: New York University Press.

Tanski, Kate. 2016. "Fat Positivity in Comics: What I Need from Faith." *Women Write about Comics*, December 21. Available at http://womenwriteaboutcomics.com/2015/12/21/what-i-need-from-faith/.

Tori. 2011. "The Temptation to Play 'Good Fatty.'" Anytime Yoga, May 14. Available at https://anytimeyoga.wordpress.com/2011/05/14/the-temptation-to-play-good-fatty/.

Valiant Entertainment. 2018. "*Harbinger*." Available at http://valiantentertainment.com/comics/harbinger/.

Wood, Caitlin, ed. 2014. *Criptiques*. Portland, OR: May Day.

5

New and Improved? Disability and Monstrosity in Gail Simone's *Batgirl*

Charlotte Johanne Fabricius

In 2011, in a move both praised and condemned, DC Comics relaunched the *Batgirl* title under "The New 52" initiative. Comics writer Gail Simone and artists Ardian Syaf and Vicente Cifuentes spearheaded the title for four years, between 2011 and 2014, and their run was debated extensively,[1] in particular the choice to cast Barbara Gordon as Batgirl. Barbara Gordon, who was introduced to the DC Comics Batverse in 1967, was shot through the spine by the Joker in Alan Moore and Brian Bolland's 1988 *Batman: The Killing Joke*. For the next twenty-three years, Barbara was a paraplegic, trading acrobatics for computer genius under the moniker Oracle. The Batgirl name was taken up by other characters and Barbara became one of very few disabled superheroes, and a woman at that, fighting crime and forming social bonds with other female superheroes while operating out of a wheelchair. In the rebooted *Batgirl* title, Barbara was given a miraculous surgery and gained back the use of her legs, all the while erasing much of her history as Oracle. Simone herself argued that while Oracle was a powerful character, it seemed unfair that, in a framework in which almost all male superheroes have recovered from devastating injuries or come back from death, Barbara Gordon wasn't extended the same healing power (Cocca 2016, 78–79). The run's reception was divided between readers who missed Oracle and her powerful example of a disabled superhero, and readers who were excited to see Barbara as Batgirl once again. Simone included explicit discussions of Barbara's time as a paraplegic (though not a superhero) and the ensuing struggles associated with her recovery process and PTSD. These themes are, however, centered on an (at least seemingly) able-bodied superhero.

In this chapter, I will examine how able-bodiedness and disability are framed in narrative and visuals in the first six issues of Simone's *Batgirl* run, which features art by Ardian Syaf and Vicente Cifuentes, collected in the trade paperback titled *The Darkest Reflection* (2012). As Barbara is rehabilitated and reconfigured as both an able-bodied subject and a superhero, her embodiment and identity are called into question and undergo a repositioning with regard to social norms and genre conventions. Barbara's path to becoming Batgirl is lined with personal struggles and highly symbolic villains who serve to frame her as a recognizably normative hero. The inclusion of variously disabled and nonnormative bodies and the uncertainty surrounding Barbara's own bodily status, however, provide moments of slippage within the comics. It is particularly productive, I will argue, to think of Barbara and her antagonists through the figure of the monster in order to account for these slippages and to examine more clearly how they work to orient Barbara within the normative framework of the comics page, the superhero genre, and the cultural expectations pertaining to able-bodied womanhood. The monster, according to scholars such as Barbara Creed and Jeffrey Jerome Cohen, is a destabilizing figure that serves to highlight cultural boundaries and norms (Creed 2015; Cohen 1996). Thinking of Barbara Gordon/Batgirl as both a monstrous figure and a slayer of monsters enables me to explore how Barbara's recovery and return to superheroics are facilitated in part by coding disability as monstrous. These explorations take place within a methodological framework based on a queer-phenomenological approach to the lines and orientations of the comics page, linked to a theoretical combination of disability studies and monster theory. This framework allows me to critically explore how able-bodiedness and superheroism are linked, as well as how these links are both challenged and upheld, in one of the most anticipated and controversial superhero reboots in recent years.

The methodological approach in this chapter is based on Sara Ahmed's notion of orientation as discussed in *Queer Phenomenology: Orientations, Objects, Others* (2006). Ahmed builds on Maurice Merleau-Ponty's phenomenology, which considers the body as both medium and metaphor for our understanding of and interaction with the world. Ahmed transfers this argument to the realm of queer theory by taking Merleau-Ponty's metaphor of orientation literally, suggesting that our upright bodily orientation makes us "see straight"(2006, 65). Ahmed takes "straightness" to mean both able-bodied and upright bodily orientation in "straight lines" (as opposed to "slantwise lines," which become a metaphor for nonnormative embodiment) and "straight" as in heterosexual orientation. "Seeing straight," in other words, means falling in line with normative expectations of embodiment and social interaction. Falling out of line, conversely, marks one as different or divergent. I propose, with regard to considering comics, a move to further concretize the metaphor and investigate how actual lines work to orient characters and objects on the page and within the world of the story. Those who fall out of line with norms of identity, desire, and representation, I argue, are coded as other, even as monstrous, in the comics narrative through their "slantwise" orientation on the page. It is not a question of reading straight lines as coding for straightness and diagonal lines as somehow inherently subversive or queer-coded, but rather a way of looking at panel structure and layout as a normative framework in which characters are constrained in boxes, and have their identities constructed before our eyes by the orienting principles of the pages.

Part of what makes superheroes recognizable is their placement within visual and narrative structures with predetermined orientations, like the depiction of a superhero standing in a power pose. As an example of the orienting principles of the superhero comic page, we might consider a mainstay of the genre: the full-page panel. The format of mainstream superhero comics caters to certain forms of embodiment, restricted by the size and dimensions of the page and layout. Full-page panels might seem to be some of the least restrictive pages in comics, as they contain no panel borders or demarcations. They are often used in superhero comics to display the main character in a power pose, highlighting their body and trademark skills or traits, allowing the superhero to take up the entire page and draw the full attention of the reader. Further, full-page panels often create a break in the narrative, a pause for the reader to dwell on the page (Cortsen 2014, 408–9). Upon closer reflection, however, the full-page panel reveals itself as a limiting feature. Although the superheroic body could take on a myriad of shapes, certain shapes are privileged by the format, layout, and narrative structure. Superhero comics are traditionally drawn in portrait format rather than landscape, giving the characters space to unfold mainly in a vertical direction. Bodies that are not tall and upright will fit less well into this format. Convention also dictates, as mentioned, the depiction of the superhero in a power pose, meaning that they must be physically able to do so. Full-page panels rely on a normatively able-bodied subject for maximum effect, a body that is able to extend vertically and take up space on the page in a dynamic power pose.

That is not to say, however, that nonnormative forms of embodiment do not exist on comics pages. On the contrary, and in line with Ahmed's argument, normatively oriented bodies and objects become visible as normative in contrast with those that appear slantwise across the straight lines. Ahmed writes: "If Merleau-Ponty accounts for how things get straightened up, then he also accounts for how things become queer, or how 'the straight' might even depend on 'queer slants' to appear as straight" (2006, 106). In other words, a straight line only appears straight in the context of other, nonstraight lines, in the same way that heterosexuality becomes recognizable only in contrast to nonnormative sexual orientations. In the case of comics, we might deliberately look not only for the structuring principles of the pages but also for what does not immediately fall in line: a stray panel, an alternative form of embodiment, conflicting or contradictory information presented by text and images, and so forth. Comics orient their readers but often also contain traces of alternative lines of sight, which are worth following in an analysis of normative and monstrous embodiment on the comics page.

Of all the structuring principles to which superheroes are subject, none is more spectacular than what disability scholar Robert McRuer terms "compulsory able-bodiedness," the idea that the default human being is assumed to be able-bodied and that able-bodiedness becomes the norm of being in the world (2006). The question of bodily capability is heightened within the superhero genre, as superhero vigilantism is, as a rule, based on moving through a city at high speed and altitude and engaging in physical fights with adversaries. A superhero's agency—their identity, even—is based on the expectation of their bodily capability. If their able-bodiedness is somehow taken away from them, as it was for Barbara after the events of *The Killing Joke*, their identity is no longer valid. Although disabled superheroes have existed and still do, they often take the form of what comics scholar José Alaniz calls "supercrips," whose superpowers are mostly framed as "compensating" for the perceived "lack" of their disability: blind Daredevil has heightened senses, paraplegic Professor X possesses telekinetic and telepathic powers, and so forth (Alaniz 2014). Barbara Gordon as Oracle gained prodigious computer skills, which allowed her an omnipresence and virtual mobility to compensate for her being less mobile in person.[2] Barbara was precluded from the Batgirl identity after losing the use of her legs, however, revealing the name "Batgirl" to be contingent upon capability. Thinking about this through the lens of orientation makes it apparent that Barbara Gordon's struggle to reclaim both her bodily capability and her identity as Batgirl can be read as struggles to fit back into the orienting principles of superhero comics pages, following the normative lines for what superheroic embodiment is meant to look like and what narrative trajectory it is meant to follow. Along the way, Barbara is placed in situations in which she is coded as monstrous—as not quite "fitting" on the pages. She also, however, realigns herself with the normative orientation of the superhero comic by defeating villains coded as monstrous Others.[3] These issues are foregrounded by Simone, Syaf, and Cifuentes, who spend many a comic book page exploring how to transform the once-disabled character of Barbara into the able-bodied superhero Batgirl.

Becoming Batgirl

When reading the opening pages of the first issue of *Batgirl: The Darkest Reflection*, one could assume that the transition from Barbara Gordon to Batgirl was largely unproblematic. We first meet Barbara accompanied by the proclamation that tonight, she is not Barbara Gordon, she is Batgirl. The Batgirl identity is presented with exuberance; as the reader turns the page, they are met by a full-page image of Batgirl in a power pose and with a wide grin on her face. The angles of her body and the line of the rope by which she is swinging lead the eyes of the reader from the top left-hand corner, in which a text box proclaims "Tonight, I'm BATGIRL" (Simone et al. 2012, 10), down the page to her pointed foot and deep into the streets of Gotham below her. The page is bold and dramatic, heavily featuring Batgirl's signature purple color. The lines point to her belonging in this space, the Gotham of Bat-vigilantes who make their way through the night swinging from ropes across the rooftops. In no way are we in doubt that this is a superhero, almost as classic as they come. And yet, there is something novel in Barbara's assumption of the cowl and cape in this run.

We are told and shown that the old-new Batgirl is back on her feet, but with wobbly legs. Her recovery may be framed as gaining back an old capability, but as it turns out, nothing is familiar or easy. This foregrounding of trial-and-error seems out of place for an experienced hero, instead giving Barbara the story arc of a new hero trying to adapt to her new identity. In the early issues, Barbara is repeatedly shown struggling in her body. Her uncertainty and difficulty in gauging the strength and tone of her body are shown in her internal monologue (Simone et al. 2012, 30), in the use of dramatic angles to emphasize her almost falling or being knocked out (16, 31, 32), and in the visual choices used to show her fighting and acrobatics. While Barbara can hardly be described as passive, Syaf has chosen not to show her in the technique known as simultaneous figuration, in which a body is shown several times at different stages of movement within a single panel, giving a dynamic feel to the depicted action. The technique is utilized a couple of times, but only by other characters, mainly Nightwing, Batgirl's hypercapable colleague (65). Batgirl, on the other hand, is shown in snapshots, rarely with movement lines and more commonly in stills, which gives the sequences a staccato effect (see, e.g., 76 [fig. 5.1]). In several fighting sequences, Batgirl is instead framed by lines representing heavy rain. Her surroundings bear down upon her, giving weight to the background and emphasizing a downward motion in the line work. Barbara/Batgirl is therefore weighed down, drawn toward the ground, not allowed to fully take flight.

Figure 5.1: Batgirl pausing to catch her breath before leaping off a building in pursuit of a suspect. *Batgirl: The Darkest Reflection*, p. 76, by Gail Simone, Ardian Syaf, Vicente Cifuentes, and Adam T. Hughes. Copyright 2012, DC Comics.

Failure is a prevalent theme, not only as it pertains to Barbara's actions as a superhero and getting used to her "new" body but also in a broader sense. Simone's narrative explores an understanding of the disabled body, especially one coded as female. According to critical disability scholars such as McRuer and Rosemarie Garland-Thomson, able-bodiedness is a fleeting state, one that we are all eventually going to lose. Garland-Thomson writes that "we will all become disabled if we live long enough," a sentiment echoed by McRuer (Garland-Thomson 1997, 14; McRuer 2006, 200). Just because Barbara has miraculously gained back her ability, she won't necessarily be allowed to keep it; in fact, the comic repeatedly emphasizes the fact that Barbara does not trust her body and ability. Barbara Gordon as Batgirl may no longer be a disabled superhero,[4] but the stories do critique the impossible standard of the able body that never fails by emphasizing Barbara's uneasy transition out of her wheelchair and the many near misses her vigilante work entails.

The Monstrous Superhero

We can see how the *Batgirl* comics engage with the question of precarious able-bodiedness by returning to the full-page panel. As mentioned, these are formatted to accommodate a certain shape and bodily orientation: the upright, the dynamic, the vertical. In one instance, we do see Barbara (dressed as Batgirl) in a wheelchair on an opening splash page (Simone et al. 2012, 71 [fig. 5.2]), but this is part of a nightmare sequence illustrating Barbara's struggle with survivor's guilt and feeling like she got a second, unfair chance when given back the use of her legs. She is the focal point of the page, but not in a confident manner. Rather, she seems boxed in by the blank space around her, a stark contrast to how her able-bodied self is depicted in the more classical full-page panels, where her legs are often emphasized in dynamic angles (e.g., 10, 93). Even so, the number of full-page panels depicting her in situations out of her control outnumber the ones depicting her in a classical power pose.[5] Batgirl is characterized as an able-bodied but vulnerable superhero whose capability is precarious and whose body does not flow as freely as it might across the pages.

The *mise-en-page* utilized throughout by Syaf reinforces this depiction of Barbara. The panel structure relies heavily on short, wide panels stacked on top of each other, which are often used to show close-ups of Barbara's face, especially her eyes. This brings us closer to her but also boxes her in, constraining her movement on the page (Simone et al. 2012, 50, 80). We are witnesses to Barbara's struggle to fit back into a genre made for bodies not quite like hers. She fits in "slantwise" on the pages, squeezed into panels that

Figure 5.2: Splash page of Batgirl in a wheelchair. *Batgirl: The Darkest Reflection*, p. 71, by Gail Simone, Ardian Syaf, Vicente Cifuentes, and Adam T. Hughes. Copyright 2012, DC Comics.

don't seem to fit her body, moving between them in the stop-motion staccato described above. The lines of the comic and the lines of Barbara's body seem at odds, marking her as out of place despite her passing privilege as a seemingly normative superhero. Batgirl should align with her narrative, but she doesn't quite manage to do so. What both pages illustrate is that Barbara's in-between status complicates how we read and interpret her body and how it is staged as superheroic and able. The hybrid nature of the splash page (fig. 5.2), where Barbara-as-Batgirl is posed in the wheelchair, positions Barbara in a doubly objectified situation. According to Garland-Thomson, the disabled woman is freed from the male gaze but becomes instead the object of "the stare"; that is, the disabled woman becomes a freak in the eyes of the observer, rendered sexless and barren due to her disabled body (Garland-Thomson 1997, 26). Barbara is seemingly exempt from this logic, because she now is, or at least passes as, able-bodied. Removed from the logic of the stare, however, Barbara is also removed from an identity in which she had agency, identity, and purpose, without being overtly sexualized (Cocca 2014). As once again able-bodied, she is back in the male gaze, occasionally posed in sexually suggestive ways. This is more than a little uncomfortable, given her epithet of "girl," but nevertheless par for the course in the world of superhero comics. And when she appears in the wheelchair in her Batgirl costume, clearly uncomfortable and looking defeated, the visual orientation of the body on the splash page, which invites a combined gaze *and* stare, code Barbara as a monstrous hybrid body with little agency and a precarious relation to her able-bodied privilege.

As a result of her precarity, Batgirl appears to her readers as an ambivalent embodiment of cultural anxieties surrounding the female superhero and the disabled woman. Being the object of both gaze and stare marks her body as hybrid and difficult to contain within the logic of superhero comics, which link heroism and normative embodiment. To quote Creed, the function of the monster is "to bring about an encounter between the symbolic order and that which threatens its stability" (2015, 10–11). Connecting Barbara visually to the monstrous hybrid destabilizes ideas about what superheroic bodily capability looks like.

In the *Batgirl* comics, we witness Barbara Gordon/Batgirl's struggle to reenter the world of superhero comics as a legible superhero. This bodily work is presented as traumatic, as we witness Barbara's struggles in both text and images, through the layout and the use of antagonists as mirrors to her struggles. Barbara is tasked with proving the capability of her newly abled body through superheroic acts, which might cause her to slip back into the realm of the disabled body. Many superheroes teeter on this edge in their death-defying exploits, but for Barbara, the threat is tangible in both text and visuals, as we are privy to her many near misses. Here, a monstrous temporal logic is tied to superheroic existence. As discussed by Umberto Eco in his seminal essay on superheroes and temporality, superheroic existence is, classically, characterized by recurrence (1972, 17). Superman, claims Eco, cannot ever truly progress, but must relive the same story each week in order to secure the longevity of the character and, more importantly to publishers, the series. Superheroic temporality, in other words, combines a linear, causal narrative logic with the cyclical nature of myth. Even though superhero comics increasingly employ a complicated and sprawling continuity, remnants of a repetitive logic still linger in the genre and continuities past impact upon present stories. Alaniz notes in *Death, Disability, and the Superhero* that serialized temporality poses a particular threat to disabled superheroes, framing their bodies as inherently unstable and in danger of "slipping back" into despair or villainy (2014, 114). According to Cohen, in the introduction to *Monster Theory*, the body of the monster folds traumatic past into the present, making the monster the focal point for temporal confusion (1996, ix). Barbara's memory of her shooting and former life creep into her able-bodied present, marking it as multiple, dissonant, monstrous. Despite her reboot, Barbara is still connected to her past identities as a not-yet-violated Batgirl, a disabled woman, a disabled superhero (Oracle), and a person in recovery. Not all these are mentioned explicitly, but neither are any of them definitively ret-conned by Simone and her team.[6] Rather, we are left with a Batgirl whose past identities haunt her embodiment. The body of Barbara/Batgirl inhabits the immortal space of the superhero, but also the mortal space of the woman injured almost to death. Barbara is oriented, by the genre and her own narrative, toward her disabled past and an able-bodied future simultaneously. The monstrosity of her former self is figured as monstrous disability, the threat of a life less desirable than the one she gained from being "cured."[7]

The superhero genre works here as a form of interpellation, providing a framework for us to understand the protagonist as a superhero, recognizable within an established history of similar protagonists who have, by and large, been able-bodied white men. A disabled superhero may not be inherently monstrous, but, as discussed above, they do highlight the fact that the genre conventions must be bent in order to accommodate superheroic disability, thus disrupting our orientation toward the normative body as heroic and the disabled body as villainous. When traits usually relegated to the realm of the monstrous are embodied by characters identified as heroes, our understanding of what belongs to the normal and what can be termed monstrous is shaken up. Monstrous, nonnormative figures create alternative lines of orientation within the normative framework, but, more often than not, these "slants" are "straightened out" by the force of genre conventions and social norms. Barbara succeeds not only in convincing the reader that she deserves to be recognized as a hero but also in erasing almost all traces of her perceived monstrosity. However traumatic her road to recovery is, it is just that—a variation on the "road to recovery" trope—which leaves her disconnected from any ties to a disabled body. She is not, as Cohen describes the monster, a "form suspended between forms that threatens to smash distinctions" (1996, 6), at least not for very long. Re-abling Barbara is, despite the uncertainty created in the comics, ultimately an act of "straightening out," in Ahmed's terms. Her conformation to an able-bodied superhero ideal is managed largely through overcoming villains who embody various forms of survivor's guilt, disability, and rogue vigilantism.

Villainous Others

Despite the limitations on female-coded superheroes, we should not necessarily lament the fact that Batgirl cannot truly be claimed a monster. In looking for traits coded as monstrous, we run the risk of permanently relegating those traits to a nonhuman status (Cohen 1996, 11). Claiming something or someone as monstrous is an abjection, what Creed calls "a means of separating out the human from the non-human and the fully constituted subject from the partially formed subject" (2015, 8). The monster is not recognizable as a subject, and so monstrosity must eventually be located in some other body than the protagonist. As McRuer writes: "Since queerness and disability both have the potential to disrupt the performance of able-bodied heterosexuality, both must be safely contained—embodied—in others" (2006, 24). The coding of "potentially disruptive" bodies as monstrous, scholars such as Creed and Cohen would claim, can hold promise. Reading with McRuer, however, and revealing that Barbara is steadily aligned away from the monstrous and toward a "healed"—that is, able-bodied—normative identity means that the disruptive potential of monstrosity is confined to the margins of the comics, identified only in antagonists. Instead of being aligned with monstrosity and a nonnormative heroic body, Barbara is steadily realigned with an able-bodied identity, both visually and in the narrative.

An example of this is Batgirl's confrontation with the villain Gretel, a young woman who has gained mind control powers after being shot in the head. She exacts her revenge on men in power by making them kill for her but remains friendless, alone, and wanting to die. She uses her powers, we are told, in place of her beauty, as the emergency surgery left her bald and with a large scar on her scalp (Simone et al. 2012, 124–25). Unlike Barbara, she awoke alone and deserted in the hospital, robbed of her beauty and social status. She had no billionaire protector or loving father to help her recover. Barbara trumps her in all possible privileges, class, gender conformity, and acceptable sexuality. Gretel is framed as a truly monstrous woman, but not as far removed from our hero as we might expect. She can tell her own story, allowing us to empathize with her and understand further the privileges that separate her fate from Barbara's. We are also shown a sequence in which Gretel is the narrator. The layout and color scheme remain almost unchanged in the transition from Barbara to Gretel, orienting them along parallel lines for a brief time. "She's so damn near me that I don't know where I begin and she ends. [. . .] I could have been Gretel," Barbara reflects, coming shockingly close to a critique of her own privilege (Simone et al. 2012, 133–34). The moment of monstrous solidarity in which Barbara and Gretel are aligned is, however, brief. The normative force of the narrative contains the monstrous within Gretel, exempting Barbara from the position of monstrous outsider. As Gretel begs Batgirl to let her fall to her death rather than live without the powers that "make up" for her disfigurement, Batgirl is overshadowed by the figure of Batman (134). The imposing form of Barbara's figurative father reorients her away from solidarity with Gretel and back in line with able-bodied vigilantism.

The monstrosity of disability, of alternative embodiment, and of the nonnormative may haunt the *Batgirl* story lines, but it is increasingly marginalized and symbolically overcome as Batgirl defeats more and more enemies who suffer from what one might term "villainous disabilities"[8]—ones who, like Gretel, have had their lives permanently altered by accidents or violent crime and suffer a physical and/or mental disability as a consequence and turn to crime out of desperation or delusion. Barbara Gordon/Batgirl moves increasingly closer to the center of normative embodiment, removing herself from the taint of monstrosity by figuratively exorcising it one villain at a time. In this view, our privileged insight into Batgirl's struggles with her bodily capability and identity denaturalize able-bodiedness and reveal the contingency of superheroic capability. The recurring attempts at contrasting Barbara's body, agency, and morals with disabled villains, however, point to a different and rather more problematic reading of the comics. The promise of monstrosity as disruptive remains unfulfilled, and the coding of disability as monstrous and other remains uncontested, as the narrative and panels orient Batgirl away from uncertain hybridity and toward an able body. Barbara Gordon had the potential to be a monster subject but instead becomes a monster slayer, fighting for and not against normativity.

Conclusion

Batgirl is a series about identity and who gets to be a hero, on what terms, for how long, and at whose expense. Barbara's former disability is projected onto Others, who become antagonists as a direct consequence of their otherness. This is not an unfamiliar strategy in superhero comics—in fact, one could easily argue that it is one of the founding tropes of the genre—but in Simone's *Batgirl* run, it is foregrounded. Barbara's rehabilitation means relocating her disability—which, as McRuer and Garland-Thomson remind us, could be a valuable site of critique—to villains, in whose bodies it becomes a signifier of evil. The stories are presented as cathartic and emancipatory, but when read "slantwise," it becomes clear that what Simone, Syaf, and Cifuentes imagine for Barbara comes at a very high price. Not only is her "road to recovery" traumatic and taxing upon her body and sense of self, it also happens at the expense of those less privileged than Barbara. No matter how much tragic backstory Simone and her team give Batgirl's villains, they never let us forget that these are Bad Cripples[9] who have chosen evil and only deserve to be aids in Barbara's journey to able-bodiedness. *Batgirl* may present a world where capability functions on different terms than the ones we know, but these terms should not go uncritiqued when encountered in superhero narratives—the perhaps most spectacular source of cultural imaginings of capability and its links to agency and identity.

However tenuous the link is becoming, we should not completely let go of the idea of Barbara as a monstrous woman. Barbara's disabled past lurks on the edges of the Batgirl mythos, orienting her struggles with her body and the villains representing various nonnormative traits, which she can then symbolically overcome. This is not in itself a very progressive strategy—quite the contrary—but neither is it a strategy that goes uncritiqued within the work itself. Aligning Batgirl with her villains, if temporarily, causes slippages in the narrative in which alternative lines of orientation become visible. Although the conclusions to Batgirl's struggles with her past, her body, and her villains adhere to a normative understanding of the able-bodied superhero, the work in between shows us the work necessary to uphold those norms. The questions asked are not simple; the villains have complicated backstories, and Barbara doubts herself and her right to a recovery more than once. Thus, I have attempted to read both with and against the grain of the comics, uncovering both the moments of critique and the adherence to normativity expressed in Simone's rebooting of Barbara Gordon as Batgirl. By blurring the lines between normative hero and divergent villains, Simone, Syaf, and Cifuentes attempt to reorient the compulsory able-bodiedness on which the figure of the superhero is premised. Barbara may not be utterly monstrous, but she is a catalyst for monstrosity, both tainted by and fighting against it. We need not stand on our heads to see this, only to read a little slantwise.

Notes

1. See Cocca 2014 for a detailed discussion.
2. The narrative in this way systematically downplays the mobility afforded to Barbara by her wheelchair, consistent with the ways in which Western society frames mobility aids as "limiting" rather than enabling users.
3. I capitalize "Others" to signify my use of it to mean outsiders, outcasts, or those who otherwise fail to pass as normative subjects.
4. Carolyn Cocca, in *Superwomen*, does suggest, in a similar argument to mine, that the foregrounding of Barbara's struggles in "finding her feet" can lead her to be read as still somehow disabled (2016, 79).
5. Out of a total of sixty-two full-page panels in the first twenty-six issues, nineteen show Batgirl in various power poses, whereas twenty-three show her in a situation in which she is in some way compromised.
6. Ret-conning, short for "retroactive continuity," refers to the practice common to publishing houses such as DC Comics through which the backstories of characters are retroactively changed or erased, breaking with the established continuity of an ongoing story.
7. José Alaniz has discussed the body politics of the Batgirl ret-con in more detail in a chapter included in *Disability in Comic Books and Graphic Narratives* (Foss, Gray, and Whalen 2016).
8. In other words, the classic comic book malaise in which one's evil/amoral tendencies stem from one's bitterness over being disabled or otherwise excluded from society (e.g., the depiction of the Penguin in the Batman mythos).
9. See Garland-Thomson 1997, 50–51, passim, for a discussion of the moral valorization of disabled persons and their status as "productive members of society."

Bibliography

Ahmed, Sara. 2006. *Queer Phenomenology: Orientations, Objects, Others*. Durham, NC: Duke University Press.
Alaniz, José. 2014. *Death, Disability, and the Superhero: The Silver Age and Beyond*. Jackson: University Press of Mississippi.
Cocca, Carolyn. 2014. "Re-Booting Barbara Gordon: Oracle, Batgirl, and Feminist Disability Theories." *ImageTexT* 7, no. 4: n.p.
Cocca, Carolyn. 2016. *Superwomen: Gender, Power, and Representation*. New York: Bloomsbury Academic.
Cohen, Jeffrey Jerome, ed. 1996. *Monster Theory: Reading Culture*. Minneapolis: University of Minnesota Press.
Cortsen, Rikke Platz. 2014. "Full Page Insight: The Apocalyptic Moment in Comics Written by Alan Moore." *Journal of Graphic Novels and Comics* 5, no. 4 (October): 397–410.
Creed, Barbara. 2015. *The Monstrous-Feminine: Film, Feminism, Psychoanalysis*. Abingdon, Oxon, England: Routledge.

Eco, Umberto. 1972. "The Myth of Superman." Translated by Natalie Chilton. *Diacritics* 2, no. 1 (Spring): 14–22.
Foss, Chris, Jonathan W. Gray, and Zach Whalen, eds. 2016. *Disability in Comic Books and Graphic Narratives*. New York: Palgrave Macmillan.
Garland-Thomson, Rosemarie. 1997. *Extraordinary Bodies: Figuring Physical Disability in American Culture and Literature*. New York: Columbia University Press.
McRuer, Robert. 2006. *Crip Theory: Cultural Signs of Queerness and Disability*. New York: New York University Press.
Simone, Gail, Ardian Syaf, Vicente Cifuentes, and Adam T. Hughes. 2012. *Batgirl*, vol. 1: *The Darkest Reflection*. New York: DC Comics.

6

Horrible Victorians: Interrogating Power, Sex, and Gender in *InSEXts*

Keri Crist-Wagner

Outside of her popular titles for DC, Marvel, and Image, comic book writer Marguerite Bennett conceived a narrative that portrays women with unchecked power and provides a glimpse of the monstrous and subversive lurking beneath the repressive sexualities and (re)strict(tive) gender roles of the Victorian era. *InSEXts* reflects Donna Haraway's notion that "organisms are not born; they are made in world-changing technoscientific practices" (1992, 297) through the intentional metamorphosis of Lady Bertram and Mariah from mere humans into something "other." The transformation itself, a stunning form of body horror drawn vividly by artist Ariela Kristantina, is juxtaposed with scenes of sex, love, and family, which makes it all the more subversive and monstrous. Margrit Shildrick speaks of the monstrous as being both like us and not like us, that it "is precisely this ambiguity that lies at the heart of what makes the monstrous body transhistorically both so fascinating and so disturbing" (2000). That the protagonists of *InSEXts* are women in love with each other is significant. Queer theorist Alexander Doty points out: "Considering the interests of patriarchal heterosexual culture, it is not surprising most of its media should want to devalue any potential site of women-centered pleasures in mass culture" (1993, 41). *InSEXts* offers a vison of women's lives that serves as an emancipatory project, resisting normative presentations of women as subject to the male gaze and agenda. In this chapter I offer a quantitative close reading of *InSEXts* to illuminate the persistently queer and monstrous example that Bennett brings to the page, and to document both the number and quality of change agent actions the characters demonstrate. This method allows the reader to nuance the repeated violence of the text and excavate its (monstrously) queer potential to transform patriarchal and heteronormative edicts.

Women who are too strong, too frightening, or too independent face consequences in literature, particularly in comics. Punishment takes many forms, such as the paralysis of Batgirl (Moore and Bolland 1995), the rape of Captain Marvel (Layton and Perez 1980), Thor's fight with the cancer she developed as a direct consequence of her power (Aaron and Dauterman 2016), and a number of other consequences set to counter women's agency. The treatment of characters who are not identified as cisgender heterosexual white men in traditional comic books is marginalizing at best and deadly at worst (Gray and Wright 2017). Women in the horror genre (films/books/comics) seldom fair better: "The image of the distressed female most likely to linger in memory is the image of the one who did not die; the survivor, or Final Girl" (Clover 1992, 35). As the Final Girl is overwhelmingly portrayed as having the least sexual experience or displays of sexuality, this leaves little doubt as to what role or value women play in the horror genre. They are the prize, an object to be claimed. The dichotomy of the virgin (Final Girl) and the whore highlights rigid gender roles at play. Be the good girl and you may survive. Embrace your sexuality, or in any way deviate from what a good girl should do, and you will die, usually in long, drawn-out, bloody ways. Eroticized violence as punishment for sexuality is perhaps the most common trope in horror (Welsh 2010).

InSEXts traverses both comic books and horror. The protagonists of *InSEXts* are women of the Victorian era (or an *InSEXts* alternative-universe version of it), portrayed initially as victims of an abusive patriarchy. The two leading women, Lady Lalita Bertram and her lady's maid Mariah, are also lovers who "discover a form of body horror that allows them to escape and transcend the confines of their lives, and punish those who harmed them and others like them" (Morris 2015). While their original goal seems to simply rid themselves of Lady's abusive husband, what follows quickly escalates into a mission of near superhero proportions (if superheroes were wont to transform into insect-like creatures and kill in visceral ways).[1]

Lady and Mariah are monstrous in two very specific ways within the world of *InSEXts*. First, they have the ability to transform into insect-like creatures, complete with pincers, claws, teeth, and wings. A notable scene depicts the horrifying transformation of beautiful woman into monster, complete with glowing eyes and snarl. Insectoid legs rip from her back and grope toward the reader. Even the sound effects used are insect "chitter"s, which a human could not ordinarily make. Additionally, the text "Let me show you how exotic I can be" displays Lady's rage at being treated as a solely sexual object, or as chattel.

She is a monster in the classic sense; she and Mariah are creatures outside of the bounds of ordinary nature and humanity. Perhaps more importantly, they are monstrous in their queerness. The sociopolitical climate of the Victorian era saw women as the property of men. Wives, daughters, servants, and prostitutes were all defined by their relationship to men and given varying value as seen through the male gaze. The terms "queer" and "queerness" have many uses and definitions, but here Doty's classification of queerness as something to "challenge and break apart conventional categories" (1993) seems apt. Mariah and Lady challenge the status quo. And by removing them from the sphere of men's control, having them love each other, raise a family together, and embrace power that is uniquely their own, *InSEXts* is "queering" the dominant narrative and making Lady and Mariah truly monstrous.

InSEXts's narrative is outside the typical comic book or horror storytelling conventions in its displays of unchecked power, violence by women, and same-sex relationships. As such, the purpose of this study is to explore these themes in depth through a quantitative close reading and analysis. Such an undertaking seems best situated within a bricolage framework. Bricolage, "as conceptualized by [Norman] Denzin and [Yvonna] Lincoln and further theorized by [Joe] Kincheloe and [Kathleen] Berry, can be considered a critical, multi-perspectival, multi-theoretical and multi-methodological approach to inquiry" (Rogers 2012).

This study seeks to measure incidents of violence and queerness in relation to gender, power, and genre by utilizing the tools of multiple disciplines, including quantitative frequency from social science, visual rhetoric from English and film studies, and queer theory from women's and gender studies. Within this bricolage research framework, I tested the following three hypotheses:

Hypothesis 1: *InSEXts* functions as a revenge/vigilante narrative, with women-identified characters committing most of the violence.

Hypothesis 2: The violence enacted by Lady and Mariah is in response to violence against themselves or other women.

Hypothesis 3: Lady's and Mariah's queerness functions in opposition to the toxic heteronormativity portrayed within the comic. They are "other," different from women they come into contact with, and through their otherness they are able to act as change agents.

I developed this set of hypotheses from a larger set of assumptions and questions revolving around the roles and functions of women in traditional comic book narratives. For instance, the revenge/vigilante narrative is common but seldom involves women in anything other than a victim role. *InSEXts* felt different, both in that these women do not appear to fall into the victim category, and in that they revisit violence in a way that seems justified. How is their violence justified; who does it serve? Additionally, I had questions about the queerness of these characters. Do their subject personalities queer the comic norm, or are there other ways they are queering the norm? Intensity? Motive? Target? Outcome? How does their monstrous form allow them to escape the powerlessness of other women in the narrative, women who are disempowered by convention and physical (in)ability? While the hypotheses do not address all these questions, they explore much of the meaning behind them. A quantitative method allows this chapter to chart more holistically the subtle differences and changes in the relationship between expressions of violence and queerness.

Method

Sample

The sample for this study consists of issues 1–7 of the comic book *InSEXts*. The creative team is composed of Marguerite Bennett (writer), Ariela Kristantina (artist), Bryan Valenza (colorist), Jessica Kholinne (colorist), and A Larger World (letterers). These issues were published between December 2015 and August of 2016 by AfterShock Comics. Sampling was conducted on individual "floppy" issues. Issues 1–7 of *InSEXts* were selected as they represent a complete story arc.

Unit of Analysis

When applying the term "violence," I used the World Health Organization's definition: "The intentional use of physical force or power, threatened or actual, against oneself, another person, or against a group or community, which either results in or has a high likelihood of resulting in injury, death, psychological harm, maldevelopment, or deprivation." I felt that this was a good starting place, as the WHO is a global organization and I wanted as broadly applicable a definition as possible. I also found the prominent inclusion of nonphysical forms of violence to be particularly useful, as I was tracking microaggressions and verbal expressions of violence.

For the purposes of this study, I created the Diamond of Violence (DoV) as an instrument to measure violence toward and by women (fig. 6.1). The DoV is a scoring system that rates incidents of violence based on level of intensity, with positive numbers reflecting violence toward women and negative numbers

Interrogating Power, Sex, and Gender in *InSEXts*

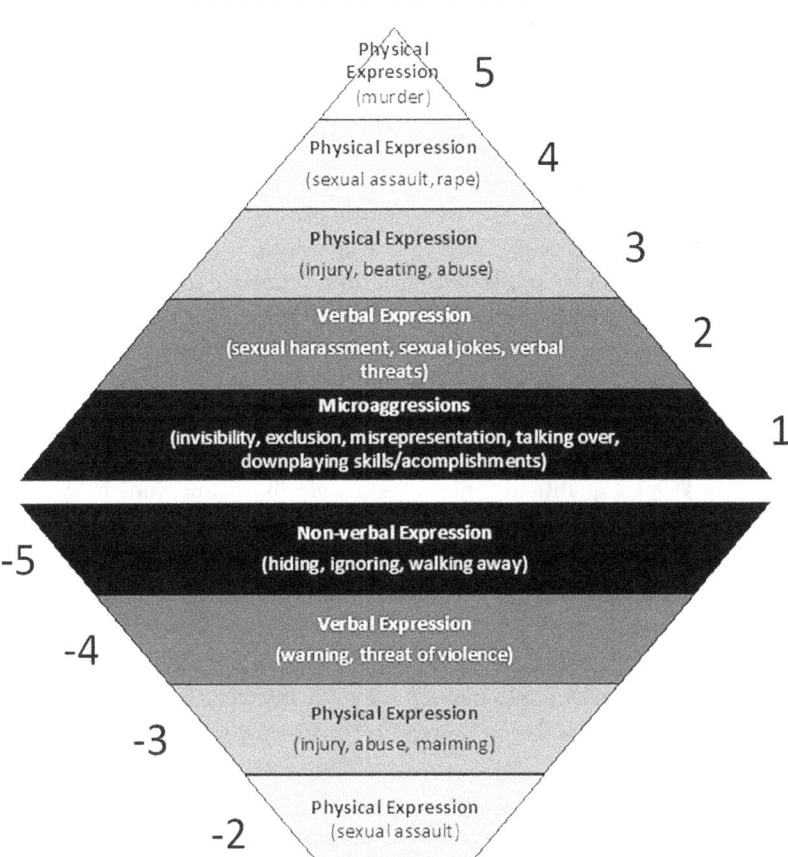

Figure 6.1: The Diamond of Violence, an instrument created for this study to measure incidents of violence involving women.

indicating expressions of violence by women. Assuming that zero is a neutral state with no violence, the scoring is as follows:

> Physical expressions of violence toward women resulting in murder score a 5. Physical expressions of violence toward women resulting in sexual assault or rape

score a 4. Physical expressions of violence toward women resulting in injury, beating, or abuse score a 3. Verbal expressions of violence toward women resulting in sexual harassment, sexual jokes, or verbal threats score a 2. Microaggressions of violence toward women resulting in invisibility, exclusion, misrepresentation, talking over, or downplaying of skills/accomplishments score a 1.

Nonverbal expressions in response to violence manifesting in hiding, ignoring, or walking away score a −1. Verbal expressions in response to violence manifesting in warning or threat of violence score a −2. Physical expressions in response to violence manifesting in injury, harm, or maiming score a −3. Physical expressions in response to violence manifesting in sexual assault score a −4. Physical expressions in response to violence manifesting in killing or murder score a −5.

The DoV scoring tool helps to nuance the motive alongside the impact of violence. It depicts a holistic view that situates violence within a larger context of justice. Using a quantitative numbering scale allows this study to map and track escalating violence toward and by women.

Additionally, incidents of same-sex romantic interaction were tracked and coded throughout *InSEXts*. These incidents are defined as acts of a romantic or sexual nature (including but not limited to shared looks, conversation, and physical touching) between two characters who do not identify as opposite gender. For each incident of same-sex romantic interaction, I assigned a score based on a Scale of Escalating Romance. The scoring is as follows:

Nonverbal expressions of queerness including looks, shared or not, score a 1. Verbal expressions including flirting, declarations of love, attraction, and devotion score a 2. Casual physical expressions including light touches, hand-holding, hugs and embraces, and light kissing score a 3. Passionate physical expressions including intense touches, sexual acts, and making love score a 4.

This measure of same-sex romantic interaction is a way of studying an aspect of queerness that allows me to make a more subtle and broad definition of the term. That is, to be queer is not only to participate in same-sex romantic interaction; it is to intentionally subvert societal expectations. Within *InSEXts*'s setting of Victorian London, for women to express physical and sexual attraction to each other, an attraction that in no way constitutes the role of woman as wife and subordinate to a male husband, is already pushing boundaries of normalcy. In that way, romantic expressions of love between two women queer social expectations of gender roles. Queerness is not reduced to sexual attraction, but sexual attraction between two women in this time and

Scale of Escalating Romance

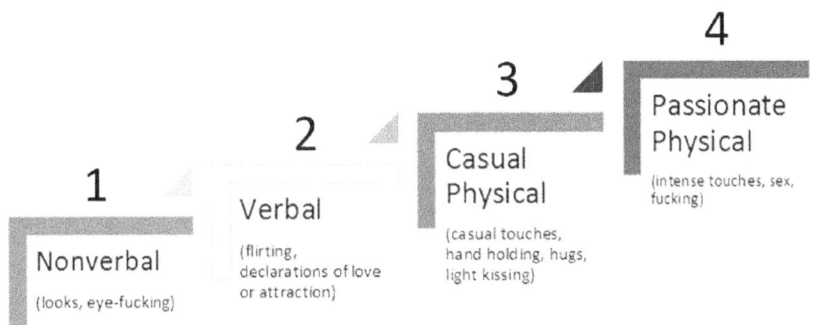

Figure 6.2: The Scale of Escalating Romance, an instrument created for this study to measure incidents of same-sex romantic interaction.

in this place *is* queer. Queer in this sense is anti-establishment and subversive, forging new ways of being and doing in the world.

Coding Protocol

I collected data from issues 1–7 of *InSEXts*. For every incident of violence found, I tracked and coded six variables. Each entry also included a brief description of the incident. A description of each variable is provided below:

1. DoV score. Scores based on a scale of −5 to 5.
2. Gender of the character acting as the agent of violence. Gender variables were male, female, or other.
3. Gender of the character acting as the target of violence. Gender variables were male, female, or other.
4. Was the incident of violence in response to violence committed against the target character? Variables were yes or no.
5. Was the incident of violence committed by either Lady or Mariah? Variables were yes or no.
6. Did the incident of violence occur off the page? Variables were yes or no.

For every incident of same-sex romantic interaction found, I created an entry giving a brief description of the incident and a Scale of Escalating Romance score. Scores were based on a scale of 1 to 4.

DoV Score

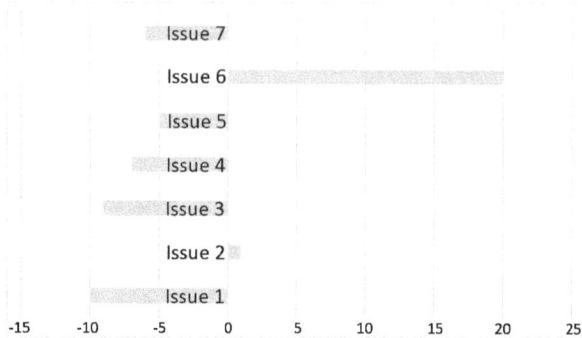

Figure 6.3: Numerical scores for each issue of *InSEXts* based on the Diamond of Violence.

Coder Reliability

All coding and data collection was completed by the primary investigator. All coding was conducted twice, first during February 2017, and then again during April 2017, to ensure accuracy and reliability.

Observations

Sample Overview

Figure 6.3 presents the general DoV scores for each issue in graphic form. Issues 6 and 2 both indicate a positive score in terms of the number indicating violence toward women. Issue 6 displays the highest score (20), whereas issue 2 is just slightly over the neutral line with a score of 1. Issues 1, 3, 4, 5, and 7 all display negative scores, indicating violence by women, with issue 1 displaying the lowest DoV score of −10.

Hypothesis 1: Women Commit Most of the Violence

I first hypothesized that women-identified characters in *InSEXts* act as the agent of violence most of the time. Figure 6.4 presents the frequency of violent incidents involving women from issues 1–7. Women-identified characters committed 74 percent of the violence. Conversely, women also were the target of violent incidents 64 percent of the time.

Variable		Women	Men	Total
	Incidents of violence involving women			
Agent of Violence		74% (43)	26% (15)	58
	Off Page			
	Yes	3% (2)	9% (5)	
	No	70% (41)	18% (10)	
Target of Violence		64% (37)	36% (21)	58
	Off Page			
	Yes	11% (6)	2% (1)	
	No	54% (31)	33% (20)	

Figure 6.4: A breakdown of women's roles, both as agent and as target of violence, in *InSEXts*.

Hypothesis 2: Violence Enacted Is in Response to Violence

I then hypothesized that the violence in which Lady and Mariah, the protagonists of *InSEXts*, act as agents of violence is in response to violence against themselves or other women. Figure 6.5 displays the incidents of violence tracked in *InSEXts* that are coded as "in response." Violent incidents committed "in response" to other acts of violence make up 61 percent of the total incidents of violence coded. Lady and Mariah are the agents of violence in twenty-eight of the fifty-eight tracked incidents of violence, committing 48 percent of the total violence in issues 1–7. Of the twenty-eight incidents, all twenty-eight are coded as "in response." Lady and Mariah act as agents of violence 100 percent of the time "in response" to other acts of violence against themselves or others.

Hypothesis 3: Queerness Enables Change

Finally, I hypothesized that the queerness displayed by Lady and Mariah, set in opposition to toxic heteronormativity, enables them to act as change agents in *InSEXts*. Throughout the seven issues of *InSEXts* sampled, the only characters who display "queerness" as defined for this study are Lady and Mariah. This serves to set them apart from the other characters in the comic.

Discussion

Overall, all three hypotheses were supported by the study, suggesting that despite their monstrous appearance, the women of *InSEXts*, specifically Lady and Mariah, are violent queer vigilantes with a just cause. The study presents

Violence committed in response to other violence

Variable	L&M	Other Women	Men	Total
Agent of Violence	48% (28)	26% (15)	26% (15)	58
Violence in response				
Yes	28	6	2	61% (36)
No	0	9	13	39% (22)

Figure 6.5: The motivation of agents of violence. Note that Lady and Mariah are scored as a group.

quantitative support that Lady's and Mariah's violence is *always* in response to violence committed against themselves or other women. Conversely, the violence committed by men in *InSEXts* is overwhelmingly unprovoked (87 percent). From issue 1, *InSEXts* sets its protagonists, Lady and Mariah, up in opposition to the toxic heteronormative society they exist in. Their relationship is portrayed as loving, equal, and trusting, whereas Lady's relationship with her husband, William, is portrayed as cold, abusive, and horrific. Other examples of toxic heteronormativity, such as Lord Bertram's abuse of Mariah, Colonel Fitzgerald's pursuit of Lady, and the various scenes of sexual assault at the House of Madame H., show men in general with few positive characteristics. Dr. Taylor, Talal, and Adom are notable exceptions. Talal and Adom have small but powerful roles, both standing up to their fellow men in order to side with Mariah and Lady. It is interesting that both are presented as outside of the dominant white male patriarchy, Talal as part of the werewolf pack and Adom as a man of color. Dr. Taylor, however, is a card-carrying member of the white cisgender boys' club and features frequently in the comic, appearing in all seven issues studied. He is portrayed as a friend to Lady and Mariah but also as a man in love with Lady. He is aware of Lady's and Mariah's actions, specifically their murder of Lord Bertram, but instead of leveraging this in order to win Lady for himself, as would many of the men featured in *InSEXts*, he helps them, pledging his friendship in issue 4: "This is not what you fear . . . I don't . . . I don't threaten your freedom. Let me protect you as much as I can. Let us remain friends . . . we can go into hell together." This protection and friendship show how Dr. Taylor views Lady as his equal, not a woman to be subordinated to his opinions and actions. He wants to stand next to her, not in front of her. It is a total queering of what a man "should" do in the world of *InSEXts*.

Unlike traditional comic book narratives found in DC, Marvel, and Image comics, Lady and Mariah experience few negative consequences, none of which can be defined as punishment, once they come to power. The only possible activity that might be interpreted as punishment is Lady's need for rest and possible metamorphosis in her cocoon at the end of issue 7. Even that seems more a case of chosen consequences, the result of using her power to

Scale of Escalating Romance

VARIABLE	SCORE	FREQUENCY
ISSUE 1	24	9
ISSUE 2	10	3
ISSUE 3	8	4
ISSUE 4	6	2
ISSUE 5	7	2
ISSUE 6	3	2
ISSUE 7	7	3

Figure 6.6: The results of the Scale of Escalating Romance, both in score and in frequency.

exhaustion in order to defeat the Hag. It is a natural and chosen consequence of her own agency rather than a narrative punishment by an outside force. By virtue of Lady's and Mariah's gender, their power, and their queerness, some type of punishment should be expected. Long dominated by men in the field, "perhaps it should be obvious that comics are generally exploitive of women" (Gray and Wright 2017, 3), and yet the highest price Lady and Mariah pay is the death of a cisgender, heterosexual, white, male friend.

The intersection of queerness and violence is of particular interest, as the DoV score and Scale of Escalating Romance results, when considered side by side, reveal some interesting patterns. Issue 1 displays the lowest DoV score (−10), indicating that much of the violence committed in that issue is done by women. Issue 1 also displays both the highest score on the Scale of Escalating Romance (24) and the greatest frequency of queerness (nine incidents). Issue 6, conversely, displays the highest DoV score (20) as well as the lowest Scale of Escalating Romance score (3). Taken together, this suggests an inverse correlation between Lady's and Mariah's power and their queerness. In fact, several incidents in *InSEXts*, specifically in issues 4 and 5, indicate that the two women have sex in order to increase Mariah's power at tracking. Again, *InSEXts* is juxtaposing Mariah and Lady's relationship with the unhealthy (in this world) heteronormative relationships of others. For instance, rape, specifically the alluded-to rape of Mariah by Lord Bertram, is used to show his power over her, and to a point, over his wife. The sex between Mariah and Lady is loving, reciprocal sexual energy that also increases their power. Power that is creative, not destructive. Power that is consensual and amplifying. Power with, not power over.

An interesting plot point occurs in issue 7. The concept of "fridging" a character, or killing off the best friend, love interest, or sidekick of the hero in order to motivate them, gets its name from an incident in the comic book *Green Lantern*, no. 54 (Marz et al. 1994). The original incident involved the main character, Green Lantern, finding the body of his girlfriend, Alexandra DeWitt, stuffed into a refrigerator. Writer Gail Simone popularized the term and set up the website Women in Refrigerators in order to track similar occurrences in popular culture (Simone 1999): specifically, the way books, movies, television, and comics treat women as plot devices rather than fully formed and fleshed-out characters in their own right. *InSEXts* flips the particulars of the trope, killing off Dr. Taylor in a gruesome and bloody set of panels as a way to motivate Lady.

After Dr. Taylor dies in the arms of Lady and Mariah, Lady's eyes go red with fury, and she transforms into the most extreme version of herself yet. The switched gender "fridging" of Dr. Taylor and Lady positions *InSEXts* further in opposition to the traditional gender tropes of comic book characters. It is a queering of the traditionally white cisgender male superhero, who in cases like this would go on to seek righteous vengeance upon the "monster" who had murdered his loved one. But what happens when the hero is a monster? Lady's transformation following Dr. Taylor's death is horrifying in every sense of the word, painful and graphic, but while fighting Madame H., Lady clarifies why she is the "better monster" with the lines, "You prey on the weak and the wounded. You slither in through our broken hearts and injured pride . . . and you make us hate the very things that we are, until we are your puppets. You spoke of knights and ladies and those who die against dragons. Your hubris was thinking that you were the dragon . . . and that there were no better monsters to bring you down" (Bennett et al. 2016f). Her monstrosity is a source of power gleaned.

Conclusion

Comic books such as *InSEXts* provide a counternarrative to the traditional storytelling of mainstream US comics. By imbuing the characters of Mariah and Lady with power (that, yes, is sometimes very violent), compassion, and sexuality that exists outside of the structure and limits of patriarchal gender roles, the creators of *InSEXts* have given reign to a new type of comic book "monster." This study has found a link between power and queerness within *InSEXts* and highlighted the difference between the motivations of men and women when committing violence. The twofold monstrousness of Lady and Mariah, in terms of their physical monstrosity and their queer monstrosity, allows them to cause material impact and damage to the patriarchy and to change their world and circumstances, almost completely without punishment. There is a larger application possible for this bricolage-based research framework, especially within comics studies. A larger study could reveal more about gender-based violence, creative team makeup, and positive queer representation.

This study was born out of a love for comics, for the joy of finding queer women representation, and from a desire to explore how themes of social justice can be used effectively in comic books. But it is also the product of frustration with the comics industry and the gatekeeping mindset of so many fans. As a woman, the number of times I have been ignored, talked over, or treated with outright hostility when discussing comic books is countless. The reinforced message of foregrounding the stories of white heterosexual cisgender men as heroes translates to the fanbase. Fans reproduce their own indoctrination. The work of visionaries like Marguerite Bennett, G. Willow Wilson, Kelly Sue DeConnick, Roxane Gay, Marjorie Liu, and more is changing how fans read comic books as well as who those fans are. Further study of the relationship between queerness and violence is a must, and quantitative instruments like the ones used here are important tools in measuring these effects and ultimately working for change.

Notes

1. "Lady" is treated as a first name throughout the comic. Lady Bertram casually remarks that she does not care for her first name or her last (her husband's), but loves that Mariah calls her simply "Lady."

Bibliography

Aaron, Jason, and Russell Dauterman. 2017. *Mighty Thor*, vol. 1: *Thunder in Her Veins*. New York: Marvel Comics.
Bennett, Marguerite, Ariela Kristantina, Bryan Valenza, and Jessica Kholinne. 2015. *InSEXts*, no. 1. Sherman Oaks, CA: AfterShock Comics.
Bennett, Marguerite, Ariela Kristantina, Bryan Valenza, and Jessica Kholinne. 2016a. *InSEXts*, no. 2. Sherman Oaks, CA: AfterShock Comics.
Bennett, Marguerite, Ariela Kristantina, Bryan Valenza, and Jessica Kholinne. 2016b. *InSEXts*, no. 3. Sherman Oaks, CA: AfterShock Comics.
Bennett, Marguerite, Ariela Kristantina, Bryan Valenza, and Jessica Kholinne. 2016c. *InSEXts*, no. 4. Sherman Oaks, CA: AfterShock Comics.
Bennett, Marguerite, Ariela Kristantina, Bryan Valenza, and Jessica Kholinne. 2016d. *InSEXts*, no. 5. Sherman Oaks, CA: AfterShock Comics.
Bennett, Marguerite, Ariela Kristantina, Bryan Valenza, and Jessica Kholinne. 2016e. *InSEXts*, no. 6. Sherman Oaks, CA: AfterShock Comics.
Bennett, Marguerite, Ariela Kristantina, Bryan Valenza, and Jessica Kholinne. 2016f. *InSEXts*, no. 7. Sherman Oaks, CA: AfterShock Comics.

Carroll, Tobias. 2016. "'I Wanted to Corrupt the Imperialist Narrative': An Interview with *InSEXts* and *Animosity* Writer Marguerite Bennett." *Paste*, August 19. Available at http://www.pastemagazine.com/articles/2016/08/i-wanted-to-corrupt-the-imperialist-narrative-an-i.html.

Clover, Carol J. 1992. *Men, Women, and Chain Saws: Gender in the Modern Horror Film*. Princeton, NJ: Princeton University Press.

Doty, Alexander. 1993. *Making Things Perfectly Queer: Interpreting Mass Culture*. Minneapolis: University of Minnesota Press.

Gray, Brenna Clarke, and David N. Wright. 2017. "Decentering the Sexual Aggressor: Sexual Violence, Trigger Warnings and *Bitch Planet*." *Journal of Graphic Novels and Comics* 8, no. 3: 264–76. Available at https://doi.org/10.1080/21504857.2017.1307240.

Haraway, Donna. 1992. "The Promises of Monsters: A Regenerative Politics for Inappropriate/d Others." In *Cultural Studies*, edited by Lawrence Grossberg, Cary Nelson, and Paula Treichler, 295–337. New York: Routledge.

Jorgensen, Anna, and Arianna Lechan. 2013. "Not Your Mom's Graphic Novels: Giving Girls a Choice beyond Wonder Woman." *Technical Services Quarterly* 30, no. 3: 266–84. Available at https://doi.org/10.1080/07317131.2013.785779.

Layton, Bob, and George Perez. 1980. *Avengers* (*1963*), no. 200. New York: Marvel Comics.

Marz, Ron, Derec Aucoin, Darryl Banks, and Steve Carr. 1994. *Green Lantern*, no. 54. New York: DC Comics.

Moore, Alan, and Brian Bolland. 1995. *Batman: The Killing Joke*. New York: DC Comics.

Morris, Steve. 2015. "Bennett's Shape-Shifting, Victorian Horror Series 'InSEXts' Also Has Kissing." Comic Book Resources, September 17. Available at http://www.cbr.com/bennetts-shape-shifting-victorian-horror-series-insexts-also-has-kissing.

Roberts, Jude. 2015. "Girly Porno Comics: Contemporary US Pornographic Comics for Women." *Journal of Graphic Novels and Comics* 6, no. 3: 214–29. Available at https://doi.org/10.1080/21504857.2015.1011398.

Rogers, Matt. 2012. "Contextualizing Theories and Practices of Bricolage Research." *Qualitative Report* 17, no. 48: 1–17. Available at https://nsuworks.nova.edu/tqr/vol17/iss48/3/.

Shildrick, Margrit. 2000. "Monsters, Marvels and Metaphysics: Beyond the Powers of Horror." In *Transformations: Thinking through Feminism*, edited by Sarah Ahmed et al., 303–15. New York: Routledge.

Simone, Gail. 1999. Women in Refrigerators. Available at https://www.lby3.com/wir/.

Welsh, Andrew. 2010. "On the Perils of Living Dangerously in the Slasher Horror Film: Gender Differences in the Association between Sexual Activity and Survival." *Sex Roles* 62, nos. 11–12 (June): 762–73. Available at https://doi.org/10.1007/s11199-010-9762-x.

Wickens, Corrine M. 2011. "The Investigation of Power in Written Texts through the Use of Multiple Textual Analytic Frames." *International Journal of Qualitative Studies in Education* 24, no. 2: 151–64. Available at https://doi.org/10.1080/09518398.2010.495363.

Part 3
Childbearing as Monstrous

7
Kicking Ass in Flip-Flops: Inappropriate/d Generations and Monstrous Pregnancy in Comics Narratives

Jeannie Ludlow

This chapter is rooted in a desire to reconceptualize pregnancy toward a goal of defending a broad range of reproductive experiences from overdetermination by a politicized prochoice/prolife binary. Toward this end, I seek narratives that explore uncomfortable possibilities that move readers beyond narrowly defined acceptability via a wider array of pregnancy outcomes. This means, in part, embracing the monstrous aspects of pregnancy, drawing particularly on an understanding of the monstrous as chimeric, simultaneously marked by hybridity and tension. Rosi Braidotti explains that "to be significant and to signify potentially contradictory meanings is precisely what the monster is supposed to do" (1996, 135). Pregnancy, circumscribed by patriarchy, is monstrous; as Donna Haraway argues in "The Promises of Monsters," when patriarchal discourses of reproduction separate pregnancy from the fetus, "discursively reconstitut[ing]" each pregnant person as a "maternal environment" rather than "a partner in an intricate and intimate dialectic of social relationality," monstrosity becomes a logical extension of reproduction (1992, 299). And, she reminds us bluntly, "it is crucial to remember that all of this is about the power of life and death" (312). This chapter explores the potential for graphic narratives, with their grotesque bodies and narratives that exceed the frame of normalcy, to intervene in the politics of pregnancy, reclaiming life, birth, and abortion from easy binarizations.

Reading comics narratives that recover pregnancy from what Adrienne Rich calls the "institution of motherhood" (1976, 13) via the power of the monstrous pregnant body will demonstrate the ability of graphic narratives to expand or describe the limits of acceptability. Beginning with an examination of the politics of normalization in Leah Hayes's graphic abortion handbook, *Not Funny Ha-Ha* (2015), the chapter then turns to several portrayals of monstrous pregnancy in comics, each of which narratively deconstructs the maternal/fetal relational dialectic. Finally, I revisit Hayes's text, rereading through the lens of these deconstructions, in order better to see moments of oppositionality emerging stealthily from gaps in the normal. These analyses demonstrate how graphic narratives function as part of what Drucilla Cornell calls the "imaginary domain," the psychic space of symbolic forms that inspire us to perceive ourselves as individuals. As such, these texts have the power to (re)shape our ability to challenge sexist ideology and authorize individual subjectivity. As Cornell writes, "our sense of freedom is intimately tied to the renewal of the imagination as we come to terms with who we are and who we wish to be" (1995, 7). Rosemary Betterton concurs, noting how artistic representations of pregnancy "negotiate the relations between the socially constituted maternal body and the particularities of the embodied materiality of pregnancy" (2006, 82). The power of representation is a power of expanded imagination.

Not Funny and Normalization

The 2015 publication of Leah Hayes's graphic narrative *Not Funny Ha-Ha: A Handbook for Something Hard* was praised for its realistic and depoliticized presentation of abortion, the "something hard" in the book's title. A *Los Angeles Times* review describes the book as "the story of two characters [. . .] who are getting abortions" told "[i]n simple, sketch-style drawings." Hayes

> takes the reader, step by step, through different aspects of the procedure, covering everything from the confused emotional feelings that can accompany the decision to abort, to what a woman might expect at the doctor's office before, after and during an abortion. (For the record: this is a graphic novel, but it isn't graphic—Hayes does not show the procedure). (Miranda 2015)

As an abortion counselor, I couldn't wait to get my hands on a copy.

Among the many challenges of abortion counseling, helping patients recognize the effects of the social stigmatization of abortion and work toward resolution of those effects is primary. Almost every abortion patient I have counseled has reiterated stigmatizing messages that having an abortion is unnatural, inhuman, even monstrous. Hayes is clearly aware of this concern. In a review in *Bustle*, Hayes "explain[s] that she 'wanted to create something that other girls (and men!) could read and feel a connection with'" (Weiss 2015). She chose the genre of handbook deliberately and precisely: "I was picturing a girl [sic] going through this procedure, thinking 'What would she want to read?' So it was an attempt to write something comforting, but also something that was helpful" (Miranda 2015). *Bustle* describes the book as "informative" and "emotionally engaging," with "friendly, accessible dialogue and narration and engaging illustrations"; in short, Hayes's graphic narrative "humanize[s]" abortion (Weiss 2015). Hayes herself explains how her book could mitigate the stigmatization that equates abortion with the monstrous: "I wanted it to feel like a friend or a family member was putting a hand on your shoulder saying, 'It's OK'" (Miranda 2015). In thirteen years of work as a prochoice counselor in abortion clinics, I have listened to scores of patients who would have loved to have had one friend or family member providing the kind of support Hayes describes. I imagined copies of Hayes's book in clinic waiting areas, spreading comfort and information among our more anxious patients.

Nonetheless, when I first read *Not Funny Ha-Ha*, I was disappointed. While the simple line drawings were indeed humanizing, the color scheme—a bilious yellow with accents of pale orange and gray—seemed somewhat sickly. The narrative framing was engaging, but the text-heavy single-panel pages did not allow the characters to emerge fully until well into the story. I was unable to get through the entire book in one sitting, which suggested that many clinic patients—usually nervous, distracted, and nauseated—would put the book down before completing the story. I took my copy to the clinic with me and showed it to several coworkers, most of whom were counselors, nurses, or doctors; none of them read beyond the first ten pages. To be fair, the book landed in the middle of several competing discourses about abortion, and I am sure I am not the only abortion advocate who hoped against hope that it would positively intervene in each one, triumphantly shifting common assumptions about abortions and those who have them, eradicating abortion stigma once and for all! It doesn't. The book is not a superhero; it is, as the title says, a handbook, written to help people facing abortion know what to expect and feel supported. The book is, more than anything, a testament to the normalcy of abortion.

Normalcy and the "Good" Abortion

As someone who theorizes abortion stigma and works to diminish it, particularly among those of us who identify as prochoice, I often think about normalization, especially in relation to US political culture, in which abortion discourse is circumscribed by the prochoice/prolife binary. While I appreciate Hayes's desire to help those having abortions to feel normal, I do not read normalization as incontrovertibly liberatory, as she seems to. As I have argued elsewhere (Ludlow 2008), the "normal" for US abortion discourse is apologetic, at best. Even in prochoice spaces, abortion narratives that are generally deemed most culturally acceptable and politically effective describe "good" abortions occurring, paradoxically, in the absence of fully realized choice: in cases of sexual assault, birth control failure, fetal anomaly, and teenage pregnancy. Even in prochoice narratives, the choice to abort is often framed apologetically, as a sad reality of some people's difficult lives or as a necessary tragedy in our society. This framing is problematic on two fronts. First, the "good" abortion represents a very small percentage of abortion experiences in the United States; abortion providers know that, while very few abortion patients use the language of empowered choice to describe their pregnancy decision-making, nearly 90 percent of abortions in the United States are elective—chosen by the pregnant patient (Biggs, Gould, and Foster 2013; CDC 2017; Guttmacher Institute 2014). The framing of the "good" abortion, then, effectively erases or stigmatizes by comparison the majority of abortion experiences. Second, the framing around "good" or acceptable abortion narratives represents a very narrow range of pregnancy decision-making experiences, thereby contributing to an ever-shrinking definition of abortion acceptability and a correspondingly expanding sense of abortion as monstrous. I argue that this shrinking margin of abortion acceptability correlates with shrinking access to abortion via a tightening of state and federal regulations.

The ways a narrowing definition of acceptable abortion participates in a politics of shaming can be seen in Hayes's book nearly from the very beginning. *Not Funny Ha-Ha* follows two women, Lisa and Mary, through very different abortion experiences. Lisa, who is drawn to appear white (with straight, shoulder-length hair and unshaded skin), has an in-clinic procedure, which the text calls "surgical." Mary is drawn as a woman of color, with curly dark hair and gray-shaded skin, to represent a darker complexion; she uses medication abortion and passes her pregnancy at home. For both characters, though, the book is almost defiant in its attempts to normalize abortion: "[W]hatever your reason is: it's **fine**, it's your reason" (Hayes 2015; emphasis in the original). A couple of pages later, the text reemphasizes: "The important thing to remember is that the decision is **yours**, and no one is allowed to tell you what to do"; anyone who disagrees "can go screw." In fact, the repeated insistence that the choice is "fine," in the context of cultural normalization of abortion stigma, serves to draw attention to just how un-fine it might be. This interpretation is reinforced by the fact that the text consistently presents reproductive choice as definitionally hard, sad, confusing, and shameful. "**Remember**," the text insists, "this is *not* an *easy thing* to go through." Neither character experiences unqualified relief or happiness after her abortion, as I did after mine, and neither expresses that deciding to have an abortion was the right thing to do, even though 95 percent of US abortion patients reported feeling this way in a longitudinal study (Rocca et al., 2015). Instead, the text tells us that, following her in-clinic procedure, Lisa felt physically fine but "didn't feel like seeing anyone . . . she just wanted some time by herself" (Hayes 2015). Mary, whose at-home medication abortion is carefully detailed in the text, knew that a moment of "**very** heavy" bleeding "meant that the abortion had really happened. It was intense and made her a little sad. She didn't know why." There is, of course, a wide range of healthy emotional responses to abortion, as has been documented by empirical study (Rocca et al., 2015), and Hayes's inclusion of feelings of sadness and isolation could be read as verisimilitude. However, the absence of context for these feelings coupled with the absence of any positive postabortion responses lends the text a dolorous air. It also echoes dominant cultural messages that having an abortion is unnatural and emotionally damaging, and that a "good" abortion is a regretful abortion (Rapp 2000; Allen 2014; Ludlow 2008). By drawing even inadvertent attention to abortion stigma within the context of normalizing choice, the text risks imbricating normalization and stigmatization in ways that echo dominant cultural narratives. In this way, "normalization" participates in a poetics of concession.

The Radical Promises of Monsters

As Stefanie Snider argues elsewhere in this volume, normalization—particularly of a monstrous character—effectively defangs her, constraining her ability to subvert patriarchal demands. Snider's work suggests one reason for my initial response to Hayes's book; perhaps I was not so troubled by the book's normalization of abortion as by its normalization of the graphic narrative. Realism, after all, is not comics creators' only (or perhaps even their best) platform for social commentary. As Hillary Chute has noted, comics as a medium works narratively via defamiliarization rather than mimesis; graphic narratives are "patently artificial," "never suggest[ing] transparency." In fact, comics' narrative power is rooted in gaps—both the gutters between panels and the "constant, active, uneasy back-and-forth" of the "*internally*, conspicuously dialogic" tension between words and images (Chute 2015, 198–99). In this way, comics narratives are, themselves, artificial, strange, marked by internal contradictions, not unlike monsters.

The ability to represent and exceed borders, to imagine im/possibilities, makes the medium of comics effective for replacing sacred images with those that are, simultaneously, unfitting, excessive, and generative—with "inappropriate/d others" (Haraway 1992, 301). As Andrea Wood and Brandy Schillace write in their introduction to *Unnatural Reproductions and Monstrosity*, the "female reproductive body" has long been a representational locus for cultural anxiety around questions of what (who) comes next, in terms of culture change (2014, 2). This anxiety is imbricated, as is the fear of the monstrous, with desire, as Jeffrey Cohen reminds us (1996, 16–18). Given US culture's (conflicted) veneration of pregnancy and motherhood and attendant stigmatization of abortion, comics narratives should be an incredibly productive space within which to revision gestation, abortion, and motherhood through the figure of monstrosity. Indeed, as Jeffrey Brown has argued, "maternity in the comics has been cast as an example of femininity as both literally and figuratively monstrous" (2015, 138). So I went looking for examples of comics narratives that disrupt sacred images of maternity either through accounts of reproductive choice or through representations of inappropriate/d m/others. It is important to note here that while I do not elide motherhood with abortion, I do recognize that any textual/discursive containment of pregnancy always already applies to abortion. As Betterton explains, "the pregnant body exceeds regulatory social norms in certain respects" (2006, 82). The aborting body must, by definition, exceed those same norms. At the same time, abortion materially returns the body to its normative state. Thus, the very condition that designates the body as unregulatable becomes the mechanism for control over that body. The radical promise of these comics narratives stems from their advancement of representations of the "monstrous-feminine" (Brown 2015, 140). In these texts, pregnancy and abortion reflect Haraway's monstrous promise, via artifactual pregnancies and diffracted choice(s), which are inappropriate/d (1992).

Diffracted Choices

As a reproductive justice scholar, of course, I was looking for heroic representations of choice. The texts I found were simultaneously heroic and disruptive of the dominant prochoice narratives. Haraway tells us that "[d]iffraction is a mapping of interference, not of replication, reflection, or reproduction. A diffracted pattern [. . .] maps" not difference but "where the effects of difference appear" (1992, 300). If graphic narratives are going to teratologize choice, they must do so through strategies of interruption and interference. For example, in *Baby Talk*, Jessica Drew/Spider-Woman is shown in a flashback, wrestling with a difficult decision early in her pregnancy. In an asymmetrical eight-panel sequence, she talks herself into an important sacrifice.

Alone in her garage, lit by a single light from above, face shadowed and contorted, Jess vacillates between indignation—"I shouldn't have to do this"—and refusal—"No. I'm not doing this! I refuse to become some kind of . . . just because . . ." (Hopeless and Rodriguez 2016). Because the narrative has previously established that she is pregnant, readers are invited to imagine that Jess is working through a process of pregnancy decision-making (deciding whether to have a baby or an abortion). The complexity of the decision process is expressed in the tension between the text and the images; larger panels are textually thin while smaller panels are rendered tight—nearly claustrophobic—and full of words. At the moment when the decision is set, the panel is a narrowly shaped, tight close-up of Jess's right eye and cheek; within this intimacy, her decision seems to waver one final time: "It's . . ." In the next panel, Jess is shown full-bodied (both full-length and obviously pregnant), covering her motorcycle with a tarp, placing it in storage for the duration of her pregnancy. As a diffracted choice, this scene demonstrates a differential mapping of desire, a refusal to naturalize pregnancy as a state of maternal protectiveness. At the same time, because this scene maps the process of pregnancy decision-making neatly onto the motorcycle decision-making, it locks Jess Drew (in contradistinction to her superhero persona) into a decision to stop working while she is pregnant, thereby propelling her story toward one typical superhero/mom plot: "giving up superheroics to become a full-time parent" (Brown 2015, 144). Spider-Woman's reproductive choice falls short of any potential for radical redefinitions of pregnancy and work that a truly diffracted choice would allow.

Earlier in the story, Dennis Hopeless and Javier Rodriguez provide a more monstrous—and thus more radical—narrative of pregnancy and work. *Baby Talk* opens with Jess Drew, six months pregnant, lugging groceries through town, wearing flip-flops, jean shorts, a T-shirt stretched across her distended abdomen, and her Spider-Woman uniform jacket. The jacket gapes open like a too-small cardigan, simultaneously invoking and neutralizing its power. Her Spider-Woman sunglasses are pushed up onto her forehead. Hands dangling grocery bags, Jess chats on her cell phone with Carol Danvers while Captain Marvel (Danvers's superhero alter ego) fights and subdues a two-headed robot monster in space. As they talk about how annoying Jess finds the "never ending parade" of "human shields" that "po[p] out . . . to hold open every single door" for her, Captain Marvel tightens restraints around the robot monster's wrists. After kicking open a door (with no help) in what looks like an apartment building, Jess faces three minor villains in the kitchen, apparently making tea. This two-page spread is organized into a quarter-page row of panels across the top of a single panel that bleeds off the edges. In the foreground of the large panel, the three villains face our hero, back to the readers, whose point of

Figure 7.1: Jess Drew defeats three minor villains, pregnant, in flip-flops, and while explaining how terrifying pregnancy is. *Spider-Woman: Shifting Gears*, vol. 1: *Baby Talk*, by Dennis Hopeless and Javier Rodriguez. Copyright 2016, Marvel Comics.

view is looking through their legs at Jess. Midground, three images of Jess, who suddenly seems much more Spider-Woman-like, in various fighting stances, one facing each villain, represent her fight with them. By putting multiple images of Jess/Spider-Woman in the same panel, Hopeless and Rodriguez invite readers into the energy and movement of the fight (McCloud 1993, 112). Cell phone tucked between ear and shoulder, flip-flops revealing her painted

toes, Jess throws her groceries at the villains. Inset into the large panel are three small square panels, each of which shows a villain's face seeming to explode into red and pink foodstuffs: tomatoes, beans, soup, sausages. While fighting the villains, Jess explains between breaths just how terrifying she finds impending motherhood: " . . . I'm **quite** clearly terrified . . . more terrified in fact—than I've ever been in my entire—shockingly insane—life" (fig. 7.1).

Epitomizing the "constant, active, uneasy back-and-forth" between words and images that Hillary Chute argues is a source of comics' monstrous power, this panel is intended to represent the impotence of superpowers against the anxieties of impending motherhood. The tension between Jess's descriptions of her fear and her almost nonchalant defeat of three foes provides a much more radical narrative about pregnancy and work, one in which our hero can acknowledge her fears without subverting her competence. Indeed, the synchronicity of anxiety and competence locates Jess's pregnancy narrative (like most pregnancies) at a radical intersection of normalcy and monstrosity.

Haraway suggests that the radical potential of diffraction is rooted in its challenge to verisimilitude: "These diffracting rays compose interference patterns, not reflecting images" which, in turn "mak[e] potent connection that exceeds domination" (1992, 299). A. K. Summers's graphic memoir, *Pregnant Butch: Nine Long Months Spent in Drag*, suggests that comics narratives can offer diffracted patterns of interference rather than reflections of reality. One way that the text does this is through oscillating representations of Teek, the eponymous pregnant butch. Although Summers frequently renders Teek as a Tintin double, the text periodically presents her more realistically—sometimes on the same page. The opening scene of the memoir, for example, shows Teek looking like "just another fat guy on the subway" (2014, 2). In the top two-thirds of the page, Teek and the other people on the subway are rendered realistically. Noses, lips, and eyes are detailed, cross-hatching creates shadows and body hair, and facial expressions are clearly defined. The bottom third of the page is divided into two panels. On the left is a spare drawing of pregnant Teek looking like a round-torsoed Tintin: Teek's round face is mouthless; her nose is an upside-down 7 below eyes that are simple dots; and three curved lines suggest upswept bangs. In the right-hand panel, pre-pregnancy Teek is drawn realistically, with a more square-shaped face and defined ears, nose, facial lines, fingernails and knuckle lines. These very different representations "in the space of a single page" serve to "collaps[e] or protrac[t] temporal dimensions" of Teek's pregnancy experience at the same time that they "force [readers] to confront a [. . .] proliferation, or multiplicity, of selves" (Chute 2015, 200). Chute explains that these concerns—"positionality, location, and embodiment"—exist at the intersection of feminist theory and the grammar of comics, thereby marking comics texts as methodologically feminist (200). These diffracted images of Teek exist side by side with more overtly monstrous representations. For example, when her partner gives Teek "Good Earth tea" in place of her coffee, pregnant Teek morphs into a Hulk-like form in tattered clothing. As the swelling panel bursts out of its quarter of the page and her swelling biceps "pop!" her T-shirt sleeves, Teek Hulk growls: "You no take Teek coffee!!

Beer gone . . . coffee **stay**!!" The more reasonable narrative voice, scrolling across the top of the panel, explains: "It was the **principle**! Whose body was it anyway?" (Summers 2014, 45). This direct invocation of prochoice discourse in a humorous description of pregnancy's inconveniences should remind readers that "prochoice" is not as simple as have/don't have a baby. Within the context of Teek's frank examinations of the dialogic between her pregnancy experience and her butch identity, it should also remind us that previously held assumptions about gender and pregnancy are no longer ineluctable. As her body transforms in ways that refuse "normalizing mechanisms," Teek embodies the "*deformative* and *misappropriative* power" in "oppos[ition to] society itself" that defines queerness (Eng, Halberstam, and Muñoz 2005, 1; Butler 1993, 21; Warner 1993, xxvii; emphasis in the original). In this moment, Teek Hulk becomes a queer reproductive justice superhero, pushing back against the easy political binarizations defining gender and choice.

Later, Teek metaphorizes her inability to "let go" of her control over labor to fear of going off the high diving board at the pool. In a two-page sequence of small, neat panels in four even—straight—rows of three, readers follow Teek's thought processes while in active labor. Pregnant Teek, represented in simple, almost cartoonish lines as a naked, round-torsoed, large-breasted Tintin, sits on the edge of a high diving board, which protrudes into the panel, baseless, from the left. While Teek ponders some other way "out of this," the order of panels on the page contrasts with the gaiety that exceeds each panel (Summers 2014, 96–98). As Teek catalogs her fears, a thin man in a hat, dark tie, and flared pants backs onto the high dive behind her. Music notation floats below the board as the man's dancing partner, a willowy blonde wearing a long, swinging skirt, bobby socks, and chunk heels, comes into view. The man lifts the woman across his back and flips her into the air as the lyrics to a World War II–era jazz standard scroll around Teek. The dancers push Teek off the edge of the board as she shouts, "Pesky swing dancers!" After invoking the source of her inability to let go—"masculin-féminin yin-yang assholes," she shouts, drawing attention to the complexity of her own butch identification—she dangles, tries to pull herself back up, loses her grip, flaps her arms frantically like a bird, and finally begins to fall, cursing, down through the panels. The music changes first to the chorus of Cole Porter's "Let's Do It" and then to Culture Club's "Karma Chameleon," suggesting, perhaps, an increasingly queered labor and delivery process as Teek continues to fall into "transition" labor for nearly two full pages. Read in the context of Teek's proud butch presentation, these pages present an interruption of US society's heteronormative sanctification of maternity, which Haraway describes as "the reproduction of the sacred image of the same [. . .] mediated by the luminous technolog[y] of compulsory heterosexuality"

(1992, 299). The humorous explorations of diffracted identity in *Pregnant Butch*, represented by the changes in Teek's pregnant body and the shifts in her position on the page, thus constitute a kind of desacralization, an artistic transition enabling readers to accept and identify with a queered pregnancy.

Artifactual Pregnancies and Inappropriate/d Others

These shifts also serve to draw attention to the artifactuality of pregnancy in terms of gender. As Haraway describes it, artifactuality reveals the constructedness of nature; therefore, that most "natural" of states for some bodies—pregnancy—must be a construct of our assumptions about gender, generation, family, love, sex, and a whole host of other ultimately undefinable concepts. The artifactual is the location for an "elsewhere" simultaneously grounded in and deconstructive of binarized epistemological categories (Haraway 1992, 297). Positing the deconstruction of the embodied/socially constituted binary, the artifactual challenges the naturalization of pregnant embodiment by highlighting the ways all pregnancy experiences are socially constituted. Artifactualism offers what Haraway calls "serious political and analytical hope" (1992, 295) in the face of cultural anxiety—magnified by desire—that defines the monstrous reproductive body (Wood and Schillace 2014). Jessica Jones's 2005 pregnancy in *The Pulse* certainly inspires anxiety and desire in the city hospital. When Jones presents at the city hospital in labor, Carol Danvers (in *The Pulse*, identified as "ex-Avenger Ms. Marvel") is asked to leave because the "energies" she is "emitting" are "not safe for the baby" (Bendis and Gaydos 2005b). This concern for the baby's safety is controverted minutes later by a hospital administrator, who yells for "[o]rderlies [to] [r]oll that woman out of here and onto the street!" (Bendis and Gaydos 2005b). When challenged by the doctor who has been attending Jessica, the administrator says, "We cannot give birth to whatever she has in there!" This declaration underscores the artifactual nature of all pregnancies, which are (by experience if not by legal definition) simultaneously physical, psychological, and social. Note that the administrator does not say, "*She* cannot give birth to whatever she has in there"; she says, "*We* cannot," thereby revealing monstrous birth to be not the product of the maternal body but of the entire culture. As Braidotti explains, this cultural reproduction often reveals "deep-seated anxiety that surrounds the issue of women's maternal power of procreation in a patriarchal society" (1996, 82). In this case, that anxiety is clearly racist anxiety over biraciality and white erasure within a white supremacist patriarchal context. The father of Jessica's baby is Luke Cage; the baby is biracial (Bendis and Gaydos 2005a). If monsters represent our cultural anxieties over who comes next, surely Jessica's monstrous pregnancy draws attention to the increasing minoritization of white people in the United States. As the gestator of a hybrid fetus, she must be ejected from the hospital. If we follow Haraway and "rethin[k] social relationality" through the hospital administrator's speech, we confront the artifactuality of the "privacy" of pregnancy. These disruptions become the "interference patterns" that Haraway suggests might make up the "elsewhere" of "a differential, diffracted feminist allegory" of "inappropriate/d others" (1992, 301). By highlighting the tension between racist anxiety on one hand and natalist concern for the unborn on the other, Jessica Jones's genetically "different" pregnancy and her expulsion from the presumably safe space of the hospital interfere with our understanding of reproduction as natural, knowable—as appropriate.

Haraway reminds us that Trinh T. Minh-ha's term "inappropriate/d others" asks us to reconsider "the relations of difference among people and among humans, other organisms, and machines" in ways that disrupt long-accepted hierarchies and oppositions (1992, 301). Being inappropriate/d is about being simultaneously inappropriate and not appropriable—not (able to be) appropriated or contained by dominant discourses. The end of Jessica Jones's pregnancy narrative in *The Pulse* dwells in perhaps uncomfortable (therefore potentially productive) ways on the inappropriate/d family that Jones and Luke Cage are building (Bendis and Gaydos 2006b). In a three-page flashback sequence of Luke's proposal of marriage, the narrative shifts from a conversation with a lot of silences to a strung-together sequence of rapid short sentences and then to a series of repetitions that set up an echo effect. The first page uses a regular arrangement of two columns of four panels of medium close-up representations of Jessica holding the baby and Luke entering (or leaving) the panel on the right. There is no text in half of the eight panels, and the images in the panels change very little, except for Jessica's looking up at Luke and then back to front several times, giving the impression of a double take. The second page is drawn in landscape orientation, with two short, wide panels to the page; the top panel looks over Jessica's shoulder to Luke's face while the bottom looks over Luke's shoulder to Jessica, in a comics staging of a shot reverse shot. This page has a lot of text, strung along in small speech balloons, all attributed to Luke. On this page, he justifies his proposal to a shocked Jessica, explaining that he hopes their marriage will help normalize their daughter in the eyes of culture. He says, in part, "We're two 'super hero' parents and this is a biracial relationship . . . For some people out there that is about a million different reasons to hate us . . . Why the hell does this girl, this perfect little baby girl, have to contend with being **illegitimate** on top of all the other crap that's going to come her way because of her **biracial, super hero**

parents??" (Bendis and Gaydos 2006b). The framing on this page represents how difficult it is for Luke to have this conversation about racism with his white lover. We cannot see both their faces at the same time, suggesting both an intensity of response and an incongruity of focus. The strung-together short phrases suggest that he is talking kind of fast, in bursts of phrases. In the scene, Jessica is clearly more focused on the baby, while Luke is thinking about seemingly abstract concerns like legitimacy, biraciality, and otherness. This difference draws attention to the ways Luke Cage is racially marked in the series as well as the ways Jessica represents white privilege. In a racist sociopolitical context that simultaneously erases Black fatherhood and blames Black men for being absent fathers, Cage's concerns about illegitimacy read less like an example of patriarchal ownership than like an antiracist counternarrative.

Just when we start worrying that Jessica Jones and Luke Cage are headed for the suburbs, the writers remind us that Jessica has not yet named her baby (Bendis and Gaydos 2006b). If, as Cohen argues, the monstrous defies categorization, then our naming of monsters functions to capture them, to discursively contain their disruptive potential. Perhaps "their perfect little girl" is perfect not because she has escaped being a monster but because monsters escape social confines. In fact, as Cohen reminds us, escaping is a monster's act. We may never know. *The Pulse* story line—"Jessica's own series"—ends with no. 14, in which Luke proposes, with Jessica speaking speculatively to her unnamed daughter (Brown 2015, 144). Jessica Jones may have successfully given birth, but the writers discontinue her story, leaving this family suspended between marriage and illegitimacy, simultaneously undefined and marked by potential.

In contrast to the nebulous promise of *The Pulse*'s monstrous family, *Pregnant Butch* proposes monstrous embodiment to represent inappropriate/d family. Summers gives Teek a dream of a birth education class full of truly inappropriate/d others/mothers, "filled with queers" who "carved out their roles as 'birth givers' and 'birth partners' without the obfuscations of Ina May Gaskin and Dave Barry." In this dream childbirth class, "there'd be at least one other pregnant butch. And some femme-on-femme, butch-on-butch action. A hot single, a bearded lady. Some highly idiosyncratic classifications. At least one threesome . . ." (Summers 2014, 73). In a full-page panel, this dream class consisting of ten visibly queer characters performs a human pyramid, literally standing on one another's shoulders and hoisting an upside-down acrobatic pregnant person to the top of the page. The annoying performance artist–cum–childbirth coach approaches from a distance, carrying pompons and shouting "Rah! Rah! Rah!" Presented in the context of Teek's desire for queer support—the pyramid page is titled "Reinforcements"—this dream childbirth class ends up looking an awful lot like a party in the bottom layer of transgender theorist

Kate Bornstein's Gender/Identity/Power Pyramid, as drawn by feminist comics artist Diane DiMassa, best known for *Hothead Paisan: Homicidal Lesbian Terrorist* (Bornstein 1998, 44). In this panel, the "queers" are simultaneously contained by the conventionality of a birth class, as represented by the borders of the frame, and centered in relation to conventionality, which is marginalized via the placement of the coach to the side and in the background (fig. 7.2). Unrestrained in their joy, their physicality and visible generativity renders them doubly monstrous, both *in* space and *as* space. Haraway reminds us that "the womb of a pregnant monster" is "a foreign, allotopic place" within which our notions of normalcy and appropriateness are situated and from which they can be deconstructed (1992, 295).

The Monstrous in the Mundane

These figures are surely inappropriate/d: inappropriate and inappropriable in their queerness and freakness. Even as their physical and social positionalities— teetering in a human pyramid suspended within the panel; participating in socially respectable institutions like family and parenthood within the story— suggest hierarchies, readers know that this is Teek's dream. Dream status refuses normalization, so their inappropriateness provides balance vis-à-vis the hierarchy. In their unrealness, they promise to be an inappropriate/d family for Teek, her partner Vee, and their baby. Teek's dream of the monstrous generative queer can not be limited by the normal/deviant binary; it reminds us that, in Haraway's words, "[t]o be 'inappropriate/d' does not mean not to be in relation with" nor innocent of. "Rather to be an 'inappropriate/d other' means to be in critical deconstructive relationality" (1992, 299) with the narratives that shape and limit us. Perhaps monstrosity within institutions, rather than being contained, normalized, and defanged, is rendered more monstrous, more powerful by its proximity to the mundane. Like Jess Drew kicking ass in her maternity top and flip-flops, or like just about any creepy movie villain walking through our homes when we can't see them, the monstrous imbricated into our daily lives may actually be more shocking. In fact, it may be the juxtaposition of normalcy and aberration that distinguishes the monstrous from the monster; as Stephen T. Asma writes of Frankenstein's creature, "It is the failure of [. . .] society generally to provide a space for him in the human family that turns the creature into a monster" (2009, 11). Perhaps conversely, it is the ability to move seamlessly into and among the human family that gives the monstrous its power.

Inspired by this realization, I return to Hayes's *Not Funny Ha-Ha* to find that within the normalization that I originally perceived in the book, she has

Figure 7.2: In Teek's dream childbirth class, queer pregnancy is simultaneously the center of attention and contained by convention. *Pregnant Butch: Nine Long Months Spent in Drag*, p. 73, by A. K. Summers. Copyright 2014, Soft Skull Press.

imbricated two narrative moments that turn toward a critical deconstruction of "normative" and thus "inflexible" abortion narratives (Allen 2014, 53, 61). These monstrous declarations, emerging with shocking ease from the disarming harmony between words and images in Hayes's book, promise (like monsters) to "issue in something other than the sacred image of the same," something potentially "inappropriate/d" (Haraway 1992, 300). Early in the book, as she introduces her protagonists Mary and Lisa, Hayes explicitly turns from a standard prochoice narrative trope: that of the "unintended pregnancy as an accident or understandable mistake" onto which the pregnant one can map an abortion experience as "moral" and "empowering" (Allen 2014, 47). In *Not Funny Ha-Ha*, Hayes writes about Mary: "Since this is a book about what it's like to go through an abortion, we won't get into why or how she **got** pregnant. For all intents and purposes . . . it doesn't really matter" (2015). These hand-lettered words make up about half the page, hovering box-less above a three-quarter image of Mary and a head-and-shoulders image of Lisa. Mary's speech bubble says, seemingly in conversation with the narrative voice, "Yep! and it's also none of your business!" The narration continues, " . . . and the same goes for Lisa." "Yeah," Lisa's speech bubble reads, "that's a different kind of book!" The defiant stance taken by Hayes and her characters here represents a refusal to conform to "contemporary middle-class values regarding personal responsibility, sexuality, and motherhood," which Mallary Allen finds circumscribing prochoice "movement norms" and, ultimately, limiting prochoice storytelling (2014, 43).

Similarly, Hayes resists allowing her characters' abortion narratives to reify heteronormative expectations for sexual relationships. Mary's sexual choices are completely under erasure in the text; her only relationship is a warm and caring one with a woman the text names her "best friend." Lisa, by contrast, does call her former partner to tell him about her impending abortion. This act does not, however, shift the focus from the pregnancy or abortion experience onto their relationship, as often happens in prochoice narratives. Lisa's former partner offers to "take [her]" to her appointment, and she refuses him because she would rather have her sister there. He then, appropriately, offers to pay, and Lisa tearfully accepts and thanks him. This brief moment of relationship drama is closed, however, by a turning of the page. In the next panel, we see Lisa very competently, albeit with a worried expression on her face, calling the clinic for an appointment, asking about anesthesia. According to Mallary Allen's analytic frame, these narrative choices are as oppositional to the prochoice movement as sharing an abortion story is to dominant cultural standards. Allen notes that prochoice storytelling has become schematized. "As a cause gains public attention," she writes, "formulaic understandings become widespread, and those with ambiguous experiences [. . .] learn to emphasize those elements [. . .] most consistent with dominant social movement stories" (2014, 45). In other words, by refusing to conform her narrative to what Allen calls "basic [. . .] sympathetic pro-choice storytelling" (2014, 47), Hayes resists the reification of the "good" abortion. More importantly, by explicitly invoking the tropes of basic sympathetic prochoice storytelling as an element of this resistance, Hayes visibly injects her monstrous refusal into the normalcy of her graphic novel. In so doing, she reproduces contextually one of the strengths of comics texts. As Chute describes, the power of comics to defamiliarize an experience for readers resides in a productive tension between words and images that moves the narrative along. It is this very tension that makes comics a perfect medium/art form for expressing the monstrous simultaneity of aberration and mundanity. Leah Hayes has reproduced this tension in *Not Funny Ha-Ha*, situating it between prochoice standards and realistic experiences, thereby representing the monstrous simultaneity of the mundanity of pregnancy and the aberration of abortion. Maybe Hayes's book really is a superhero, and I was unable to see past its mild-mannered alter ego.

Bibliography

Allen, Mallary. 2014. "Narrative Diversity and Sympathetic Abortion: What Online Storytelling Reveals about the Prescribed Norms of the Mainstream Movements." *Symbolic Interaction* 38, no. 1: 42–63.

Asma, Stephen T. 2009. *On Monsters: An Unnatural History of Our Worst Fears*. Oxford: Oxford University Press.

Bendis, Brian Michael, and Michael Gaydos. 2005a. *The Pulse: Fear, part 1*. Vol. 1, no. 11 (September 14).

Bendis, Brian Michael, and Michael Gaydos. 2005b. *The Pulse: Fear, part 2*. Vol. 1, no. 12 (November 9).

Bendis, Brian Michael, and Michael Gaydos. 2006a. *The Pulse: Fear, part 3*. Vol. 1, no. 13 (January 6).

Bendis, Brian Michael, and Michael Gaydos. 2006b. *The Pulse: Finale*. Vol. 1, no. 14 (March 8).

Betterton, Rosemary. 2006. "Promising Monsters: Pregnant Bodies, Artistic Subjectivity, and Maternal Imagination." *Hypatia* 21, no. 1 (Winter): 80–100.

Biggs, M. Antonia, Heather Gould, and Diana Greene Foster. 2013. "Understanding Why Women Seek Abortions in the US." *BMC Women's Health* 13. Available at https://doi.org/10.1186/1472-6874-13-29.

Bornstein, Kate. 1998. *My Gender Workbook: How to Become a Real Man, a Real Woman, the Real You, or Something Else Entirely*. Illustrations by Diane DiMassa. New York: Routledge.

Braidotti, Rosi. 1996. "Signs of Wonder and Traces of Doubt: On Teratology and Embodied Differences." In *Between Monsters, Goddesses, and Cyborgs: Feminist Confrontations with Science, Medicine, and Cyberspace*, edited by Nina Lykke and Rosi Braidotti, 135–52. Atlantic Highlands, NJ: Zed Books.

Brown, Jeffrey A. 2015. "Supermoms? Maternity and the Monstrous-Feminine in Superhero Comics." In *Beyond Bombshells: The New Action Heroine in Popular Culture*, 136–51. Jackson: University Press of Mississippi.

Butler, Judith. 1993. "Critically Queer." *GLQ* 1, no. 1: 17–32.

Centers for Disease Control and Prevention (CDC). 2017. "CDC's Abortion Surveillance System FAQs." Available at https://www.cdc.gov/reproductivehealth/data_stats/abortion.htm.

Chute, Hillary. 2015. "The Space of Graphic Narrative: Mapping Bodies, Feminism, and Form." In *Narrative Theory Unbound: Queer and Feminist Interventions*, edited by Robyn Warhol and Susan S. Lanser, 194–209. Columbus: Ohio State University Press.

Cohen, Jeffrey Jerome. 1996. "Monster Culture (Seven Theses)." In *Monster Theory: Reading Culture*, edited by Jeffrey Jerome Cohen, 3–25. Minneapolis: University of Minnesota Press.

Cornell, Drucilla. 1995. *The Imaginary Domain: Abortion, Pornography and Sexual Harassment*. New York: Routledge.

Eng, David L., with Judith Halberstam and José Esteban Muñoz. 2005. "Introduction: What's Queer about Queer Studies Now?" *Social Text* 23, nos. 3–4 (Fall–Winter 2005): 1–17.

Guttmacher Institute. 2014. "An Overview of Abortion Laws." Available at https://www.guttmacher.org/state-policy/explore/overview-abortion-laws.

Haraway, Donna. 1992. "The Promises of Monsters: A Regenerative Politics for Inappropriate/d Others." In *Cultural Studies*, edited by Lawrence Grossberg, Cary Nelson, and Paula Treichler, 295–337. New York: Routledge.

Hayes, Leah. 2015. *Not Funny Ha-Ha: A Handbook for Something Hard*. Seattle: Fantagraphics.

Hopeless, Dennis, and Javier Rodriguez. 2016. *Spider-Woman: Shifting Gears*, vol. 1: *Baby Talk*. New York: Marvel Comics.

Ludlow, Jeannie. 2008. "The Things We Cannot Say: Witnessing the Trauma-tization of Abortion in the United States." *Women's Studies Quarterly* 36, nos. 1–2 (Spring): 28–41. Available at https://doi.org/10.1353/wsq.0.0057.

McCloud, Scott. 1993. *Understanding Comics: The Invisible Art*. Northampton, MA: Kitchen Sink Press.

Miranda, Carolina A. 2015. "*Not Funny Ha-Ha*: Leah Hayes' Graphic Novel about Abortion Goes beyond Politics." *Los Angeles Times*, August 25. Available at http://www.latimes.com/entertainment/music/la-et-cam-leah-hayes-graphic-novel-about-abortion-20150824-column.html.

Rapp, Rayna. 2000. *Testing Women, Testing the Fetus: The Social Impact of Amniocentesis in America*. New York: Routledge.

Rich, Adrienne. 1976. *Of Woman Born: Motherhood as Experience and Institution*. New York: W. W. Norton.

Rocca, Corinne H., Katrina Kimport, Sarah C. M. Roberts, Heather Gould, John Neuhaus, and Diana G. Foster. 2015. "Decision Rightness and Emotional Responses to Abortion in the United States: A Longitudinal Study." *PLOS ONE*, July 8. Available at https://doi.org/10.1371/journal.pone.0128832.

Summers, A. K. 2014. *Pregnant Butch: Nine Long Months Spent in Drag*. Berkeley, CA: Soft Skull Press.

Warner, Michael. 1993. Introduction to *Fear of a Queer Planet: Queer Politics and Social Theory*, vii–xxxi. Minneapolis: University of Minnesota Press.

Weiss, Suzannah. 2015. "Artist Leah Hayes' *Not Funny Ha-Ha: A Handbook for Something Hard* Lets Those Who Get Abortions Know They're Not Alone." *Bustle*, July 10. Available at https://www.bustle.com/

articles/96365-artist-leah-hayes-not-funny-ha-ha-a-handbook-for-something-hard-lets-those-who-get-abortions.

Wood, Andrea, and Brandy Schillace, eds. 2014. *Unnatural Reproductions and Monstrosity: The Birth of the Monster in Literature, Film, and Media.* Amherst, NY: Cambria Press.

8

The Monstrous Portrayal of the Maternal Bolivian Chola in Contemporary Comics

Marcela Murillo

In his book *Monster Culture*, Jeffrey Jerome Cohen analyzes the creation of monsters to help us understand the cultures that have created them. As he argues, the monster "is best understood as an embodiment of difference, a breaker of category, and a resistant Other" (1996, x). It is through this awareness that motherhood has been depicted as monstrous by scholars such as Jeffrey Brown (2011), Ross Murray (2011), Leo Loveday and Satomi Chiba (1983), Marilyn Francus (2012), and others in a variety of contexts. The Bolivian case is no different, as indigenous mothers in contemporary Bolivian comics are represented as fat, crass, and ignorant. This chapter focuses on the monstrous representation of the Bolivian chola mother and the graphic and narrative mechanisms by which this is accomplished.

Bolivian cholas are indigenous Aymara or Quechua women who wear a distinctive and easily recognizable outfit. They are mainly peasants who have migrated to urban areas and work as domestic workers or market vendors. Spanish tends to be their second language, while an indigenous language such as Aymara or Quechua is often their primary mode of communication. Historically, they have been marginalized; however, their social condition has changed significantly since the turn of the twenty-first century because of revised government policies (Farthing and Kohl 2014, 66). Twentieth-century literature represents the chola in two distinct ways. On the one hand, popular theater presents her positively as a caring woman, whereas novelists tend to present her negatively as an egotistical, opportunistic woman. These contradictions should be taken into account when focusing on the depiction of the chola in twentieth-first-century graphic narratives.

The chola as a mother figure in the Bolivian context is illustrated in three contemporary comics: Corven Icenail and Rafaela Rada's *La Estrella y el Zorro* (2014), Álvaro Ruilova's *Noche de mercado* (2005), and Rafaela Rada's *Nina cholita Andina* (2016a). In these comics, the chola's grotesque representation is positioned within one of the twentieth century's defining intellectual discourses: *mestizaje* (Albó 2008, 19; Shakow 2014, 30; Stephenson 1999, 35–36), a nationalist identity project that has shaped Bolivian history. At the same time, the Andean woman, or chola, has been central to this process as an intermediary in cultural exchange between Spanish colonizers and indigenous colonized populations (Money 2012). This chapter argues that these representations illustrate the cultural and social discursive formations that shape the chola as a monster in Bolivian society, and reflect her social position in Bolivian imagery as the Other.

First, I provide a brief historical overview of cultural representations of the Bolivian chola. Following this, I demonstrate how she is depicted primarily as a maternal figure in Bolivian literature. Third, I offer an analysis of her representation in the three aforementioned Bolivian comics; and finally, I explain how the monstrous representation of the chola fits within *mestizaje* ideology. The chola figure in pop culture provides an insight into current society's appraisal of this historically marginalized population. This is important for Bolivia, as more than 60 percent of the population is indigenous. This type of study fills an academic void because it not only considers commonly overlooked texts such as comics but also focuses entirely on an indigenous figure: cholas. The fictional vilification of the chola speaks of the negativity that is still associated with the indigenous population in Bolivia despite the recent adoption of a pro-indigenous political discourse, accompanied by policy changes.

Historical Overview

To understand who the cholas are, it is necessary to consider how Bolivian women lived during the twentieth century. According to Bolivian historian Ximena Medinaceli (1989), Bolivian women were divided into two groups: upper-class women, whose lives revolved around the domestic sphere and family; and cholas, the working-class women. Dressing styles helped define the difference between these two groups. Upper-class women dressed in European-style garments, while cholas wore the outfit imposed by the Spanish during the colonial period: a big skirt (known as a pollera), a shawl, a bowler hat, and hair styled into two braids. Medinaceli, in her analysis of the Bolivian chola and upper-class women, argues that the main difference between them is the former's active labor status: "Cholas are almost by definition a sector that participates in economic activities that go beyond the domestic sphere" (1989, 82). Commonly, cholas work as domestic employees, cooks, and weavers. The economic remuneration for their work is crucial for their freedom: "In general *cholas* lived much more independently than women of the upper classes. [. . .] It was not uncommon for a woman to maintain economically her household" (Stephenson 1999, 29). This is dissimilar to upper-class women, who considered work done outside the domestic sphere as socially beneath them. Additionally, according to Medinaceli and Stephenson, cholas distinguished themselves from upper-class women not only through their clothing and working status but also through the legality of their partnerships. Upper-class women conceived of marriage and child-rearing as the key components of their lives. In contrast, cholas were and still are known for living and having children out of wedlock. These choices are socially frowned upon by the predominant Catholic Bolivian society.

Thus, cholas experienced freedoms and consequences that were uncommon to upper-class women. But despite their relative economic independence, cholas were systematically discriminated against and looked down upon. This discrimination was often inscribed into laws. For example, in 1925, a municipal ordinance prohibited the entrance of all Natives to public squares, and cholas were included in this categorization. This restriction prevailed for twenty years. In 1935, cholas were also prohibited from using the trams. The reasoning behind this was to prevent middle- and upper-class passengers from having to smell the cholas' body odor. The law declared the following:

> IN ORDER TO AVOID INFECTIONS ON THE TRAMWAY. It is strictly forbidden to allow the entrance of anyone with any bulky items to come into contact with other passengers, as well as people with visible signs of disgust or whose clothes can contaminate other passengers or give off bad smell. (Wadsworth and Dibbits 1989, 67)

Julia Kristeva (2010) argues that the "abject" is the human reaction (horror, vomit) elicited by the impossibility of distinguishing between subject and object, or between oneself (the upper-middle class) and the Other (the chola); this theory may be useful to frame the reasoning of such laws. The "bulky items" that the law refers to are the cholas' polleras; this prohibition shows how the cholas were imagined as dirty and unsanitary. The same year, municipal authorities mandated that everyone who intended to work as a domestic worker or cook had to obtain a "sanitary card." Cholas almost exclusively performed these jobs. This sanitary card necessitated a medical examination for venereal diseases and required that women undress completely. The office in charge of this exam was also responsible for the accreditation of prostitutes' hygiene, thus establishing a sordid connection between indigenous women and sex workers.

Such laws are examples of the structural discrimination and dehumanization that cholas endured. To resist and reject these measures, the cholas formed unions. Within these associations, they fought discriminatory practices such as the sanitary card through public demonstrations, which were occasionally successful. Moreover, in the twenty-first century, the government of Evo Morales, the first indigenous Bolivian president, has increased female presence in politics with the appointment of several cholas as heads of government ministries. Many of them have been elected to positions in municipal offices:

> What is most remarkable is the upsurge in indigenous women involvement. Nemesia Achacollo, minister of rural development; Silvia Lazarte, president of the Constitutional Assembly; Leonilda Zurita, head of the MAS in Cochabamba; Nilda Copa, justice minister; and Cristina Mamani, head of the Magistrates Council, are all indigenous women. At the same time, the indigenous and peasant women's federation has emerged as a critical player among social movements. (Farthing and Kohl 2014, 66)

In 2010, an antiracism law was passed to protect cholas and indigenous people from discrimination. In 2013, the municipal law of La Paz declared the chola figure as a national intangible cultural heritage (Baldivieso 2013), and now the image is legally protected. In addition, cholas are now working in traditional male occupations, employed as traffic officers, bus and taxi drivers, construction workers, and government workers. While performing their duties, they are allowed to wear their traditional clothing, thus showing an increased social awareness and appreciation of its symbolic significance. Despite these new laws, however, discrimination against cholas persists. In December 2015, the city of Caquiaviri sanctioned its mayor for corruption by dressing and displaying him as a chola in the public square (Calle 2015). This humiliation demonstrates the persistence of the association of the chola with notions of shame, which lies at an intersection of gender and ethnicity deemed as problematic for many in Bolivia. Later, in an attempt to demonstrate that wearing a chola outfit is not a shameful act and that it should not be considered a punishment, higher state authorities on a public occasion dressed up in traditional chola clothing.

This brief overview highlights the challenges cholas have faced and the difficulties they have endured throughout history. In recent years their situation has improved, but racism is still latent. This paradoxical context is reflected in contemporary literature and popular culture.

Chola Literature

Bolivian literature of the twentieth century evinces a contradictory representation of the chola. In venues such as the theater, she is depicted as a loving and forgiving mother, as in Juan Barrera's *Me avergüenzan tus polleras* (I am ashamed by your skirts) (1993) and Raúl Salmón's *Hijo de chola* (Son of a chola) (1991). Both plays are affirmative of cholas but also display the social burden of wearing polleras. The first play involves a daughter who renounces the maternal world of the chola and the use of polleras; the second play is about a son who is repulsed by his chola mother. Both the son and the daughter fail in their attempt to ascend socially, and they are mocked by society, as they are unable to erase their indigenous heritage. At the end of both plays, the respective children accept the chola as their mother, and the familial union is reconstituted. The chola mother is always happy to take them back and is shown as a benevolent, loving, and forgiving woman.

Conversely, various novels depict the chola as a cruel and calculating woman. Carlos Medinaceli's *La Chaskañawi* (Star eyes) (1947) and Jaime Mendoza's *En las tierras del Potosí* (In the lands of Potosí) (1911) show the chola as a cold woman who seduces upper-class men. The men who fall for her end up financially ruined and alienated from their social class. The warning is evident: cholas are perilous.

These descriptions are diametrically opposed. Plays' depictions of cholas are related to motherhood, while novels depict cholas as lovers. In a bid to better understand dichotomous representations of cholas—on the one hand, as the forgiving mother in theater, and on the other, as the dangerous lover-woman who brings misfortune to men in novels—I suggest that another source of cultural production be examined: contemporary comics. Specifically, I will examine three Bolivian comics that, unlike novels (Guzmán 1938; Soruco Sologuren 2011), have been largely unstudied even though Bolivian comics are a prolific site of cultural production and reflection. Such comics will visually demonstrate the ways the chola has been portrayed as a monster in the multiethnic and multicultural Bolivian context, as well as how the current Bolivian political climate contributes to that portrayal.

Comics and Cholas

The Bolivian comics industry is small but has grown significantly in the twenty-first century. Comics are mainly disseminated through small publishing houses, such as Pseudogente Editores, the publisher of *Noche de mercado*. I will analyze three comics that present the chola figure, all three portraying the chola as a mother: Corven Icenail and Rafaela Rada's *La Estrella y el Zorro* (2014), Álvaro Ruilova's *Noche de mercado* (2005), and Rafaela Rada's *Nina cholita Andina* (2016a). The authors are all young, urban Bolivians who reside in the city of La Paz. Icenail and Rada are a married couple, and both are illustrators. Icenail is also a fiction writer, although Rada works exclusively on comics. Both work primarily with the Japanese manga style. Their manga *La Estrella y el Zorro* (The star and the fox) narrates the story of Wara, a teenager who lives in the Bolivian highlands with her mother. Wara is an outstanding student who attends a school run by German nuns in her rural community. Aside from being an excellent student, she is also a great person who is well liked in school and who treats the animals in her stable with love and care. Thanks to her academic excellence, she is offered a scholarship to pursue higher education in Germany.

Wara's mother, who is never given a name throughout the comic, is characterized as rude, clumsy, and coarse. In the early vignettes, Wara's mother is presented as an angry woman who beats foxes with stones to keep them away from her property and cattle. She does not support her daughter's desire to pursue education and is always asking her to do more of the stable work; she views school as a distraction. The vignettes in which she interacts with her daughter show a distant relationship. She always addresses her daughter using a loud and imperative tone and focuses mainly on farm work. When Wara finds out about the scholarship, she fears telling her mother and eventually withholds this information from her. Ultimately, a German nun visits Wara's mother and convinces her to let Wara go to study abroad. These initial scenes mark the roughness and aggressiveness in her representation, qualities that are emphasized throughout the comic strip. From the start, it is clear that Wara is different from her mother: while Wara shows a deep connection to her cattle and animals in general, even foxes, her mother shows none. Other panels, in which she interacts with Wara, show her reprimanding her daughter for focusing on school and spending her time reading. In one instance, she interrupts her daughter, who is reading, saying: "I AM TALKING TO YOU!! SURELY, YOU WERE READING THOSE THINGS THAT THE NUNS GIVE YOU!!!" (Icenail and Rada Herrera 2014, 26). Wara's mother is clearly upset because Wara uses the bulk of her time to study, rather than work on the farm. The numerous exclamation marks emphasize the severity of her reprimand. Interactions such as this stress an apparent lack of affection or parental warmth.

Wara's mother is depicted as a bulky woman with a wide neck. Her face has rugged features with pronounced and raised cheekbones. Graphically, her facial expressions, furious gaze, and even speech bubbles indicate a harsh temper. Wara's winsomeness contrasts with her mother's physical and verbal roughness.

Wara's mother's priority is clearly working in the fields. Her practical world view as a farm woman, however, changes after the German nun's visit. This situation echoes an asymmetrical power relationship that situates European values as superior, and education as an exclusively European value. Wara's opportunity to study abroad grants her access to the European world, but in return she must leave and renounce her maternal/native world, which she does willingly and happily. Wara's mother's harsh portrayal does not take into account extenuating factors for her utilitarian approach toward work and animals. Unlike her daughter, she cannot afford a romantic relationship with animals because of her precarious financial position as a single mother and sole breadwinner. Her quotidian circumstances force her to view animals as her livelihood, and not a pleasant distraction. The namelessness of Wara's mother cements her as a subaltern (Spivak 1988) and as an unimportant character in Wara's life. The chola's voice is entirely absent, as the narrative silences her agency by not contextualizing her life conditions or her social position. The only possibilities for speech that the chola has are within a framework embedded in monstrosity, in the sense that she only speaks in a harsh manner or down to her daughter. The comic never shows her in a loving way.

Rafaela Rada's *Nina cholita Andina* (Nina, Andean chola) tells the story of a young chola girl named Saturnina. She is an aspiring model who lives with her mother, Mercedes, also known as Doña Mecha. Saturnina faces mockery in her modeling classes because of her voluptuous figure and her chola outfit. Her modeling career takes off when a French promoter chooses her as the face of a recognized shampoo brand in France. Doña Mecha is presented as a loud, clumsy, and unpleasant woman who is critical of her daughter's modeling dreams. Throughout the comic, she harshly mocks her daughter's intentions to be a model. She urges Saturnina to quit modeling because it is not a customary occupation for cholas, and to focus on the market stall instead. Like Wara's mother, Doña Mecha's priority is work. The similarities between the protagonists' mothers are also physical, as Doña Mecha is illustrated as being physically stocky and short. She has small eyes and a wide, swollen nose. When she talks, she spits and reveals sharp and uneven teeth. Various shades of gray indicate layers of dirt that cover her teeth, emphasizing her lack of care and grooming. The physical difference between mother and daughter is remarkable in this comic as well; the juxtaposition in figure 8.1 shows how Saturnina's poise differs strikingly from her mother's hunched body and rough speech. The dismissal of Saturnina's modeling aspirations by her fellow model classmates and her mother echo the prevailing aesthetic values of Bolivian modeling, which posits European beauty ideals as central and desired and relegates nonconforming examples to the margins.

Figure 8.1: Doña Mecha sets up her market stall in the early morning and calls for her daughter to assist her. Next, Saturnina sadly leaves her room. The last panel shows mother and daughter together at the market stall. *Nina cholita Andina*, no. 1, p. 3, by Rafaela Rada Herrera. Copyright 2016, Axcido.

Saturnina stands out initially because of her chola outfit, which visually translates into a marker of subaltern femininity. Also, because of her voluptuous figure, she does not fit the European ideal of beauty. Despite these obstacles, Saturnina pursues her dream and proves everyone wrong. Like Wara, she, too, leaves Bolivia for Europe, in this case France and not Germany. To fulfill her career aspirations, she leaves Bolivia behind, renouncing the stall and her mother. In both comics, *La Estrella y el Zorro* and *Nina cholita Andina*, European values triumph, as Wara and Saturnina fulfill their aspirations in Europe while their chola single mothers are deemed monstrous and left behind in Bolivia. In these narratives, both chola mothers fail in their attempt to reproduce chola womanhood and values in their daughters. This double failure renders cholas doubly monstrous, as their womanhood is discredited and their femininity posited to the margins, but also because of their inability to reproduce this discarded femininity in their offspring, leaving their motherly role unfulfilled. This double monstrosity demonstrates marginality in both facets, acknowledging nonconformance to the *mestizaje* ideals of a woman and of a mother.

The last comic I will analyze is *Noche de mercado* (Market night) by Álvaro Ruilova. Like Icenail and Rada, Ruilova is a well-known illustrator in Bolivia, whose work ranges from comic novel adaptations to Bolivian zombie-themed comics. *Noche de mercado* narrates the story of Pedro, an alcoholic teenager from La Paz. One day, he discovers that his estranged mother, Antonia Mamani, has died, so he goes to the cemetery to visit her tomb. At the graveyard, a group of criminals knock him unconscious and tie him up. They intend to offer him as a sacrifice as part of an Andean rite to free a local market of an evil demon that has been haunting them: this chola-monster demon has been causing their produce to rot. The night of rite, when Pedro is about to die, his mother's soul appears and saves him. Antonia offers her own soul to the chola demon so her son can live. The depiction of the chola demon as the personification of pure evil is an extreme example of disparaged portrayals of indigenous women. This story of ultimate maternal sacrifice portrays Antonia when she was alive as a cold and work-driven mother. We learn about Antonia through her son's memories. These recollections show her working late at her street-side food stall and kicking him out of the house when he descends into alcoholism. One panel depicts Antonia yelling at Pedro when he is still only a child: "What are you looking at with that idiot face? Get to it" (Ruilova 2005, 11). Pedro argues that his lack of memories of her is due to her "lack of merits to be remembered" (12). Graphically, she is drawn with protruding eyes with swollen blood vessels, and always with an enraged expression. Other panels show her screaming and kicking her son out of the house. Antonia Mamani, like the maternal characters examined earlier in this chapter, is a working single mother who demands help from her child. She does not have a close relationship with him and often treats him harshly. Therefore, monstrous representations in this comic show the chola as both mother and demon. Monstrosity is expressed through the demon, while Antonia embodies the daily vilification of the chola. Both, to different degrees, show their marginality though their monstrosity. This comic reinforces the idea of the chola as a monster and offers two degrees of disparagement, equally nefarious. The demon haunts the market and prevents the daily activities of society, while Antonia is a cold mother whose bad parenting leads her offspring to alcoholism. Both results are detrimental to society in general. Through the political lens of *mestizaje*, the nation-building project of the twentieth century, cholas through their demeanor and clothing choice reject ideal European society. Therefore, cholas' anomic behavior, in terms of the hegemonic ideology, is read as monstrous in comics.

In all three comics, similar strategies are employed to facilitate the chola's characterization as a monster. First is the grotesque depiction: all of them are drawn in a manner that dehumanizes them by exaggerating their physical features and evoking horror. Wara's mother is short and bulky and has stark facial features; Doña Mecha's teeth are sharp and unclean, resembling a beast's jaw when she talks; and Antonia Mamani looks like a deranged women with deorbited, protruding eyes. These brutalized representations convert these women into monsters, lacking any congruence to the figure of a loving mother. The second strategy utilized is dissociation from children; none of these mothers get along with their offspring. Their children neither enjoy their company nor appreciate them, and criticize their performance as parents. Wara prefers to spend time at the stable and at school rather than with her mother, and states that she is misunderstood; Saturnina feels misunderstood, too, and dreams of escaping a future as a market-stall vendor; and Pedro prefers to live on the streets rather than living under his mother's rules, to the extent that he runs away and never sees his mother again. Finally, the last strategy used to demonize cholas is to provide narrative benefit to the children, who distinguish themselves from their mothers. The mother-child difference is celebrated through the success of the child: Wara goes to Germany to study, Saturnina goes to Paris and becomes a model, and Pedro demonstrates his independence at an early age. The children's lives are favored by the narrative because they are different from their mothers in the sense that they do not want to reproduce the chola lifestyle, and therefore they will not become monsters. All of them desire different paths in life, such as becoming a model, studying abroad, even being alcoholic, rather than living the life of a working chola.

The contrast in representation becomes even more evident when comparing the chola mother to the idealized, Europeanized mothers depicted by the same authors. The manga *Otaku* (2016b), Rafaela Rada's latest work, narrates the life of an urban teenager, Otaku, who lives with both of her parents and attends college. In this case, the mother, who is not a chola but a Europeanized Bolivian woman, plays a vital role in supporting her daughter. She is routinely

Figure 8.2: Antonia Mamani yells at her son, Pedro. Note her protruding eyes. *Noche de mercado*, no. 1, p. 12, by Álvaro Ruivola. Copyright 2005, Pseudogente Editores.

depicted in the domestic sphere as cooking or gently addressing her child. The paternal figure, who is notably absent in chola comics, is present here and always involved in his daughter's life in this middle-class family portrayal. Rada's understanding of Europeanized femininity, as it is displayed in this comic, seems to be informed by 1950s notions of womanhood—confined to the roles of homemaker and housewife. Otaku's mother exemplifies this Europeanized femininity and is rewarded for it with the love and respect of her daughter. The contrasted depictions of the chola and the Europeanized mother highlight the differences in the respective societal and cultural statuses of these women. Upper-class women are envisioned as belonging to the domestic sphere, while cholas belong to the world of the working class. The chola, however, defies this notion of Europeanized femininity (originating in the 1950s) through her employment status and financial independence. The lifestyle of the cholas and their historical lack of regard for social norms such as marriage and staying in the domestic sphere seem to propel their monstrous depictions in contemporary Bolivian comics. *Mestizaje* prioritized European values and institutions, such as the ideal, heteronormative marriage, which became hegemonic. Under this framework, the cholas' lifestyle was deemed nonconformist and rebellious. The comics' vile depictions of chola motherhood hint at the core of the representational problem: the positionality of Bolivian womanhood with regard to nation building. In other words, these comics highlight the endemic hierarchy found in Bolivian femininity that positions the Europeanized mother as a hegemonic figure while disparaging the nonconforming cholas.

Mestizaje, Cholas, and "the Monstrous Maternal"

The monstrosity of the chola's maternal representation in comics can be interpreted as a graphic reflection of problematic gender norms within *mestizaje*. *Mestizaje* is part of an intellectual discourse that tries to resolve the conflict that many see in Bolivia between two coexisting nations: one white and one Indian (Ströbele-Gregor 1994). The so-called Indian and peasant cultures were identified and understood by the then-ruling elites as responsible for national backwardness (Stephenson 1999, 35). The aim of this ideology was to address the "Indian problem," the vast population of indigenous people, through assimilation of the Indians into the dominant European culture.

Early twentieth-century Bolivian thinkers were divided in their approaches to a possible solution to the indigenous problem, and offered different solutions. On the one hand, liberal discourses that were informed by positivist notions and Darwinian ideology maintained that the indigenous must be brought into the light of European culture and thought.[1] In contrast, radical intellectuals advocated for a different approach that revolved around the autochthonous heritage of Bolivia and tried to relocate the indigenous within the construction of the Bolivian nation.[2] This "ideal *mestizaje*" conceived of the indigenous population without vilification and valorized their will and character as virtues (Sanjinés C. 2016, 270). These two approaches were fundamentally different in so far as the former took a condemnatory and fatalistic view of the indigenous population, whereas the latter proposed to recover and incorporate the vitality and resilience of Bolivia's indigenous people. In spite of their substantial differences on the conception of *mestizaje* and the place of indigenous people in Bolivia's national identity, both shared a disdain for *encholamiento* (the process of becoming a *cholo*, of lowering one's social status). As explained by Javier Sanjinés:

> [Franz] Tamayo, no different from [Alcides] Arguedas, attacked *cholaje*, the process of forming cholos. Indeed, Arguedas had argued for liberating the Indian, the local *Homo sylvestris*, from the social scourge of the cholo. Tamayo, too, looked down on the cholo with profound disdain, but was much more cautious in promoting the liberal civilizing project. (2016, 278–79)

These different approaches toward *mestizaje* ultimately coalesced into a shared disdain of *encholamiento*. Salvador Romero Pittari, in *Las Claudinas*, distinguishes *mestizaje* from *encholamiento* and argues:

> They are historically and socially close to each other, however, different. *Mestizaje* is a wider process through which biological, social, and cultural features of groups mix. Different racial groups are mixed, permanently reshaping the social order. The *mestizaje* leaves its fruits in men, behaviors, and values of all levels of society. The *encholamiento* refers, on the other hand, more closely to a sexual relationship of certain permanence and visibility with people considered of inferior social status, in the specific case of someone who is cholo. [. . .] On the other hand, the cholo is a social state, with its own values and behaviors. (2015, 29)

Mestizaje implies the hegemonic adoption of European behaviors and values, while *encholamiento* rejects them and visualizes this dismissal. The chola, through her clothing and lifestyle, personifies this refusal to conform to hegemonic standards. As such, the historical dimension of *mestizaje* and the visualization of the Bolivian nation become central to the configuration of the chola as monstrosity. Douglas Cowan (2008) understands monsters as a reflection of their society, and Scott Poole (2014), building from Cowan's notion, argues that monsters emerge from the collective and public imagination. They are born out of social experiences such as historical events and social change. For Poole:

> [Monsters] are part of the genetic code of the American experience, ciphers that reveal disturbing truths about everything from colonial settlement to the institution of slavery, from anti-immigrant movements to the rise of religious fundamentalism in recent American politics. They are more than fantastical metaphors because they have a history coincident with a national history. (2014, 18)

In the case of Bolivia, national identity is a topic of public anxiety, and the question of the indigenous is central to this national angst. Discourse about the indigenous and the degree of acculturation that is an inescapable part of the national project is mainly the province of Bolivian elites, but the anxiety with which *encholamiento* is perceived is unanimous. Unfortunately, the two dominant perspectives of *mestizaje* view *encholamiento* with contempt, and for them, the chola is the embodiment of this derision. The chola, aesthetically and performatively, rejects *mestizaje* and distances herself from it. The resistance of the chola lies mainly in two aspects: her clothing and her lifestyle. The clothing, which is a remnant of the colonial period, defies modern Europeanized dress and visually distinguishes the chola from contemporary, urban Bolivians. Her lifestyle, the fact that she works and is generally not married, challenges and rejects present-day social norms and defies hegemonic stereotypes of femininity.

The chola constitutes a threat to the project of national identity because she is neither Indian nor mestizo but a hybrid, whose nature can change circumstantially (Seligmann 1989; Paulson 1991). In a political sense, and from a historical perspective, the monstrosity of the chola is shaped by her rejection of the national identity project of the twentieth century: *mestizaje*. Her maternal role adds another layer to her monstrosity, given her reproductive possibilities. The maternal modality menaces *mestizaje* due to its reproductive function. Its reproduction implies the multiplication of culprits who hinder the success of *mestizaje* and therefore Bolivia as a modern state (if one understands *mestizaje* as the path to modernity and state progress).

Conclusions

Jeffrey Cohen's fifth thesis, "The Monster Polices the Borders of the Possible," in his "Monster Culture (Seven Theses)" (2007), argues that the monster has a preventive function that warns about the crossing of social conventions. In this sense, the monstrosity of chola mothers serves to prevent their offspring from following in their mother's footsteps and inhibits the violation of the norms found in the modern state. The comics discussed above show the triumph of children who decide to adopt European values while leaving their chola mother behind in Bolivia, or dead. This narrative reaffirms *mestizaje* as the hegemonic nation-building project and continues to discredit the womanhood of nonconforming female subjects within this framework. In his fourth thesis, Cohen (2007) argues that the monster dwells at the gates of difference and states that the monster is the "Other." This difference brands and builds the monster. Cohen also posits that the nature of the monster escapes any kind of categorization, thus requiring a plural system (1996). The monster is seen as the embodiment of the anxieties, fears, and collective desires of a particular society at a given moment. It resists any categorization within a hierarchical system, and it serves as a warning to prevent transgression of cultural edges. Like Cohen's monster, the chola resists the classification devised by the national project of the twentieth century, and she is marked by her cultural difference. Her otherness is registered in contemporary Bolivian comics as monstrous. Chola femininity is framed as monstrous under the *mestizaje* gaze. The chola, through her dress and attitude, rejects assimilation and stays as "in between," neither white nor Indian (Seligmann 1989; Paulson 1991).

This undesirable femininity elicits disdain and disqualification from aspirational Bolivians, and from the chola's own children. The chola resists fitting into the model proposed by *mestizaje* and is chastised through her monstrosity while Europeanized femininity is celebrated. These representations show an adherence to the national identity project that persists even in the twenty-first century. The prevalence of these national discourses echoes in contemporary maternal representations, emphasizing the validity of Eurocentric notions of modernity that displace the "Other" in Bolivia. While this monstrous motherly image of the chola remains, it is important to acknowledge that a new chola image has emerged and coexists with the monstrous figure. The comic *Super Cholita*, which features a chola heroine with superpowers, is an example par excellence of this new and empowered chola representation. The elements that worked as markers of her marginality in the comics discussed above are here depicted instead as markers of change for a new wave of cholas. Political shifts in Bolivia, from the nation-building project of *mestizaje* to the recent multiculturalist, nation-building project adopted by the Morales government, makes viable this new empowered vision. In conclusion, similar to definitions of the monster from the field of monster studies, the representations of the chola cannot be thought of as only liberatory or as exclusively marginalizing. All dimensions must be accounted for, which lends the perspective that there is not one sole depiction of the chola in comics. Due to recent cultural and political shifts in Bolivia, such monsters must not be viewed through a single lens but rather with an awareness of the ways designations of monstrosity are tied up with power.

Notes

1. See, for example, Alcides Arguedas, an exponent of this idea, in his book *Pueblo enfermo* (2000), first published in 1909.
2. Franz Tamayo's *Creación de la pedagogía nacional* (1975), first published in 1910, is a pillar of this discourse.

Bibliography

Albó, Xavier. 2008. "The 'Long Memory' of Ethnicity in Bolivia and Some Temporary Oscillations." In *Unresolved Tensions: Bolivia Past and Present*, edited by John Crabtree and Laurence Whitehead, 13–34. Pittsburgh: University of Pittsburgh Press.

Albro, Robert. 2010. *Roosters at Midnight: Indigenous Signs and Stigma in Local Bolivian Politics*. Santa Fe: School for Advanced Research Press.

Arguedas, Alcides. 2000. *Pueblo enfermo*. La Paz: Anthropos.

Baldivieso, Gina. 2013. "La chola paceña ya es patrimonio cultural." *La Razón* (La Paz), November 1. Available at http://www.la-razon.com/la_revista/chola-pacena-patrimonio-cultural_0_1935406512.html.

Barragán, Rossana. 1992. "Entre polleras, lliqllas y ñañacas: Los mestizos y la emergencia de la tercera república." In *Espacio urbano y dinámica étnica: La Paz en el siglo XIX*. La Paz: Hisbol.

Barrera G., Juan. 1993. *Me avergüenzan tus polleras*. La Paz: Librería Editorial Juventud.

Brown, Jeffrey A. 2011. "Supermoms? Maternity and the Monstrous-Feminine in Superhero Comics." *Journal of Graphic Novels and Comics* 2, no. 1: 77–87.

Calle, Guiomara. 2015. "En Caquiaviri visten al alcalde con ropa de mujer como castigo." *La Razón* (La Paz), December 15.

Cohen, Jeffrey Jerome, ed. 1996. *Monster Theory: Reading Culture*. Minneapolis: University of Minnesota Press.

Cohen, Jeffrey Jerome. 2007. "Monster Culture (Seven Theses)." In *Gothic Horror: A Guide for Students and Readers*, edited by Clive Bloom, 2nd ed., 198–216. Basingstoke, Hampshire, England: Palgrave Macmillan.

Cowan, Douglas E. 2008. *Sacred Terror: Religion and Horror on the Silver Screen*. Waco, TX: Baylor University Press.

Farthing, Linda C., and Benjamin H. Kohl. 2014. *Evo's Bolivia: Continuity and Change*. Austin: University of Texas Press.

Francus, Marilyn. 2012. *Monstrous Motherhood: Eighteenth-Century Culture and the Ideology of Domesticity*. Baltimore: Johns Hopkins University Press.

Guzmán, Augusto. 1938. *Historia de la novela boliviana*. La Paz: Revista México.

Icenail, Corven, and Rafaela Rada Herrera. 2014. *La Estrella y el Zorro*. La Paz: Artexbol.

Kristeva, Julia. 2010. *Powers of Horror: An Essay on Abjection*. New York: Columbia University Press.

Loveday, Leo, and Satomi Chiba. 1983. "At the Crossroads: The Folk Ideology of Femininity in the Japanese Comic." *Fabula* 24, no. 3: 246–63.
Medinaceli, Carlos. 1947. *La Chaskañawi*. Buenos Aires: Fundación Universitaria Simón I. Patiño.
Medinaceli, Ximena. 1989. *Alterando la rutina mujeres en las ciudades de Bolivia, 1920–1930*. La Paz: Centro de Información y Desarrollo de la Mujer.
Mendoza, Jaime. 1911. *En las tierras del Potosí*. Barcelona: Imprenta Viuda de Luis Tasso.
Money, Mary. 2012. "La Mujer Andina en el mestizaje: La Chola Cuencana y Paceña en la construcción de la identidad (siglos XVII–XX)." In *Historia de la Provincia del Azuay: Estudio de casos*, 183–98. Cuenca, Ecuador: Universidad de Cuenca.
Murray, Ross. 2011. "The Feminine Mystique: Feminism, Sexuality, Motherhood." *Journal of Graphic Novels and Comics* 2, no. 1: 55–66.
Paulson, Susan. 1991. *Women in Mizque: The Heart of Household Survival*. Binghamton, NY: Institute for Development Anthropology.
Poole, W. Scott. 2014. *Monsters in America: Our Historical Obsession with the Hideous and the Haunting*. Waco, TX: Baylor University Press.
Rada Herrera, Rafaela. 2016a. *Nina cholita Andina*. La Paz: Axcido.
Rada Herrera, Rafaela. 2016b. *Otaku*. La Paz: Axcido.
Romero Pittari, Salvador. 2015. *Las Claudinas: Libros y sensibilidades a principios del siglo XX en Bolivia*. La Paz: Plural Editores.
Ruilova, Álvaro. 2005. *Cuentos de cuculis: Noche de mercado*. Cochabamba, Bolivia: Pseudogente Editores.
Salmón, Raúl. 1991. *Hijo de chola: Comedia criolla en 2 actos*. La Paz: Librería Editorial Juventud.
Sanjinés C., Javier. 2004. *Mestizaje Upside-Down: Aesthetic Politics in Modern Bolivia*. Pittsburgh: University of Pittsburgh Press.
Sanjinés C., Javier. 2016. "Foundational Essays as 'Mestizo-Criollo Acts': The Bolivian Case." *Latin American and Caribbean Ethnic Studies* 11, no. 3: 266–86.
Seligmann, Linda J. 1989. "To Be In Between: The Cholas as Market Women." *Comparative Studies in Society and History* 31, no. 4 (October): 694–721.
Shakow, Miriam. 2014. *Along the Bolivian Highway: Social Mobility and Political Culture in a New Middle Class*. Philadelphia: University of Pennsylvania Press.
Soruco Sologuren, Ximena. 2011. *La ciudad de los cholos: Mestizaje y colonialidad en Bolivia, siglos XIX y XX*. La Paz: Fundación para la Investigación Estratégica en Bolivia; Lima: Instituto Francés de Estudios Andinos.
Spivak, Gayatri Chakravorty. 1988. "Can the Subaltern Speak?" In *Marxism and the Interpretation of Culture*, edited by Cary Nelson and Lawrence Grossberg, 271–313. Urbana: University of Illinois Press.
Stephenson, Marcia. 1999. *Gender and Modernity in Andean Bolivia*. Austin: University of Texas Press.
Ströbele-Gregor, Juliana. 1994. "From *Indio* to Mestizo . . . to *Indio*: New Indianist Movements in Bolivia." *Latin American Perspectives* 21, no. 2 (Spring): 106–23.
Tamayo, Franz. 1975. *Creación de la pedagogía nacional*. 3rd ed. La Paz: Biblioteca del Sesquicentenario de la República.
Wadsworth, Ana Cecilia, and Ineke Dibbits. 1989. *Agitadoras de buen gusto: Historia del Sindicato de Culinarias (1935–1958)*. La Paz: Tahipamu/Hisbol.
Weismantel, Mary. 2001. *Cholas and Pishtacos: Stories of Race and Sex in the Andes*. Chicago: University of Chicago Press.

9

The Monstrous "Mother" in Moto Hagio's *Marginal*: The Posthuman, the Human, and the Bioengineered Uterus

Tomoko Kuribayashi

Moto Hagio (active 1969–present), a major Japanese manga author, has posed many poignant questions about gender, including how women are defined by their reproductive capacities. Often, her graphic narratives depict women who fail to be "good" mothers or who even behave monstrously toward their children; the narratives not only reveal the devastating consequences of such "failures" often suffered by children but also critique the rigidity with which standards of proper motherhood are imposed on women. Hagio's explorations of problematic maternal figures, and of equally if not more problematic expectations imposed on mothers, extend to her highly imaginative science fiction narratives. Some of these texts feature characters who appear to bypass or undermine prevalent sexual and gender binarism, either because they are biologically unisex until they reach puberty (as in the case of Frol, a young alien character in 1975's *Juuichinin iru!* [We are eleven!]), or because they have been bioengineered to be able to switch between two sexual identities depending on the occasion (as in the case of Kira, a character found in *Maajinaru* [Marginal], to be discussed in detail below). Perhaps it could be argued that such characters still end up reinforcing sexual and gender binarism; in the first case, the aliens with a unisex childhood become male or female in adulthood, and in the second case, the bioengineered character visually presents as male most of the time but is revealed to have a female reproductive function that is activated under certain conditions. Nevertheless, both scenarios can be seen as explorations of how posthumanity may reconfigure sexual and gender identity and relations in that they depict beings whose sexual and reproductive development and functions go beyond the existing definition of humanity.

This chapter will explore what Hagio's narrative in *Marginal* suggests will be the effects of the arrival of the posthuman (as embodied by Kira) on sexual and gender dynamics on Earth—in particular, how the process of human reproduction may be reshaped and whether women will figure at all in that process (and if so, how). By presenting a new "maternal" being that is a product of genetic engineering and is thus seen as both posthuman and monstrous, Hagio's narrative underscores the traditional intersection of the monstrous and the feminine/maternal (or feminine fecundity). Kira's posthuman monstrosity, inseparable from "her" female fecundity, may merely be a futuristic version of the age-old patriarchal equation of women's fertility with monstrosity. Or, instead, it can be a technological breakthrough that can counteract and vanquish such sexist fear of, and efforts to contain or even destroy, women. Intertwined with the above questions, what Hagio's narrative suggests as to the future relationship between the posthuman and the human on Earth, especially in terms of how the human may help tame or control the posthuman's monstrosity, will also be explored.

The Posthuman and Biopunk Narratives

The term "posthuman" has a wide variety of indications depending on the context in which it is used; in addition, it necessarily raises questions about what it means to be human. For example, in her book *The Posthuman*, Rosi Braidotti explains that the term can be used in "hardnosed business discussions of robotics, prosthetic technologies, neuroscience and bio-genetic capital to fuzzier new age visions of trans-humanism and techno-transcendence," but she also considers its academic use, as well as how it provokes "anxiety" about the "de-centring of 'Man'" (2013, 2). Her chapter titles indicate various meanings of the term: it can mean "post-humanism: life beyond the self" (a challenge/end to the European, phallogocentric concept of humanness); "post-anthropocentrism: life beyond the species"; "the inhuman: life beyond death"; or "posthuman humanities: life beyond theory." Lars Schmeink uses the term "posthuman" to indicate "life beyond the species" in his 2016 volume *Biopunk Dystopias: Genetic Engineering, Society and Science Fiction*, in which he discusses Margaret Atwood's *MaddAddam* trilogy and Paolo Bacigalupi's *The Windup Girl*, both of which fall into the genre of science fiction or speculative fiction (Schmeink uses the term "sf"). Elsewhere in his book, Schmeink distinguishes cyberpunk from biopunk, declaring that a shift from the former to the latter happened less than twenty years ago, in the 1990s, in the world of (presumably Western) sf works:

> I believe that with the beginning of the twenty-first century there has been a shift in sf away from a cyberpunk imaginary best embodied in [Donna] Haraway's cyborg and the visceral technology of mechanical implants, [and] body augmentations [. . .] and towards another technocultural expression of scientific progress: One that favors genetic engineering, xenotransplantation, and virology and is thus best expressed in the metaphor not of the cyborg but of the splice. (2016, 7)

In the following discussion of Hagio's speculative fiction narrative *Marginal*, the term "posthuman" will be used to refer to entities that combine usual human characteristics with bioengineered traits (what Schmeink says belongs in "biopunk") rather than entities that have mechanical and/or artificial intelligence enhancements (what Schmeink sees as part of "cyberpunk"). Even though Hagio's *Marginal* was originally serialized in 1985–1987 and thus predates the shift that Schmeink delineates in his discussion of "biopunk" by about fifteen years, Octavia Butler's *Xenogenesis* trilogy was also published in the late 1980s, and the two authors' works together indicate that the global public discourse that centered on the possibility of bioengineering (which also, in the case of their narratives, incorporated the intervention of extraterrestrial beings or non-earthlings), and the anxious questions that it provoked, were already exerting strong influence on the imagination of creators of sf narratives on both sides of the Pacific in that decade. In the sense that biopunk denotes more permanent, deeply ingrained changes to human bodies (and possibly minds) than cyberpunk does, it is important to note that already in the 1980s popular culture narratives like *Marginal* and Butler's trilogy were raising questions about potential consequences of biopunk alterations to human bodies, and especially to human reproductive functions, making their readers at least somewhat aware of how the arrival of posthumanity via bioengineering and xenotransplantation might impact human reproduction and gender relations in general. As Jane Caputi summarizes in *Goddesses and Monsters: Women, Myth, Power, and Popular Culture*, popular culture can both enforce hegemonic values and undermine them: "Pop culture is not only a meaning system enforcing the status quo [. . .] it is also a place where things usually unspoken, things that go against established canons, can be said" (2004, 5). In the latter sense, manga and sf narratives like Hagio's and Butler's serve as (often covert) platforms where subversive questions can be asked and resistance against mainstream authorities may begin.

Moto Hagio's *Marginal*

In *Marginal*, one of Hagio's many complex speculative fiction narratives, the reader is introduced to an Earth in the year 2999 where women have disappeared after a deadly plague several hundred years earlier and the planet itself has lost much of its fecundity due to human-induced pollutions. The only "woman" on Earth, called the Holy Mother, is the sole source of new life for earthlings, who submit their blood and semen in the hope that they will soon be given offspring, who are invariably male. She is eventually revealed to be a sham created to enable non-earthlings to exploit Earth's mineral resources. Simultaneously, an androgynous being called Kira, also artificially created, is found, possibly to replace the Holy Mother as the future procreator of human (or human-like) life on Earth. At the end of the three-volume narrative, Kira is considered the only human—or somewhat human—being on Earth who has the ability to "conceive" new life. Scientists working for the interplanetary colonialist administration (headquartered in a building called the Center), who manage both humans and resources on Earth, have collected Kira's eggs to produce 1,600 babies, and they plan to examine them to find out which parts of Kira's DNA make it possible for Kira to conceive in the arid/hostile environment of Earth. The scientists also release Kira to the care of the two men who have more or less acted as "her" guardians as well as lovers in the recent past, possibly to bear children by one or both of the two men in the future.

The story of *Marginal* suggests that in order to survive in the now arid world on Earth, humankind must undergo radical genetic transformation; that is, they must become posthuman by accepting Kira, a biologically engineered being (therefore possibly of a monstrous nature), as the "mother" of their future offspring. One of the major questions that Hagio's narrative asks is whether the posthuman future will bring with it a radical reorganization or even total erasure of sexual differences and of gender roles and dynamics. On one hand, as an androgynous being who usually presents as a male but possesses female reproductive organs, Kira may prefigure a revised definition of the human—or, more accurately, posthuman or human/posthuman hybrid— that does not abide by traditional sexual binarism (male-female) and thereby radically reconfigures, if not completely does away with, gender roles. On the other hand, Kira's ability to revive the fertility of the natural environment on

Earth seems to reinforce the conventional view that identifies women (or at least female reproductive capacities) with the natural environment (Mother Nature), thereby essentializing women and reinforcing the traditional sex/gender matrix. Likewise, while Kira's "ability" to choose with whom "she" mates for possible procreation seems to suggest more sexual/reproductive autonomy for women, it can also be argued that Kira has little control over "her" own body since "her" uterus and the rest of "her" reproductive organs are accorded a sort of independent life (independent of Kira's wishes and desires) according to the vision of the male scientist who created "her." What is also highlighted throughout *Marginal* is Kira's possible monstrosity: the posthuman is often perceived as monstrous because of its radical differences from the human, including its superhuman abilities, but such monstrosity also resonates with monstrosity that has often been associated with the feminine, especially human women's reproductive powers.

Monstrous Markers of Posthumanity: Genetic Engineering, Multiplicity of the Self, and Superhuman Powers

Kira is a product of genetic engineering, which is a distinct marker of posthumanity. Ivan, a genius but unethical scientist, created Kira after many failed attempts from the eggs of his female partner, Arlene, and sperm from Mayard, a man who had genetically inherited special sensitivities as well as grave risk factors. Ivan's genetic engineering was conducted without Mayard's knowledge, while Arlene's consent was gained by Ivan without fully disclosing his ultimate intention, which was eventually to create offspring between Kira and Ivan himself, a path Arlene later saw as incestuous (because Ivan is Arlene's sexual partner and Kira is Arlene's child). Arlene's eventual discovery of Ivan's true intentions caused her to seek help from the interplanetary authorities, which led to the burning of the woods on Earth in which Ivan and Arlene secretly lived with Kira. Thus, the existence of Kira asks the reader to consider ethical questions about genetic engineering, given the way Ivan chose to conduct the whole project. E. Ann Clark points out "the imprecision and instability that characterizes genetic engineering," which can lead to a "humanist nightmare" (quoted in Didur 2003, 112). Genetic experiments, when carried out without regard to ethical considerations, often become exploitative and abusive. In her discussion of colonial literature, Diane M. Nelson compares colonies to laboratories where "the colonizers were scientists and the colonized the mice and the guinea pigs" (2003, 254). In that light, what Ivan the scientist has done in creating Kira parallels what the interplanetary government has been doing to earthlings in the back story of *Marginal*: both Ivan's project and the Center's manipulation and exploitation of Earth's human population and resources remind the reader that science is often used as a tool of oppression, be it colonization or biological experimentation. And both forms of oppression are shown to be fundamentally patriarchal. Kazue Harada states that "the scientist characters Ivan and Meyard [sic] [who is the head of the Center as well as later revealed to be Kira's biological father] reflect a male-centered biomedical discourse" (2015, 117). The title of the narrative, *Marginal*, which is also what Earth is called in the narrative, highlights the fact that Earth is a colony that is seen to exist on the margin of civilization, which other, more "scientific" and "knowledgeable" groups of humans (who live elsewhere, away from the pollution and aridity of Earth) feel entitled to control and profit from. In addition, the narrative has Ivan declare that the uterus is also the "marginal" of the female body, which indicates an explicit link between the colonization of (feminine) Earth by the interplanetary administration and the colonization of the female reproductive organ or function via patriarchal scientific experimentation conducted by male scientists.

The narrative also poses a question about Kira's multiplicity, another possible posthuman trait. Kira is supposedly Ivan's "dream child," who is never unhappy or afraid, but there is more than one Kira. Originally, there were quadruplets with individual names, but they did not have separate individualities, as their mother Arlene came to find. If one of them was taught something, all the other three also learned it. They also possessed the ability to read people's (Ivan's and Arlene's) thoughts, and could communicate with each other telepathically. Three of the four underwent normal physiological development, while the fourth remained a baby, who functioned as a brain for them all. The Kira who appears in most of the narrative of *Marginal* is one of the three "normally" developed children, and also one of the two who survived the burning of the woods. By the end of the narrative, the first Kira has died or disappeared, but the other Kira who survived the burning replaces the first Kira, whose memories of the recent events and whose attachment to the two lovers are shared/inherited by the second Kira. In addition to the questions about the ethics of genetic engineering, then, the identity or personhood that is shared initially by all the four children, and then by the two survivors of the burning/bombing, poses an explicit challenge to the traditional idea of selfhood as singular and separated from others. Scholars of science fiction narratives, like Laurel Bollinger, have raised questions about selfhood by examining cases of symbiosis and symbiogenesis. Bollinger acknowledges that, while because of the possibility of pregnancy "female identity is always coded as at least potentially plural, and as such potentially incapable of exerting full agency over itself [. . .], to see all individuality as fundamentally plural calls into question the very notion of a self/other split, and reaffirms our connectedness to the natural processes by which life evolved" (2010, 36). In other words, "a plural selfhood—individuality by incorporation—becomes a feminine selfhood with fluid boundaries and unclear definitions," unlike the traditional (masculine) selfhood with clear boundaries (36). Feminine selfhood, in Bollinger's view, "incorporates rather than excludes the other" (50). Such fluidity and multiplicity, which have marked women and female fertility as monstrous for millennia, are, in Hagio's narrative, graphically embodied and amplified by Kira's posthuman (bioengineered) origin and superhuman powers. While such "abnormalities" have typically been abhorred and persecuted in human history, Hagio's narrative suggests that, by virtue of what it has in common with femaleness and female reproductive ability, Kira's posthuman monstrousness—multiplicity, shared selfhood, and ESP—enables the regenerative impact that Kira ends up having on Earth's environment toward the end of the narrative.

Kira possesses (but does not know how to control) superhuman abilities including some kinetic powers, but the most notable ability according to scientists at the Center is Kira's possible fecundity as a "woman." The first Kira is found to be pregnant by one of her two earthling lovers, and for that reason the Center tries to capture Kira without causing physical harm. Instead of giving birth to a human child, however, Kira ends up merging into Earth's environment, more specifically the nearby ocean, after a cat-and-mouse chase with a man with ESP abilities who has been hired by the Center for the specific purpose of capturing Kira alive. Kira evades the hunter and disappears into the ocean, thereby (evidently) reversing the horrible pollution that has plagued the ocean for the prior centuries (fig. 9.1). After Kira's "cleansing," the ocean is found to be regaining its life-giving powers. Thus, in the narrative of *Marginal*, Kira's ability to conceive a child is explicitly connected to the life-giving power of the ocean and, by extension, the natural environment as a whole. In that sense, Kira is a life principle itself, a contemporary or futuristic "feminine divine." Despite Kira's ambiguous sexual presentation, Hagio's text presents Kira's posthuman body as a bioengineered version of female monstrosity long associated with goddess figures, with the posthumanness underscoring the monstrosity (nonhumanness) of female fertility. Also, Hagio's text indicates that Ivan's fundamental belief about human fecundity led him to "conceive" Kira in the image of fertility goddesses.

Ivan's parents divorced when he was a small child and lived on a planet that was not Earth. The father went away with another woman but came back a few years later, hoping to be taken back by his ex-wife. She refused, which led to his strangling her and raping her while she was unconscious. Ivan, still a young

Figure 9.1: Kira escapes the hunter, to merge into and rejuvenate the ocean. *Maajinaru* (1985–1987), vol. 3, p. 296, by Moto Hagio. Copyright 1999, Shogakukan.

child at the time, witnessed the incident, which left him with lifelong trauma. He questioned why his mother's mental state radically declined after being attacked by her ex-husband even though she could not possibly remember being raped; he mused, "Does the uterus have its own mind, apart from the woman in whose body it belongs?" and wondered whether his mother's uterus remembered the violation and caused her decline (Hagio 1999, 2:53–54). In fact, Ivan named Kira after his mother, which both indicates his desire to resurrect his mother and burdens Kira with his peculiar belief that the uterus, or female fertility, can be separated from the woman. In the latter sense, Ivan's creation Kira stands for the uterus—or female fertility itself. If the uterus has its own mind and life apart from the woman's, then human fertility, at least as far as the female body is concerned, can be possibly separated from the individual woman—from what she thinks, believes, wants, and seeks out. This is a dangerous argument, akin to what anti-abortion activists may assert: that the uterus, and what it may contain (including a fetus), does and should have its own autonomy beyond what the woman herself has the right to choose. That logic can end up turning a woman's body against her. At the same time, it can possibly liberate the individual woman from the biological "burden" of being the sex to carry and then give birth to new life.

Kira, for instance, only becomes a fertile female when in a sexual situation with a male partner who resonates with Kira; at other times, which is most of the narrative, other characters assume Kira to be male. This may be partly because all earthlings are male, but the narrative also indicates that Kira usually has a male appearance, or at least is androgynous in appearance, as many teenage boys are on Earth. In that sense, Kira is not limited or defined by "her" female fertility unless or until a pregnancy occurs. "Her" uterus usually does not define her; it defines itself, separate from Kira's identity, and it is not always a recognizable part of Kira. Kira may embody the kind of freedom that Shulamith Firestone envisioned women would enjoy in "a future when pregnancies will happen in laboratories, thus freeing women from the reproductive task" (quoted in Puleo 2012, 355). Harada describes the two sides of Ivan's view of the uterus this way: "Ivan's idea of the connection between wombs and women's (un)conscious suggests the possibility of a collective and transcendent feminized space, although his concept essentializes women and equates them with their reproductive organs (wombs)" (2015, 107). Harada continues: "Ivan believes that uteruses function in a woman's body like another brain and use another kind of language like dreams" (107). When Kira "cleanses" the sickened ocean, the scientists follow Ivan's reasoning and speculate that Kira and Earth have shared the same "dream," a dream of regeneration, of new life.

Thus, the figure of Kira potentially reconfigures both "human" and "female" in multiple ways. For one, Kira is posthuman in being a product of genetic engineering, especially problematic because the engineering was conducted without proper authorization, beyond what interplanetary laws allowed, and was also otherwise unethical. Kira is also posthuman in not having the traditional well-demarcated selfhood, being multiple and possessing collective thoughts and memories. Additionally, Kira has superhuman or ESP abilities that make Kira both monstrous and fecund—a combination of characteristics commonly found in powerful female figures like goddesses. The fact that Kira cannot control the powers may highlight a significant problem that comes with genetic engineering. It may also evoke the historically prevalent view of women's—and nature's—fertility as powerful, uncontrollable, and superhuman as well as terrifying. Just as goddess figures, representing the fecundity of women as well as of nature, have inspired admiration as well as fear, and have been seen as monstrous, genetic engineering that purports to augment or substitute for "natural" fecundity (of humans in the case of Hagio's narrative, but more generally, as in our current sociopolitical discourse, both of humans and of other organisms) can end up wreaking havoc by overshooting its aim and losing control, becoming monstrous. At the same time, the figure of Kira suggests the possibility of making human fecundity independent of femaleness or female bodies. Since human fecundity has traditionally been inseparably linked to women's bodies, both to empower women and to justify limiting (often severely) their choices and freedom, Kira's existence can further disempower women, or it can liberate women from such limitations.

Holy Mother

Even before Kira appears on the devastated and colonized Earth, Hagio's science fiction narrative problematizes the concepts of humanity, femaleness, and fertility in the figure of the Holy Mother. Arguably, prior to Kira's arrival, the male-only environment on Earth also signals a significant reorganization of sexual relations and gender dynamics. In a fashion reminiscent of ancient Greece, older men often mate with younger, androgynous-looking men, whether such couplings take the form of one-time transactions at brothels or that of a committed relationship that involves sustained financial support and conferring of social status. The Holy Mother, however, seemingly counteracts the normalization of homosexual relations on Earth—and erasure of gender binarism—by reemphasizing the centrality of the female/maternal for the continuation of human life. Yet Hagio's narrative reveals that the aged Holy

Mother, called "the mother of all humankind" (1999, 1:29), is not at all divine or reproductively viable. After her assassination, the non-earthling scientists at the Center, which forms the core of the sacred building that sits in the middle of "the City," are shown to be taking elaborate steps to create a new Mother by injecting hormones into an androgynous-looking young man abducted for that very purpose. The officials also hypnotize the new Mother into believing that "she" is the holy source of all life. The reader thus learns that the Holy Mother is a lie concocted by humans living on the moon and on other planets in order to exploit the mineral resources of Earth. In the absence of women on Earth, male earthlings submit their blood and semen to the administration in the hope that the Mother will provide them with offspring. The truth is that the colonial officials buy eggs from women who live on the moon and create test-tube babies in the underground depths of the Center.

The Holy Mother, like the Virgin Mary, is divine and asexual ("pure") while also essentially defined by her fertility, which normally would presuppose sexual—especially heterosexual—activity. Historically, prior to the rise of patriarchy, goddess figures across cultures—or the feminine divine—were understood to be a "source of life and death and regeneration" (David Leeming and Jake Page, quoted in Caputi 2004, 317), but "as the patriarchy takes hold[,] femaleness, animality, sexuality, nature, death, and darkness are increasingly seen as something abject, chaotic, 'dirty,' to be feared and controlled if not eradicated. For example, dutiful motherhood and (exploitable) fertility are honored while free sexuality is labeled 'whoredom'" (Caputi 2004, 317–18). In the narrative of *Marginal*, the figure of the Holy Mother symbolizes the patriarchal valuation of female fertility that is solely based on its usefulness to the regime, or in this case, more accurately speaking, the colonizers. The fact that the Holy Mother is not biologically female but is a product of biochemical (and also psychological) manipulation emphasizes the artificial nature of the patriarchal version of the sacred female: "she" is not a woman at all but a patriarchal idea of what a woman should be like. Given the fact that, in the narrative of *Marginal*, males who are more androgynous or feminine-looking are chosen to be made into and paraded as the Holy Mother, one might argue that the Holy Mother is actually a sort of drag queen, which emphasizes the potentially parodic nature of the construction of femininity/maternity via performance. At the same time, the exploitative use of the Holy Mother as a tool with which to manipulate Earth's population parallels the exploitation of Earth's mineral resources, which suggests that the exploitation of the "feminine" goes hand in hand with the exploitation of nature or the environment, which is also usually seen as feminine. It is not a coincidence that the Holy Mother as a manipulation tool was made possible in the first place by the devastation of both human fertility and natural fecundity: the human female population was wiped out by a plague several centuries earlier in tandem with the devastation of the environment on Earth, which has left the oceans too polluted to produce life. The discussion of the exploitation of Earth by those who live elsewhere can also be extended into an exploration of colonialism where the Natives are seen as naïve—in reality, intentionally left in the dark—and superstitious. The irony is that, while they occupy a stereotypically feminine (powerless) position, the Natives are all male in the story, and a feminine figure, the Holy Mother, is used by colonizers to manipulate them via religion. Alicia H. Puleo's name for this kind of manipulation is "the Eternal Feminine as an oppressive mystification" (2012, 354). In *Marginal*, it oppresses not women but colonized, feminized men via the figure of the Holy Mother.

Once the Holy Mother is revealed to have been a sham, the reader sees that the monstrosity of the Holy Mother resides in the intentions of those who use her as a tool of colonization. The Mother has no superhuman powers that cannot be controlled, nor has she ever possessed reproductive powers. Kira has both. Kira is bioengineered much more thoroughly than the Holy Mother, whose feminization is not done at the genetic level. Kira's genetically engineered fertility apparently makes her an improved replacement for the Holy Mother, but also the question arises of whether Kira's posthumanness may prove to be truly monstrous, in the sense of being destructive rather than regenerative. Kira has individual agency and a developing awareness, whereas the Mother is deprived of the ability to think or act for "herself" and is essentially a puppet. While such agency can be promising in that it may lead to the development of an ability to make ethical judgments and act conscientiously, it can also cause trouble and chaos, especially if one is endowed with superhuman powers. While the Holy Mother's monstrosity is both a product of human (male) scientific experiments and under human control, Kira's monstrosity, also a product of such experiments, may turn out to be truly posthuman, in that it comes with posthuman powers and goes totally beyond human control. Notably, though, the narrative of *Marginal* closes by suggesting that Kira's two human lovers, Ashijin and Grinja, will play essential roles in making Kira's posthumanness viable on Earth, that their human influence will somehow "tame" Kira's posthuman, monstrous unpredictability.

Kira's Human Consorts

For a discussion of Kira's relationship with her two human consorts, their ethnic/racial identities as suggested by Hagio's visual presentations of the three characters are of significant import. Kira supposedly introduces posthuman elements into life on Earth and yet is portrayed as very human-like and also very European/Caucasian-looking. Many characters in Hagio's narratives are presented as Caucasian via their names and/or places of residence/origin, but many other characters Hagio has created are Caucasian-looking even when their names and other traits suggest that they are Japanese. Therefore, it cannot be easily determined whether Hagio meant Kira to be Caucasian. Both of Kira's genetic parents, however, have European names—Arlene and Mayard—and arguably possess Caucasian facial features. Kira's human-like appearance makes it easier for the reader (and earthlings in the narrative) to accept "her" as a possible mother of future life on Earth. Kira may be a posthuman being who has been bioengineered from human genes and is therefore possibly monstrous, but that posthumanness or possible monstrosity is not immediately apparent; it is only when Kira exerts kinetic powers, without intending to, or shows signs of female fertility that the question of super- or posthumanness and attendant monstrosity arises. On the other hand, Kira's Caucasian looks are a marked contrast with some characters, including "her" two human lovers, who have non-European-sounding names, Ashijin and Grinja, which sound Middle Eastern or South Asian. Also, at least Ashijin comes from an area whose desert landscape strongly suggests non-Europeanness, while Grinja also comes from a small village far away from the City. The fact that Kira looks very Caucasian, in contrast to the more "exotic" looks of the two men (especially Grinja, the more benevolent and less volatile of the two) who may become fathers of Kira's future children, may make the reader feel that the posthuman is more advanced or civilized than the "mere" human (fig. 9.2). These assumptions resonate with the historical colonialist way of thinking, which maintains that lighter skin color and Caucasian facial features indicate intellectual and other kinds of superiority, while darker skin and non-Caucasian features indicate various kinds of inferiority. In other words, the reader may be led to feel that the Caucasian-looking posthuman is more civilized or more "human" than the non-Caucasian-looking human. In many of Hagio's other graphic narratives (and in fact in much of Japanese manga, especially manga that is targeted toward the female reader), European-looking characters can both add to the romantic allure of narratives and help distance the realities of problems/abuse being presented, but in the case of *Marginal*, the contrast in racial identity between Kira and the two male companions raises questions about the implied hierarchy between the posthuman and the human (with the former being seen as more advanced and more viable). It also reminds the reader of how thoroughly colonized Earth already is by humans who live elsewhere (and Ivan's unbridled genetic engineering experiments mirror that colonization, as discussed above).

Figure 9.2: Grinja nurses injured Kira in Ashijin's cave. *Maajinaru* (1985–1987), vol. 1, p. 59, by Moto Hagio. Copyright 1999, Shogakukan.

At the same time, Hagio's narrative's suggestion that for survival and personal development Kira needs the companionship and guidance of the two men, and that Kira's future viability depends on their "humanizing" influence, complicates the picture further. The narrative indicates that the posthuman, while endowed with special abilities that may enable them to overpower and dominate (if not totally replace) the human, cannot survive on their own in the environment of Earth but need to merge with (elements of) the human to create a species suitable for new life. The colonial scientists have determined that Grinja and Ashijin are able to control or help Kira control the ESP, even though the scientists can only speculate as to why the two men exert that influence over Kira. Is it that the two and Kira have compatibility, or is it because they have had sexual relations, or is it because Kira trusts them? In any case, the two human males seem able to help tame Kira's posthuman monstrosity. The narrative of *Marginal* ends with Ashijin (the younger and more volatile, but also less pessimistic of Kira's two human consorts) declaring that Kira should be given a new name on the morrow, which suggests that Kira's future identity and character will be shaped by the two male earthlings, keeping in check if not totally eliminating the influence of Ivan's original intention for Kira. The narrative ends by positing the intriguing question of whether the guidance of Ashijin and Grinja prefigures yet another version of patriarchal ("human") control over monstrous ("posthuman") female fertility. So, although Harada asserts that "Hagio creates the reproductive system that distances itself from women's biological reproduction [. . .] to circumvent a binary-opposed system between 'men/culture/technological reproduction' and 'women/nature/biological reproduction'" (2015, 106), *Marginal* does not provide conclusive evidence that gender binarism on Earth will be erased via the figure of Kira.

A Posthuman Future?

In a number of ways, Kira is an emblem of the posthuman—as a product of genetic engineering (not a product of "natural," heterosexual mating), as multiple instead of singular, as possessed of superhuman abilities, and as a fertility principle independent of a human (female) body/self. Kira's offspring can fundamentally reconfigure humanness on Earth while possibly ensuring the continuation of life on Earth (in whatever forms it may take). When Kira replaces the Holy Mother as a source of all new life, Kira replicates and even outdoes the Mother's medically altered, androgynous body but jettisons the predecessor's asexual holiness that has been constructed and exploited by the patriarchal, colonial administration. Kira's uncontrolled powers, or monstrosity, may resemble the powers traditionally associated with the feminine divine, but they are a product of bioengineering and therefore are posthuman rather than mythical. (It should be noted that science begets its own mythology, a topic worthy of extensive discussion elsewhere.) The figure of Kira also calls into question the femaleness and, furthermore, the humanness of fertility itself, but the offspring that Kira may bestow on Earth are posited to be a hybrid of the bioengineered posthuman and the human, the influence of the latter, in the form of two human companions, being presented as an indispensable component to the viability of the posthuman. So, while the question as to whether Kira will reconfigure or eliminate gender binarism on Earth seems to hang in the balance at the end of *Marginal*, the question about whether the posthuman will utterly replace the human seems answered in the negative, given the narrative's final emphasis on Kira's dependence on the grounding influence of Ashijin and Grinja. After presenting Kira's posthumanity as a futuristic version of monstrosity ascribed to female fertility for millennia, and after hinting at the liberatory potential for gender relations that Kira represents, Hagio's text ends on an ambiguous note by predicting that human male (and also non-Caucasian) influence will exert control over posthuman female (and also apparently Caucasian) addition to life on Earth. Possibly it will be a balanced, egalitarian coexistence of complementary elements, as the last pages of *Marginal* seem to suggest. At the same time, by highlighting how bioengineering may exploit as well as be exploited and by suggesting that such exploitation may well extend to female fertility—and also let us not forget that Earth is still a colony, albeit now under a more benign administration—Hagio's narrative warns us that all may not be well in our very scientific, possibly posthuman future.

Bibliography

Bollinger, Laurel. 2010. "Symbiogenesis, Selfhood, and Science Fiction." *Science Fiction Studies* 37, no. 1 (March): 34–53.

Braidotti, Rosi. 2013. *The Posthuman*. Cambridge: Polity Press.

Caputi, Jane. 2004. *Goddesses and Monsters: Women, Myth, Power, and Popular Culture*. Madison, WI: Popular Press.

Didur, Jill. 2003. "Re-Embodying Technoscientific Fantasies: Posthumanism, Genetically Modified Foods, and the Colonization of Life." *Cultural Critique* 53 (Winter): 98–115.

Hagio, Moto. 1994. *Juuichinin iru!* Tokyo: Shogakukan.

Hagio, Moto. 1999. *Maajinaru*. 3 vols. Tokyo: Shogakukan.

Harada, Kazue. 2015. "Japanese Women's Science Fiction: Posthuman Bodies and the Representation of Gender." PhD diss., Washington University in St. Louis.

Nelson, Diane M. 2003. "A Social Science Fiction of Fevers, Delirium and Discovery: *The Calcutta Chromosome*, the Colonial Laboratory, and the Postcolonial New Human." *Science Fiction Studies* 30, no. 2 (July): 246–66.

Puleo, Alicia H. 2012. "From Cyborgs to Organic Model and Back: Old and New Paradoxes of Gender and Hybridity." *Comparative Critical Studies* 9, no. 3: 349–64.

Schmeink, Lars. 2016. *Biopunk Dystopias: Genetic Engineering, Society and Science Fiction*. Liverpool: Liverpool University Press.

Part 4

Monsters of Childhood

10
SeDUCKtress! Magica De Spell, Scrooge McDuck, and the Avuncular Anthropomorphism of Carl Barks's Midcentury Disney Comics

Daniel F. Yezbick

> *She lived in any age . . . She's that powerful and evil force: the lady with the black hair. We've seen her in all art forms.*
> MAILA NURMI (VAMPIRA), in Mark Voger, *Monster Mash*

As Scrooge McDuck's foremost female rival, Magica De Spell has developed an unequivocally slippery and enjoyably outré reputation in Disney comics. Throughout her frequent face-offs with Scrooge, Magica endures as a sensually sinister, comically campy, adamantly feminine antagonist closely associated with the taboo, the arcane, and the supernatural. As such, she is perhaps the most subversively monstrous of Carl Barks's plentiful, vice-ridden villains. She certainly stands among his most perennially popular creations. I.N.D.U.C.K.S., the most comprehensive online database of international Disney comics, calculates that Magica De Spell appeared in 153 stories in forty-one separate American publications between 1961 and 1992, slightly more than 10 percent of all Disney comics during that period. Internationally, Magica has been featured in 1,472 stories, including 570 in her home nation of Italy, 359 in Denmark, and 127 in the Netherlands, where Disney Ducks remain a seminal component of family entertainment (I.N.D.U.C.K.S. 2018). Judging from such numbers, Magica seems uniquely prevalent in Disney's Barks-built Duckverse.

This chapter explores Magica De Spell's relevance as a monstrously gendered villain within Barks's frequently sexist, largely xenophobic, anthropocentric, or "anthroparchial" Disney milieu, where predominantly male, hetero, white-feathered humanoid ducks enjoy privileged dominance and heedless agency over other grotesquely satirized genders, ethnicities, and species. Focusing first on Magica's close thematic association with monstrous and abject femininity, I examine Barks's use of Magica De Spell within specific Duckberg stories to emphasize how her witchy ways continually trouble not only Scrooge but also the patriarchal hierarchies of Barks's story world and, by extension, the carefully surveilled and sanitized simulacra of Disney's family entertainments. Throughout such texts, Magica's consistent reliance on age, gender, and species-shifting transformation provides intriguing perspectives on how the codes of anthropomorphic—or, more accurately, therianthropic—creature comics construct and market fantasies of commoditized charisma, cuteness, and cruelty (Baker 1993, 108).[1]

Magica represents a potent blend of monstrous femininity, therianthropic animality, and menacing abjection. In most cases, she arrives as an ambitious, alluring entrepreneurial female, well aware of her singular talents for seducing, swindling, and enslaving victims. She also exudes a particularly oppositional, often militant, and sometimes parasitic sexuality rooted in radical exaggerations of gender and power. Magica continually distracts and disarms her typically straight, male quarry by developing elaborate, performative heists or swindles that trade on her manipulative sensuality. These are usually rooted in the exploitation of egotistical males and their conventional assumptions concerning female behaviors and appearances. She proudly indulges in hypergendered disguises and metamorphic deceptions that exploit established conventions of sex and identity, making her a decidedly #mefirst feminist presence in Barks's pre-#metoo world populated largely by presumptive drakes. Such moments not only encourage deconstructive and queer interpretations of Magica's brash femininity but also invite further scrutiny of her role as a provocative monster of abject rebellion and revolt within Disney's generally sanitized "funny animal" franchise.

As both an anthropomorphic duck and an abject witch, Magica De Spell threatens the conventional frameworks of anthropomorphic comics that repurpose iconic therianthropic characters like Scrooge and Donald across multiple commercial formats. Recent advances in animal studies interrogate the role of such funny animal properties in the general erasure of actual animal presence.[2] Building on what Jean Baudrillard identifies as the simulacral removal of human-animal awareness in late capitalist culture, meaningful *animalséant*—or animal-conscious—links with other species and their habitats are then replaced with what Jacques Derrida conceives as anthropomorphically *chimerical* fantasies celebrating the charisma or charming ingenuity of unreal human/animal hybrids or virtual surrogates (Baudrillard 1994, 130; Derrida 2008, 4). With the construction and consumption of captivating commercial creatures like Jessica Rabbit, Kermit the Frog, Rainbow Dash, or Peter Porker, *animalséant* sensibility and female agency are epistemologically divested and systematically debased as ideologically thin, intellectually shallow, or simply transposed over other commercial concerns. Glenn Willmott traces this avoidance, removal, and replacement of the truly wild or *umwelt* animal experience with what he conceives as more addictively artificial, or zoomorphic models of anthropocentric privilege within enthralling media myths (Willmott 2012, iv). One of the most enduring and influential of these is certainly Barks's ornery Scrooge McDuck and his eternal struggles against the sly seducktress, Magica De Spell.

Barks's scheming "knock-out" of a sorceress adopts many malicious personae in her one duck-woman's war against the complex "anthroparchial" politics behind Barks's "funny animal-themed" mediation of human deception, danger, and desire (Cudworth 2014, 29). Yet, Magica also represents a monstrous therianthropic sign of abjected feminine resilience whose every action seems to threaten the foundations of Scrooge's Duckberg, Barks's ambivalent satires of feminism, and perhaps even the greater matrix of Disney entertainments. A ferocious feminine foil to Scrooge's primacy as the Duck family's patriarch and Duckburg's resident plutocrat, Magica also signifies an equally abject threat to Carl Barks's role as an artistic arbiter or craftsman who renders entertainments mediating both female identity and animal experience "at the mercy of anthropocentric societies" (Creed and Hoorn 2016, 96). From story to story, Magica terrorizes Duckburg's hierarchies of gender and power.

As a ruthless witch, Magica also personifies each of Jeffrey Jerome Cohen's seven theses of monstrous signification. Across a variety of duck tales, her metamorphic body is spectacularly orchestrated to intimidate, deceive, and ultimately ridicule more normative opponents, but Magica also dwells gleefully "at the gates of difference" where she doles "out rebuke to traditional methods of organizing knowledge," especially those relating to McDuck's gargantuan global empire and the Duck family dynasty (Cohen 1996, 7). When she is not spelunking Circe's cave or "refueling evil eyes," her sassy sorcery, furious temperament, and catastrophic capabilities also speak to a perversely abjectified reversal of theriomorphic forms and visons. Early surrealists like André Breton and Georges Bataille first embraced the abject animal experience of the abattoir and the zoo to better question human anthroparchial arrogance and general ignorance of organic interspecies experiences (Bataille et al. 1995, 60). Later theorists including Derrida, Julia Kristeva, Donna Haraway, Suzanne Keen, and Erika Cudworth have wedded these concerns to the intersections of gender diversity and animal empathy to further explore what Jack Morgan labels an "anxiety of organism," in which the transformative biological realities of actual living creatures crash down ruthlessly on chimerical spectacles and their anthroparchial signifiers with emphatic shock waves of darkly driven humor, horror, and abjection (Morgan 2002, 110).

Here lies the seminal difference between the ferocious threat of Magica De Spell and the bulk of Barks's rogues' gallery—her schemes emphatically recruit the agency of other uncivilized or exploited animals like screeching jungle birds ("The Unbreakable Bin"), stray dogs ("The Many Faces"), and farm flocks ("Isle of the Golden Geese"). They also include heady doses of sexual seduction and sadistic control, themes that work directly against the generally asexual, sentimentalist codes of Disney media and Dell/Western Comics. Finally, most of Scrooge's enemies are more inclined to steal his fortune or assume his title as the World's Richest Duck. Magica, however, strives to completely annihilate the root of Scrooge's fortune, his prestige, and especially his genuine devotion to thrift, industry, and influence. She is Barks's radical threat to McDuck's establishmentarian privilege, and her methods emphasize her close connections to subversive modes of espionage, terrorism, and sabotage.

Her villainous arsenal is amply diversified and artfully concealed within her "little black" dress. Its sleeves are crammed with Cold War spy tech ranging from her infamous "foof" bombs to paralyzing stun rays. Her equally wicked witchcraft also includes weather-wrangling wands, philters of love, animal charms, and secret recipes for mayhem and mutation stolen from the Greek gods themselves. Magica's most potent weaponry involves her fusion of the femme fatale's manipulative menace, the pinup's seductive sensuality, and the vamp's cunning couture. In this sense, she is more akin to the devious desires kindled by Terry's Dragon Lady, Steve Canyon's Madame Lynx, or more recently, the mischievous manias of Poison Ivy and Harley Quinn. Ironically, Magica's predatory sexuality arose as a less contentious alternative to other forms of offensive humor. Throughout the 1950s, Barks's thrilling blend of global "swashduckling" and frantic slapstick helped make Dell/Western Publishing's Disney duck titles the most popular in the nation.[3] Clever Natives and quirky tribes often left Barks's supposedly superior "Great White" Ducks bamboozled, but his broad ethnic satires seemed more disconcerting after the Fredric Wertham/Estes Kefauver comics witch hunts of the mid-1950s (Hajdu 2009, 55). Unaware of his seminal role in Disney/Dell's success, Barks was beginning to take editorial heat for the xenophobic caricatures and grotesques exaggerating the postcolonial conflicts within whatever emerging nations his ducks explored and exploited. Disney and Western were now more sensitive to Barks's parodies of multicultural difference, especially whenever he emphasized the questionable methods involved in acquiring raw materials, natural resources, and indigenous treasures: "I was not allowed to poke fun at countries and people as I used to" he lamented in a 1968 interview (Barks, quoted in Willits, Thompson, and Thompson 2003, 7).[4] To reinvigorate his satires, he returned to popular villains such as the "terrible, terrible Beagle Boys," Flintheart Glomgold, and Porkman DeLardo. He also conjured up the fiercely feminine threat of Magica De Spell from a variety of sources, old and new.

Female villainy arises periodically in Barks's previous work, but two early stories focusing on sinister duck women offer revealing harbingers of Magica's later malevolence. In a rare moment of genuine romance, Scrooge's sentimental reunion with Glittering Goldie, the opportunistic saloon siren of 1953's "Back to the Klondike" from *Four Color*, no. 456, softened the bitter miser into the more affably thrifty curmudgeon who delighted readers of all ages. Although something of a literal gold digger, Goldie proved that Scrooge could know love, empathy, and ultimately forgiveness. Years later, Magica would strategically exploit each of these chinks in the fantasticajillionaire's gruff exterior to facilitate her pursuit of power and prestige. In many stories, Magica becomes more vampishly duplicitous than Goldie. For example, in "The Ten Cent Valentine," she bewitches the adult males with perfume-laced letters that leave McDuck actually "whinnying" with desire as he exclaims: "Attar of Araby! Essence of the Mystic East! Man bait of fabled sirens from Circe to Brigit Barduck!"

Even more famously in 1955, Barks remixed the story of Jason and the Argonauts to develop "The Golden Fleecing" from *Walt Disney's Uncle Scrooge*, no. 12. Among his most celebrated works, the topsy-turvy tale finds the Ducks encountering a strange group of orientalized, quasi-Arabic brothers later revealed as the giggling Larkies, hideous cross-dressing bird sisters who once kidnapped the great kings of old, then tortured them as judges in nauseating cooking competitions. Now, the Larkies abduct both Scrooge and Donald to settle their culinary rivalry in the most ghastly cook-off yet. Western feared that the original term, "harpy," might recall prostitutes or streetwalkers despite the creatures' hooked noses and gap-toothed grimaces, and famously forced Barks to concoct the supposedly less predatory "Larkie." Even so, the Larkies satirize not only classical myth but also midcentury homemaking contests, barbecues, and bake sales. Barksian Larkies also signify a decidedly "weaker" and more miserably gendered monstrosity. Unlike Magica, who thrives proudly on the opportunities and advantages her sexuality provides, the crone-ish, bickering Larkies are defeated by the most clichéd of sexist assumptions about skittish women. To save their uncles, the courageous nephews refuse to harm these women in any way, so they scare the monstrous girly birds out of their wits with mice tied to parachutes.

Glittering Goldie's sentimentality and the Larkies' gleeful sadism each inform Barks's introduction of Magica De Spell in 1961's "The Midas Touch," the lead story from *Walt Disney's Uncle Scrooge*, no. 36. Magica saunters into the opening pages of her premiere, entering Scrooge's office with all the casual confidence of an independent professional. She begins as a fashionable, liberated working woman negotiating the sexist assumptions and misogynistic habits of corporate America.

As Barks himself explained, "One dreadful day in 1961, the slithery slinky Magica De Spell entered Uncle Scrooge's office and announced that she was a sorceress. Uncle Scrooge thought that was very funny, and he laughed and laughed. He hasn't laughed since" (Barks 1987, 294). As Magica invades McDuck's world, Scrooge's struggles, Duckberg's patriarchal order, and perhaps even the Disney/Western enterprise's chimerical manimal fantasies seem oblivious to these first fateful tremors of change. Barks himself often dismissed Magica as little more than a convenient pinup lacking substantive ideological bite, but fans remarked on the chilly shift in any narrative that features her disruptive presence (Chalker 1974, 72). For the first time in Barks's work, the steadfast establishmentarian mogul must face off against an antithetical female equal whose threats are rooted in arcane lore and literally "shifty" disguises of gender and species.

Like Goldie in her prime, Magica is unequivocally fetching, a fresh seductive foil to Scrooge's gruff seniority, yet McDuck's immediate dismissal of her sorcery turns our sympathies from the start. Ignoring Donald's wary concerns, McDuck scoffs, "Anyone wacky enough to think herself a sorceress is bound to be harmless," and gladly mansplains away her "great experiment" in magical wealth management.

Barks's *mise-en-page* emphasizes Magica's patient scorn through carefully orchestrated medium two-shots, pairing her as Scrooge's visual equal despite his authoritative, oversize desk. Her icy response is typical of someone all too familiar with workplace harassment and gender-driven ridicule: "Laugh! I am not bothered by your jeers and derision." As Barks warned, Scrooge's self-confidence is short-lived. In his braggadocio, he unwittingly sells Magica his most treasured single possession—Old Number One, the first dime he ever earned from supposedly staying "tougher than the toughies and smarter than the smarties." The Ducks quickly recover the mistaken coin, but Magica becomes obsessed with reclaiming its totemic fortune-founding potential, and so begins the most dynamically gendered power struggle in the history of Disney comics. No other story line in Disney's Scroogiverse would enjoy as much success, influence, or variation as Magica's lifelong quest to reclaim Old Number One, and aside from the plethora of Beagle Boys yarns, no other plot is so often revised or recapitulated across Disney duck media. Later Disney auteur Don Rosa would also exaggerate the troubled love triangle between Scrooge, Magica, and Old

Figure 10.1: Scrooge McDuck's first encounter with Magica De Spell, from Barks's "The Midas Touch." *Walt Disney's Uncle Scrooge*, no. 36, p. 2, by Carl Barks. Copyright 1961, Western Publishing.

Number One in his prequel story, "Of Ducks and Dimes and Destinies," for the mock epic *The Life and Times of Scrooge McDuck* (2006). Rosa's work, unlike Barks's, teems with powerful and important female heroines and villainesses who add exciting depth and gendered diversity to the Disney duck franchise, but for a time only Magica truly equaled Scrooge in cunning and ferocity.

As with her first appearance, Magica is almost always introduced in positions of considerable strength and aptitude. Testing her nefarious (and hilarious!) inventions, she proudly prepares to (sometimes literally) rain hell down upon her "ducktagonists." Barks confirms: "She is capable of so many things and it brought in an opportunity to kid this Superman stuff—the super witches and the weird things that you find in some of the other comics" (Barks, quoted in Willits, Thompson, and Thompson 2003, 15). Her creator's recollections relate to his own jealous disdain for more celebrated cartoonists whose overdetermined works of megaviolence and superegoism gave them considerable notoriety outside of the Disney-brand animal farm.

Magica's witchy chic also allows Barks to comment on scandals surrounding mid-1950s horror comics and capitalize on the rising Monster Kid culture of the early 1960s. Thanks to their squeaky-clean reputation for quality family entertainment, Western Publishing and the Dell imprint had weathered the popular backlash brought on by Wertham and his followers and the industry-crushing Senate hearings that condemned the "horror craze." Even after the Comics Code Authority was established in 1954, Dell/Western products were not submitted for approval (Nyberg 1998, 116).[5] Still, Western discouraged any use of the weird, ghostly, or monstrous; Barks relates: "They did tell me from the office to be awfully careful. Don't put in anything that suggests any kind of horror. Don't use the word 'Horror.' I never did use the word 'death'" (Ault 2003, 12). Postcode Disney editors carefully policed gothic and crime stories, but as so often happens in cultural production, politely repressed or subverted pleasures eventually bleed through as brilliantly weird and surprisingly provocative.[6] Barks's emphasis on both Disney's and his own omission of death-based scenarios also provides fascinating confirmation of the Kristevean perspective on patriarchal illusions and spectacles that subdue, erase, or eliminate the complex realities of gender and mortality.

Similarly, Barks's perpetual reuse of Magica in his later work signals a crucial shift toward more "rich and strange" manifestations of monstrous femininity and outlandish animalism. Although he declared Magica's many narrative possibilities "strictly non-political in any language," Barks's sultry Italian "seducktress" compounds several contemporary trends and tensions relating to ethnicity, gender, and culture. Barks's earlier career as a pinup and gag man for cheesecake humor titles like *Coo-Coo* and *The Calgary Eye-Opener* also informs his construction of dishy ducks like Magica. In fact, he had a knack for infusing blatantly innocuous material with the whiff or hint of licentious titillation and, of course, ethnic parody. His audition sketch for Disney Studios depicts Snow White beset by seven less-than-gentlemanly dwarfs, one of whom, a Mahatma Gandhi caricature, exposes himself to her. He also regularly practiced pinup and nude sketches that fused female and animal features "trying to get action into girlie poses" that presented new, "more perky" perspectives on sensual objectification (Barrier 1982, 76).[7]

Barks first conceived Magica as an anthropomorphic analogy to the gothically glamorous matriarch Morticia featured in Charles Addams's grimly goofy *New Yorker* cartoons. Building on Mother Addams's svelte charm, Barks's winsome witch also channels the disarming smolder of celebrity bombshells like Gina Lollobrigida, Sophia Loren, and Yvonne De Carlo (who later contributed to the same "playful monster" fad portraying TV's Lily Munster) (Andrae 2006, 242). Yet, the Disney duck diva arrived a full two years before the influential ABC TV adaptation of *The Addams Family* and three years before *The Munsters* aired on CBS. At times, Carolyn Jones's delightful, deadpan portrayal of Morticia even wants a bit of Magica's fuss and flare.

Barks may also have drawn inspiration from other evocative blends of horror and desire. Magica's signature saunter certainly recalls Gloria Holden's slinky performance of Countess Marya Zaleska in Lambert Hillyer's 1936 *Dracula's Daughter*, as well as the charismatically creepy 1954–1955 vignettes invented by KABC-TV's shock horror host, Vampira (Maila Nurmi). Nurmi also modeled her iconic character on a strategic fusion of Charles Addams's Morticia and the "waist-cinching bondage art" of John Willie's *Bizarre* fetish magazines (Voger 2016, 20).[8] Magica's knack for finding herself in oddly compromised positions *à cause de* her own gizmos, charms, and accoutrements also seems to—somewhat oddly—channel the S&M aesthetics of Irving and Paula Klaw's fetish media made infamous by Bettie Page, whose bobbed coiffure clearly mirrors Magica's. I do not suggest that Barks was in any way knowingly appropriating Vampira's camp performances or indulging in the Klaws' fetish pornography. Yet, Magica's revolutionary role as a young, feminine foil to Scrooge's older, avuncular dominance seems couched or cloaked in a repeating series of vampiric, witchy, and "bitchy" codes of monstrosity that simultaneously empower and vilify, entice and repel, arouse and undermine her appearance and her behaviors in outré forms that clearly speak to the cultural concerns and gender crises of the times. Morticia, Vampira, Lily Munster, Bettie Page, and the harrowed heroines of the Klaw and Wylie fetish media were all surprisingly interconnected in their blending of monstrous identity, alluring sexuality, and curious kink.

By the mid-1960s, the creatures of movies, network television, and *New Yorker* cartoons were matched with Aurora's best-selling monster and victim models, proto-goth pop songs like Bobby Pickett's "Monster Mash," Forrest J. Ackerman's *Famous Monsters of Filmland,* and related Warren Publishing black-and-white creepfests like *Creepy* and *Eerie.* These all erupted with revolutionary themes of queer camp and polymorphous pleasure, a mode that Barks enjoyed incorporating into his hetero-animal comics via Magica De Spell (Strzyz 2003, 113). The Duck Man continued to play with his most popular seducktress well into the 1960s, and Magica's revolutionary menace would increase with each new skirmish in her rollicking feud with Scrooge.

Present-day Duck artist Don Rosa identifies Magica as the most inherently treacherous of Barks's three major antagonists (Rosa 2017). The "terrible, terrible Beagle Boys" make it a "family affair" to breach McDuck's iconic Money Bin. Flintheart Glomgold, a jealous plutocrat, strives to tarnish Scrooge's excruciating status as the World's Richest Duck. Meanwhile, Magica fixates on a single coin from Scrooge's vast horde, the famously named "Old Number One," which she considers his primary talisman of limitless thrift, luck, and fortune. Although many Barks stories emphasize the mythic import of Scrooge's first dime, the coin did not earn its proper name, "Old Number One," until Magica De Spell's arrival in 1961's "The Midas Touch." The character and the prop define each other in the manner of Kristeva's "object of phobic desire" or Bataille's "disprivileging" *informe* (Creed and Hoorn 2016, 101). Through her arcane studies, Magica discovers how to unlock the dime's moneymaking karma. In early stories like "The Midas Touch" and "The Many Faces," she hopes to forge it Tolkien-style in the fires of Mount Vesuvius into an all-powerful moneymaking amulet.[9] Later tales like "Raven Mad" introduce more bizarre schemes like blasting it directly into the sun. Regardless of which wacky strategy she invents, Magica's acquisition of Scrooge's first dime holds crucial monstrous purpose. Her fixation on the agency-defining dime also introduces other subversive agendas.

First, in possessing Old Number One, Magica hopes to indulge in or even supersede the infinite pleasures of capitalist indulgence, a wild extension of the destabilizing Kristevean abject (Creed and Hoorn 2016, 101). Second, as a perversely alluring sorceress—whose interests, talents, and powers are coded as suspiciously perverse—she exalts in the humiliating, coin-centered castration of Scrooge's primacy as an agent of "avuncular" wealth, power, and prestige. There is also considerable queer friction in the way her hunt for the dime perpetually places her at odds with hetero codes of romantic, maternal, and domestic behavior. Magica often excels at seductive performances and impersonations, adding still more "anxiety of organism" to Barks's simulacral animal comedies. Yet, she is generally bored by or contemptuous of most straight behaviors and cis perspectives. In "Ten Cent Valentine," she is disgusted by the thought of raising children, and in 1963's "Isle of the Golden Geese" she shrivels with revulsion at the sight of Scrooge's shepherdess ally, a sweet, ultrafeminine ingenue.

In these later stories, like the wild goose quest from *Uncle Scrooge*, no. 45, or 1964's "Rug Riders of the Sky" from *Uncle Scrooge*, no. 50, Magica's fixation on McDuck's primary dime also gives way to her general delight in foiling or embarrassing her capitalist quarry's postcolonial expeditions. In such cases, Magica's urge for gendered vengeance moves beyond her hunt for Old Number One, pushing her into more seditious territory where "the animal, along with the woman," can fight back with "the power to disturb identity [and] system order" (Creed and Hoorn 2016, 92). In such stories, her many animal allies, including exotic birds, bats, cats, and especially her familiar Ratface the Raven, all emphasize repressed organic anxiety as naturalistic unspeaking animals arise at her command to assail Scrooge's defenses and defile his treasures.

Barks's seducktress also indulges in increasingly ignominious impersonations and monstrous metamorphoses. In every case, she transgresses normative boundaries of gender, body, and species, always drawing attention to the chimerical elements of Disney's overwrought simulations of therianthropic pleasure. Thomas Andrae rightly argues that such moments of shape-shifting "polymorphousness" provide anxious evidence of how "new forms of identity" and gender threatened "rigid forms of masculinity" in midcentury American culture (2006, 244).

As a signifier, Magica remains as slippery as any duck-woman gets. In "The Midas Touch," she transforms into Gina Luluduckita, an exotic celebrity "damsel een distress"; a gray-haired matron in autumnal attire; a plump double agent working for McDuck himself; and a meager fishwife who humiliates Scrooge, Donald, and the nephews by stuffing them into dead tuna delivered to a cat food factory. In this case, the gag is doubly perverse. Magica terrifies her petrified "catch" by monologuing about the factory. Once freed from their humiliating fish-prisons, however, the ducks find that she has sent them to a paper flower mill instead. Staffed largely by men doing a traditionally feminine job, Scrooge and his family find themselves thoroughly flummoxed by her deceptive manipulations of expectations relating to gender, work, and power.

In "For Old Dime's Sake," she saunters past McDuck's guards and "private dicks" as a fetching blonde stewardess, then morphs into another helmet-haired matron before impersonating the porcine Mayor of Duckburg, and ultimately Scrooge himself. In the kooky holiday yarn "Ten Cent Valentine," Magica avails herself of the endearing charms of a harmless "little old lady" to infiltrate McDuck's money bin, where she bugs his office Cold War style.

Then, fearing an "unladylike" altercation with the ducks, she assumes the form of a "strong, agile, muscle girl" marathon runner who bullies Donald into a tantrum of machismo. Calling her "a scrawny crow" and "feeble female," he chases down the strange "musclewoman," "just to teach her a lesson in manners," before falling painfully into her trap. Few monstrous females are more parasitically performative in their attacks on the identity-driven presumptions of others.

Magica's knack for transgressive transference reaches its zenith in two of Barks's zoomorphic masterpieces: 1963's "For Old Dime's Sake" from *Uncle Scrooge*, no. 43, and 1964's "The Many Faces of Magica De Spell" from *Uncle Scrooge*, no. 48. One full page from "For Old Dime's Sake" firmly establishes Magica's dominance as a monstrous "modern sorceress" whose fiendish talents have now "coagulated enough wallop to fracture the cosmos." As she cackles and cavorts through a thrilling eight-panel salvo, Barks crams his panels with cats, bats, shooting stars, lightning bolts, and awe-inspiring astronomical terrors. Like never before, Magica's villainous potency has made her "so ornery the world will tremble at [her] slightest scowl."

Barks's powerful *mise-en-page* toys with traditional elements of witchcraft, villainy, and catastrophe to mediate what Kristeva might call comedic "jouissance" (1982, 9). Magica's power trip equates well with Kristeva's conception of "a time of oblivion and thunder, of veiled infinity and the moment when revelation bursts forth" for subjects impelled to recognize their own phobias, limitations, and boundaries either within or beyond patriarchal signification, even though Barks ultimately undermines Magica's egomaniacal rant.

Magica savors her own abject amplitude as a Kristevean "Female Who Can Wreck the Infinite." As readers skate along the iconotextual edges of Barks's waffle-like grid, its "conformed" sequential focalization emphasizes the constancy and clarity of his revelation of Magica's newfound abilities, but coolly and critically. It mediates Magica's grand indulgence in her own monstrous potential from a detached and dominant narrative distance (Peeters 2007).

In other words, Barks's scene empowers Magica as a female monstrosity fueled by her taste for chaos and conflict, but his matter-of-fact presentation of her wickedness ultimately tames or familiarizes her transgressive strength. At the end of this cautiously structured satire of a driven, empowered female, he punctuates the gendered gag emphasizing that her evil arises not from genius or industry, but from crabbiness. She becomes, in effect, doubly monstrous because she is both ideologically malevolent and socially incorrigible. Melding her monstrosity to "unladylike" rudeness, the very structures of Barks's comics limit and label the otherwise ludic extremes of abjection and desire fueling Magica's witchy rebelliousness.

Figure 10.2: A more fearsome and adamantly "ornery" Magica De Spell prepares to "wreck the infinite" in Barks's "For Old Dime's Sake." *Walt Disney's Uncle Scrooge*, no. 43, p. 5, by Carl Barks. Copyright 1963, Western Publishing.

At times, Magica herself exalts in the extremity of her foul moods and ingenious hexes, especially in one shocking moment of self-satisfied cruelty from "The Many Faces." On her way to engage McDuck with her new face-shifting charm, she abuses an ornery street dog by switching its "ugly annoying" face with her own. After constructing this freakish, disquieting cross-species homage to her own "bitchiness," she exits with Larkie-like glee, reflecting, "Hee, hee, hee! Circe's formula is such an amusing toy to play with." Barks's Larkies also giggled as they sadistically manipulated their prey, but they never approached Magica's rampant narcissism or her penchant for ruthless mayhem. Although the dog is left to suffer as an *animalséant* freak among more balanced and orthodox therianthropic simulations, its amblings eventually alert the ducks to Magica's whereabouts, providing them with valuable strategic advantage later in the tale.

Barks also enjoys wedding Magica's grumpiness to other faults and vices. Although she constantly uncovers dangerous secrets, hatches new plots, and perfects powerful charms, he consistently codes her as lazy, irritable, and shallow. This last flaw seems especially ironic considering that her primary rival is a fantastically wealthy elder male who swims through cubic acres of cash for recreation and obsessively covets a single heirloom coin. In "The Midas Touch," Scrooge scoffs at her amulet plan: "Har! Har! Of all the ways to get rich, **YOUR** way takes the cake!" And in 1962's "Raven Mad" from *Walt Disney's Comics and Stories*, no. 265, he dismisses her desperate plot to "get **extra-rich** every time I get a sun-burn" from basking in the magical light of good fortune, as the "**laziest** way to make money I ever heard of." Barks scholar Geoffrey Blum notes that such moments reveal Magica as the ideal "psychological double for Scrooge, a dark twin who shares his lust for treasure," but whose ideology and methods are "fundamentally different from those of the tycoon," who emphasizes "work, thrift, and self-sacrifice" as "national virtues." Instead, Magica works hard at devising hacks and cheats rooted in style, image, and convenience, believing that "wealth inheres in objects" of luxury and status (Blum 1994, 1).

She stands as the industrious Barks parody of "the perfect modern consumer, convinced that ownership of the right objects, luxuries that Scrooge would never covet," will bring her glory, joy, and power (Blum 1994, 1). Barks's early life was marked by backbreaking labor, periods of itinerant poverty, and desperate need. The experience left him particularly skeptical of conspicuous consumption, indulgent privilege, and pampered intellectualism (Blum 2000, 55). Furthermore, Barks's bouts between Scrooge and Magica parallel the dichotomies of repression that define Kristeva's patriarchally policed female/animal abjections. Compared to Scrooge's avuncular dominance and limitlessly diversified wealth, Magica's role as a "capable woman" provocateur vested with "dark, abominable, and degraded power" linked to unorthodox sensuality, seditious ingenuity, and arcane knowledge is broadly satirized (Kristeva 1982, 168–69).

Ultimately, the feud between Uncle Scrooge McDuck and Ms. Magical De Spell apes Kristeva's own claims relating to the controlling and surveilling of Célinian abjection: "The ideal figure is nevertheless not completely absent; it is the uncle—the maternal one of course [. . .] the hope of righteous families" (1982, 172). Although Kristeva focuses specifically on "family life" in Céline's *Death on the Installment Plan*, her insight applies productively to Barks's righteously straight, white, and ludicrously repressed Disney Duck family, among whom the unspecified orthodoxies of sexless Disney entertainment require the removal of direct hereditary relationships (1982, 170). All children are narratively orphaned of their biological parents and serve as the strangely asexual wards of uncles and aunts. All "avuncular" adults dutifully raise their oblivious nieces and nephews, leaving Scrooge and Donald each as oddly maternal patriarchs implicit within the simulacral erasure of sexual reproduction and multigendered parenting common to chimerical entertainments like animated cartoons and funny animal comics. Perhaps powerfully eroticized female monsters like Magica threaten to steal more than dimes and topple bigger assets than fortunes when they invade Disney's politely neutered media or Barks's blatantly homogenized Duckburg contexts.

By the end of most Magica stories, Barks also takes zealous pleasure in rendering her hysterical. She may gloat with fits of heel kicking or Larkie-like "tee hee hee's" during her brief triumphs, but her final moments in "The Midas Touch," "The Unsafe Safe," "For Old Dime's Sake," "Raven Mad," and "Rug Riders in the Sky" leave her not only foiled but furiously defiled. In each case, she exits in frenzied misery, her glamorous locks ravaged by exhaustion, her once proud monologues reduced to sublingual, monosyllabic drivel like "fzt! Sft! Spt!," and her sorceries diminished from grand "foofs" to nearly Neanderthal rock tossing.[10]

In some stories, Barks playfully rubs his therianthropic animal metaphors against each other to deploy new transspecies tortures that further reduce and ridicule Magica's threat to dogmatic Disney Duckdom. This particular use for Magica becomes especially important in moments of magical metamorphosis within Barks's zoomorphic tour de force. In "The Many Faces of Magica De Spell," "the human strays on the territory of the animal" in grotesque mutations involving both anthropomorphized humanoids and realistically rendered animals (Ayra and Chare 2016, 7). Even the comic book's unorthodox cover design warns of something especially insidious within Magica's next scheme.

Most Dell pamphlet covers featured a mundane "flexible form of sight gag based on nuances of posture, facial expression, and characterization" that were generally unrelated to the stories within. This issue depicts Barks's regular company of hetero ducks facing down strangely personal reflections of Magica, who schemes in the background from behind a shrub (Eronen 31). Even before the story begins, we find heady emphasis on "an exploration of borders or luminal, fragile states where the subject's identity is directly threatened by the abject [. . .] through the process of metamorphosis" (Creed and Hoorn 2016, 91). Thanks to Magica's zoomorphic "hex juice," any living creature who encounters her potion must suddenly swap faces with whatever animal it encounters. The outrageous results lead to Barks's most peculiar parade of satiric switcheroos.[11] Before the face-swapping farce concludes, Magica's jumble juice has made monstrously incongruous cat-birds, duck-dogs, monkey-Scrooges, and, most disturbing of all to the established order, transgendered McDuck/De Spells—funny but unpleasant debasements of conventional anthropomorphic fantasies that clash against orthodoxies of identity, patriarchy, and taxonomy.

Magica's shocking behaviors and disgraceful denouements arise from Barks's interest in humiliating her ambitious femininity and eroticized menace. As he told Michael Naiman in 1993, "Magica De Spell was a villainess. She had mean thoughts. She was acquisitive. The same way with the Beagle Boys and Flintheart Glomgold—they were people I had no sympathy with, and I love to use them in stories in order to humiliate them, frustrate them" (Ault 2003, 159). Such frustrations—the push and pull of desire and debasement—are vividly, insistently obvious in his "Many Faces" story. As Creed and Hoorn argue, "the roles of the woman and animal" are deeply "interrelated" in such chimeric fantasies of subjection and control (2016, 91). In this story, Barks's renderings of Magica are always introduced or associated with animal familiars, from bats and cats to her loyal raven, Ratface, whose name is itself a literalized hybrid rooted in the judgment of appearance, ethics, and human/animal bonds.

Although Peter Schilling finds her merely "another mediocre female in the Barks universe" (2014, 6), Blum observes that Barks's "Magica stories assume a very different tone" from his previous postcolonial farces (1994, 1), and Andrae devotes nearly twenty pages of his seminal *Carl Barks and the Disney Comic Book* to dissecting the myriad ways in which "Magica combines the sexual threat of the femme fatale with the image of the [Disney] witch," not to mention obvious nods to the parasitic vamp and the bad girl pinup (2006, 244). Finally, though, we might see Magica De Spell as the most significant sign of Barks's own ambivalent attitudes toward not only powerful women and outlandish satire but also the dynamics of his own artistic agency within the Disney simulacrum factory.

Magica's ferociously independent, flagrantly untraditional performance of sexual sorcery assaults the primacy of the hetero-drakes who drive Barks's Duckburg stories. She is a monstrous woman of comics who reveals the monstrous masculinities that mock and marginalize her. As a mash-up of the wicked witch and the therianthropic fatale; a consumerist *grotesque* who compulsively equates getting and spending with owning and winning; and an *abjectified* she-animal who parasitically pursues "the power and wealth of others," Magica is Barks's most intriguing combination of humor, horror, and humiliation as they relate to the most enduring element of his Disney comics—their inherently sardonic, lavishly rendered, inscrutable Duckiness (Andrae 2006, 245; Blum 1994, 1).

Notes

1. Steve Baker's groundbreaking study *Picturing the Beast* draws the useful distinction between therianthropic creatures that blend human and animal characteristics such as Barks's ducks or Hasbro's My Little Pony characters, and theriomorphic animal disguises or costumes like that of Batman or Spider-Man, which suggest the forms and abilities of beasts (1993, 108).

2. For more thorough discussions, see Chaney 2011, Haraway 1992, Haraway 2008, Herman 2011, Keen 2013, Willmott 2012, Willmott 2018, Witek 2016, and Yezbick 2018.

3. For historical discussions of the dominance of Dell/Western Publishing's Disney titles, especially those featuring Barks's uncredited material, see Andrae 2006, Barrier 2015, Wright 2003, Gabilliet 2005, and Yezbick 2018.

4. Barks's frequent use of exotic locales and emerging nations has remained a contentious topic in cultural studies. For various contributions and refinements of the debate, see Dorfman and Mattelarte 1991, Andrae 2006, and Yezbick 2013.

5. For comprehensive discussions of Dell's relationship with the Comics Magazine Association of America and the Comics Code Authority, see Nyberg 1998, Barrier 2015, Hajdu 2009, and Whitted 2019.

6. For more extended discussion of the non-CAA approved content of Dell/Gold Key/Whitman comics of all genres, see Barrier 2015 and Kunka 2019.

7. For closer analysis of Barks's pinup and gag work for men's magazines as Barkie, see Spiegelman 1998, and Barrier 1982.

8. David J. Skal goes into even more dreadful detail concerning Nurmi's extreme body modifications to further enhance the monstrous proportions of her Vampira figure, another very human corollary to the many metamorphoses, mutations, and magical fetishes circulating around sultry signifiers like Magica De Spell (Skal 2001, 35).

9. Barks was fond of Tolkien's world-building (Ault 2003).

10. See Stjernfelt and Østergaard 2013 for a revealing analysis of Barks's elegant use of signature sound effects in his comics narration.

11. Barks loved to remix and trouble his own therianthropic metaphors, and some of his most bizarre extensions of human/animal hybrid disguise plumb strange, uncanny, adamantly abject territory even without Magica. These include "Donald's Worst Nightmare" (*Walt Disney's*

Comics and Stories, no. 101, February 1949); "The Think Box Bollix" (*WDC&S*, no. 141, June 1952); "Wispy Willie" (*WDC&S*, no. 159, December 1953); and the story that introduced Scrooge McDuck himself, "Christmas on Bear Mountain" (*Four Color*, no. 178, December 1947).

Bibliography

Andrae, Thomas. 2006. *Carl Barks and the Disney Comic Book: Unmasking the Myth of Modernity*. Jackson: University Press of Mississippi.
Arya, Rina, and Nicholas Chare. 2016. "Introduction: Approaching Abjection." In *Abject Visions: Powers of Horror in Art and Visual Culture*, edited by Rina Arya and Nicholas Chare, 1–13. Manchester: Manchester University Press.
Ault, Donald, ed. 2003. *Carl Barks: Conversations*. Jackson: University Press of Mississippi.
Ault, Donald. 2013. "Life among the Ducks." In *Walt Disney's Donald Duck: The Old Castle's Secret*. Seattle: Fantagraphics.
Baker, Steve. 1993. *Picturing the Beast: Animals, Identity, and Representation*. Champaign: University of Illinois Press.
Barks, Carl. 1974–1975. "The Unknown Carl Barks." *Funnyworld*, no. 16 (Winter): 12–19.
Barks, Carl. 1987. *Uncle Scrooge McDuck: His Life and Times*. Berkeley, CA: Celestial Arts.
Barks, Carl. 1998. "The Duck Man." In *The Comic-Book Book*, edited by Don Thompson and Dick Lupoff, 211–27. Iola, WI: Krause Publications.
Barrier, Michael. 1982. *Carl Barks and the Art of the Comic Book*. New York: M. Lilien.
Barrier, Michael. 2015. *Funnybooks: the Improbable Glories of the Best American Comic-Books*. Oakland: University of California Press.
Bataille, Georges, Michel Leiris, Marcel Griaule, Carl Einstein, and Robert Desnos. 1995. *Encyclopedia Acephalica*. London: Atlas Press.
Baudrillard, Jean. 1994. "The Animals: Territory and Metamorphoses." In *Simulacra and Simulation*, 129–41. Translated by Sheila Faria Glaser. Ann Arbor: University of Michigan Press.
Berenstein, Rhona J. 1995. *Attack of the Leading Ladies: Gender, Sexuality, and Spectatorship in Classic Horror Cinema*. New York: Columbia University Press.
Berger, Arthur Asa. 1973. *The Comic-Stripped American*. Baltimore: Penguin.
Berger, John. 1992. "Why Look at Animals?" In *About Looking*, 3–28. New York: Vintage.
Blum, Geoffrey. 1993. *Carl Barks and the Disney Ducks*. Prescott, AZ: Another Rainbow.
Blum, Geoffrey. 1994. Introduction to *Walt Disney's Uncle Scrooge: The Many Faces of Magica De Spell*. Prescott, AZ: Gladstone Publishing.
Blum, Geoffrey. 2000. "A Letter from the Duck Man." *Comics Journal*, no. 227 (September): 55–56.
Carroll, Noël. 1990. *The Philosophy of Horror; or, Paradoxes of the Heart*. New York: Routledge.
Chalker, Jack L. 1974. *An Informal Biography of Scrooge McDuck*. Baltimore: Mirage Press.
Chaney, Michael. 2011. "Animal Subjects in the Graphic Novel." *College Literature* 38, no. 3: 129–49.
Cohen, Jeffrey Jerome, ed. 1996. *Monster Theory: Reading Culture*. University of Minnesota Press.
Creed, Barbara, and Jeanette Hoorn. 2016. "Animals, Art, Abjection." In *Abject Visions: Powers of Horror in Art and Visual Culture*, edited by Rina Arya and Nicholas Chare, 90–105. Manchester: Manchester University Press.

Cudworth, Erika. 2014. "Beyond Speciesism: Intersectionality, Critical Sociology, and the Human Domination of Other Animals." In *The Rise of Critical Animal Studies: From the Margins to the Centre*, edited by Nik Taylor and Richard Twine, 19–35. Abingdon, Oxon, England: Routledge.

Dean, Michael. 2000. "In Tribute: Carl Barks, 1901–2000." *Comics Journal*, no. 227 (September): 38–81.

Derrida, Jacques. 2008. *The Animal That Therefore I Am*. New York: Fordham University Press.

Dorfman, Ariel, and Armand Mattelart. 1991. *How to Read Donald Duck: Imperialist Ideology in the Disney Comic*. New York: I. G. Editions. Available at https://fadingtheaesthetic.files.wordpress.com/2012/03/33788991-how-to-read-donald.pdf.

Eronen, Matti. 2017. *A Study from Shadows: Carl Barks' Surviving Comic Book Covers*. N.p.: Matti Eronen.

Gabilliet, Jean-Paul. 2005. *Of Comics and Men: A Cultural History of American Comic Books*. Translated by Bart Beaty and Nick Nguyen. Jackson: University Press of Mississippi.

Grennan, Simon. 2017. *A Theory of Narrative Drawing*. New York: Palgrave Macmillan.

Hajdu, David. 2009. *The Ten-Cent Plague: The Great Comic-Book Scare and How It Changed America*. New York: Picador.

Haraway, Donna. 1992. "The Promises of Monsters: A Regenerative Politics for Inappropriate/d Others." In *Cultural Studies*, edited by Lawrence Grossberg, Cary Nelson, and Paula A. Treichler, 295–337. New York: Routledge.

Haraway, Donna. 2008. *When Species Meet*. Minneapolis: University of Minnesota Press.

Herman, David. 2011. "Storyworld/Umwelt: Nonhuman Experiences in Graphic Narratives." *SubStance* 40, no. 1 (January): 156–81.

I.N.D.U.C.K.S. 2018. Search results for "Magica De Spell." I.N.D.U.C.K.S. International database, February 10. Available at https://inducks.org/simp.php?d1=Magica&d2=&d4=&creat=Carl+Barks&exactpg=&kind=0.

Keen, Suzanne. 2013. "Fast Tracks to Narrative Empathy: Anthropomorphism and Dehumanization in Graphic Narratives." *SubStance* 40, no. 1 (January): 135–55.

Kristeva, Julia. 1982. *Powers of Horror: An Essay on Abjection*. New York: Columbia University Press.

Kunka, Andrew J. 2019. "Adaptation and Racial Representation in Dell/Gold Key TV Tie-Ins." In *The Oxford Handbook of Comic Book Studies*, edited by Frederick Luis Aldama. Oxford Handbooks Online. Available at https://www.oxfordhandbooks.com/view/10.1093/oxfordhb/9780190917944.001.0001/oxfordhb-9780190917944-e-33.

Lippit, Akira Mizuta. 2000. *Electric Animal: Toward a Rhetoric of Wildlife*. Minneapolis: University of Minnesota Press.

Lyons, Mike, and Tom Tumbusch. 1995. "Carl Barks: The Old Master in His Disneyana Prime." *Tomart's Disneyana Update*, no. 7: 12–15.

Maynard, Patrick. 2012. "What's So Funny? Comic Content in Depiction." In *The Art of Comics: A Philosophical Approach*, edited by Aaron Meskin and Roy T. Cook, 105–24. Oxford: Wiley-Blackwell.

McHugh, Susan. 2011. *Animal Stories: Narrating across Species Lines*. Minneapolis: University of Minnesota Press.

Morgan, Jack. 2002. *The Biology of Horror*. Carbondale: Southern Illinois University Press.

Nyberg, Amy Kiste. 1998. *Seal of Approval: The History of the Comics Code*. Jackson: University Press of Mississippi.

Peeters, Benoît. 2007. "Four Conceptions of the Page." Translated by Jesse Cohn. *ImageTexT* 3, no. 3. Available at http://www.english.ufl.edu/imagetext/archives/v3_3/peeters/.

Rosa, Don. 2006. *The Life and Times of Scrooge McDuck*. Timonium, MD: Gemstone.

Rosa, Don. 2017. Unpublished interview. Planet Comicon, May 5.

Schilling, Peter, Jr. 2014. *Carl Barks' Duck: Average American*. Minneapolis: Uncivilized Books.

Skal, David J. 2001. *The Monster Show: A Cultural History of Horror*. New York: Farrar, Straus and Giroux.

Spiegelman, Art. 1998. "A Real Eye-Opener." In *The Unexpurgated Carl Barks*, by Carl Barks, 1–2. Prescott, AZ: Hamilton Comics.

Stjernfelt, Frederik, and Svend Østergaard. 2013. "Fonk! Honk! Wham! Oof! Representation of Events in Carl Barks—and the Aesthetics of Comics in General." In *Picturing the Language of Images*, edited by Nancy Pedri and Laurence Petit, 483–508. Newcastle upon Tyne: Cambridge Scholars Publishing.

Strzyz, Klaus. 2003. "An Interview with Carl and Garé Barks." In *Carl Barks: Conversations*, edited by Donald Ault, 109–19. Jackson: University Press of Mississippi.

Summer, Peter. 1987. "Garé Barks: A Recollection." In *Uncle Scrooge McDuck: His Life and Times*, by Carl Barks. New York: Celestial Arts.

Voger, Mark. 2016. *Monster Mash: The Creepy, Kooky Monster Craze in America, 1957–1972*. Raleigh, NC: TwoMorrows.

Weisberg, Zipporah. 2009. "The Broken Promises of Monsters: Haraway, Animals and the Humanist Legacy." *Journal for Critical Animal Studies* 7, no. 2: 22–62.

Whitted, Qiana. 2019. *EC Comics: Race, Shock, and Social Protest*. New Brunswick, NJ: Rutgers University Press.

Willits, Malcolm, Don Thompson, and Maggie Thompson. 2003. "The Duck Man." In *Carl Barks: Conversations*, edited by Donald Ault, 3–18. Jackson: University Press of Mississippi.

Willmott, Glenn. 2012. *Modern Animalism: Habitats of Scarcity and Wealth in Comics and Literature*. Toronto: University of Toronto Press.

Willmott, Glenn. 2018. "The Animalized Character and Style." In *Animal Comics: Multispecies Storyworlds in Graphic Narratives*, edited by David Herman, 53–73. London: Bloomsbury.

Witek, Joseph. 2016. "If a Way to the Better There Be: Excellence, Mere Competence, and the Worst Comics Ever Made." *Image and Narrative* 17, no. 4: 26–42.

Wright, Bradford W. 2003. *Comic Book Nation*. Baltimore: Johns Hopkins University Press.

Yezbick, Daniel. 2013. "Uncle Scrooge." In *Icons of the American Comic-Book*, edited by Randy Duncan and Matthew J. Smith, vol. 2, 773–80. Santa Barbara, CA: ABC-CLIO.

Yezbick, Daniel. 2018. "Lions and Tigers and Fears: A Natural History of the Sequential Animal." In *Animal Comics: Multispecies Storyworlds in Graphic Narratives*, edited by David Herman, 29–52. London: Bloomsbury.

11

On the Edge of 1990s Japan: Kyoko Okazaki and the Horror of Adolescence

Novia Shih-Shan Chen and Sho Ogawa

> *"Love" isn't that tepid and lukewarm thing people like to talk about. I don't think. It's a tough, severe, scary and cruel monster. So is "capitalism." But being scared of them, like a kid who can't swim is scared of a swimming pool, is lame.*
>
> KYOKO OKAZAKI

Kyoko Okazaki is a Japanese woman manga writer who has created narratives that bluntly address issues of sexuality and anxieties of female adolescents and young adult women in 1990s Japan. First discovered by the social critic Otsuka Eiji, one of Japan's most renowned scholars on adolescent women (*shōjo*), Okazaki contributed to his cutting-edge *hentai* magazine. Her subsequent works were released in similarly unconventional publications such as ladies' comics, edgy women's fashion magazines, and men's tabloid magazines. Despite being a prolific, critically and commercially acclaimed writer, her works are rarely discussed in English-language scholarship. In the afterword to her early work *Pink*, she signals her conscious authorial intent to reveal the hardships of existence and self-searching in the debilitating social and economic contexts of 1990s Japan. She shows how the period's commodification of underage women, idealization of women as sites of reproduction, and prevalent consumer culture exposed a heightened anxiety and alienation among youth, especially teenage girls (Okazaki 2010, 255). Love and capitalism had become the unexamined means for young and independent women to find self-assurance and assertion.

In this chapter, we trace Okazaki's career during the 1980s and 1990s and examine the social values ascribed to women's roles in *Pink* (1989), *River's Edge*

(1993–1994), and *Helter Skelter* (1995–1996). We examine the ways in which Okazaki's work displays both the Western conceptualization of the monstrous-feminine and Japanese female ghosts (*yurei*) characterized by hyperbolic sexual difference, violence, women's abjection, emotional breakdown, and, ultimately, death. In her important work "Horror and the Monstrous-Feminine," Barbara Creed defines the monstrous-feminine through gender difference and abjection. Creed contends that Julia Kristeva's *Powers of Horror* provides insights into the understanding of women's roles and functions in horror films (Creed 2002, 68). The monstrous-feminine is particularly marked by signifiers associated with female sexuality such as puberty, pregnancy, and menopause. In addition, women's sexual perversions and immorality are elements that are religiously, socially, and culturally projected onto a mature yet dangerous female body that simultaneously elicits dread and desire from men. The stereotypical depictions of women in horror, often encapsulated in the virgin/whore duality, the two polarizing roles that are offered to women in a patriarchal society, are examples of how the monstrous-feminine is fabricated by men and for men. The connection between female sexuality and horror perpetuates the undesirability of women's consciousness and expression of sexuality. In a similar vein, adolescent horror also manifests in the fear and anxiety toward female puberty that must be contained in order to appease male viewers.

Japanese horror films are also rooted in the fear and containment of femininity. The trope of female ghosts has been prevalent in Japanese horror cinema and literature, in which women who are victims of violent treatment at the hands of their samurai husbands who break the samurai moral codes become unquiet souls and return to haunt the guilty, living husband (Richards 2010, 16). The grudging souls of the wives reemerge in postwar Japanese cinema, when films such as *Ugetsu* and *Onibaba* epitomize society's anxiety of economic recession, the irretrievable loss of the warrior spirit, and the hierarchical social order (Richards 2010, 22–23). The men in these Japanese horror films are portrayed as incapable of restoring their economic and social status, and the women in turn obtain their revenge as either ghostly or demon-like figures.

Centering on female protagonists, *Pink*, *River's Edge*, and *Helter Skelter* deal with monstrosity in disparate ways and are intricately tied to the expression of a commodified female body. In the investigation of these portrayals of female characters in the three comics, we present that the concept of monstrosity takes different forms in each of the three, ranging from the unruly female body to phantasmic presences, an insatiable desire for capitalism, and bodily excess. These representations simultaneously reflect and deflect the monstrous-feminine, and yet we maintain that monstrosity is not inherent in the characters but is socially and culturally constructed, and functions as a critical reflection on Japan's national agenda for a productive and reproductive future.

Okazaki's Comics and Monstrosity

Okazaki started her career writing for *Manga Burikko*, a porn comic magazine for male readers. *Manga Burikko* at the time was one of the two best-selling *lolicon* (characters with caricatured, child-like features) porn magazines with an ambitious editorial policy that featured young, female comic writers such as Okazaki and Erica Sakurazawa. The magazine's primary editor, Eiji Otsuka, states that Okazaki's comics were different from other contemporary works because they integrated "something like feminism" (Hayami 2000, 66). Otsuka's statement, which is from a male perspective, should be read in two ways. One acknowledges a rising awareness of female subjectivity and the foregrounding of female sexuality in the traditionally male-dominated manga industry. The second recognizes a sense of anxiety toward a burgeoning girls' culture, cautioning how it could potentially destroy the patriarchal nationhood upheld by male artists, critics, and readers alike.

Okazaki's start in a porn comic magazine is a signal of how unconventional her career would be. She wrote narratives about young women in varied outlets such as men's weeklies and newsmagazines, women's comic magazines, and fashion magazines. Her works were praised not only in the manga industry but by literary writers and academics, in particular for their intertextuality. Her works have also been featured in various art exhibitions, demonstrating that they are representative of not just Japanese comics but overall cultural production in the 1980s and 1990s. Okazaki was permanently disabled by an automobile accident in 1996, which left her unable to express herself except through eye-operated communication systems. Except for several short statements, Okazaki has remained silent since her accident. Her lack of a media presence has given her and her works an air of mystery and enduring popularity, demonstrated by film remakes and reprintings of her past works.

Okazaki's comics arguably straddle *shōjo* manga and ladies' comics. In all the three works analyzed, the unsettling mental and physical states of young women are boldly represented. Her rise to fame coincides with female manga artists' increased participation in the male-dominant industry, particularly within the two genres: *shōjo* and ladies' comics. Japanese manga culture has adhered to a coherent readership-based genre system across gender and age. This system is a reaction to diversified and niche tastes developed by postwar baby boomers. The commonly known categories specifically referring to the demographics each genre is targeted to include *shōnen* (adolescent boys), *seinen* (adult men), *shōjo* (adolescent girls), and *redicomi* (adult women).

The emergence of *shōjo* culture in the 1970s cultivated new subjects, discourses, and types of role models for young female readers. Female comics writers created narratives that centered on young girls' dreams and fantasies, enabling these writers to explore new identities and shape their own distinct subculture. Deborah M. Shamoon, in her extensive research on Japanese girls' culture (*shōjo bunka*), demonstrates that "a discrete discourse on the social construction of girlhood" is consistently represented from the prewar *shōjo* literature to the postwar *shōjo* manga (2012, 1). Despite the varying themes, representations, aesthetics, and styles across different *shōjo* manga products, Shamoon argues that purity and innocence are still viewed as ideal qualities of girlhood and are widely circulated among the *shōjo bunka*, whether female readers identify with them or not (2012, 3). Okazaki's works deviate from the conventional portrayal in most *shōjo* manga by drawing attention to the female body, displaying menstruation, the use of tampons, and female sexual pleasure and displeasure.

Following the proliferation of *shōjo* manga, the early 1980s marks the inception of the fourth gender- and age-specific readership category, ladies' comics, targeting female readers of reproductive age. The themes of these comics vary from falling in love to romance, mate selection, family life, female friendship, extramarital relationships, sex, violence, and lust (Ito 2008, 43). According to Kinko Ito, the emergence and proliferation of *redicomi* coincided with the economic expansion of the early 1980s, resulting in financially independent women seeking entertainment or identification through the diverse adult (but not necessarily pornographic) content that reflected their everyday social activities and emotional states (Ito 2011, 12). Okazaki's comics deal with themes and stories similar to those seen in ladies' comics. Yet her works mostly feature female adolescent or young adult women and do not shy away from displaying female nudity and sexuality, to some extent blurring the dichotomous distinction between *shōjo* manga and ladies' comics.

From her debut in 1983 until her accident in 1996, Okazaki completed more than thirty works. *Pink* solidified Okazaki's status as a reputable manga artist and exemplifies how she traverses the rigidly defined boundaries between manga genres. *Pink* was released in 1989 and first serialized in *New Punch Zaurus*, which was the foundational men's magazine *Heibon Punch*'s short-lived attempt to reinvent its image. *Pink* follows an artistic tradition that resembles *shōjo* manga, in which characters are less realistically proportioned than they are in *River's Edge* and *Helter Skelter*. However, unlike traditional *shōjo* manga, *Pink* contains explicit nudity and sex scenes. *Pink* features a female protagonist,

Figure 11.1: Okazaki intercuts between Kanonzaki cheating on Haruna with Rumi, while Yamada reveals his secret treasure to Haruna. Dialogue translated by the author. *River's Edge* (2000), pp. 60–61, by Kyoko Okazaki. Copyright 2000, Takarajimasha, Inc.

Yumi, who works two jobs—as an office lady by day and as a call girl whenever available and physically capable—in order to raise her pet crocodile, an embodiment of Yumi's monstrous femininity and a representation of her defiance against patriarchal norms of decency. She also shares a boyfriend, Haruo, who is a novelist and happens to be her stepmother's secret lover. The story climaxes when Yumi's stepmother murders Yumi's crocodile and turns it into a leather suitcase. The devastated Yumi decides to cope with her sorrow by planning a trip to an unnamed tropical island with Haruo. While she awaits the long overdue getaway trip at the airport, her boyfriend is killed in an accident on the way there. The last panel displays her relaxing and waiting for the ultimate happiness to arrive, which is imaginatively located in a mysterious, exotic place outside of Japan, accompanied by the leather suitcase made of her deceased crocodile.

River's Edge was first serialized in the women's fashion magazine *Monthly Cutie* in 1993–1994. The plot revolves around an urban high school girl, Haruna, and her friends as they deal with lives filled with boredom, despair, and lust. Haruna is in a relationship with Kanonzaki, whom she treats with annoyance and indifference. Kanonzaki also sleeps with Haruna's girlfriend

Rumi. Haruna befriends a closeted gay boy, Yamada, whom she repeatedly saves from Kanonzaki's relentless bullying. Yamada, in turn, shares with her his secret treasure, a corpse he found in a deserted field on the outskirts of their school. As their friendship develops, Haruna promises to keep his treasure and sexuality a secret from his girlfriend, Tajima. In the second half of the comic, the story deteriorates quickly. Rumi gets pregnant and is assaulted by Kanonzaki and her sister successively. Tajima commits suicide after Yamada ruthlessly shuts her off. After a series of events, most characters drift apart, except for Haruna, Yamada, and a bulimic celebrity/classmate who reappears in Okazaki's later work, *Helter Skelter*.

Helter Skelter was serialized in *Monthly Feel Young* from 1995 to 2003 and was later adapted for film by the Japanese female director Mika Ninagawa. Rie Karatsu draws connections between the film adaptation and Okazaki's original comics. Specifically on the manga itself, she argues that *Helter Skelter* could be "read as a feminist subversion of traditional Western fairy tales as well as the Western beauty standardized in *shōjo* manga and the patriarchal world" (Karatsu 2016, 967–83). In *Helter Skelter*, Okazaki delineates men's and women's obsession with youth as well as their anxiety about losing their youthful attractiveness and healthy skin. The story revolves around a short-tempered, self-centered, and disrespectful young supermodel, Liliko, whose glamour gradually crumbles after the effects of plastic surgical substances begin to wear off. Eventually, the facts of her surgery, which she had kept secret, are unraveled by the tabloid press. While the public amusingly awaits her confession at a press conference, she magically vanishes, leaving an enigmatic pool of blood with a single eyeball in its center. A few years later, Liliko is sighted in Mexico performing for a local show. The last panel shows her breaking the fourth wall, gazing out of her single eye as she lounges in an armchair wearing an eye patch and joined by a giant snake and a sculpture of a flayed man just over her shoulder. The deformity and the exotic elements accentuate her monstrosity, which is no longer concealed but proudly displayed.

The three comics connect to the idea of monstrosity in different ways. *Pink* deals with the insatiable desires that arise from living in a market-driven society, evidenced by the croc's appetite, Yumi's moonlighting sex work to make ends meet, and the stepmom's desire for youthful bodies. Furthermore, the narrative keeps Yumi from following a normative life path in accordance with the national ideal such as forming a family unit, signaling a rejection of the ideal womanhood expected by the state. Such deliberate rejection of reproduction is shared by many characters in the works examined, including the adolescents' desire for the monstrous in *River's Edge*. The vexed relationships shown in *River's Edge* do not pose serious plot complications, but rather the

Figure 11.2: The last panel of *Helter Skelter*. *Helter Skelter* (2003), p. 316, by Kyoko Okazaki. Copyright 2003, Shodensha Publishing Company.

story invites the readers to voyeuristically gaze into the characters' messy and unspeakable desires. The provision of this voyeuristic (dis)pleasure seems to lend a critical lens in unpacking and demystifying why these characters indulge themselves in these vague and indifferent emotions. As a group of outcasts, they manage to resist compliance with the consumer culture of the 1990s that tells them what to desire, what to devour, and what to discard. *River's Edge* is less about embodied monstrosities and more about the stifling social relations and norms that draw the high schoolers to the dead, the abject, and the monstrous. Monstrous accessories symbolize the adolescents' co-optation in and rejection of commodification. Consuming is a way of living, if not survival; at the same time, the characters retain a sense of agency through their consumption of monstrous objects. *Helter Skelter* inverts *River's Edge*'s reflection on the desire of monstrosity to examine the production of the monstrous by pursuing and desiring social ideals for women's bodies.

While a feminist reading of Okazaki's works is tempting, none of the three comics present strong-willed and powerful female characters. All three female protagonists generally lack agency and capability to counter or disrupt capitalist patriarchy. Yet, it is exactly from this standpoint that we propose to read her works and characters beyond mere representations but in relation to the social and economic backdrop of 1990s Japan. We probe the social construction of anxiety—the reactions and actions in response to the unattainable expectations imposed upon the adolescents tragically delineated by Okazaki. Okazaki's depiction of women and their bodies reflects and relentlessly criticizes the reductive quality of the prevalent social roles of women in late capitalist Japan. The various representations of monstrosity such as unruly bodies, ghostly presences, and bodily excess remind us of various characteristics that are erased in prescribed roles for women. Okazaki brings back the reproductive body to the teenager, active sexuality to mothers, and unhinged rage to women as they are commodified and disenfranchised. In response to social constrictions that demand women to be accessible, commodifiable, or reproductive, Okazaki presents the exhilarating appeal of being monstrous.

Reproductive Futurity: Consumerism and the Low Birthrate in Japan

Okazaki's frank depiction of women's sexuality subverts the invisibility of active female sexual desire, fixating on sexuality in a way that displaces reproduction. In her discussion of the invisibility of lesbianism in Japanese society, Sharon Chalmers argues that the distinct separation between the categories of wife/mother, unmarried young women, and sex industry workers in Japan works to produce married female bodies that deny, displace and replace female sexual desire in favor of reproduction. For it is in this bodily form that heterosexual women gain privilege and it is this body that is then set in direct opposition to active and autonomous female sexual desire which is represented as a lack or excess, both of these latter portrayals characterized in negative terms. (2002, 73)

It is precisely this sanitized conceptualization of women's bodies through the separation of reproduction and sex that Okazaki addresses in her representation of women's lives. Okazaki's emphasis on the messy realities of women's bodies through depictions of bulimia, plastic surgery, and menstruation breaks from the reductive conceptualizations of bodies that underlie the separation of women's social roles in Japan.

Okazaki's depiction of women also responds to the discourse on women's sexuality in 1990s Japanese media, where these boundaries between wife/mother, unmarried young woman, and sex industry worker were shown to be in flux but never eradicated. In the 1990s, there was a moral panic surrounding schoolgirls who were involved in sex work, which was referred to as "compensated dating" (*enjo-kōsai*). Sex work among trendy, fashion-forward schoolgirls called *kogyaru* increased due to the popularization of "telephone clubs," through which men take phone calls from women in individual booths for conversation, phone sex, or setting up dates (Leheny 2006, 320). The entry of middle-class underage women in the sex market for luxury consumption was met with paternalistic condemnation and criticism from the mainstream media. Feminist scholar Chizuko Ueno lauds young ideologues who resisted the condemnation of *enjo-kōsai* by highlighting their agency and self-determination in their own commodification. However, she comments that *enjo-kōsai* ultimately supports patriarchy, "leaving the assumption intact that women's body is served for the male desire as an object" (2003, 323). Ueno's argument demonstrates that schoolgirls' self-commodification entrenched them within a patriarchal and capitalist system that commodified female bodies, but also led to the transgression of firmly defined categories among women. The unruly female bodies that inhabit Okazaki's comics transgress the boundaries that separate sexual from nonsexual bodies, and so become monstrous. Bodily functions that are staples in the horror genre such as menstruation, promiscuity, and puberty are not only represented but prominently featured in her work. The corporeality of Okazaki's characters renders them transgressive beings who resist conforming to feminine roles idealized in patriarchal society. Their bodies are marked by excess.

Similar to the expansion and consolidation of young women's roles as sexual objects, women's bodies as a site for reproduction was further reinforced when the Japanese birthrate hit an all-time low in 1989. Dubbed the "1.57 shock" after the total fertility rate calculated for that year, this decrease in women bearing children threatened Japan's myth of motherhood, which is intimately tied to conceptualizations of the nation. The Meiji-era government (1868–1912) had promoted the importance of women's role as mother, installing the slogan "good wife, wise mother" (*ryōsai kenbo*). The concept was based on a sexual egalitarianism that promoted the importance of women as educators and installed a modern form of nationalism in which women contributed to the state through their role as mother (Niwa and Yoda 1993, 75). The significance of motherhood increased as women's centrality in the domestic sphere was recognized during the Second World War, with the deployment of men overseas. Motherhood was further idealized and institutionalized with the professionalization of the housewife in the postwar period to support men's labor in the effort to sustain high economic growth. It was widely understood that women's role in the domestic sphere as mothers was intimately tied to the national interest and growth.

The 1.57 shock aroused strong anxieties about the future of the nation, which was simultaneously facing the consequences of an aging population. Miho Ogino notes that during this period "Japanese women found themselves bombarded by both open and hidden calls to have more children for the future of Japan," and political and economic leaders criticized women who would not bear children for their "selfishness" (Ogino 1994, 89). The discourse on the future of the nation mobilized women's bodies for the purpose of reproduction, and sex was increasingly more intimately connected to childbearing. At this junction, Okazaki drew female characters whose bodies and sexualities did not exist solely for the sake of reproduction, constantly transgressing rigidly defined women's roles. For example, Yumi in *Pink* maintains both a stable heterosexual romance and her job as a call girl. Meanwhile, Yumi's lover continues his sexual and financially dependent relation with Yumi's stepmother, his two-timing known by Yumi but not her stepmother. The frank depictions of women infringing prescribed female roles exposes the fallacy and hypocrisy of patriarchal and nationalistic paranoia generated by the 1.57 shock.

The Disrupted Monstrous-Feminine

In Okazaki's comics, women's bodies are not only commodified under the guise of self-expression—the young female adolescents caught in the state of nonreproductivity also embody an association with monstrosity, or feminine horror. Their unmarried status is rendered uncomfortable and unbearable not only to themselves but to their society. Such a portrayal resonates well with the representation of women in horror films in both Western and Japanese contexts. A female ghost story makes its appearance in *River's Edge*, in which two fishing teenage boys gossip about an urban legend in which a woman was violently murdered and turned into a *yurei* who wears heavy makeup, waiting to devour male virgins. Like the monstrous-feminine, Japanese women's sexual obsession is presented as an enduring threat to men and can only exist in supernatural form. Later in the narrative, Yamada's girlfriend, Tajima, kills herself through self-incineration and is turned into another *yurei* legend, quickly spread to scare male schoolmates. However, Tajima's death does not affect Yamada in the same way as other male students. The closeted Yamada resented Tajima's affection when she was alive, but their relationship changes after she dies. As both of them are equally ostracized, Yamada finds serenity in her death. He comments to the protagonist Haruna: "I saw Yamada's *yurei*. Compared to the living Tajima, I prefer the Tajima who is now burned to a crisp" (Okazaki 2000, 227). In *Helter Skelter*, Liliko's mystical disappearance also turns her into a ghost/monster, worshipped in awe by female teenagers but intimidating to men (Okazaki 2003, 307). Women who reject normative expectations can exist on the supernatural continuum, and that existence continues to threaten heterosexual men and serve as a moral admonition that enacts women's self-regulation.

Helter Skelter demonstrates a stronger and more direct interconnection than *River's Edge* with feminine horror, both literally and symbolically. To an extent, *Helter Skelter* is a psychological horror that teases out two levels of tension, a sociological one and a generational one. The story touches upon social instability built upon fame, materialism, and consumerism. On the other hand, *Helter Skelter* sheds light on mother-daughter issues; Liliko has become a puppet controlled by her agent, whom she refers to as her "mother." Liliko becomes obsessed with youth and appearance, which is ultimately a service for the patriarchal gaze in the guise of self-expression. On several occasions, Liliko is addressed as the embodiment of a monster. Physically speaking, Liliko's post-op facial expressions are perceived by others as flat, replicative of popular female icons in the media. She is referred to as "that gorgeous monster," beautiful yet dangerous (Okazaki 2003, 122). In addition, Okazaki makes a self-reflexive comment through two police officers investigating a surgical clinic frequented by Liliko for its violation of pharmaceutical laws. Recognizing how Liliko's stardom is built upon numerous rounds of touch-ups, they state sarcastically that "[s]tars are perpetually fascinating because stars are a type of deformity, like cancer" (119). The correlation between stardom, beauty, and monstrosity pins down Liliko's role as menacing, pitiful, and undesirable. Liliko's and her agent's fear of a degenerating body represents the pervasiveness of the subordination of women to a normative body image limited to youth, reproduction, and appearance. The obsessive pursuit of self-maintenance reflects the internalization of normalized beauty but also transforms women into monstrous and ludicrous beings. Jane Ussher states that "women subject their bodies to punishing regimes of diet and exercise to maintain the illusion that they can contain and control outward signs of feminine excess" (2006, 6). What drives Liliko's fame and wealth hinges on perfectly maintained facial and bodily features. After Liliko's secret is revealed, her reputation plummets, and her existence becomes a joke as well as a threat that needs to be immediately extinguished from the public discourse. Liliko thus represents a literal connection to the feminine horror, and both the plot development and characterization work to reinforce her presence as a threatening and objectionable entity that needs to be destroyed.

In the case of *River's Edge*, the link between the female characters and the monstrous-feminine takes another turn. Monstrosity has become a form of accessory that is irresistible to urban adolescent individuals. The female protagonist, Haruna, is a relatively normal, average high school student who has a boyfriend just for the sake of it. Her life does not seem as hectic as that of her peers. However, her monstrosity is accentuated by her close connection to a closeted gay man and his fetish treasure, a corpse, and a bulimic classmate who is also a TV celebrity. By grouping together with marginalized characters—a gay man and a girl with an eating disorder—Haruna becomes the center that channels between unwanted societal tumors. Besides Haruna, Okazaki extends the expression of monstrosity to other, secondary characters, including Haruna's girlfriend's socially reclusive sister, who ends up murdering her own sister for her oblivious behavior. Monstrosity in teenage women works as a signifier of unruly femininity that is abnormal and problematic and should be contained.

In *Pink*, the intimacy between the monstrous crocodile and the young female protagonist teases out the possible bonding between femininity and monstrosity. It manifests not only in the female protagonist's lifestyle, which can be characterized as sexually active and purposeless, but also in the alligator's insatiable appetite for meat. This monstrous appetite reflects upon how capitalism has turned women with disposable incomes into consumers and desiring subjects. However, the limited social roles available to women restrict the ways in which this desire and agency can be manifested. Their subjectivities can only be expressed through consumption, turning them into unproductive civilians. This lack of productivity is discouraged by the Japanese state.

From the delineation of a symbolic alligator, marginalized groups, and a fake body, all three comics shed light on the uneasy relations between female adolescents and monstrosity. Nonetheless, a nuanced reading enables us to see how these marginalized female adolescents resist and successfully disrupt a reproductive future that is sustained by nationalism and patriarchy. The female characters in Okazaki's comics embody the monstrous-feminine through their ample sexual appetite and immorality, which are deemed outside the norm of proper femininity. The characters are thus incapable and incompatible with adulthood and a reproductive future. This incapability and incompatibility, masquerading as personal choices under the neoliberal agenda, are a result of capitalist and sexist commodification and objectification of young women's bodies. In her analysis of the social regulation of the reproductive body, Ussher illustrates how

> women who fail in this [natural reproduction], who fail to perform femininity within the tight boundaries within which it is prescribed at each stage of the reproductive life cycle, are at risk of being positioned as mad or bad, and subjected to discipline or punishment, which masquerades as treatment or rehabilitation to disguise its regulatory intent. (2006, 4)

The coercive social pressures that aim to reinforce acceptable and appropriate models of femininity are reflected in the characters' physical and mental vulnerability, rendering the monstrous essence as products of the unreasonable social expectations and control upon female adolescent bodies. The adolescents in Okazaki's comics struggle to meet the standards of feminine ideals; the only means for them to survive is to flip out, bawl, regurgitate, and have meaningless sex, and by doing so unravel the absurdity and hypocrisy of a consumer-driven culture. Many of the characters in the three comics are presented with an intrinsic, animalistic desire to destroy social expectations and the facade of adulthood by embracing and exposing their bodily functions and their raw emotions. For example, Keiko, who is Yumi's stepsister, bluntly comments on how grownups are horny, dishonest, and damn complicated but does not look away when Yumi makes out with her boyfriend or when she feeds her neighbor's dog to the pet crocodile.

Empty subjectivity is symptomatic of late capitalist Japan, which scholar Yumiko Iida writes is governed by commodified identities. Iida writes that by transforming themselves into "nameless anonymities wrapped in fashionable goods and decked out with trendy hairstyles and accessories, individuals are 'different' enough from one another to communicate the subtleties of their sameness-in-difference while simultaneously affirming their collective identity" (2002, 174). Yet, this play of identity-through-consumption that in turn creates homogeneity is what is precisely rejected in Okazaki's comics, especially in the characters' fetishizing of noncommodified objects. In *River's Edge*, the protagonists' most valued object is an unclaimed dead body by the river, which the bulimic celebrity claims to be important to her, as it proves that people "acting glamorous, adorning themselves, and acting fun" is all meaningless (Okazaki 2000, 109). Both the dead body in *River's Edge* and the crocodile in *Pink* signify a way out of this homogeneous commodification of identity, a secret crutch for the characters to maintain a sense of self through contact with unknowable others that resist commodification. These fetishized objects represent a fantasy of escape from late capitalist Japan buried within commodified signs. However, the utopian dream of an escape from commodified identities is ultimately futile, exemplified by the alligator in *Pink* murdered and transmuted into a high-end alligator suitcase by the protagonist's evil yet sympathetic stepmother. Okazaki's monsters are not frightening but embody the fantasy of escape from the commodification of women's bodies. This is why Okazaki's works endow such beauty and sense of intimacy to the dead body, the crocodile, and the one-eyed Liliko. These beings remind us of a fantastical and potential escape from the cycle of consuming and being consumed, even if it entails losing life or agency, or being exiled.

Conclusion

Okazaki's explorations of young women's sexuality were relevant in 1990s Japan, when changing gender roles, a low birthrate, and the proliferation of diverse consumerist identities situated young women's bodies in an ambivalent position in which they were sexualized, commodified, and co-opted for social and biological reproduction. The social and economic context regulates and channels desire, either toward fashioning homogeneous identities through consumption or encouraging reproduction for the sake of the future of the nation. The bulimic teen celebrity in *River's Edge* and *Helter Skelter* throws up all of what she eats. Liliko goes through numerous dangerous surgeries. Both go to great lengths to keep their desirable, commodified bodies. When they try to achieve self-realization and align with social ideals, they harm themselves. This self-harm serves patriarchal and capitalist interests. Okazaki's meditation on these acts of self-harm, bodily discharge, and abject bodies functions as a critique of this economy of desire and self-realization. Okazaki stated in a published conversation with Keiji Uejima, a scholar in the anthropology of religion, "Sex world=dystopia=dislike" and "Non-sex world=nice," expressing her skepticism toward uninhibited desire and sexual liberation (Hayami 2000, 66–71). The production and reproduction of desire are not antithetical to the fragmented subjectivity of late capitalist Japan, but they are essential components that regulate women's bodies and mannerisms. Okazaki's characters become monsters only through their acts that seek a temporary release from this economy of desire by meditating on social and bodily abjections. A release from the economy of desire remains unattainably distant, embodied by the sudden appearance of Liliko in Mexico in *Helter Skelter*, the haunted space of the dead in *River's Edge*, and Yumi's imaginary tropical island in *Pink*. *Pink* is viewed as the most cynical depiction of this unattainable utopia, where Yumi waits for her dead lover to appear while sitting next to her suitcase made from the hide of her pet alligator. The alligator, once Yumi's sign of defiance against social norms, has been transformed into a luxury travel item. Yumi holds this dead signifier of defiance while anticipating a departure from the "sex world=dystopia" of Japan that will never occur. Yumi's symbol of her monstrous femininity and unruly, sexualized body is domesticated and converted to a lifeless commodity.

Okazaki undoubtedly puts forward important female roles in her comics, yet we recognize that the portrayals of feminine horror observed in many female characters reinforce the nexus between monstrosity and women's sexuality. Nonetheless, Okazaki's works allow us to interrogate the capitalist construction of femininity and reproduction in 1990s Japan, and the fear of this wildly arrested adolescence becomes a potential site to disrupt the idealized progression toward adulthood and parenthood. Love and capitalism, notwithstanding the dangerous and monstrous elements in both, become young, independent women's bold yet futile means of seeking new identities.

Bibliography

Chalmers, Sharon. 2002. *Emerging Lesbian Voices from Japan*. London: RoutledgeCurzon.
Creed, Barbara. 2002. "Horror and the Monstrous-Feminine: An Imaginary Abjection." In *Horror, The Film Reader*, edited by Mark Jancovich, 67–76. London: Routledge.
Hayami, Yukiko. 2000. "Mangaka Okazaki Kyoko." *Aera* (October 30): 66–71.
Iida, Yumiko. 2002. *Rethinking Identity in Modern Japan: Nationalism as Aesthetics*. London: Routledge.
Ito, Kinko. 2008. "Manga in Japanese History." In *Japanese Visual Culture: Explorations in the World of Manga and Anime*, edited by Mark W. MacWilliams. Armonk, NY: M. E. Sharpe.
Ito, Kinko. 2011. "Chikae Ide, The Queen of Japanese Ladies' Comics: Her Life and Manga." In *Mangatopia: Essays on Manga and Anime in the Modern World*, edited by Timothy Perper and Martha Cornog. Santa Barbara, CA: Libraries Unlimited.
Karatsu, Rie. 2016. "Female Voice and Occidentalism in Mika Ninagawa's *Helter Skelter* (2012): Adapting Kyoko Okazaki to the Screen." *Journal of Popular Culture* 49, no. 5: 967–83.

Leheny, David Richard. 2006. *Think Global, Fear Local: Sex, Violence, and Anxiety in Contemporary Japan*. Ithaca, NY: Cornell University Press.
Niwa, Akiko, and Tomiko Yoda. 1993. "The Formation of the Myth of Motherhood in Japan." *U.S.-Japan Women's Journal*, English Supplement, no. 4: 70–82.
Ogino, Miho. 1994. "Abortion and Women's Reproductive Rights: The State of Japanese Women, 1945–1991." In *Women of Japan and Korea: Continuity and Change*, edited by Joyce Gelb and Marian Lief Palley, 69–94. Philadelphia: Temple University Press.
Okazaki, Kyoko. 2000. *River's Edge*. Tokyo: Takarajimasha.
Okazaki, Kyoko. 2003. *Helter Skelter*. Tokyo: Shodensha.
Okazaki, Kyoko. 2010. *Pink*. Tokyo: Magazine House.
Richards, Andy. 2010. *Asian Horror*. Harpenden, Herts, England: Kamera Books.
Shamoon, Deborah Michelle. 2012. *Passionate Friendship: The Aesthetics of Girls' Culture in Japan*. Honolulu: University of Hawai'i Press.
Ueno, Chizuko. 2003. "Self-Determination on Sexuality? Commercialization of Sex among Teenage Girls in Japan." *Inter-Asia Cultural Studies* 4, no. 2: 317–24.
Ussher, Jane M. 2006. *Managing the Monstrous Feminine: Regulating the Reproductive Body*. London: Routledge.

12

Chinese Snake Woman Resurfaces in Comics: Considering the Case Study of *Calabash Brothers*

Jing Zhang

For some two thousand years, snake women, both good and bad, have appeared in Chinese folklore stories and fairy tales. Folklore stories in China have reflected cultural, historical, and social conditions, often showing the cruel hardships and vicissitudes of the common people. Especially in ancient China, due to the central government's authority, folklore stories could be the only way for common citizens to express and record their experiences and project their wishes. "They illuminate the Chinese social order through the structured relationships that defined it: emperor and subject, father and son, husband and wife (or wives), official and peasant, human and beast" (Roberts 1979, xv). In modern times, snake women have appeared in operas, films, and television. A cartoon version of the evil snake woman has also become a leading protagonist in the popular Chinese animated TV series *Calabash Brothers* (*Hulu Xiongdi* in the Chinese phonetic romanization system for Mandarin in use since 1958), produced by Shanghai Animation Film Studio in 1986. In adjacent episodes, one or two brothers are born from ripened calabash gourds with various powers and vulnerabilities; eventually, through their sacrifices, Snake Woman is defeated. Today, a new comic book, movie, and TV series have been adapted from the original story, showing its ongoing relevance to modern Chinese culture. Online discussions of these interpretations reveal misunderstandings about the story that make a thorough art historical analysis of this story timely.

This chapter covers several representative snake women in Chinese popular folklore and fairy tale history. It looks at what makes them both repugnant and appealing with their sleek power, manipulative qualities, and dangerous intellect. The chapter analyzes how snake woman stories are embedded within and can explain the significance of this "monster" in Chinese culture. A retelling of the story of *Calabash Brothers* with explanations and analyses of the production aspects of the animation and comics—character design, setting design, imagery technical solutions, and frame compositions—all help locate this particular Snake Woman within a larger narrative.

The Definitions of Monster in Chinese Culture

Monster (*yaoguai*) in Chinese culture has a different meaning from ghost, spook, giant, undead, devil, demon, fiend, evil spirit, elf, goblin, bogy, or fairy in English. *The Commentary of Zuo* (*Zuo Zhuan*), an ancient Chinese narrative history published around the late fourth century BCE, defined monsters as abnormal things on earth (Liu, Xiaofeng 2017). "Monster" was then interpreted as the general term for weird appearance, suggestive language in songs and poems, or the strange shape of plants and trees, in *Explaining Graphs and Analyzing Characters* (*Shuowen Jiezi*), an early second-century CE Chinese dictionary from the Han Dynasty (Pianzhu 2016). These could be the definitions for monster in a general sense. Conversely, in a more specific sense, both *On Numerous* (ca. 80 CE; *Lunheng*) and *Book of the Master Who Embraces Simplicity* (ca. 317 CE; *Baopuzi*) claim that everything that lasts beyond its normal age limit, that shape-shifts into a human figure, or that confuses and deludes common people's minds is a monster (Pianzhu 2018). Chinese monsterology is often categorized as a subculture under Chinese mythology, associated with chorography, totemism, and object worship as well as art creation in folk custom, local beliefs, and the reproduction of historical memories.

The Origin and Development of Snake Culture in China

From snake images of ancient times to Sino-Western snake image comparisons, from literary records to unearthed relics, there has been much research on snake beliefs. In Buddhist legend, a multiheaded snake-and-dragon king covered Buddha during a storm for seven continuous days while he was under a bodhi tree. Nüwa, a snake goddess, is one of the representative snake women of Chinese mythology of the late Paleolithic period. She renewed the sky, set up the four sky pillars, and stopped a flood in remote antiquity, as recorded by An Liu's *Huainanzi* (ca. 139 BCE) (Yang and An 2008, 10–11). Her snake-like figure can be seen in book illustrations, murals, and sculptural works. She also created men and women from the mud left over after she renewed the sky. Nüwa is therefore admired as an ancestor of the whole Chinese nation. In primitive society, it was hard for human beings to avoid snake attacks. This ever-present danger cloaked snakes in suspense and mystery. Also, snakes could boast strong reproductive capacity. Articles like "The Fairy Tales of Fuxi[1] and Nüwa and Ancient China's Worship of Snakes" (Fan, Lizhou 2002, 455–58) and "Textual Research on the Totem of the Southern Snake, Ancient Snake, and Dragon" (Yang, Qing 1992, 9–15) analyze and integrate images of both snakes and dragons, maintaining that dragon images were inspired by snakes. Because it was associated with the dragon, the snake remained associated with divinity. Both Huili Fan's "The Image of the Snake in *Classic of Mountains and Seas*" (2013)[2] and Ruijuan Lu's "Exploration of 'the Snake Phenomena' in *Classic of Mountains and Seas*" (2010) state that nine out of fifty-eight totem worships are snake totems in the subject book series. And among the 454 human characters, 138 are related to snake images as well (Wang 2010, 47).[3]

Ke Mo's "Snake Culture in China" (1993, 17–18), Xiaoyan Liu's "On the Origin of the Snake Totem" (1990, 118–19), and Lihua Chen's "Brief on the Worship of the Snake Totem" (2003, 36–38) discuss the fundamental features of snake belief in China in general terms. Developing through the Qin and Han Dynasties (221 BCE–220 CE), dragon belief came to represent government power and the emperor. Taoism was the major local religion before Buddhism was introduced to China. As Buddhism spread through China during the Wei, Jin, Northern, and Southern Dynasties (220–581), snake beliefs continued to diverge from the worship of dragons (Zhang, Chunfang 2016, 20). With gradual acquisition of knowledge about productive forces, people became more knowledgeable about snakes. As a cold-blooded, ecdysial, footless creature with no vocal cords, snakes also came to represent unpredictability, coldness, evil, cruelty, cunning, and even wisdom. Snake images were associated with the monstrous and supernatural.

During Sui and Tang Dynasties (581–907), administrative regions of various sizes called "countries" coexisted with the central government. There was expanded communication between these regions; people had more chances to exchange ideas and beliefs. Snake belief grew in popularity in folk belief systems. As men became the center of society, the snake's negative characteristics were associated with women. Stories about snake men are very rare. The negative association of dangerous snakes and women was connected to the blossoming of the prostitution industry, which has a reputation in China for figuratively "poisoning" men. No matter their occupation, women are often associated with snakes in folk wisdom.

A snake spirit woman features in one episode of the Chinese novel *Journey to the West* (*Xiyouji*). The novel is based on events during the Tang Dynasty (618–907) even though it was not published until the sixteenth century, during the Ming Dynasty (1368–1644); it is attributed to Cheng'en Wu (ca. 1500–1582). As one of China's longest-lasting and most widely disseminated works of literature, the novel has been adapted in the form of picture books, TV series, video games, and manga series produced in mainland China, Hong Kong, Korea, Japan, the United States, and Australia.

In the story, in their journey to obtain the Buddhist sutras, Tang Tripitaka Master and his three disciples (the Monkey King, the Pig of Eight Prohibitions, and Friar Sand) help local inhabitants they encounter by defeating various monsters and demons who try to obtain immortality by eating the Master's flesh. A snake spirit woman is among them. This red-colored snake woman maintains her young appearance by frequently drinking the blood and eating the flesh of human beings. She disguises herself as a female human, speaks the local language, and is accomplished at lying. She approaches local people without raising their suspicions. She then kills some of them in secluded locations, becoming a nightmarish figure among nearby villagers. Tang Tripitaka Master's three disciples confront her in battle; she swallows the Monkey King but then dies when he ruptures her belly from inside out, using his golden magic cudgel. This particular snake woman is a monster for the community, and the hero of the story defeats her.

However, not all snakes are considered monstrous in Chinese culture; sometimes they have medicinal or religious significance. Zhenyue Zhang (2009, 38–39, 52) discusses the divinity of snakes in community conversations and their applications as folk characters. In Chinese culture, the snake's symbolic significance incorporates luck and sacrosanctity, productivity, long life, the ability to control water and wealth, and more. Due to a snake's ability to recognize different herbs, from time to time in various regions the Chinese folk medicine industry has also elevated the snake as a deity with powers of healing. *Record of the Listener* (*Yijianzhi*) is a collection of Song Dynasty mystery and supernatural tales, written by Mai Hong (1123–1202) during his later years and based on "stories of the strange" circulated in the oral tradition. Its rich content includes topics such as gods and ghosts, injustice and retribution, fantasy and the uncanny, and regional customs. Among its 420 chapters, there are eighty-one stories about snakes shape-shifting into other animals, humans, and snake spirits.

The number and size of snake temples in China tremendously increased during the Song Dynasty. In order to gain more believers and achieve mutual benefit, Buddhist monks and Taoist priests often built snake temples near their own temples. Some Buddhist principles were also incorporated into snake belief (Zhang, Chunfang 2016, 31, 97–98). And, when called upon, Buddhist monks and Taoist priests were quite capable of acting as snake exorcists and restrainers, using their own religious sutras, incantations, and magical talismans.

The other major symbolic significance of the snake is as an indicator of love and happiness. "The Legend of the White Snake," also known as "Lady White Snake," is a Chinese legend that existed in the oral tradition long before its earliest written compilation during the Ming Dynasty. The story has been reiterated in Chinese operas, stage musicals, modern dance, picture books, and numerous films and TV series in mainland China, Hong Kong, Taiwan, Japan, the United States, and Germany. The original story pitted good against evil, with the Buddhist monk Fahai setting out to save Xian Xu's soul from the white snake spirit, who was depicted as an evil demon. Over the centuries, the legend has evolved into a romance story, with Lady White Snake and Xian Xu being genuinely in love with each other even though their relationship is forbidden by both societal moral standards and Buddhist principles.

In Xian Xu's past life, he saved a small, white-colored snake's life, and centuries later that white snake became a spirit named Suzhen Bai, called Lady White Snake by the populace. In order to return Xian Xu's favor, she shape-shifts into a human form and offers a pure, faithful, and unconditional love to the poor scholar, helping him operate a medical clinic. Monk Fahai tries to separate them by exploiting Xian Xu's dithering and imprisoning him in the Gold Mountain Temple. Lady White Snake fights with Fahai to rescue her husband. She uses her powers to flood the temple, in the process drowning many innocent people. Fahai defeats Lady White Snake and captures her in his golden magic alms bowl, imprisoning her in the Leifeng Pagoda. Twenty years later, Mengjiao Xu, the son of the couple, earns first place in the imperial examinations and returns home in glory to visit his parents. At the same time, Lady White Snake's blood-oath sister goes to confront Fahai and defeats him. Lady White Snake is freed and reunited with her husband and son, while Fahai flees and hides inside the stomach of a crab. The early versions of this story spend more time describing Lady White Snake as a terrible creature causing mayhem. However, over the decades, especially after the establishment of the People's Republic of China in 1949, literary critics have widely expressed their opinion on the feudalist power represented by Monk Fahai, arousing readers' hatred toward Fahai and establishing the common preference to read this story as more about true love. Readers regularly praise the fact that a snake spirit knows how to return love when not every human does. The original monster here is sympathetic in later readings.

Snake Woman and the Calabash Brothers

In modern times, a cartoon version of the evil snake woman has become a leading antagonist in the animated TV series *Calabash Brothers*. *Calabash*

Brothers won the 1986–1987 outstanding film award of the (national) Radio, Film, and Television Bureau, awarded in 1988; the outstanding cartoon film award (the third Gold Cattle Award) for Chinese children's and youth films; the Little Red Flower Award; the third-class film award of the First Nationwide Film and TV Animation Show's Broadcast Exhibition in 1989; and the third-class award at the Cairo International Film Festival for Children in 1992 (Tong 2017, 12–13). This chapter's discussion is based on the comic series created by the Shanghai Animation Film Studio, published by Foreign Language Teaching and Research Press (Beijing) in 2014. The comics follow the plot of the original animation film, borrowing and integrating the dialogue and voice-over transcriptions;[4] the pages are organized in a screen-shot-like style that records all the key sequences along with the development of the storytelling of the original film. My analysis of the animated film also applies to the comic series. It is important to first understand the plot of the tale and identify the monstrous qualities of Snake Woman.

Legend has it that two demons were jailed in a cave in the Calabash Mountains, one a snake spirit and the other a scorpion spirit. One day, a pangolin happens to dig a tunnel into the slope, and the two spirits escape from the cave, causing grave harm to nearby residents. The pangolin hurries to an old man and tells him that only by growing calabashes in seven colors can they annihilate the spirits. The old man spares no time in growing seven calabashes. They ripen sequentially, falling off their stems to the ground and transforming into seven boys. Each has a unique superhuman ability as well as weaknesses and vulnerabilities. Snake Woman exploits the specific weaknesses of each brother.

Before the first calabash brother, Red Brother, is ripened, Snake Woman sends the snake, spider, and bat spirits to kidnap the old man, whom the calabash brothers call "grandpa." Red Brother has superstrength; he tries to rescue his grandpa from the spirits' cave, where he is being held. At the end of the mountain tunnel, Snake Woman accompanies him to see his grandpa, actually just a projected image of his grandpa that she had prepared. Red Brother does not notice this deception, running to approach what he believes to be his grandpa. He then falls into a mud pool and loses the ability to use his power. Snake Woman then seals his navel to lock down his power and ties him up in a huge web of a spider spirit (fig. 12.1).

Snake Woman leads the second calabash brother, Orange Brother, into a mirror maze and uses reflections to blind his eyes and almost deafen him, which successfully destroys his enhanced hearing and sight. Later, both Orange Brother and his grandpa escape from Snake Woman's cave; a squirrel, a frog, and some birds bring him dew to heal his eyes. Snake Woman figures out the

Figure 12.1: "Unexpected Encounter at Fairy Peak." *Calabash Brothers*, vol. 1, pp. 28–29, by Shanghai Animation Film Studio. Copyright 2014, Foreign Language Teaching and Research Press.

Achilles' heel of Yellow Brother, the third calabash brother's sword- and spear-proof body; she uses multiple snake-like twisted swords to limit his movement and tie him up. Before this, Yellow Brother fought with heroic determination. He first helps his grandpa and second elder brother to escape, then defeats Scorpion Man and chases him to his cave, but Snake Woman's grasses tangle him up.

In Chinese culture, women belong to yin in the yin-and-yang principles of Taoism, the negative, hidden, secret, sinister, and feminine side. Therefore, after witnessing the powers of Green Brother and Cyan Brother, Snake Woman knows immediately when they meet that she should not confront them directly. Instead, she persuades the brothers to sit down with her and Scorpion Man for dinner. She convinces the brothers that she intends to clear up their miscommunication and establish a genuine friendship. But in fact, Snake Woman uses her magic *ruyi*[5] to produce a bottle of "cold spring cool wine" to overcome Green Brother's ability to generate and control fire. She then joins Scorpion Man in laughing at Green Brother's capacity for liquor, to irritate Cyan Brother into accepting her "rapture wine" challenge, trying to dry up an endless wine fountain. She thereby defeats Cyan Brother's ability to create and control water at will, by getting him drunk.

Snake Woman begins her battle with the youngest brother, Purple Brother, before he is even born. He was first brought to the cave of Snake Woman and Scorpion Man when still inside his gourd on the stem. Snake woman fertilizes him with poison, which makes him believe that she and Scorpion Man are his parents. He is born with the ability to manipulate others' emotions and thoughts and is equipped with his own magic gourd. He is the most powerful of all the brothers, but he cannot resist Snake Woman's mental pollution. Purple Brother's betrayal becomes a turning point in the story. Even though the sixth calabash brother, Blue Brother, has the power of invisibility, which makes him the only calabash brother who has never been directly defeated by Snake Woman and her allies, he cannot trick Purple Brother.

In the final battle, the old man uses a magic seven-colored lotus plumule given to him by the mountain god to help all seven brothers reconnect. They capture Snake Woman and Scorpion Man in Purple Brother's magic gourd, throw the gourd into a canyon, then seal themselves into a seven-colored mountain that sits atop the gourd. Sealing her away at the sacrifice of their own freedom is the only way to ensure that she will not poison people further.

Similar to some plants and animals, the snake is also considered "toxic" in Chinese traditional medicine. There are five toxicities in Chinese custom—snake, scorpion, centipede, toad, and bat. People believe that any one of these five creatures can cause human infection and death when it is not countered by an intervention. But the release of Snake Woman and Scorpion Man indicates the rise of another spirit power, something different from traditional evil. Traditional evil is comparatively pure and desiring to simply destroy, but the evil of Snake Woman and Scorpion Man is more rational, more like a dark political organization that has precise structures and hierarchies of authority and management. At every order given by Snake Woman, the corresponding weapons—bee spirits, bat spirits, spider spirits, centipede spirits, and toad spirits—stand by immediately, ready to act. She patiently observes the weaknesses of her enemies, including their kindness, then undertakes focused attacks on those weaknesses, using lies, tricks, and armed forces. She achieves her goals step by step, planning far ahead but also responding promptly to unforeseen situations.

Snake Woman is both extremely rational and overly ambitious; when these two qualities are combined, a monster is born. The golden mean is a formula for wisdom in the Confucian school that advocates impartiality, reconciliation, and compromise in one's approach to people or circumstances. It guides people to pursue balance and harmony in life; otherwise, one may jeopardize one's human nature. One might become a monster under certain social systems and historical conditions. However, Snake Woman is more Machiavellian; it does not matter if people are her own kind or her enemy, they will all be treated as pieces on her chessboard. In the story, nearly all the commands and decisions are made by Snake Woman. Scorpion Man, titled "the King," has the right only to supervise work, not to command; Snake Woman's interests always come first. Her precise schemes, thorough observation, and frightening execution make her the most dangerous evil spirit. Her endless capacity for betraying and using others shows her sneaky and devious nature.

In her tough battles with the calabash brothers, Snake Woman gains the upper hand most of the time. She is always capable of exploiting the specific weakness of each brother in the first moment of encounter, which is reminiscent of intelligent battles based on strategy more than raw courage, as in the Japanese manga series *JoJo's Bizarre Adventure* (Araki 1987–) or *Hunter × Hunter* (Togashi 1998–). When needed, Snake Woman also uses political charm to beat down her enemy. She could be in a violent rage in one moment, then turn on a radiant and pleasant smile in the next. There are people who make others cry, and then there are those who cause others to bleed; Snake Woman definitely belongs to the latter category. She inflicts thorough harm and damage on her enemies. She is also the gloomy nightmare present in all the brothers' minds; therefore the *otaku* (people with obsessive interests, in this context anime and manga fandom) see Snake Woman as a female version of Paul von Oberstein in the Japanese series of science fiction novels *Legend of the Galactic Heroes* (Michihara 1986–2000). She is such a flawless character that the creation team made a clone sister in the sequel *Little Calabash Warriors* (Shanghai Animation Film Studio 1991, "Hulu Xiaojingang"). Her popularity outlives even the character herself.

Snake Woman changes to fit expectations. When Scorpion Man calls her "queen," Snake Woman presents her feminine self. When the youngest calabash boy calls her "mom," she presents her maternal self. When she uses her magic *ruyi* to conquer her enemies, she presents her strategist self. Femininity and maternity could be components of her strategies; her ruthless obsession molds her into a strong figure, but also causes her to lose her life.

In the 1980s, the series was one of the most popular animated shows in China. While it has been praised as highly as the celebrated Chinese animated feature film *Havoc in Heaven* (1965), domestically, it was released during a time when the Chinese animation industry was at a relatively low point compared to animated films being produced elsewhere in the world. The episodes were produced with a vast amount of paper-cut stop-motion animations, directed by Jinqing Hu, Keqin Zhou, and Guiyun Ge.

The creation team borrowed ideas from both Chinese opera and traditional New Year's paintings for their character design. People recognized Chinese opera costume styles in the character design for both Snake Woman and Scorpion Man, as well as the bright and sharp colors used for the seven calabash brothers. The creation team kept Snake Woman's hairstyle, makeup

Figure 12.2: Human figure paper puppet. "The Art of Paper-Cut Animation of the 'Chinese School,'" by Huwan Tong. Copyright 2017, Xi'an Polytechnic University.

style, jewelry style, skin tone, face shape and facial features, hand gestures, and body language loyal to the characteristics of Chinese opera as well. Director Hu took references from the look of Sudhana Kumārachose, one of the disciples of Avalokiteśvara, as well as a subject of Chinese New Year's paintings for his character design of the seven calabash brothers (Baidu, n.d.). He kept a country-boy design to show their wild nature. Each calabash brother combs his hair up and wears a hairpin version of his corresponding calabash and two green leaves. There are echoes of green leaf decorations on their necks and waists; each looks keen witted and capable.

The character movements take their references from traditional shadow play and puppetry. In order to save money, the production team created separate body joints for each character. For the human figures of the calabash brothers, there are joints in the neck, shoulders, arms, wrists, legs, knees, and ankles (fig. 12.2). Snake Woman's joints are arranged at the neck, shoulders, arms, wrists, waist, and tail. The production team then created different sets of body parts for different motion actions, especially for the fighting actions. The background setting applied many solutions borrowed from traditional Chinese painting and engraving. The production team used not only the contrast from bright and dark colors in the same scene to create environmental depth, but also bright light sources to enhance the vivid atmosphere. They placed every single action on the corresponding background and photographed them frame by frame. The thirteen episodes of the animated series contain thousands of scenes, and it took the production team more than two years to produce. All this hard work made *Calabash Brothers* a classic Chinese animation film and comic series. These design choices show that the team echoed a traditional Chinese cultural aesthetic; the philosophy that follows is similarly traditional.

Snake Woman as a Monstrous Woman, and Misunderstandings of Her Symbolism

Snake Woman is a transgressive female figure from Chinese culture and history who emerges from the long-standing tradition of snake culture and belief in China. She has a dubious moral standing when contrasted with that of the calabash brothers, in both the animation and its comic book adaptation. Her monstrous qualities are revived as the proper counterpart to the brothers' superhuman feats. As Shiwen Sun agrees, the core significance of snake culture reflects Buddhism's, Taoism's, and Confucianism's deep influence and proverbial currency in Chinese literature, opera, folklore, and folktales.[6]

The Monkey King in *Journey to the West*, Monk Fahai in "The Legend of the White Snake," and Purple Brother in *Calabash Brothers*, as snake women's restrainers, all recited religious sutras or incantations while deploying their magic talismans—a golden magic cudgel, a golden magic alms bowl, and a magic gourd, respectively. Reciting incantations and controlling magic talismans are the daily practice of Taoist priests (Xu 2015, 68). Each of the calabash brothers has certain superhuman abilities; they appeared one by one, each displaying one of the Monkey King's powers. These stories all involve a traditional religious or magical key used to defeat Snake Woman.

Snake Woman continues to be relevant in online internet discussions. New interpretations of *Calabash Brothers* have appeared regularly on Chinese threaded discussion forums, such as during 2015–2016 on websites like zhihu.com and baidu.com. These online communities discuss the show and its symbolism at length. The posts are not always serious analysis; one drew an analogy between seven calabash brothers and seven weekdays, but the post's author also admitted that they were just kidding. Some posts make particular assumptions about human nature and women. One tried to use character-color theory to analyze the seven calabash brothers as the seven characteristics of a "normal" human being. Here, Snake Woman and her allies were seen as the dark side of humankind. Whoever the discussion groups' authors are, their posts do not support the *Calabash Brothers* creators' original intent. Their logic does not hold up, since it does not address many representative characteristics of human beings—the brothers and Snake Woman alone do not adequately represent human nature.

Several of the online discussions came to the general conclusion that the seven calabash brothers, in seven colors of the rainbow, represent seven different individual characteristics; any single one cannot make up a complete personality, but all seven must be joined together. For example, Purple Brother's color is much closer to black than any of the other six colors—a color symbolizing gloomy, speculative thinking, according to traditional sources. Although Snake Woman is the one who pushed him to become a turncoat, and it was her pollution that enlarged the dark side of his heart, Purple Brother can also expect a dark outcome for himself. One discussion group contributor concluded that overemphasizing any specific characteristic in a personality may eventually create a paranoid streak in that personality and provide a chance for the darkness, represented by Snake Woman and her allies, to destroy the inner self and create a psychological tragedy.

These discussion group posts do not demonstrate an awareness of the full story of Snake Woman or the calabash brothers. The original *Calabash Brothers* series was adapted from a novel about ten brothers, not seven rainbow-colored brothers (Wen and Zhai 2010, D03). Furthermore, considering the character-color theories discussed above, some associations made between a calabash brother's color and his character are not accurate and may even be contradictory. The culture behind Snake Woman and Chinese snake culture is deeply influenced by Buddhism's, Taoism's, and Confucianism's proverbial currency. In order to fully engage the characteristics of Snake Woman and the other legendary figures in *Calabash Brothers*, interpreters need to pay close attention to the forces behind them. Snake Woman is not a simple force of monstrous evil; she is a complex character with roots in traditional Chinese folklore and medicine, and a more sympathetic interpretation is possible.

Notes

1. Fuxi is an ancient Chinese god (ca. 2,600 BCE) who is said to have shown the ancient Chinese people how to hunt, cook, domesticate animals, and other tasks.

2. *Classic of Mountains and Seas* is a Chinese classic text, a compilation of Chinese mythology and mythic geography. It was written between the middle of the Warring States period (475–221 BCE) and the early Han Dynasty (206 BCE–220 CE) and is divided into eighteen sections, describing more than 550 mountains and 300 channels.

3. The translations of Chinese texts are by the author unless otherwise mentioned.

4. In the comics version of *Calabash Brothers*, phonetic transcriptions of the romanization system for Mandarin are provided along with the Chinese characters, in order to better serve young readers still in the process of learning Chinese characters.

5. A *ruyi* is a piece of an ornamental scepter, a kind of amulet. Its shape is streamlined, and its handle is a little bent.

6. Shiwen Sun is retired from School of Chinese Language and Literature, College of Humanities and Sciences, of Northeast Normal University, and his academic research mainly focuses on Chinese folklore. This chapter's author interviewed him three times on animal culturology in late May 2018.

Bibliography

Araki, Hirohiko. 1987–. *JoJo's Bizarre Adventure*. Weekly *Shōnen Jump*, 1987–2004; *Ultra Jump*, 2005–.
Baidu. n.d. "Jinqing Hu." Available at https://baike.baidu.com/item/%E8%83%A1%E8%BF%9B %E5%BA%86.
Chen, Lihua. 2003. "Brief on the Worship of the Snake Totem." *Journal of Nanping Normal College*, no. 3: 36–38.
Fan, Huili. 2013 "The Image of the Snake in *Classic of Mountains and Seas*." MPhil diss., Yunnan University.
Fan, Lizhou. 2002. "The Fairy Tales of Fuxi and Nüwa and Ancient China's Worship of Snakes." *Journal of Yantai University*, Philosophy and Social Science edition, no. 4: 455–58.
Liu, Xiaofeng. 2017. "Monsterology Study." China Folklore Network. Available at http://www .chinesefolklore.org.cn/web/index.php?NewsID=15732.
Liu, Xiaoyan. 1990. "On the Origin of the Snake Totem." *Jiangxi Social Sciences*, no. 4: 118–19.
Lu, Ruijuan. 2010. "Exploration of 'the Snake Phenomena' in *Classic of Mountains and Seas*." MPhil diss., Chongqing University.
Michihara, Katsumi. 1986–2000. *Legend of the Galactic Heroes. Chara*, 1986; *Shōnen Captain*, 1986–2000.
Mo, Ke. 1993. "Snake Culture in China." *Journal of the Snake*, no. 4: 17–18.
Pianzhu, [Zaixia]. 2016. "Chinese Monsterology: It's Time to Talk about Monsterology." Available at https://culture.china.com/history/records/11170645/20161114/30037258_all.html.
Pianzhu, Zaixia. 2018. "Chinese Monsterology, Lecture One: What Is Monster? (The First)." Available at https://kknews.cc/zh-my/culture/aaxjm9v.html.
Roberts, Moss, ed. 1979. *Chinese Fairy Tales and Fantasies*. New York: Pantheon.
Shanghai Animation Film Studio. 1991. *Little Calabash Warriors*. Directed by Guiyun Ge. Beijing: China Central Television.
Shanghai Animation Film Studio. 2014. *Calabash Brothers*. Beijing: Foreign Language Teaching and Research Press.
Togashi, Yoshihiro. 1998–. *Hunter × Hunter*. *Weekly Shōnen Jump*.
Tong, Huwan. 2017. "The Art of Paper-Cut Animation of the 'China School.'" MPhil diss., Xi'an Polytechnic University.
Wang, Linmei. 2010. "Comparison of the Sino-Western Cultural Meaning of 'Snake.'" *College English*, no. 1: 47.
Wen, Bianhui, and Lu Zhai. 2010. "Who Is the Calabash Brothers' Natural Father?" *Democracy and Legislation Times*, June 14, D03.
Xu, Yangyang. 2015. "Cultural Implications of the *Calabash Brothers* Creation: A Calabash Mythological Perspective." *Journal of Jingchu University of Technology* 30, no. 5: 68.
Yang, Lihui, and Deming An. 2008. *Handbook of Chinese Mythology*. New York: Oxford University Press.

Yang, Qing. 1992. "Textual Research on the Totem of the Southern Snake, Ancient Snake, and Dragon." *Journal of Yiyang Normal College*, no. 1: 9–15.

Zhang, Chunfang. 2016. "Study on Snakes and Snake Belief in the Literacy Sketches of the Song Dynasty." MPhil diss., Hebei University.

Zhang, Zhenyue. 2009. "An Interpretation of the Auspicious Connotation of 'Snake' Culture in China." *Progress in Textile Science and Technology*, no. 3: 38–39, 52.

Part 5

Taking On the Role of Monster

13

Monochromatic Teats, Teeth, and Tentacles: Monstrous Visual Rhetoric in Stephen L. Stern and Christopher Steininger's *Beowulf: The Graphic Novel*

Justin Wigard

Beowulf is an Old English epic that has proven popular enough to be preserved for centuries, retold in various forms and formats, all due in no small part to its monstrous triumvirate: Grendel, Grendel's mother, and the dragon. While there is a sizeable number of illustrated versions within children's literature, only a small number of comic adaptations of *Beowulf* have been published. Beginning in 1975 with *Beowulf: Dragon Slayer* by Michael Uslan and Ricardo Villamonte, the Old English poem has been adapted to the comics medium infrequently, finding particular purchase in the 2000s by such authors and artists as Gareth Hinds, Santiago García, and David Rubin, and even a comic version of Neil Gaiman and Roger Avary's film adaptation. These adaptations must necessarily depict each of the three monsters on the comics page, and of particular import to *Beowulf* is the depiction of Grendel's mother. As an adaptation of Francis Barton Gummere's 1910 translation of *Beowulf*, writer Stephen L. Stern and artist Christopher Steininger's *Beowulf: The Graphic Novel* stands out as an attempt "to remain as faithful to the original as the graphic novel form allows," particularly as an adaptation of a translation published some ninety-three years prior (Stern and Steininger 2007, 4). Although each of the monsters, and even Beowulf himself, warrants their own analysis in other avenues, the visual depiction of Grendel's mother bears particular critical attention because of Stern and Steininger's adaptive changes. In this adaptation, Grendel's mother is visually characterized by four phallic tentacles where each arm should be; a similarly phallic and extended tongue; an enlarged bust devoid of any further details other than size; and a letter *M* between her legs that draws attention to the space where the vagina should be located anatomically (fig. 13.1). Even though countless retellings of *Beowulf* exist, Stern and Steininger's construction of Grendel's mother is, at first glance, shockingly and unapologetically monstrous, given the assemblage of tentacles, monstrous bust, and elongated tongue.

What follows is an attempt to make sense of the various adaptive changes that lead to the phallically monstrous figure at the heart of this graphic novel by tracing *Beowulf: The Graphic Novel* to Gummere's poetic translation and even to the original manuscript's Old English. To do so, I employ a three-pronged critical approach (combining monster theory, visual rhetoric, and adaptation) to unpack this odd text, a graphic adaptation of an adaptive translation of an ancient Old English epic. Jeffrey Jerome Cohen's (1996) monster theory finds that monsters can be viewed as representations of the cultural and historical time in which they were produced. Likewise, Scott McCloud's (1993) theory of the visual rhetoric making up comics can provide insights into the visual significance of these unique aspects of the characterization of Grendel's mother. Furthermore, Linda Hutcheon's (2012) theory of adaptation will be introduced to further explicate the significance of the adaptive process involved in this palimpsestuous relationship. Although the text complicates the role of Grendel's mother by visually depicting her as a powerful and transgressive monstrous woman facing a patriarchal hero, a close reading of Stern and Steininger's *Beowulf: The Graphic Novel* will reveal that the visual rhetoric used to represent Grendel's mother proves deeply problematic in its performance of anxieties about female sexuality and traditional gender roles. Ultimately, the text suggests that even with one thousand years of progress, insidious patriarchal fears about female sexuality, power, and agency still pervade the human consciousness as modern adaptors perpetuate a cycle of monstrous (visual) rhetoric.

Teratology and Old English

Hutcheon notes that every adaptation, whether visual, textual, or otherwise, is "[a]n acknowledged transposition of a recognizable other work or works; a creative *and* an interpretive act of appropriation/salvaging; an extended intertextual engagement with the adapted work" (2012, 8). To adapt *Beowulf* is to adapt the narrative of each of the monsters, which means adapting the process of meeting Grendel, and then meeting Grendel's mother. Thus, according to Hutcheon, in order to fully realize the unique position of Stern and Steininger's graphic adaptation, and particularly that visualization of Grendel's mother, we must first understand the context surrounding Grendel's mother in the original manuscript as well as in Gummere's translation.

Figure 13.1: Beowulf confronts Grendel's mother, whose tentacular visage dominates the comics page and the reader's eye in more ways than one. *Beowulf: The Graphic Novel*, p. 39, by Stephen L. Stern and Christopher Steininger. Copyright 2007, Markosia Enterprises, Ltd.

Although *Beowulf* is centuries old, critical engagement with its monsters is relatively new. As Paul Acker notes, one of the most notable such studies, J. R. R. Tolkien's "*Beowulf*: The Monsters and the Critics," has "for many readers achieved one of its stated intentions, that of placing the monsters at the center of the poem rather than at the periphery" (2006, 702). Tolkien's impact on the study of *Beowulf* cannot be overstated, to be sure, but what Acker highlights as particularly significant is what Tolkien left out: meaningful analysis and conversation on Grendel's mother. M. Wendy Hennequin (2008) has similarly synthesized the varied readings and critical traditions of Grendel's mother (also beginning with Tolkien's seminal reading on *Beowulf*), ranging from those that identify her as a narrative placeholder between the battles of Grendel and of the dragon, to analyses that find Grendel's mother to be something inhuman or bestial. Her synthesis of research on Grendel's mother uncovers a critical trend in which Grendel's mother is often characterized as a monster (Hennequin 2008, 504). This critical trend is based on her supernatural abilities and her lair, which Hennequin refutes by noting that neither her actions nor her physical characteristics are particularly monstrous. She points to the notion that "diction and action, not superpowers, determine whether a character in *Beowulf* is good, or evil, monstrous or heroic," thereby dismissing the abilities of the characters as the critical juncture of focus (513). Instead, she finds that it is the translator or the scholar who positions Grendel's mother as a monster, rather than the diction of the original text itself.

Because of the creative work involved in any translation project, much less that involved in translating a centuries-old epic, Christine Alfano finds that many of these translations of *Beowulf* "employ monstrous imagery, although [. . .] there is little evidence for this in the Old English" (1992, 2). As an example, Alfano dissects the key Old English term *aglæwif*, which many translators (including Gummere) find to mean "monstrous ogress," "witch of the sea," or more simply "monster woman," whereas she finds it to be something much less monstrous: "warrior-woman" (1992, 2). What Alfano highlights here is a trend among *Beowulf* translators to deliberately transpose terms and phrases associated with female power or strength into phrases of monstrosity.

This makes sense in some ways as, according to Cohen, monsters can be seen as embodiments of the cultures in which they are present; to illustrate this, Cohen offers seven working theses as methods of understanding what cultural meanings these monsters signify. His primary assertion, Thesis I, "The Monster's Body Is a Cultural Body," claims that "the monster's body quite literally incorporates fear" (1996, 4). Through this, the monster (Grendel's mother) is often analyzed as a signifier of the cultural fears in which it is produced, thus embodying societal anxieties. To illustrate, Acker argues that

Grendel's mother represents Anglo-Saxon anxieties, particularly those over maternal vengeance and agency, that threaten "not just an individual man's dominance but the whole system of male dominance" (2006, 708). Similarly, in Thesis IV, "The Monster Dwells at the Gates of Difference," Cohen discusses how monsters are seen to correlate with a kind of difference, whether "cultural, political, racial, economic, [or] sexual" (1996, 7). The monster exists outside of the norm and thus is to be seen as a figure from the margins. In a patriarchal culture, therefore, Grendel's mother, so marked by difference, will inevitably reflect men's fears of female agency.

Barbara Creed states that her notion of the monstrous-feminine, "what it is about woman that is shocking, terrifying, horrific, abject," is "related intimately to the problem of sexual difference and castration" (1993, 1, 2). She asserts that the monstrous-feminine warrants a significant distinction from "female monster," which instead "implies a simple reversal of 'male monster'" (3). Here, Creed theorizes the monstrous-feminine in terms of how the monster is characterized both by gendered/sexual differences and by its terrifying and deadly nature. This aligns with Cohen's theory that monsters embody difference, although Cohen's Thesis IV is more of an umbrella category that folds sexual difference in with other markers of identity (1996). Whereas Cohen ties monsters to the cultural moment in which they appear, Creed takes this notion one step further by connecting gender and sexuality to the monster's construction, noting specifically "that when woman is represented as monstrous it is almost always in relation to her mothering and reproductive functions" (1993, 7). It is not enough to understand how the sexual and gendered differences mark the monstrous-feminine as Other, but one must push to understand what it is that makes the monstrous-feminine dangerous. Thus, for a classical figure of monstrosity like Grendel's mother, who is literally defined by her maternal characteristics, the monstrous-feminine becomes integral to understanding the figure, particularly in a visual context like Steininger's drawings. Alfano suggests care in reading contemporary fears, anxieties, and even prejudices within Grendel's mother as a monster, cautioning to be mindful of the "original Anglo-Saxon context" and the original Old English text (1992, 1). This concern is certainly valid, given the historical gaps between the Anglo-Saxon historical placement of the original manuscript believed to have been created "sometime between the middle of the seventh and the end of the tenth century of the first millennium" (Heaney 2000, ix). Because these adaptations still hold contemporary fears and anxieties, even if these fears are not exactly parallel to the ones held by Anglo-Saxons, much less those of the seventh century, we can and should still examine these adaptations for their gendered and sexist anxieties. Thus, when examining *Beowulf: The Graphic*

Novel, what emerges are the historical-cultural anxieties imbued into the text by modern translators, as well as Stern and Steininger's own explicit or latent anxieties as modern adaptors, and dissecting these provides valuable insights into the perplexing construction of such a figure as this conception of Grendel's mother.

Wolf of the Waves and Alliterative Rhetoric

In his article "The Translation of Beowulf, and the Relations of Ancient and Modern English Verse," Gummere (1886) discusses the merits and possibilities of a successful translation of *Beowulf*, which eventually prompted his own full translation thirty years later that served as the source for Stern and Steininger's adaptation. Here, Gummere disagrees with the prevalent notions at the time that the original meter and alliteration of *Beowulf* should be ignored when translating, as he argues that "alliteration *is* rime" within Old English poetry (72). He argues that it is not that the original verse must be avoided, but rather that the majority of previous translations failed due to the use of blank verse. Gummere advocates for the use of the original meter in order to adhere to the general movement of the verse itself, discounting the popular notion that the meter is either impossible to translate or that it detracts from the integrity of the poem. Instead, he suggests that there must be a conjoining of "the rhythm of the old and the rhythm of the new" in order to pay homage to the original poem through translation (76). To illustrate this, Gummere includes a short translation of the first fifty-four lines of *Beowulf*, in an attempt to balance the alliteration of the original with more modern Anglo-Saxon styles of poetry that utilize end rhymes.

Gummere's translation of *Beowulf*, written some thirty years after his discussion of the process of translating, stands as an example of this emphasis on adherence to the original meter and movement of the text. The opening lines of the translation convey the alliteration that Gummere fixated on, as he translates and emphasizes the alliteration of the front syllables: "LO, *praise* of the *prowess* of *people-kings* / of *spear*-armed Danes, in days long *sped*" (1910, 7). The poetic rhetoric involved in Gummere's translation showcases his attempt at a faithful translation, as he utilizes alliteration to create rhyme. In these first few lines, Gummere emphasizes the hard stops generated when the letter *p* is used, framing the rest of the translation as a version that will focus on this alliterative rhyme scheme. Thus, Gummere's poetic rhetoric is established within the first two lines, a notion that will be discussed in conjunction with the visual rhetoric in this adaptation of *Beowulf*.

The depiction of Grendel's mother in Gummere's translation bears special analysis, as it is this translation that Stern claims to be the foundation for his adaptation in *Beowulf: The Graphic Novel*. One of the most defining physical characteristics of Grendel's mother in Gummere's translation is that of her "claws," which she uses to drag Beowulf down into underwater depths unknown (1910, 495). These claws signify to the reader that a nonhumanness should be attributed to Grendel's mother, quite simply because humans do not use or have claws; although Steininger's version does not have claws, the tentacles perform the same function, grasping Beowulf and constricting him. Elsewhere in this section, Gummere describes Grendel's mother several times with lupine rhetoric as a "wolf-of-the-waves" (527), "brine-wolf" (497), and "wolf-of-the-deep" (501). While no other physical descriptors are offered beyond these, the combination of these two physical characteristics (grasping claws and the lupine descriptors) mark Grendel's mother as an Other, a being that is decidedly not human. According to Cohen (1996), this position as an Other designates her as a monstrous figure within Gummere's translation.

Returning to Hennequin's notion of the monstrous rhetoric at work within *Beowulf*, this rhetoric of nonhuman characteristics also serves to classify Grendel's mother as a monster because of Otherness (2008, 504). According to Cohen, this notion of the Other defines monstrosity as the monster dwells among humans but is aberrant in its Otherness (1996, 7). In addition, this frequent use of rhetoric that draws attention to Grendel's mother as part wolf or as a sea wolf positions her to be read through Thesis III, "The Monster Is the Harbinger of Category Crisis," signifying her as "dangerous, a form suspended between forms" (Cohen 1996, 6). The terrestrial nature of wolves combined with the use of aquatic descriptors relegates her to hybrid stature. Furthermore, Grendel's mother is described in Gummere's translation as a "monster of women" (1910, 419) and a "monstrous" woman (501), suggesting explicitly within the rhetoric of the text that Grendel's mother embodies that which is monstrous. This is significant in that it shows the rhetoric of Stern's source material for the writing of *Beowulf: The Graphic Novel* to be grounded in a monstrous rhetoric that results not just from the actions of Grendel's mother but also from the rhetoric used in describing her that contributes to and perpetuates her monstrosity.

Stern and Steininger's Visual Rhetoric

Chris Bishop offers one of the more recent forays into analyzing a visual representation of *Beowulf* by arguing that Michael Uslan's *Beowulf: Dragon*

Slayer, a six-issue comic book series from the 1970s, represents a rather authentic interpretation of the original poem, even if the comic itself failed commercially (Bishop 2011, 73). Although Uslan embellishes Grendel's narrative by placing the monster in a contested battle against Dracula (yes, that Dracula) for control of Hell, Bishop claims that this comic nevertheless stays accurate by introducing Grendel in the same position as in the original poem: that of an antagonist to Beowulf (2011, 79). However, Bishop's analysis of Grendel is limited in only analyzing the literary elements of the two forms (poem and comic) rather than embracing an analysis of the visual elements in Uslan's comic series. Moreover, Bishop's analysis avoids analyzing the visual representation of Grendel's mother, only focusing on the traditional literary elements of Grendel and Beowulf. Examining Grendel's mother through a lens of visual rhetoric will extend Bishop's research by providing insights into new comic representations of *Beowulf*, specifically insights into *Beowulf: The Graphic Novel*, as no scholarship exists on this recent adaptation.

Scott McCloud establishes a foundational rhetoric for analyzing the medium of comics, which he defines as "juxtaposed pictorial and other images in deliberate sequence, intended to convey information and/or to produce an aesthetic response in the viewer" (1993, 9). Much like the heavy emphasis on the diction in poetry, and in the poetics of *Beowulf*, comics is a "sight-based medium" in which every visual element communicates something, akin to these elements acting as signifiers in a kind of visual semiotics (McCloud 1993, 202). Under this purview, comics become ripe for analysis, as McCloud emphasizes that the form of comics is just as significant as the content, an idea supported by Thierry Groensteen's own notion of iconic solidarity within comics. Groensteen argues that all icons, images, and space within a comic operate as a comics system, in which "all of the actualizations of the 'ninth art' can find their place and be thought of in relation to each other" (2007, 16). This notion of iconic solidarity affords an understanding of the relation between any visual elements present in comics, parsing out not just the icon but the icon in a system of other icons, page layouts, negative spaces, and so on. Whereas Creed's notion of the monstrous-feminine provides a crucial critical lens for analyzing the content of Stern and Steininger's *Beowulf* adaptation, McCloud's comics rhetoric affords a deeper understanding of the medium-specific aspects here.

As mentioned before, one of the most notable aspects of the visual rhetoric within this adaptation is the monochromatic color scheme created by artist Christopher Steininger: the visual diction of the graphic novel is that of a palette made up of different shades of white, gray, and black, with no color present except on the external cover. According to McCloud, when comics are published "in black and white, the ideas behind the art are communicated more directly. Meaning transcends form. Art approaches language" (1993, 192). The introduction of color drastically changes the composition of and content within comics, as each color carries meaning, whereas the absence of color utilizes a more direct method of imparting meaning. In much the same way that the poetic rhetoric of Gummere's translation established its emphasis within the first few lines of poetry, Steininger establishes the monochromatic elements of visual rhetoric in the graphic novel's first few pages.

The monochromatic scheme has two functions: it creates emphasis through the juxtaposition of light areas against dark areas and allows for the content of the graphic novel to be more accessible to the reader. For instance, the borders of Beowulf's first appearance are white, which carries no meaning on its own as the standard page border color (fig. 13.2). These white borders only gain meaning when juxtaposed against the black borders of pages featuring Grendel's mother later on (fig. 13.1). This contrast between the initial white borders and the later black borders signifies the shift from daytime to nighttime as the borders themselves shift from the white of daylight to the inky blackness of nightfall. Rather than devoting precious visual space to word bubbles to declare that Beowulf came to fight Grendel's mother at night, the black border of Steininger's visual rhetoric serves this same purpose. This is but one instance in which this monochromatic juxtaposition is utilized, but it is also one of the clearest uses. Contrasting light and dark elements in this way is one of the main visual rhetoric elements at play in *Beowulf: The Graphic Novel*, and one of the most accessible elements to guide the reader through the work. Through this process of juxtaposition within the monochromatic scheme, Steininger is able to highlight key elements of *Beowulf* by placing them in highly contrasting frames.

Continuing this breakdown of the visual rhetoric of Steininger's illustrations, it quickly becomes apparent that the figures and scenes are drawn in a realistic and detailed manner; Beowulf himself is drawn with a square jaw and a slight cleft chin, shoulder-length, lightly-tinted hair, broad shoulders, rustic-looking clothes, and so on (fig. 13.2). McCloud notes that the more realistic an icon or image is, the more immediately recognizable this image will be for the reader (1993, 45–46). In this way, the fully realized details of the characters' depictions leave little to the imagination and provide a straightforward representation due to the lack of color, therefore allowing meaning to be rather explicit. Based on figure 13.2, there are no aspects of Beowulf that have been left to interpretation; the reader has no room for imagination, and no room for misinterpretation, as is the case in the original poem and in Gummere's translation. The panel also employs the juxtaposition of light and dark areas discussed previously. Beowulf is surrounded by white space, which draws further focus to his darkened form. Further, he is drawn to be the heroic model of masculinity, one that the reader

Figure 13.2: Beowulf enters the court of Hygelac, King of the Geats, striding forth and exuding confidence. *Beowulf: The Graphic Novel*, p. 22, by Stephen L. Stern and Christopher Steininger. Copyright 2007, Markosia Enterprises, Ltd.

is to identify with: with bulging muscles and strong jaw, he emerges from the light to save the citizens from a monster. This short analysis of Beowulf's depiction in *Beowulf: The Graphic Novel* provides a foundation for the following analysis of the visual rhetoric of Grendel's mother, as these formal elements establish the visual rhetoric used throughout the graphic novel: deep shadows, strong light, and clear bodily details.

The Monstrous Feminine in Monochrome

In *Beowulf: The Graphic Novel*, Grendel's mother is only shown in full for one frame of the sixty-four-page work (the "primary" frame, or panel 4 of fig. 13.1), and is featured in one partial frame (the "secondary" frame, or panel 6 of fig. 13.1). As such, the rhetoric of these particular comic frames must be explored in detail. Because the primary frame takes up much more of the page than the secondary frame, the proportion of analysis of these frames will match their visual space. What I will demonstrate throughout is that the juxtaposition of dark and light areas, the perspective of Grendel's mother, and the focal points of her tentacles, tongue, teats, and symbolic *vagina dentata* reveal the monstrous rhetoric of *Beowulf: The Graphic Novel*. Creed writes that "those [images] which represent woman as monstrous also define her primarily in relation to her sexuality, specifically the abject nature of her maternal and reproductive functions" (1993, 151). Thus, following from Creed, I argue that each of the focal points outlined above articulates anxieties about sexuality and gender, deep-seated anxieties that have persisted from the earliest known recording of an Old English heroic epic into the twenty-first century. Rather than ignoring the caution raised earlier by Alfano about mapping contemporary issues onto historical texts not reflective of these issues, the contemporary *adaptations* of such historical texts as *Beowulf* do warrant analysis to understand how these anxieties about gender and sexuality manifest, particularly given how these anxieties are visually mapped in a graphic novel.

The primary frame in which Grendel's mother is shown utilizes a full black border, signifying that this encounter is taking place during the night. However, this creates a juxtaposition of the black of the frame and the white of the background, which emphasizes the dark figure at the center of this panel: Grendel's mother herself. She is revealed to have multiple phallic tentacles coming out of her arm sockets as she grapples with Beowulf. According to Creed, one crucial aspect of the monstrous-feminine is grounded in the visual iconography of Medusa, the ancient snake-haired figure of Greek mythology, as the monster has feminine features but phallic snakes protruding from her head (1993, 111). In fact, our first clear introduction to Grendel's mother is a phallic tentacle positioned dripping over Beowulf's shoulder. She is positioned in such a way that shadows are cast over much of her body, making it difficult at first to discern any details about what else defines Grendel's mother beyond these tentacles. The tentacles themselves are clearly defined with hard and bold black lines, while the rest of her body is less clear with shades of gray blending together to muddle more specific features. Moreover, each tentacle is further demarcated by the inclusion of a single row of suckers on the underbelly of the tentacle arm. They make the tentacles feel even more bestial, if possible, signaling a transitive quality to Grendel's mother and assigning a hybridity to her body. Arguably, the tentacles represent the fear of phallic invasion, creeping into Beowulf's space and rendering him helpless, akin to Medusa's own phallic snakes threatening the masculine Perseus (Creed 1993, 111). Grendel's mother dominates the battle and the panel due to her phallic tentacles, thereby signifying her masculine status. These phallic appendages and her masculine dominance prime this exploration of Grendel's mother as monstrous through visual rhetoric. Grendel's mother does not fit into any gender classification easily; according to Cohen's monster Thesis III, this allows Grendel's mother to defy societal classification, in turn positioning her as monstrous (1996, 6). Her depiction as a woman with phalluses and masculine traits indicates joint societal fears of the masculine woman and the dissolution of traditional gender roles.

Continuing this analysis of her figure, one aspect that further characterizes Grendel's mother as particularly monstrous is that of her physical position: she is drawn from a perspective such that the reader must look at her body from the ground level, which McCloud would suggest is significant. He notes that, in comics, "a 'worm's eye' view can give weight and grandeur to objects and characters," as in the case of this panel of Grendel's mother (2006, 21). By viewing Grendel's mother from this perspective, as a worm might view a human from the ground level, every aspect of her body is given more emphasis than the figure would garner if the panel had been drawn from a normal, face-to-face perspective like in Beowulf's introductory panel (fig. 13.2). Positioning the reader at eye level with Grendel's mother would imply that the two are equal, creating a connection of sameness between reader and monster. Instead, Grendel's mother is placed in a position of stature, suggesting that the monster holds power over both Beowulf and the reader. This shows Grendel's mother as an Other, indicating that she embodies Cohen's Thesis IV: "The Monster Dwells at the Gates of Difference," by exposing her difference from the reader and Beowulf through this spatial juxtaposition (1996, 7).

The primary panel featuring Grendel's mother is supported by a smaller panel that is focused on her face, revealed to be somewhat human but primarily witchlike in construction, featuring large and bulbous eyes, a hooked nose, and long, mangled hair. What truly marks this face as nonhuman, or rather as monstrous, is its most prominent feature: a long, unnatural tongue. The tongue is drawn in such a manner that it protrudes far outside of the mouth, dangling and covered in saliva, as she holds Beowulf far above her head (fig. 13.1). This becomes a focal point within the panel, as much of the hair and skin of Grendel's mother is made up of muted gray tones while the corners of the panel itself are marked off with black shadows. Dark, tonal elements of gray and black accentuate the lighter tone of the tongue and emphasize its brighter hue. However, when this focal point is combined with the unique shape of the tongue, it becomes apparent that the tongue is unapologetically phallic in design. This glistening phallic member confounds the status of Grendel's mother as a feminine creature by further associating her with masculine appendages, again drawing comparisons to the phallic nature of Medusa's own head (Creed 1993, 111). It reinforces her status as monstrous through additional evidence that she cannot be classified easily according to traditional gender norms, thereby signifying societal fears of women who make sexual advances. In a heteronormative culture that only conceives of penetration in certain ways, the phallic appendages of Grendel's mother not only threaten masculine bodily autonomy but horrify those who identify as heteronormatively masculine.

Anatomically speaking, the breasts of Grendel's mother command more attention and are more defined than most of the rest of her body. Rather than focusing on her face or giving her clothes, Steininger makes her bare chest one of the main visual focal points in this panel. There is a juxtaposition with the bustline that arises from shading the underside of the bust and highlighting the top halves of each breast, creating one of the few clearly defined areas in an otherwise blurred or shadowed figure. As mentioned before, the deliberate use of clear and realistic details renders the breasts of Grendel's mother significant to her characterization, as these are nigh unmistakable. And while the shape of her breasts is very clearly outlined, much of the detail is obscured by shadow. She is characterized by, even defined by, her sexualized body. Because each of the tentacles stems from the torso, where the arms should naturally be located, these tentacles also serve as lines that pull the reader's eyes back to the torso, therefore signifying a desire for the most feminine feature of Grendel's mother. If readers want to study the physical characteristics of Grendel's mother, then they must also be subjected to visual manipulation in this manner, gazing upon the figure and following the lines of movement toward this focal point of desire. Because "[t]he same creatures who terrify and interdict can evoke potent escapist fantasies" (Cohen 1996, 17), it is unsurprising that the visual movement of the terrifying number of phallic tentacles continually leads to the appealing breasts. Beowulf, and by proxy the reader, is terrified of the tentacles but unable to escape the visual pleasure of the breasts, because of the design of this panel. This clarifies the juxtaposition of light and dark, signifying that the light half of the breasts is ripe for escapist fantasy while the shadowy part underneath signifies fear of the forbidden and the unknown with regard to the feminine mystique and female sexuality.

Through this worm's-eye view, one of the most striking and perplexing aspects of this image is the letter M positioned between the legs of Grendel's mother, representing a marked shift in terms of the visual rhetoric that has defined her thus far. Even though contrast is created through the juxtaposition of light areas and dark areas elsewhere, there is very little contrast created in the juxtaposition of the shadows between Grendel's mother's legs and the light areas of the legs. Instead, the contrast is the symbol itself. The three examples discussed thus far (tentacles, tongue, and teats) all correspond to tangible, physical features, but this M operates as a symbol in comics. Based on its position in the exact place where a vagina would normally be located, this M could be connected to a word intertwined with the vagina: *motherhood*. While the symbol of the M reinforces her role as a mother and her position as a female figure in this instance, its position amid a patch of shadows and its lack of clear definition compared to the other, physical aspects of her body indicate an insidious underpinning: it calls forth the image of the *vagina dentata*, or toothed vagina (Creed 1993, 105). In fact, the shape of the M is drawn in a jagged, angular fashion and can conceivably be connected to or even resemble teeth.

Grendel's mother may be defined by her motherhood, but in their adaptation, Stern and Steininger instill anxieties of male castration within this icon of the *vagina dentata*. For masculine heroes, Creed argues, the appearance of female genitalia has a castrating effect on the male psyche and represents real fears of castration (1993). The performative role of Grendel's mother is complicated by this conglomeration of visual rhetoric; at once masculine through phallic appendages and feminine via an exaggerated bust, she is a monstrous woman who gives literal life to Grendel and represents sexual or genital danger to Beowulf, son of man. Due to the worm's-eye perspective, the reader must gaze upon the *vagina dentata* in awe and horror, looking at the empowered body and fearing it at the same time.

The threat of a monstrous woman armed with otherworldly tentacles and the readily apparent *vagina dentata* prove too much for Beowulf to cope with. It is not enough to slay Grendel's mother, but he must destroy her: the battle ends with Beowulf beheading Grendel's mother in an act of bodily destruction. Just as Creed reveals that "the Medusa's entire visage is alive with images of toothed vaginas, poised and waiting to strike" (1993, 110), so too is Grendel's mother embodied with tentacles covered with suckers, themselves symbolic representations of toothed vaginas along with a head visually dominated by a protruding tongue-phallus. While Beowulf could simply stab Grendel's mother, an assertive act of patriarchal dominance itself, he instead chooses an overt act of sexual denial in beheading the monstrous woman. This further renders Grendel's mother as a being of the monstrous-feminine, harking back to the figure Creed suggests is the epic ancestor of the monstrous-feminine, Medusa, who was similarly beheaded by a masculine hero, Perseus, in an act of patriarchal oppression. Visually, this translates to showing the body of Grendel's mother in shadow and the act of beheading in a blurred line of light. According to Renée R. Trilling, "[t]he appearance of Grendel's mother disrupts the strictly ordered heroic world of the text, and the narrative engages in a mad scramble to conceal the disruption behind a mask of masculine reassertion" (2007, 7). The beheading of Grendel's mother is an act of repressing these anxieties, of denying both female sexuality and the threat it poses to Beowulf's masculinity through an exaggerated act of patriarchal reassertion. The monstrous woman is too visually striking, too transgressive, and too dangerous for anything other than visual dismemberment.

As other chapters in this collection reveal, modern iterations of monstrous women in comics challenge our conceptions of monstrosity and of women in society. Comics writers and artists who adapt ancient myths and epics are no exception, bridging outdated cultural and historical anxieties about women of power with modern anxieties about sexually empowered and complicated women through visualizing ancient monstrous women. Stern and Steininger's adaptation initially suggests that the universality of the comics medium, combined with patriarchal translations and adaptations, will rhetorically position Grendel's mother as dangerously monstrous in society's eyes and Beowulf as the heroic savior. Read another way, each renewed visual adaptation will position Beowulf as patriarchal oppressor and Grendel's mother as progressive avatar of the monstrous-feminine, one who poses a threat to the patriarchy and must be confronted. Although deep-rooted anxieties about women permeate the text, so do ideas of empowerment. It would be easy to write this graphic adaptation as problematic in its visual rhetoric as a modern comic or transgressive in its depiction of Grendel's mother compared to its ancient antecedents, but, like the figure of the monster and Grendel's mother herself, *Beowulf: The Graphic Novel* defies any easy categorization.

Bibliography

Acker, Paul. 2006. "Horror and the Maternal in *Beowulf*." *PMLA* 121, no. 3 (May): 702–16.
Alfano, Christine. 1992. "The Issue of Feminine Monstrosity: A Reevaluation of Grendel's Mother." *Comitatus* 23, no. 1: 1–16.

Bishop, Chris. 2011. "Beowulf: The Monsters and the Comics." *Journal of the Australian Early Medieval Association* 7: 73–93.

Cohen, Jeffery Jerome. 1996. "Monster Culture (Seven Theses)." In *Monster Theory: Reading Culture*, edited by Jeffrey Jerome Cohen, 3–25. Minneapolis: University of Minnesota Press.

Creed, Barbara. 1993. *The Monstrous-Feminine: Film, Feminism, Psychoanalysis*. Abingdon, Oxon, England: Routledge.

Groensteen, Thierry. 2007. *The System of Comics*. Translated by Bart Beaty and Nick Nguyen. Jackson: University Press of Mississippi.

Gummere, Francis B. 1886. "The Translation of *Beowulf*, and the Relations of Ancient and Modern English Verse." *American Journal of Philology* 7, no. 1: 46–78.

Gummere, Francis B., trans. 1910. *Beowulf*. New York: P. F. Collier and Son.

Heaney, Seamus. 2000. *Beowulf: A New Verse Translation*. New York: Farrar, Straus and Giroux.

Heinecken, Dawn. 2014. "My Monster Myself: Recuperating the Maternal in Early Children's Horror by Zilpha Keatley Snyder and Phyllis Reynolds Naylor." *Children's Literature Association Quarterly* 39, no. 1 (January): 68–87.

Hennequin, M. Wendy. 2008. "We've Created a Monster: The Strange Case of Grendel's Mother." *English Studies* 89, no. 5 (October): 503–23.

Hutcheon, Linda. 2012. "Beginning to Theorize Adaptation: What? Who? Why? How? Where? When?" In *A Theory of Adaptation*, 1–32. Abingdon, Oxon, England: Routledge.

McCloud, Scott. 1993. *Understanding Comics: The Invisible Art*. New York: HarperCollins.

McCloud, Scott. 2006. *Making Comics: Storytelling Secrets of Comics, Manga, and Graphic Novels*. New York: William Morrow.

Stern, Stephen L., and Christopher Steininger. 2007. *Beowulf: The Graphic Novel*. Barnet, Herts, England: Markosia Enterprises.

Trilling, Renée R. 2007. "Beyond Abjection: The Problem with Grendel's Mother Again." *Parergon* 24, no. 1: 1–20.

14

Beauty and Her B(r)east(s): Monstrosity and College Women in *The Jaguar*

Pauline J. Reynolds and Sara Durazo-DeMoss

Since the 1930s, US comic books have utilized the spaces and people of higher education as the setting and background for stories featuring college characters (Reynolds 2017). Focusing on *The Jaguar*, an Impact Comics series from 1992, our chapter examines the monstrous representation of college women in this series, thematically revealing the visual and textual attributes of monstrosity, both explicit and implicit, through the comic book narrative. The Jaguar is a character of the Archie Comics superhero series, appearing first in the early 1960s as a male character with magnified feline powers, while the 1992 Impact series, *The Jaguar*, features a Latina superheroine, Maria de Guzman. Although the switch to a Latina Jaguar in the 1990s appears to be a more inclusive approach to characters and story lines in this male-dominated medium, the choices made by comic book writers in general regarding race and sex around this time period tended to reinforce the commodification of beauty and the popular sexualization of women (Madrid 2016), as well as drawing on dehumanizing racial stereotypes (Singer 2002).

In the comic book, Maria is an international college student from Brazil who travels abroad to fictional State University in Michigan to pursue her higher education. Soon after arrival, she learns of her Amazonian aunt's death and receives an unexpected inheritance, the bestial powers of the Jaguar. Maria's superpowers transform her into a heroine who protects those in her new community from violence and hatred, and she invokes them when she or others are in danger. No one knows that Maria is the Jaguar, causing her to have very different experiences of her new home depending on which identity she assumes, for while the Jaguar is welcomed and respected as the savior of the students and faculty of State University and the local community, Maria herself is not. Throughout the comic books, Maria's space and person are violated by a variety of actors, from the "popular girl" on campus to neo-Nazi groups. Maria, therefore, is linked to monstrosity in multiple ways—she, like many women of color in comics, has "bestial" powers, making her something of a monster herself; and, as an international female student on a college campus, she is treated monstrously.

For our purposes, "monstrosity" is not only a physical, descriptive label but one that exaggerates, exploits, and threatens marginalities, situatedness, normalities, and power (Haraway 2013; Richards 1996). As Asa Simon Mittman explains, monstrosity is located "in its embodiment [. . .] its location [. . .] [its] process(es) through which it enacts its being, but also (indeed primarily) in its impact" (2012, 7). Monsters often bear identifiable physical traits, but more important to Mittman is the way they destabilize a host of normativities; as Noël Carroll simply defines it, "they are cognitively threatening" (quoted in Mittman 2012, 7). Subsequently, monstrous depictions are one of the ways "used to abject, to reject and exclude people from the warmth of the mead hall" (Mittman 2012, 7), especially those with identities that threaten the status quo in some way.

In a context of increased access, persistence, and success for women in higher education (Goldin, Katz, and Kuziemko 2006), how college women are portrayed in popular culture can play a vital role in legitimizing, supporting, and encouraging their continued success in that milieu in reality. Unfortunately, it often does the opposite. TV shows frequently portray college women as "intellectual-lite" (Reynolds, Mendez, and Clark-Taylor 2018), while many movies represent them as fairy tale princesses (Donahoo and Yakaboski 2012) or objectified, victimized characters (Yakaboski and Donahoo 2017). Our chapter demonstrates how these tensions also play out in comic books through the example of the monstrous portrayal of college women in *The Jaguar*, where such representations exploit college women's power, threaten the validity of their presence in college, and subvert the credibility of their collegiate success. In a higher education context that deems college women to be usurping the status of college men, portrayals of college women in cultural texts such as comic books contribute to legitimizing, or stigmatizing, their presence.

The history of women in US higher education includes battles concerning access to institutions, recognition of capabilities, and validation of abilities (Evans 2007; Nash 2005; Solomon 1985). By the 1990s, college women were entering higher education more broadly at a greater rate than men (Goldin, Katz, and Kuziemko 2006), but despite the numbers of women seeking higher education, the broader perspective continued to place greater value on male participation and success. Research during the 1990s outlines how gender negatively differentiated opportunities, experiences, expectations, and compensation for female students, faculty, and administrators in higher education (Bellas 1997; Dey, Korn, and Sax 1996).[1] Alternatively, other scholarship shows that for undergraduate women to be successful, factors like friendships support educative endeavors (Wolf-Wendel 1998; Martínez Alemán 1997), and women-only spaces, such as women's colleges, are highly beneficial (Riordan 1994). The 1990s also ushered in a growing number of women's centers on US college campuses providing spaces for female activism and agency (Bengiveno 2000). During this time, feminist involvement focused less on radical activist action and more on "practical and rational responses to the social issues of the day" (Hirsch 1993, 36). These manifested as smaller efforts that, taken collectively, potentially had a larger impact on work toward equality for women (Hirsch 1993). Movements such as "Take Back the Night" or productions like *The Vagina Monologues* (1996) offered examples of women's collective power and support during a decade that in practice worked toward reclaiming women's voice and agency amid experiences and research that outlined women's continuing marginalization. One might expect, therefore, that 1990s pop culture representations of college women would include both the ways women and women's experiences of higher education continued to be marginalized, and also how certain aspects of college campuses provided women with opportunities for social activism and cultivating strong friendships. And it does, to a point. This comic challenges women's marginalization to a limited extent by providing the Jaguar with the chance to fight for and protect women, but at the expense of sustained positive female friendships and the empowerment of women to successfully act for themselves.

Also relevant to our analysis is the fact that the main character in *The Jaguar* is an international student from Brazil. American colleges during the 1990s were the most popular destination for international students. As the international student population continued to increase during this decade, campuses struggled to provide adequate space and programming to support them. During transition, foreign students commonly experience culture shock adjusting to American higher education (Yeh and Inose 2003). These students must acclimatize to a new classroom culture and social rules, and an inability to quickly adjust often leads to academic and social isolation (Sarkodie-Mensah 1998; Yeh and Inose 2003). While attempting to adjust socially, international students experience stress, which impacts their academic performance. Additionally, they face hostility when they arrive at American universities. International students of color particularly experience social distance from domestic students, facing derogatory comments about their fluency with English, isolation from professors and campus staff, difficulty finding employment, and even physical violence (Lee and Rice 2007). Rather than international and domestic students engaging in a mutually beneficial cultural exchange, the dominant culture forces international students to assimilate, which often leads to their estrangement on college campuses.

Many of the events in *The Jaguar* do indeed reflect the scholarly context concerning both women and international students in US higher education during the 1990s. The narrative sexualizes, victimizes, and sexually harasses college women, and as an international student the hero is isolated, bullied, and physically attacked. Maria hungers for social inclusion and community by seeking the approval, friendship, and camaraderie of the popular girl on campus despite numerous ongoing abuses. Generally, the women seek support from each other, with Maria particularly offering support and compassion toward others as herself, and physical protection as the Jaguar. Other than Maria's dorm room, there are no women-only spaces in the comic book, and while her social group of women rally against a hate group targeting people of color on campus in one issue (no. 13), their advocacy is ineffective and ridiculed by others; only the Jaguar can resolve the situation. Importantly, *The Jaguar* provides a rare example of a narrative concerning (international) college women in higher education, but their portrayal, and that portrayal's connection with monstrosity, are complicit with stereotypical portrayals of women and race, while complicating notions of who can be a hero and who can belong.

Higher Education in Pop Culture

Previous research describes the proliferation of higher education and its profiling across various media as a US phenomenon that seamlessly spreads from the illustrated magazine articles, short stories, and college novels of the mid- and late 1800s, to the movies, radio programs, and television shows of the 1900s (Reynolds 2014) and the video games of the 2000s (Lozano 2017). Higher education has been and remains of huge interest to audiences and consumers, but its representation (mis)educates about the purpose of higher education and ways of engaging in it, including messages about who belongs and how they belong (Byers 2005; Reynolds 2014; Tobolowsky and Reynolds 2017). Portrayals of higher education render it as a predominantly social enterprise for students, and, while actual access and engagement has obviously altered since the mid-1800s, pop culture collectively still portrays a higher education overdominated by heterosexual white men in all roles (Reynolds

2014; Tobolowsky 2017). In an extensive literature search, we found no previous research analyzing representations of international college students in US pop culture, although Brian Bourke (2013) analyzes a selection of movies to determine perceptions that international students might have of US higher education. Several studies examine women college students in novels (Inness 1995; Marchalonis 1995), movies (Yakaboski and Donahoo 2017), and TV shows (Byers 2005; Reynolds, Mendez, and Clark-Taylor 2018). Across these media, analyses reveal college women as less than their male counterparts in ways that challenge the validity of their presence in higher education intellectually, behaviorally, and axiologically (Byers 2005; Reynolds, Mendez, and Clark-Taylor 2018; Yakaboski and Donahoo 2017).

Comic books also use higher education as the setting and inspiration for stories, but to date scant research specifically examines these representations. Comic books bear some of the same (mis)educating messages in higher education narratives as other media, especially related to gender, with characters also overwhelmingly white, male, and heterosexual in the texts, containing story lines that diminish women's capabilities and punish populations striving for equality (Reynolds 2014; Reynolds 2017). There is a severe lack of gender equality in comic books set in higher education; our previous work demonstrates that professors of color and women professors are more likely to be the villain or victim of the narrative (Reynolds and Durazo-DeMoss 2016), as well to as endure physical disfigurement akin to Eric Leuschner's (2006) observations about the ways fictional narratives harm academics through ailment or accident.

Despite unequal and abundant sexist representations, college women have consistently played a role in comic book narratives from the early 1940s. College women serve as the love interest in comics such as "Dash Dillon at Hale" (*Daredevil Comics*, no. 4, 1941) or "Wally Williams" (*Popular Comics*, no. 61, 1941), in which two suitors pursue the main female student character. Etta Candy and her sorority friends attend the "Holliday College for Women" in the *Wonder Woman* comics of the early 1940s. The name of the college, paired with narratives devoid of college content other than sorority paddling and sorority women's ability to chase Nazis and other bad guys at will, suggests that women's involvement in higher education is not a serious endeavor with academic responsibilities and expectations (Reynolds 2017). Romance comics depict love, relationships, and marriage as the mainstay of college women's lives from the end of the 1940s. Comics such as *Campus Loves* and *Campus Romances* aptly illustrate the insignificance of engaging in academic work for college women, for example "Love Was My College Major" (*Campus Romance*, no. 2, 1949). Following the romance-filled 1950s, college women join the superhero craze when "Supergirl

Goes to College" (*Action Comics*, 1964) as both an undergraduate and later a graduate student ("Supergirl: Trail of the Mad Man!," 1972). Superpowered romance remains more prevalent in Supergirl's stories than those of other superheroes, as she often uses her powers to sort out relationship issues instead of physically saving the day, like her male cousin, Superman (Reynolds 2017; Reynolds and Durazo-DeMoss 2016). Other superhero comics with male leads from the 1940s portray college women in issues where the hero goes to college, but usually as peripheral characters defined by their relationship, or desired relationship, with the hero (e.g., *Superman*, *Spider-Man*, *The Atom*). In non-superhero comic book narratives, college women often remain the heterosexual "love interest" in stories with male protagonists, such as "This Little Witch Went to College" (*The Witching Hour*, 1971), where the story concerns a male professor who dates a student. More female characters headline comic books in the 1980s (e.g., *The Savage She-Hulk*), and Supergirl returns in *The Daring New Adventures of Supergirl*, with our heroine now at a fictional college in Chicago where, like many young people, she seeks to learn more about herself (no. 1, 1982). The year prior to the iteration of *The Jaguar* discussed in this chapter, *Ms. Tree Quarterly* (1991, no. 5) depicts college women as the victims of rapists on campus and as feminists. Rather than focusing on activism, the feminists in this narrative are college women who physically assault people with whom they disagree. Although Ms. Tree herself portrays a strong female character in this comic, the college women are not given the same narrative respect.

Bearing these contexts in mind, our exploratory research question for this critical qualitative study asks: how does *The Jaguar* (1992) portray (international) college women as monstrous? As comic books are cultural texts that reproduce stereotypical, gendered messaging (see, e.g., Glascock and Preston-Schreck 2004), revealing representations of college women that threaten the actual validity of women's presence and success on college campuses is an important countering action. Our analysis illuminates the ways that this fictional narrative reframes college women's success, highlighting how it exploits and sabotages their presence and power through the assignment of exaggerated images and behaviors that ally college women with monstrous messaging. In previous work, Reynolds (2017) compiled a database of comic books that feature the setting and characters of higher education, in essence creating a corpus of comic books that served as the population for this study.[2] In alignment with our research interests, we made a purposeful selection of *The Jaguar* text, in which college women are the main characters, the setting revolves around a fictional Michigan university, and the main female college student character turns into a bestial superhero.

Throughout our analysis, the monstrosity of (international) college women is expressed through dualities related to the portrayals of Maria, her alter ego the Jaguar, their comparison, and the behaviors and representations of the other college women in the comic book, particularly Tracy, the popular student on campus. The dualities of monstrosity manifest in three main ways in subthemes of monstrous hybridity, monstrous other(ing), and monstrous gendering.

Monstrous Hybridity

As an international college woman, Maria/the Jaguar faces and exhibits hybridist dualities. As a character, Maria/the Jaguar is a simple college student by day and a wild protector of others by night. She is both and separate, either and neither, an amalgam of animal and human that individually strives to be separate but adapts to work together as a hybrid whole. Vulnerable, homesick Maria, who is frightened of her Jaguar-self, becomes increasingly confident with each new issue, while her bestial-self, the Jaguar, who derives almost uncontrollable animal pleasure from the hunt and acts without thought, becomes more controlled by the infusion of Maria's reason. The juxtaposition of frames showing Maria and the Jaguar exemplify their separate parts—Maria as the earnest, still, helpless, silent, virtuous college student and the Jaguar as the active and aggressive, leaping, climbing, rolling, attacking, running, fighting, and snarling creature (figs. 14.1, 14.2).

Later issues reduce Maria's separate role as college student in the narrative and focus on the Jaguar's pursuits, reinforcing the Maria/Jaguar, animal and human, hybridity. One way the comic suggests this is by moving away from the initial, purely animalistic means of the Jaguar's communication expressed through roars, snarls, and growls to internal and external communication in English. In other words, the Jaguar starts to think and talk in English instead of making simply animalistic utterances. In the first issue, in which Maria transforms into the Jaguar, she thinks back on what happened and narrates the past, with the frames illustrating what happened. The Jaguar character makes vocal utterances over several pages. She grabs one of the men attacking her by the front of his shirt, pulling him toward her grimacing face, and says: "GRRRR!" (15). On the following page, she reacts to being grabbed with "SSNNAARLL!," and on the next leaps at her attacker with a "RRROOAARR." In later issues, the Jaguar addresses her combatants with more than animalistic utterances, demanding answers, compliance, and capitulation: "Let her go, Tony!" she demands in issue no. 10, crouched on the edge of a roof before leaping to the aid of Tracy.

Dualities of the "natural and unnatural" and "tech/science and nature" are also part of Maria/Jaguar's hybridity, the other hybrids she faces in the narratives, and her relationships to them. Maria/Jaguar is both natural and

Figure 14.1: Maria the earnest college student anxiously considers her transformation into the bestial. *The Jaguar*, no. 1, p. 23, by William Messner-Loebs, David A. Williams, José Marzan Jr., Tom Ziuko, Tim Harkins, Brian Augustyn, and Katie Main. Copyright 1991, Impact Comics.

unnatural; she is woman, she is feline, but the hybridist joining of these is not found in the natural world. Her lack of normality, her acquisition of physical power, her hybridic liminality is unnatural, monstrous. When she transforms, her Jaguar body exhibits claws (on both hands and feet), exaggerated defined musculature, huge breasts, cat's eyes, a wild abundance of hair, and fangs, all of which are absent as Maria. Their appearance and disappearance are unnatural, providing Maria/Jaguar with an unnerving fluidity of form, an instability of physical self that threatens cognitive understandings of the permanence of bodily form. However, this metamorphosis unnaturally positions college woman Maria as less than the bestial Jaguar. This occurs in numerous ways. In just the third issue, Maria is not portrayed as physically strong, and she loses herself initially within the Jaguar: "When I was fighting . . . I lost **control**. I never felt such **joy**!" (no. 3, 13). She describes the Jaguar as her better self, saying, "I have never been so alive" (no. 3, 5). She is a conscientious student who is ridiculed for being so by students and not recognized as such by her professor; indeed, in issue no. 2, Professor Ruiz berates her in class, calling her "a waste" (9), but in contrast to his dismissal of Maria, he is fascinated by the Jaguar. In the wake of her leaping to his supposed rescue through a door and then an exterior wall, he exclaims: "My God. What was that . . . creature?" (no. 3, 6). The Jaguar's wild exuberance dynamically demands the reader's attention—the beast (and her breasts) are better.

Related to other hybrids in the texts, the Jaguar faces Cyborg, a melding of military man and machine, in one of her first battles. This meeting of Cyborg and the Jaguar shifts the meaning of the natural and unnatural in that Maria/Jaguar's hybridity is now a more natural conjoining in comparison with the unnatural melding of man with machine embodied in Cyborg. Numerous oppositions in the narrative reinforce this duality: the Jaguar's claws versus the cyborg's weapons, her body of skin versus a body of metal. Arguably, Cyborg symbolizes ongoing ideas related to the threat of technology to nature in the comic book—from the rain forests in Maria's Brazilian home to the woods of Michigan in her college home. As the Jaguar, she beats Cyborg; indeed, she saves the man and releases him from the machine. What is natural rather than technological wins in this hybridist face-off.

Monstrous Other(ing)

Ideas related to locale, situatedness, norms, and roles additionally contribute to the monstrous dualities that reveal how college women other and are othered in the text. Art and text related to "belonging and not belonging" particularly reinforce Maria's immigrant status and her new presence in the United States. Led by Tracy, jealousy, hate, and intolerance from US college women herald Maria's arrival at fictional State University. Tracy and her college friends' reaction to Maria's differentiated presence results in monstrous behaviors that further alienate and marginalize Maria as a stranger at the university. There is no welcome for Maria from Tracy and her friends, who are determined that she does not belong in their university (or country). They demonstrate her lack of belonging by ridiculing her use of language, sneering at her for saying "frightmare" instead of "nightmare" (no. 1, 2). They erroneously presume that she comes from a low socioeconomic background, making assumptions about race and international students in general, and deride her for having a financial need she has not demonstrated (no. 1). They mock her clothing (no. 1, 5) and her desire to do well in her classes (nos. 1–2). Indeed, Tracy takes it upon herself to bully Maria with no provocation except her presence. As Tracy says, "Kimmy look what I found! It's LA SEÑORITA's wallet! Let's flush her ID! It'll take her months to replace" (no. 1, 11). Tracy immediately sees Maria as a threat, as an unwelcome invader who needs to be shown "her place." Sadly, her place is apparently the janitor's closet. Tracy misdirects her there instead of the registrar's office when she seeks directions when she first arrives at the university (no. 1). It appears that Maria's place is anywhere other than where she should be, as Tracy hides all her clothes behind the sports hall in a cruel prank (no. 5). Tracy even steals her classwork (no. 2). When their relationship progresses, Tracy still treats Maria poorly, as someone to be used to do her work for her rather than a friend to support her (no. 13).

Maria's difference is highlighted in the comic through narrative and illustrative mirroring. Difference is particularly mirrored between Tracy and Maria, through the distinctions in the clothes they wear, their jewelry, their expressions, their manner of communicating and voice, all of which are documented visually and textually in the comics. Maria wears large hoop earrings, in comparison with the solid, geometrically shaped earrings of Tracy and her friends. She wears long skirts and modest tops, while the American college women sport form-fitting, more revealing clothing. Tracy's facial expressions bear resemblance to the Jaguar's contorted, snarling expressions, as she sneers at Maria or others (no. 1, 7; no. 2, 5; no. 8, 13). Beyond physical descriptions, behaviorally Maria is reflective and curious, seeking assistance from religious leaders to understand her changes into the Jaguar (no. 4); while Tracy is entitled and competitive, and communicatively she demands while Maria queries, suggests, and acquiesces. Ultimately, all of the behaviors of Tracy and her friends are monstrous. Maria's presence at State University cognitively threatens their understanding of whom the university is for and how one should engage in it; as the Other, she is monstrous, and to repel her the college women behave monstrously.

Belonging and not belonging relates to another duality resulting in monstrous othering, that of the popular and not popular. After Tracy discovers Maria's secret identity as the Jaguar, she becomes jealous of her notoriety, celebrity status, and the celebration her protection of the community causes. Various frames illustrate men as frightened of the Jaguar when she battles them, either as villains and criminals (nos. 1, 12) or professors and policemen (nos. 5, 7), but women find inspiration in her heroics and seek to be her, as demonstrated by the desire to dress like her through Jaguar costumes for sale (no. 9). Unlike others in the community, rather than being inspired by the Jaguar, Tracy wants to take the mantle of the Jaguar for herself. Due to her disrespect for Maria, Tracy believes that by stealing Maria's Jaguar outfit she can become the Jaguar. Through her entitlement, Tracy can't believe that the power is something that comes from Maria herself, whom she sees as powerless, weak, and insignificant, and she steals her costume thinking it bestows powers upon the wearer, so she can then receive the accolades she feels she deserves. Doing so, she places herself and others in danger; she dresses in the costume and uses her cheerleading skills to try to engage with a villain, but ultimately she needs Maria/the Jaguar to save her. Tracy may not look like a typical monster, but her excessive behavior and othering of Maria, her attitudes toward difference, and her entitlement harmfully impact Maria and others, rendering her monstrous in our analysis.

Monstrous Gendering

The dualities revealed in our analysis of this subtheme revolve around gender, power, and transformation. These dualities exist particularly through our protagonist's identities as Maria and the Jaguar. There are many examples of dualities related to gender, but the most prominent of these revealed in our analysis are ideas of "innocent and sexualized," and "sexualized but not sexual." These dualities represent how, although Maria is linked with innocence, once she transforms into the Jaguar visual depictions sexualize her; and, while the Jaguar is sexualized in the illustrations, there is no narrative content linked with the sexual. To further elaborate, Maria is represented as a naïve, innocent young woman through association with several different visual and narrative elements including symbols of religion and childhood. For example, she seeks religious guidance as she struggles to accept her bestial powers, a cross hangs above her bed, she goes to Catholic confession, and she seeks advice from a rabbi. Panels cast her as a supplicant kneeling to pray and beholden to a greater power, emphasizing her loneliness as an international student and suggesting a feminine reliance on others. In addition to religious succor, Maria is infantilized through the omnipresent teddy bear who rests on her bed, or by her father sending Dimitri Ransom as a "baby-sitter" (no. 12) to look after her due to the criminal and "super" troubles in Michigan. Maria is always attired demurely, and the illustrations place her body in positions that do not expose her breasts or crotch. A frame in the first issue situates her next to Tracy in a classroom; with her hair tied in a demure side-ponytail, Maria is dressed in a long skirt, a top without a low neckline, and a cardigan over it, while next to her Tracy exposes lots of flesh, including significant cleavage, and her blonde hair flutters around her head. All these examples are devoid of overt sexuality and provide visual signifiers that emphasize Maria's purity.

Unlike Maria, the Jaguar is completely visually sexualized. Visual depictions inflate her breasts (they are almost their own character), and when she moves she appears to go breast first. She opens her body on display, proudly presenting her crotch, muscled arms, and taut torso. Even when restrained, reminiscent of bondage poses, she is visually presented, to a presumably heterosexual male gaze, with arched back, raised breasts, and head flung back. When fighting male baddies, panels often capture the Jaguar encountering them with openly puckered lips. She engages in the chase—she's always running to fight male villains. When the male villains exert their power, their supposed dominance, by hitting her or pinning her, she flails, with panels freezing moments of almost orgasmic intensity in which everything about her is open, exposed, like an invitation. However, although sexualized, she's not sexual. The illustrations in the comic book may sexualize the Jaguar, but the narrative does not make her a sexual actor.

Throughout the comic books, there is no narrative leering, no significant others, no pining for Maria or the Jaguar, nor does she pine for or desire others. She may chase male villains and criminals, but no one pursues anyone except to save the day. Several times, Maria's transformation is provoked by male transgression (e.g., nos. 1, 2, 13), such as when a group of men attack her while running (no. 1), but Maria hasn't sought their attention, and the text suggests that their attack is about "town vs gown" tensions. Thus, the sexualization of the Jaguar appears to be purely for the visual titillation of a heterosexual male gaze. Maria, the innocent girl, transforms into a powerful woman's body to resist male attack. The closest the narrative gets to sexual expression is Maria's delight in the power of her Jaguar body—"The song of the jungle came to me that night. It felt good . . . so incredibly good and right and true that I could scarcely move" (no. 1, 15); and, "It has been a month now since this power was passed

Figure 14.2: The Jaguar protects college student Tracy. *The Jaguar*, no. 10, cover page, by William Messner-Loebs, Rod Whigham, Pam Eklund, Tom Ziuko, and Tim Harkins. Copyright 1992, Impact Comics.

on to me . . . And still my blood pounds and my spirit exalts when I make the TRANSFORMATION" (no. 7, 3). While her illustrated sexualized body might be intended to arouse and excite the reader, narratively our heroine claims her sexualized Jaguar self through the very denial of a fictional voyeuristic male gaze in the narrative. Indeed, the Jaguar arose within Maria when she said "no"—no to the men who threw her to the floor due to her difference and supposed invasion of their town (no. 1), no to the man who watched her (and others) in the shower violating women's space and safety (nos. 1, 2), and no to the men who wished to purge women of color from this fictional Michigan community (no. 13). In essence, the Jaguar is a monstrous female response to monstrous male behavior—she has to turn into a beast to protect herself and other women from male aggression.

Conclusions

The dualities of monstrosity concerning (international) college women in *The Jaguar* are rife with complex contradictions and oppositional partnering that threatens the validity of women in higher education and exploits the marginalized presence of international college women on US campuses. In our analysis, monstrosity manifests through three different dualities that provide contrasts, extremes, juxtaposed ideas and states, fluctuations, and instabilities, reinforcing monstrosity as a state of either/or and both. The dualities of hybridity use opposing, manipulated states of being to cast Maria's Jaguar and Cyborg as cognitive threats to the normality of bodily form. The dualities in the theme of monstrous other(ing) exaggerate and exploit differences and marginalize Maria as an international college student. Specifically, monstrosity is present through Maria's identification as a threatening other, as well as in the ways college women engage in othering as a hostile activity. The dualities of gendering manifest through Maria/the Jaguar's behaviors or illustrative suggestions in the narratives that position Maria in relation to other college women and to the Jaguar. Maria contrasts with other college women and her Jaguar self through depictions of innocence that render her childlike in comparison with the more worldly college women and her sexualized super-self. In physically provocative illustrations of the Jaguar, the comic monstrously exaggerates the feline (e.g., claws, eyes) and female (e.g., breasts, crotch) for a heterosexual male gaze. Additionally, the comic reduces the Jaguar to deriving power through her body and how she uses it, although she doesn't use it sexually.

Despite research in the 1990s that validates women's presence in higher education, through its three dualities of monstrosity, *The Jaguar* positions college women as not serious about academics in general and nullifies the one student who does present herself as serious about academics by transforming her without her consent into a sexualized beast. In contrast to the importance women-only spaces held for real college women during the 1990s, women in the comic treat other women monstrously, and men violate these spaces for their own pleasure or to exercise professional power. Friendships between women are portrayed as less an area of support than a site of exploitation, competition, and jealousy. Rather than valuing collective power (Hirsch 1993), women in *The Jaguar* are rendered powerless as a group since only a super individual can challenge the villainous or criminal men, in contrast to Etta Candy's army of sorority women in *Wonder Woman*. That Maria cannot do this as just a woman, but has to be monstrously changed to have power, only emphasizes this point. Additionally, as an international student, the way Maria is treated and reacted to unfortunately aligns with research describing isolation and violence (Lee and Rice 2007). The narrative exaggerates the threat she poses actually or imaginatively to Tracy and others in the Michigan community, but the depiction of her treatment as a usurper of others' space is more real than not when cast against research describing the ways actual international students are treated. Maria counters this threat by turning into a beast, fighting back against hostility and thereby gaining acceptance. The option to transform oneself into a superhero, obviously, is not available to actual international students.

Research across media focused on representations of higher education has demonstrated that fictional higher education is overdominated by male characters (e.g., Reynolds 2014; Tobolowsky 2017). Scholarship examining representations of college women in particular find them to be frequently characterized as academically deficient, as victims, or as manipulators (Reynolds, Mendez, and Clark-Taylor 2018; Charlebois 2012; Byers 2005). *The Jaguar* confirms many of these same problematic trends. Women's intellectual contributions are diminished or sabotaged by other women, and women are victimized and manipulated in the narrative. Although Maria's transformation into the Jaguar might be seen as a positive expression of feminine power, ultimately it serves only to reinforce limiting messages about women that prolong gender and race stereotypes, and that support the objectification of female characters—beauty and the beast might be the same character in *The Jaguar*, but her beast appears to be more about her breasts. The representation of (international) college women as monstrous, through the dualities of monstrous hybridity, monstrous other(ing), and monstrous gendering, positions them as abnormal and incompatible consumers of academic space, which has implications for the legitimacy of actual (international) college women in institutions of higher education.

Notes

1. See also Drew and Work 1998; Johnsrud and Heck 1994; Leslie, McClure, and Oaxaca 1998; McElrath 1992; Park 1996; Schwartz 1997; and Smith, Morrison, and Wolf 1994.

2. Phil Francis Carspecken's (1996) qualitative methods guided our analysis for this project. Using NVivo software for data management and organization, we both used emergent coding to meaningfully and interpretatively label the text and illustrations in the comic books.

Bibliography

Bellas, Marcia L. 1997. "Disciplinary Differences in Faculty Salaries: Does Gender Bias Play a Role?" *Journal of Higher Education* 68, no. 3 (May–June): 299–321. Available at https://doi.org/10.1080/00221546.1997.11778985.

Bengiveno, Teri Ann. 2000. "Feminist Consciousness and the Potential for Change in Campus Based Student Staffed Women's Centers." *Journal of International Women's Studies* 1, no. 1: 1–9.

Bourke, Brian. 2013. "Coming to America: The Influence of College-Themed Movies on Perceptions of International Students." *College Student Journal* 47, no. 3 (September): 462–69.

Byers, Michele. 1996. "Constructing Divas in the Academy: Why the Female Graduate Student Emerges in Prime-Time Television Culture." *Higher Education Perspectives* 1: 99–118.

Byers, Michele. 2005. "Those Happy Golden Years: Beverly Hills, 90210, College Style." In *Imagining the Academy: Higher Education and Popular Culture*, edited by Susan Edgerton, Gunilla Holm, Toby Daspit, and Paul Farber, 67–88. New York: Routledge.

Carspecken, Phil Francis. 1996. *Critical Ethnography in Educational Research: A Theoretical and Practical Guide*. New York: Routledge.

Charlebois, Justin. 2012. *The Construction of Masculinities and Femininities in "Beverly Hills, 90210."* Lanham, MD: University Press of America.

Dey, Eric L., Jessica S. Korn, and Linda J. Sax. 1996. "Betrayed by the Academy: The Sexual Harassment of Women College Faculty." *Journal of Higher Education* 67, no. 2 (March–April): 149–73.

Donahoo, Saran, and Tamara Yakaboski. 2012. "Classifying Coeds: Typologies of College Women in the Movies." Paper presented at the annual meeting of the Association for the Study of Higher Education, Las Vegas.

Drew, Todd L., and Gerald G. Work. 1998. "Gender-Based Differences in Perception of Experiences in Higher Education: Gaining a Broader Perspective." *Journal of Higher Education* 69, no. 5 (September–October): 542–55.

Evans, Stephanie Y. 2007. *Black Women in the Ivory Tower, 1850–1954: An Intellectual History*. Gainesville: University Press of Florida.

Glascock, Jack, and Catherine Preston-Schreck. 2004. "Gender and Racial Stereotypes in Daily Newspaper Comics: A Time-Honored Tradition?" *Sex Roles* 51, no. 7 (October): 423–31.

Goldin, Claudia, Lawrence F. Katz, and Ilyana Kuziemko. 2006. "The Homecoming of American College Women: The Reversal of the College Gender Gap." *Journal of Economic Perspectives* 20, no. 4 (Fall): 133–56.

Haraway, Donna. 2013. *Simians, Cyborgs, and Women: The Reinvention of Nature*. New York: Routledge.

Hirsch, Deborah J. 1993. "Politics through Action: Student Service and Activism in the '90s." *Change: The Magazine of Higher Learning* 25, no. 5 (September–October): 32–36.

Inness, Sherrie A. 1995. *Intimate Communities: Representation and Social Transformation in Women's College Fiction, 1895–1910*. Bowling Green, OH: Bowling Green State University Popular Press.

Johnsrud, Linda K., and Ronald H. Heck. 1994. "Administrative Promotion within a University: The Cumulative Impact of Gender." *Journal of Higher Education* 65, no. 1 (January–February): 23–44.

Lee, Jenny J., and Charles Rice. 2007. "Welcome to America? International Student Perceptions of Discrimination." *Higher Education* 53, no. 3 (March): 381–409.

Leslie, Larry L., Gregory T. McClure, and Ronald L. Oaxaca. 1998. "Women and Minorities in Science and Engineering: A Life Sequence Analysis." *Journal of Higher Education* 69, no. 3 (May–June): 239–76.

Leuschner, Eric. 2006. "Body Damage: Dis-Figuring the Academic in Academic Fiction." *Review of Education, Pedagogy, and Cultural Studies* 28, nos. 3–4 (December): 339–54.

Lozano, Jon M. 2017. "Video Games and Anti-Intellectualism: Higher Education in Modern Video Games." In *Anti-Intellectual Representations of American Colleges and Universities: Fictional Higher Education*, edited by Barbara F. Tobolowsky and Pauline J. Reynolds, 55–79. New York: Palgrave Macmillan.

Madrid, Mike. 2016. *The Supergirls: Feminism, Fantasy, and the History of Comic Book Heroines*. Rev. ed. Minneapolis: Exterminating Angel Press.

Marchalonis, Shirley. 1995. *College Girls: A Century in Fiction*. New Brunswick, NJ: Rutgers University Press.

Martínez Alemán, Ana M. 1997. "Understanding and Investigating Female Friendship's Educative Value." *Journal of Higher Education* 68, no. 2 (March–April): 119–59.

McElrath, Karen. 1992. "Gender, Career Disruption, and Academic Rewards." *Journal of Higher Education* 63, no. 3 (May–June): 269–81.

Mittman, Asa Simon. 2012. "Introduction: The Impact of Monsters and Monster Studies." In *The Ashgate Research Companion to Monsters and the Monstrous*, edited by Asa Simon Mittman with Peter J. Dendle, 1–16. Farnham, Surrey, England: Ashgate.

Nash, Margaret. 2005. *Women's Education in the United States, 1780–1840*. New York: Palgrave Macmillan.

Park, Shelley M. 1996. "Research, Teaching, and Service: Why Shouldn't Women's Work Count?" *Journal of Higher Education* 67, no. 1 (January–February): 46–84.

Reynolds, Pauline J. 2014. "Representing 'U': Popular Culture, Media, and Higher Education." *ASHE Higher Education Report* 40, no. 4: 1–145.

Reynolds, Pauline J. 2017. "From *Superman* to *Squirrel Girl*: Higher Education in Comic Books, 1938–2015." In *Anti-Intellectual Representations of American Colleges and Universities: Fictional Higher Education*, edited by Barbara F. Tobolowsky and Pauline J. Reynolds, 33–54. New York: Palgrave Macmillan.

Reynolds, Pauline J., and Sara Durazo-DeMoss. 2016. "Super Higher Education: Academics in Comic Books, 1938–2015." Paper presented at the annual conference of the Society for Research into Higher Education, Newport, Wales, December.

Reynolds, Pauline J., Jesse Perez Mendez, and Angela Clark-Taylor. 2018. "'Do You Want Me to Become a Social Piranha?' Smarts and Sexism in College Women's Representation in the US TV Show, *Greek*." *NASPA Journal about Women in Higher Education* 11, no. 3: 313–31. Available at https://doi.org/10.1080/19407882.2018.1451754.

Richards, Evelleen. 1996. "(Un)Boxing the Monster." *Social Studies of Science* 26, no. 2 (May): 323–56.

Riordan, Cornelius. 1994. "The Value of Attending a Women's College: Education, Occupation, and Income Benefits." *Journal of Higher Education* 65, no. 4 (July–August): 486–510.

Sarkodie-Mensah, Kwasi. 1998. "International Students in the US: Trends, Cultural Adjustments, and Solutions for a Better Experience." *Journal of Education for Library and Information Science* 39, no. 3 (Summer): 214–22.

Schwartz, Robert A. 1997. "Reconceptualizing the Leadership Roles of Women in Higher Education: A Brief History on the Importance of Deans of Women." *Journal of Higher Education* 68, no. 5 (September–October): 502–22.

Singer, Marc. 2002. "'Black Skins' and White Masks: Comic Books and the Secret of Race." *African American Review* 36, no. 1 (Spring): 107–19.

Smith, Daryl G., Diane E. Morrison, and Lisa E. Wolf. 1994. "College as a Gendered Experience: An Empirical Analysis Using Multiple Lenses." *Journal of Higher Education* 65, no. 6 (November–December): 696–725.

Solomon, Barbara Miller. 1985. *In the Company of Educated Women: A History of Women and Higher Education in America*. New Haven, CT: Yale University Press.

Tobolowsky, Barbara F. 2017. "Anti-Intellectualism and Faculty: Representations of the Prime-Time Professoriate." In *Anti-Intellectual Representations of American Colleges and Universities: Fictional Higher Education*, edited by Barbara F. Tobolowsky and Pauline J. Reynolds, 161–78. New York: Palgrave Macmillan.

Tobolowsky, Barbara F., and Pauline J. Reynolds, eds. 2017. *Anti-Intellectual Representations of American Colleges and Universities: Fictional Higher Education*. New York: Palgrave Macmillan.

Wolf-Wendel, Lisa E. 1998. "Models of Excellence: The Baccalaureate Origins of Successful European American Women, African American Women, and Latinas." *Journal of Higher Education* 69, no. 2 (March–April): 141–86.

Yakaboski, Tamara. 2011. "'Quietly Stripping the Pastels': The Undergraduate Gender Gap." *Review of Higher Education* 34, no. 4 (Summer): 555–80.

Yakaboski, Tamara, and Saran Donahoo. 2017. "Titillation, Murder, and Romance: Hollywood's Objectification of Women College Students." In *Anti-Intellectual Representations of American Colleges and Universities: Fictional Higher Education*, edited by Barbara F. Tobolowsky and Pauline J. Reynolds, 101–20. New York: Palgrave Macmillan.

Yeh, Christine J., and Mayuko Inose. 2003. "International Students' Reported English Fluency, Social Support Satisfaction, and Social Connectedness as Predictors of Acculturative Stress." *Counselling Psychology Quarterly* 16, no. 1: 15–28.

15

UFO (Unusual Female Other) Sightings in *Saucer Country/State*: Metaphors of Identity and Presidential Politics

Christina M. Knopf

The truth may be "out there" but the monsters are already in here, in us. That is the theme of two science fiction comics that tackle the intersectionality of gender and race in American politics. *Saucer Country* was a monthly comic book series described as "a mad hybrid between *The X-Files* and *The West Wing*" (Young 2012) and "a dark thriller that blends UFO lore and alien abduction with political intrigue, all set in the hauntingly beautiful Southwest" (DC Entertainment 2012). Written by Paul Cornell, drawn by Ryan Kelly, and published by Vertigo in 2012 and 2013, the "cult comic book" (McMillan 2017) followed the leading Democratic candidate for president of the United States, New Mexico governor Arcadia Alvarado, while she negotiated her gubernatorial duties, presidential bid, alcoholic ex-husband, and fragmented memories of an alien abduction. In 2017, IDW began publishing Cornell and Kelly's sequel and concluding series, *Saucer State*, which features Alvarado, now America's first Latina president, navigating the possibility of aliens and the realities of global tensions and political machinations. Presented in two six-issue miniseries, *Saucer State* is designed to explore UFO mythology blended with political intrigue to comment specifically on the 2016 US election and the ensuing presidency (Cornell 2017). Together, *Saucer Country* and *Saucer State* present a compelling drama of the tensions existing between actuality and possibility and between conformity and transgression in a contemporary sociopolitical landscape that uses monstrosity to conceptualize "what it is about woman that is shocking, terrifying, horrific, abject" (Creed 1993, 1), and that has "animalized, exoticized, tokenized, and sexualized" women of color in expressing its racial anxieties (Calafell 2015, 9). Commentary on political reality is a science fiction (SF) staple. SF is an organic genre of mass culture, its generic form shaped by the combination of economic and ideological pressures upon artistic production (Rieder 2017). It has "deep roots in the narrative tradition of Western civilization, but its most immediate impetus is horror, fear, disquiet, and disaffection at the power of human intellect" (Sardar 2002, 3); the science that it fictionalizes offers an analysis of Western civilization's psyche and history, deploying "issues and angst that are immediately present" (Sardar 2002, 2). Although women's science fiction has been heralded for diversifying the feminine image in contemporary culture (Barr 1993; Larbalestier 2002; Osherow 2000), the genre itself tends to reproduce a rational and regimented masculine modernity (Sanders 1977; Stäheli 2003) in a so-called galactic suburbia, wherein strong women may be hypersexualized for male acceptance and others simply fulfill their domestic duties in support of their heroic husbands (Russ 1972, 88). In fact, despite the existence of feminist SF, it is most commonly perceived as a masculine genre because of its preoccupation with technology and warfare (Moody 2002). The same can be said of American politics, in which media and voters prefer masculine traits, such as reason, over feminine traits, such as intuition; and masculine issues, like international security, over feminine issues, like social security—even in races where a woman is a frontrunner (see, e.g., Falk 2008; Carroll 1994; Stäheli 2003).

This chapter considers the blending of feminist possibilities in SF and politics with the monstrous othering that happens in both realms, as found through the intersection in *Saucer Country* and *Saucer State*, where boundary transgressions are plentiful: legal (border crossing), political (female empowerment), physical (sexual assault), social (irrational nonconformity), and extradimensional (alien invasion). The character of Arcadia Alvarado—a woman in the masculine realm of American politics, the granddaughter of illegally immigrated Mexican Americans, and the survivor of an alien abduction—must confront the monstrous within herself, as a person society has marked as Other, in order to understand the monstrosity of powers that would subjugate and oppress. Defying personal and political monsters may be the only way to achieve justice.

The story opens when Arcadia and her alcoholic ex-husband Michael, both disoriented in a stranded car, are found by her security team headed by Fausto Aguilar. As Arcadia struggles to remember what happened to them, she and her chief of staff Harry Brooks make plans to announce her candidacy for president with the aid of Republican campaign strategist Chloe Saunders. As Arcadia makes her announcement, she experiences flashbacks to an alien abduction. Running on a pro-immigration platform, Arcadia supports the entrance of legally and illegally immigrating aliens in the United States, while simultaneously fighting what she believes is an imminent extraterrestrial alien invasion. They enlist the help of UFO mythologist Professor Joshua Kidd. Kidd believes that he is being guided by an intergalactic couple of "magical helpers" only he can see and has been recently suspended from Harvard University for publishing a book on "Flying Objects: Folklore and Fact." While Arcadia's team searches for the truth and tries to hide the incident from the public, the scandal-seeking media, and the political opposition, a team of space-travel researchers known as the Bluebird Club is looking for answers of their own. Arcadia's story unfolds through a series of flashbacks and nightmares that are visually intermingled with events of the present, immersing readers in their own search for the truth. A blend of the real and the fantastic lends credibility to the possible existence of the extraterrestrials, fairies, and ghosts that populate and motivate the narrative.

As mysteries and conspiracies intricately amass, characters experience different kinds of revelations about extraterrestrials, politics, society, and themselves. Michael is set up to believe that he is making unconscious/hypnotized assassination attempts on the campaign. As he deals with blackouts and repressed memories, he recalls childhood encounters that he and his sister had, or imagined, with fairy aliens—encounters that centered on his sister's molestation at the hands of a neighbor. (Uncovering this truth, Arcadia reveals that she was assaulted by a school janitor when she was a child.) A powerful Democratic senator—who had been favored to defeat Arcadia in the primaries—reveals that he, too, had an alien abduction experience that suggested government conspiracy. And right before the general election, the president's staff members indicate that they, inexplicably, know about Arcadia's abduction. Professor Kidd's magical helpers turn out to be actors whose images are projected to his inner ear. They were hired by an ex-military alien conspiracy theorist to make Kidd believe in UFOs, while they leaked information from Arcadia's opposition to him in order to help her win. Other factors of Arcadia and Michael's alien encounter are never resolved: footage of a bright light seen over their car the night of the incident; a mysterious "silver woman" she encounters aboard the saucer and whom Professor Kidd, alone, later sees at the security checkpoint at the governor's offices; a concession call from the president that warns, "They won't let you do what you want, you know! They won't let you find anything out! All we are to them is . . . property" (Cornell and Kelly 2013); and links made between the possible aliens and the Republican Party when the lizard people who abducted Senator Kersey reject unions and "anything left wing," and Arcadia learns that "Clinton and Carter had to ask [but] Reagan seemed to know" (Cornell and Kelly 2013). In short, nothing is what is seems and everything leads to or represents something else, not only for the characters but also for the readers of their story.

Method

Metaphor criticism recognizes that metaphors, nonliteral comparisons in which a word, phrase, or idea from one domain of experience is applied to another domain, are a major means of constituting reality through a powerful perceptual link (Foss 2009; Lakoff and Johnson1980; Bates 2004). Rhetorician Robert Ivie (1987) outlined a five-step model of metaphoric analysis: (1) familiarity with the artifact and its context; (2) selection of a representative anecdote; (3) notation of the central vehicles—the lenses through which the topic, or tenor, is being understood; (4) demarcation of the consequences of the metaphors; and (5) analysis of metaphor usage. This project focuses on isolating, sorting, and explaining (Foss 2009) the extraterrestrial alien/Monstrous Other as a metaphor in *Saucer Country*. The monstrous presence in the series has three main focuses: alien existence, alien abduction, and alien invasion. The female lead—Arcadia Alvarado, a woman in the masculine realm of American politics and the granddaughter of undocumented/alien Mexican immigrants—is the point of alien contact, linking the monstrous with the feminine. As Professor Kidd explains about (UFO) mythology, "It bridges the gap between truth and lies. It creates a disturbing liminal zone—a grey area. And in that space—all of a civilization's weak spots and shortcomings and hypocrisies are made visible" (Cornell and Kelly 2012). The metaphor of the alien reveals a monstrosity in both the world of the comic and the picture of the contemporary political world the comic shows.

Alien Existence

Alien presence and the existence of monstrous peoples are recurring cultural themes that "demonstrate what is not human the better to exemplify that which is human. Difference and otherness are the essence of aliens" (Sardar 2002, 6). They give form to divisions of race and gender ingrained in social structures of dominance and suppression (Mair 2002). Aliens define "the outer limits of the known, existing beyond the territory of the Other on the borders of [the] homeland" (Sardar 2002, 9). Those borders are "zones of transformation" that touch "both what the group is and isn't" (Marvin and Ingle 1999, 100). Borders, boundaries, or margins are dangerous; a mere shift of the boundaries, let alone a breach, alters fundamental human experience (Douglas 1966). Aliens conceptually exist at the margins of humanity, and they traverse the boundaries of the possible and impossible, passing the borders of lands, atmospheres, and solar systems. They are transgression.

Culture "routinely defines women as different, as the Other—as aliens" (Barr 1993, 64). In feminist SF, "aliens are alienated women, not interplanetary monsters" (Barr 1993, 98). Arcadia is at the center of the *Saucer Country* UFO mythology; her alien encounter is a metaphor for her own marginal position as a Mexican American woman in a white patriarchal culture and, particularly, as a Mexican American woman in the white, male-dominated political realm. Erika Falk notes that media coverage of women's political campaigns has historically argued that "women are unnatural in politics" (2008, 30). Arcadia's unnaturalness, monstrosity, or alienation is likewise represented by the imagery that appears on the cover of issue no. 2, with inhuman alien eyes peering from behind her own dark complexion (fig. 15.1). Like her alien abductors, she is a border crosser, traversing not only space but also gender lines. Moreover, as the book's visuals shift between past and present, nightmares and waking moments, hallucinations and realities, the reader, too, becomes a border crosser, sharing in Arcadia's experiences. Throughout the panels, human and alien features are blended, placing anyone and everyone as liminal by blurring the distinctions between "us" and "them."

It is not enough, however, to traverse space; space also must be conquered. "Space, the final frontier, is the recurrent frontier on which Western thought has been constructed and operated throughout history, or time" (Sardar 2002, 16). The colonizing, imperial mission is at the heart of SF (Sardar 2002). Space travelers, like aliens and those they abduct, are, therefore, pioneers. So, too, is Arcadia. Her chief of staff, Harry, tells her, "America is ready for a female, divorced, Hispanic president, if it's *you*" (Cornell and Kelly 2012), suggesting that she is uniquely situated, through some combination of timing and personal traits, to blaze a new political trail. In their study of gender, metaphor, and political identity, Karrin Vasby Anderson and Kristina Horn Sheeler note: "With respect to women governors, the first and probably most obvious metaphoric cluster used to characterize them is 'Pioneer'" (2005, 14). They were/are trailblazers in the sense that many achieve "firsts" as women in politics, which endows them with a "pioneering spirit" of populist campaigns that resemble expeditions and explorations. As heroic as the metaphor is, it also suggests novelty, as "firsts" lack the credibility of history and precedent (Falk 2008).

Arcadia's *pioneering* presidential campaign—in both the sense of its historicity and its lack of credibility—is symbolized through the shadowy guidance of "the **Pioneer** couple" (Cornell and Kelly 2012; boldface added),

Figure 15.1: Arcadia is depicted as alien/other on the cover. *Saucer Country*, no. 2, cover page, by Paul Cornell and Ryan Kelly. Copyright 2012, Vertigo.

the human figures etched on aluminum plaques attached to the Pioneer 10 and 11 space probes launched in 1972 and 1973, respectively, who appear as intergalactic "mystery helpers" to Professor Kidd, leading him down a professional rabbit hole that lands him on Arcadia's campaign team. "The norms of U.S. political culture are suspicious of women's achievements, causing their capability as executive leaders to be dismissed and further reifying the patriarchal expectations of the political sphere" (Anderson and Sheeler 2005, 16), and Arcadia's decision to employ and entrust a person with dubious credentials and sanity demonstrates her campaign as suspect.

Just as SF is most commonly perceived as a masculine genre because of its preoccupation with technology and warfare (Moody 2002), politics, too, is a man's realm, which marshals metaphors of horse races and boxing matches wherein "the president's manhood has always been a question, his manly resolve, firmness, courage, and power equated with the capacity for violence, military virtues, and a plain-living style that avoided cultivated refinement and civility" (Kimmel 2011, 29; also Iyengar and McGrady 2007). Cornell's writing directly calls out the political gender gap through Arcadia's dialogue. At one point, she reveals to Harry, "In my head now, those Grey fuckers with their torture and the **grey fuckers I have to beat**—they've become pretty much the same. None of them want me in charge" (Cornell and Kelly 2013; boldface added). And in a campaign speech, she explains, "The president's camp tried to use *that* against me, too. 'Do you want a **woman** in the White House who *tires* so easily?' One blogger called me '**unfeminine**'" (Cornell and Kelly 2013; boldface added). Racial disparities are similarly highlighted; as Fausto says in *Saucer State*, "Her being brown, the media, they have their target, they don't go looking!" (Cornell, Kelly, and Guzowski 2017d). The comics' art emphasizes the distinction between Arcadia and other political actors; Arcadia is depicted with rich brown skin and thick dark brown hair that falls to her shoulders. In government or political settings, she is frequently surrounded by men with peach- or gray-toned white skin and white or graying hair, often thinning.

Within the milieu of modern American politics, the liminality of aliens—and the question of their existence—is analogous to the era of alternative facts and "alt" movements that promote exclusion through fear, whose proponents *Saucer State* calls "the post-truth bastards" who "embrace the *big lie* and fuck the future" (Cornell, Kelly, and Guzowski 2017b), within a "post-truth environment" populated with "nutjob un-politicians who're deliberately lowering the bar" (Cornell, Kelly, and Guzowski 2017a). After becoming president, Arcadia specifically contends with Republican "nutjob" Adam Dunfries (who bears a strong visual resemblance to Donald Trump), who Harry says "can lead one to contemplate the death of meaning" (Cornell, Kelly, and Guzowski 2017a) and who "does tend to hyperbole" (Cornell, Kelly, and Guzowski 2017b), and whom a frenzied media describes as having "gone beyond 'post-truth' into full-on '*everything* is true'"—"just like the Russian media" (Cornell, Kelly, and Guzowski 2017b). Critics have argued that the use of deception and "fake news" in the Trump era are "gaslighting" the American public, just as the conspiracies surrounding aliens caused Arcadia and her advisers to question their sanity (see, e.g., Duca 2016).

Alien Abduction

SF "overtly engages with discourses of knowledge" including debates about social constructions of, and relations between, women and men (Larbalestier 2002, 8). Unnatural, fake, or alien women are those who are opposed to men or who conspire against men (Larbalestier 2002). It is, therefore, not surprising that the unmarried woman—such as the divorced Arcadia—is often treated as an alien (Crossley 1988). These alien women are, moreover, often redeemed through sexual encounters with men, wanted or unwanted, with stories that suggest that the "real" woman is better ruled by her body and physical desires than by her mind and emotional goals (Larbalestier 2002). Indeed, the alien abduction theme is essentially a rape narrative.

In the popular 1990s television show *The X-Files*, the strong female lead, Scully, who like Arcadia is a successful woman in a male-dominated profession, experiences an alien abduction. Linda Badley argues that Scully's abduction resembles a "subgenre of popular feminism, the abuse survival [and rape] narratives" (2000, 66). The same is true of Arcadia's story, both terrestrial and extraterrestrial. Her campaign strategist, Chloe, explains,

> Michael *beat* you. [. . .] "Beat you" is shorthand. You would *never* say, or even *imply*, those words. You're the brave survivor, who worked her way out of poverty, *not* the **alien**, the *epitome*. [. . .] Agree to that useful **sexism**, and I have a whole list of suggestions. (Cornell and Kelly 2012; boldface added)

Later, Arcadia agrees that she will announce her candidacy "*now*. For women like me" (Cornell and Kelly 2012). The rape survival narrative within the alien abduction is made explicit not only through the revelations of childhood molestation but also when Harry reassures her, "Whatever this was, it was something done to you. Not something you did" (Cornell and Kelly 2012), reflecting a decades-old perspective that rape is an act of violence for which the victim should not be blamed.

The narrative of rape and assault is immediately revisited in *Saucer State*. Issue no. 1 opens with Arcadia addressing the nation, telling them about her abduction. She says: "I [. . .] don't think anyone knows what 'abducted by aliens' really *means*. Apart from I'm pretty sure it involves . . . assault. Abuse. Yeah, that's under the surface of *this* too" (Cornell, Kelly, and Guzowski 2017a). The emphasis placed on "this" suggests a reference to something else with undercurrents of assault and abuse. With *Saucer State*'s overt efforts to remark on the 2016 US presidential election and its results, Arcadia might be pointing to the sexual-assault scandals surrounding Donald Trump (see, for examples, Graham 2017) and/or to the abuse, albeit verbal abuse, critics accused Trump of throughout his campaign and presidency (see, for examples, Bostick 2017). With Trump's tough stance on Mexican immigration, concerns surrounding his perceived lack of respect for women, and his female opponent in the election, a diegetic allusion by Arcadia—an abused, female, Mexican American who ran for president—to politics beyond the fourth wall seems particularly plausible. Indeed, throughout this address, Arcadia is looking directly at the reader, and she finishes with the words, "You, my fellow Americans, just aren't ready to deal with *so many things*" (Cornell, Kelly, and Guzowski 2017a).

Although both Arcadia and her ex-husband Michael were abducted, it is Arcadia who struggles with recalling the memories of it—suffering from what Badley describes as "the equivalent of hegemonic or culturally imposed repression" (2000, 66). As Michael recounts the aliens doing a rectal exam on him, he says, "People make jokes about alien abductions, about 'anal probes'— they laugh because if they took it seriously—they couldn't stand it" (Cornell and Kelly 2012). His words suggest much about rape culture in the United States wherein sexual violence is taken as a matter of course rather than something to be truly feared (see, e.g., Buchwald, Fletcher, and Roth 1993). While Michael is able to confront what happened to him as an act of violence, Arcadia is treated in a more sexualized way. As Brian Attebery notes, in SF, "[b]ecause the scientific gaze is so insistently masculine, whatever it touches upon is feminized" (2002, 51). Her body is accordingly framed as an object of prurient curiosity, seemingly observed by alien beings while she showers (fig. 15.2).

More than an object of the male gaze, Arcadia's sexuality, via its reproductive capabilities, marks her as monstrous. Writing about the 1979 film *Alien*, Barbara Creed observes

> a complex representation of the monstrous-feminine in terms of the maternal figure as perceived within a patriarchal ideology. She is there in the text's scenarios of the primal scene of birth and death; she is there in her many guises as the treacherous mother, the oral sadistic mother, the mother as the

Figure 15.2: Arcadia is displayed as a curious object for the scientific gaze, and a sexualized object for the male gaze. *Saucer Country: Run*, n.p., by Paul Cornell and Ryan Kelly. Copyright 2012, Vertigo.

> primordial abyss; and she is there in the film's images of blood, of the all-devouring vagina, the toothed vagina, the vagina as Pandora's box; and finally she is there in the chameleon figure of the alien, the monster as fetish-object of and for the mother. (1990, 128)

This archetype of the monstrous-feminine, or Terrible Mother—a force of death and devastation (Marks-Tarlow 2008)—is symbolized throughout the first volume of *Saucer Country*. Appearing in bold white-on-black letters at the start of the series are the words "aborted fetuses" (Cornell and Kelly 2012). Later, Arcadia dreams that she is being shown a fetus in a jar by a strange man who asks her, "Can you tell me where *this* goes?" before revealing, "You've heard about false memories covering up *abuse*. Perhaps you don't remember because Michael put something in your drink, then got you alone. Perhaps then he took his revenge" (Cornell and Kelly 2013). When she wakes up, she finds blood on her sheets and clutches her abdomen. Her place as a Terrible Mother or unnatural woman is reinforced when she discovers that her abduction rape could not even have resulted in pregnancy because it was anal penetration.

Like the border-crossing alien and the marginalized female politician, the pregnant body defies boundaries: it expands beyond acceptable proportions and collapses the distinctions between inside and outside and between self and other (Brown 2011). *Saucer Country*'s images of fetuses outside the womb similarly blur the distinction between private and public, as does the domesticated woman in the masculinized political realm—an idea visually represented through the metaphor of a baby in *Saucer State*. As president, Arcadia again confronts the aliens in her sleep; she finds herself holding "my baby," an infant alien, and she asks them, "Is that why there's a baby now? You think I'll fold because of *responsibility*?" (Cornell, Kelly, and Guzowski 2017c). Regardless of such inherent responsibility in maternity, motherhood and political authority are often viewed by voters as antithetical (Witt, Paget, and Matthews 1995). Despite its cultural ideal of femininity, motherhood suggests not only professional inexperience but also sexuality; menstruation carries a particular stigma in public life and the presidency with fears about "PMS going nuclear" (see, e.g., Carmon 2015, para. 6). This cultural anxiety is reflected in *Saucer Country* when a staff member for Arcadia's opposition asks, "Do you really want a president [. . .] who might build on that [UFO] fantasy"—in other words, who may behave irrationally—"with the nuclear button in her hands?" (Cornell and Kelly 2013).

Alien Invasion

There are two sides of the colonization theme implicit in SF: the Manifest Destiny drive of Western civilization toward conquest, and the fear of invasion that is "antithetical to Western credos of individualism" (Wertheim 2002, 75). During the Cold War, SF stories that emphasized ideas "of a society being taken over from the inside by an alien force and thus being made part of a hostile evil collective" symbolized political, and primal, fears of Western traditions (Sardar 2002, 10). Published during the years that would usher in the Donald Trump era of border walls and immigration bans, *Saucer Country* similarly enacts the Terror War fears of invasion, of being overrun by a hostile alien force from the outside. Invasion from *within* is also a central focus of the *Saucer State* series, which Cornell describes as being "*about* the current state of US politics," particularly the use of "psy ops" (psychological operations, or propaganda) influencing elections (quoted in Ching 2017, para. 6).

One alien menace in modern American culture is the immigrant, and this is a major theme throughout Arcadia's presidential campaign. She makes her candidacy announcement during an immigration platform speech, declaring:

> My grandparents [. . .] they were illegal **aliens**. And *that's* what *made* their children so proud to be *American*. [. . .] People talk about guarding the border, they talk about not letting in "**aliens**"—but let's say it out loud—Americans *are* **aliens**. (Cornell and Kelly 2012; boldface added)

When Arcadia reveals her abduction story to her campaign staff, Chloe chides, "Nobody *credible* gets abducted by aliens. Nobody *important* gets abducted by aliens. *Poor people* get abducted by aliens!" Arcadia challenges, "Poor people like Mexican immigrants you mean?" and Chloe retorts, "Why, yes! The aliens must be *really* racist!" (Cornell and Kelly 2012).

In describing aliens as representations of "the otherness in ourselves," Ziauddin Sardar asks, "What then is the difference between 'us' and 'them,' West and the non-West, the poor and the rich, the privileged and the marginalized? Nothing" (2002, 14, 15). Despite Sardar's affirmation of shared humanity at the center of alien representations, xenophobia has, nonetheless, been part of the SF subtext since the Cold War and is made explicit in *Saucer Country*. When Milton, an alien conspiracy theorist and New Mexico radio shock jock, learns that the presidential candidate's ex-husband believes they were abducted by aliens, he tells his listeners he has a story for them that "cuts deep to the heart of our poor state—with big government on our backs—and 'Governor Sopapilla' running for President by wanting to let the aliens in across the border—oh, you are going to hear something ironic about that!" (Cornell and Kelly 2012). The racist component of us-and-them continues into *Saucer State* when Republican opponent Dunfries repeatedly calls Arcadia the "chihuahua" (Cornell, Kelly, and Guzowski 2017a), marking her as both a Mexican and a female dog/bitch, and indicates that she is "like someone you'd hire to clean the pool" (Cornell, Kelly, and Guzowski 2017c).

Such racial tensions are further foregrounded when NASA discovers an alien saucer approaching Earth, and a representative of Black Lives Matter states, "I hope it's an *invasion*. Couldn't be worse than what we have now," a particularly strong statement against Arcadia's fears that the alien arrival will mean war and colonization (Cornell, Kelly, and Guzowski 2017b). Dunfries, too, politicizes the approaching saucer, indicating in a press conference that Arcadia cannot handle the invasion, and asks, "What, are we gonna let the aliens in and give them all green cards?" (Cornell, Kelly, and Guzowski 2017c). The presence of Black Lives Matter and debates around green cards clearly places *Saucer State* in post-2016 political discourse. Chloe refers to Dunfries's rhetoric as

> an instant scorched Earth strategy. It'll get him a huge backlash. But a huge wave of support from the hordes of the fearful—and from the fuckers who've infested the G.O.P. (Cornell, Kelly, and Guzowski 2017c)

Not only does Dunfries visually resemble Trump, but Trump's rhetoric, likewise, has been described as employing and appealing to the politics of fear (see, e.g., Ball 2016; Altman 2017). Furthermore, when Arcadia responds to Dunfries, she wants to "win Twitter" (Cornell, Kelly, and Guzowski 2017c)—another nod to Trump's communication style.

As the story heads to its conclusion in the second issue of *Saucer State* and an unidentified flying object approaches Earth, Arcadia asks, "Are they coming in force? [. . .] Because it won't be a war, it'll be a colonis—" (Cornell, Kelly, and Guzowski 2017b). Her apparent fear of colonization is, at first, almost ironic as she assumes the same xenophobic attitude expressed by the racist shock jock. From another perspective, however, her reaction is logical given the colonial history of Mexico and the American Southwest. Being part of a people who experience colonial oppression, Arcadia has reason to expect the worst in the arrival of a seemingly powerful, and potentially duplicitous, society.

Critiquing SF, Jan Mair notes: "The entire project of Western knowledge [is] knowing about the Other [to better] subsume, subjugate, and suppress them" (2002, 48). This idea, too, is found in *Saucer Country*. Mr. Brady, head of the Bluebirds, whose mission is to "[s]ecretly investigate extreme airframes, terrestrial and otherwise," indicates a desire to communicate with the aliens he believes have been visiting since at least World War II, "[b]ecause then I'd finally know them. Then I could finally *hate* them" (Cornell and Kelly 2013).

Another alien menace to modern society is the threat of feminism to the patriarchy. Although immigration is the overt theme of *Saucer Country*'s invasion metaphor, feminism is its primary subtext. In SF, "the process of imagining a world in which women are [or may become] the dominant sex immediately exposes many of the processes that normally operate to keep women subordinate; it renders these processes of power *visible*" (Larbalestier 2002, 8). The alien woman is the unnatural woman who conspires against or has power over men (Larbalestier 2002). Michael, Arcadia's ex-husband, gets drunk in a bar and laments his loss of power in his relationship with Arcadia, casting her as a space traveler in the process:

> One day you're married, to the girl you fought alongside for so long, the two young radicals—then suddenly it's years later. And she's . . . **light-years** away. And you're left on the cold hillside. (Cornell and Kelly 2012; boldface added)

As with the metaphor of alien abduction, representations of the monstrous-feminine, via the *vagina dentata*—a cultural mythos that indicates social anxiety about emasculation in the presence of a powerful woman (Marks-Tarlow 2008; Robertson 2015)—play into the series' metaphor of alien invasion. Seeking answers about the aliens, Michael tells a hypnotherapist that he has suffered erectile dysfunction since his forgotten night with Arcadia, placing her at the root of his impotency. Indeed, Michael's rape may be read as a challenge to his masculinity, one that is reflected by Arcadia's eclipsing him professionally. This idea becomes more apparent when Michael's story is challenged by Chloe, who accuses: "**You** were made *powerless*, and you think that gives you a reason to make *her*—[powerless]!" (Cornell and Kelly 2012; boldface added).

Discussion

Another comic book story of alien invasion and abduction, *Mars Attacks!*, has been described as "an ironic story about politics, populism and popular culture [which] marks a classical problem of inclusion and exclusion," wherein the Martians are excluded from the political system until there is a means and process of translation that is supported by the desires of the general public (Stäheli 2003, 276). Citizenship, inclusion, and access are at the heart of *Saucer Country*, too. Arcadia calls for "[a]mnesty for all those immigrants in honest employment, already contributing *to* our society, but without the *right*[s]"—"bringing those individuals into the *tax* system" (Cornell and Kelly 2013). Like the Martians, illegally immigrating Mexican American aliens are excluded from the political system. But, whereas the whole world wanted to hear from the Martian ambassador, in *Saucer Country* "[s]omeone's willing to kill to stop what's soon going to be the brown majority from having their first president" (Cornell and Kelly 2013), and in *Saucer State* social media is ablaze with accusations that "[s]he wants to let in the greys like she lets in browns" (Cornell, Kelly, and Guzowski 2017d). The connections made between conservative politics and the alien invaders, or aliens' aversion to liberal policies, further points to issues and debates of inclusion and exclusion—or what can also be considered "political Othering."

Whereas many modern comics with strong female leads depict the protagonists embracing monstrosity—whether supernatural (e.g., *Pretty Deadly, Monstress, Rat Queens*) or attitudinal (e.g., *Lady Killer, Bomb Queen*)—*Saucer Country*'s Arcadia finds her strength in resisting the monstrous. As her chief of staff, Harry, tells Arcadia: "It gave you the chance to show them all, even the out-of-this world 'them'—exactly how strong you are" (Cornell and Kelly 2013). Extraterrestrials, a monstrous other with a mythos of invasion, represent oppression. Her paranormal encounter is, therefore, symbolic of how an abused, divorced, Mexican American, female politician negotiates the Other and struggles with her own alien identification. In Arcadia's flashbacks, a green creature resembling the Greys says, "You are us. You belong to us" (Cornell and Kelly 2012). In feminist SF, women as Other tend to side with aliens as Other (Badley 2000; Barr 1993), but Arcadia interprets the alien's words not as an expression of holistic community or commonality but as "a clear threat, to national security" (Cornell and Kelly 2012)—one that exploits her historically repressed and marginalized roles as woman and Mexican American. Her defiance of a monstrosity is an effort to rehumanize the oppressed, subjugated, and marginalized. The initial series ends with her words, "Today is the day a brown woman *took* power. So the needs of the grey men don't interest me. Not today" (Cornell and Kelly 2013). Arcadia's campaign triumph is, therefore, not merely one for an office, but one for humanity—her humanity and the humanity of those like her.

Bibliography

Altman, Alex. 2017. "No President Has Spread Fear Like Donald Trump." *Time*, February 9. Available at http://time.com/4665755/donald-trump-fear/.

Anderson, Karrin Vasby, and Kristina Horn Sheeler. 2005. *Governing Codes: Gender, Metaphor, and Political Identity*. Lanham, MD: Lexington Books.

Attebery, Brian. 2002. *Decoding Gender in Science Fiction*. New York: Routledge.

Badley, Linda. 2000. "Scully Hits the Glass Ceiling: Postmodernism, Postfeminism, Posthumanism, and *The X-Files*." In *Fantasy Girls: Gender in the New Universe of Science Fiction and Fantasy Television*, edited by Elyce Rae Helford, 61–90. Lanham, MD: Rowman and Littlefield.

Ball, Molly. 2016. "Donald Trump and the Politics of Fear." *Atlantic*, September 2. Available at https://www.theatlantic.com/politics/archive/2016/09/donald-trump-and-the-politics-of-fear/498116/.

Barr, Marleen S. 1993. *Lost in Space: Probing Feminist Science Fiction and Beyond*. Chapel Hill: University of North Carolina Press.

Bates, Benjamin. 2004. "Audiences, Metaphors, and the Persian Gulf War." *Communication Studies* 55, no. 3: 447–63.

Bostick, Dani. 2017. "Donald Trump: Verbal␣Abuser-in-Chief." *Huffington Post*, June 29. Available at http://www.huffingtonpost.com/entry/donald-trump-verbal-abuser-in-chief_us_5955177ee4b0c85b96c65f9b.

Brown, Jeffrey A. 2011. "Supermoms? Maternity and the Monstrous-Feminine in Superhero Comics." *Journal of Graphic Novels and Comics* 2, no. 1 (June): 77–87.

Buchwald, Emilie, Pamela R. Fletcher, and Martha Roth. 1993. *Transforming a Rape Culture*. Minneapolis: Milkweed Editions.

Calafell, Bernadette Marie. 2015. *Monstrosity, Performance, and Race in Contemporary Culture*. New York: Peter Lang.

Carmon, Irin. 2015. "Donald Trump Draws on Long History of Period Stigma." MSNBC, August 10. Available at http://www.msnbc.com/msnbc/donald-trump-draws-long-history-period-stigma.

Carroll, Susan J. 1994. *Women as Candidates in American Politics*. 2nd ed. Bloomington: Indiana University Press.

Ching, Albert. 2017. "Politics Not Weird Enough? Saucer State Pits the President vs. Aliens." Comic Book Resources, May 23. Available at http://www.cbr.com/saucer-state-paul-cornell-interview-saucer-country-return/.

Cornell, Paul. 2017. "The Week of Saucer State." Paul Cornell: Novelist, Screenwriter, Comics Writer, May 22. Available at https://www.paulcornell.com/2017/05/the-week-of-saucer-state/.

Cornell, Paul, and Ryan Kelly. 2012. *Saucer Country: Run*. New York: Vertigo.

Cornell, Paul, and Ryan Kelly. 2013. *Saucer Country: The Reticulan Candidate*. New York: Vertigo.
Cornell, Paul, Ryan Kelly, and Adam Guzowski. 2017a. *Saucer State*, no. 1, May. San Diego: IDW Publishing.
Cornell, Paul, Ryan Kelly, and Adam Guzowski. 2017b. *Saucer State*, no. 2, June. San Diego: IDW Publishing.
Cornell, Paul, Ryan Kelly, and Adam Guzowski. 2017c. *Saucer State*, no. 3, July. San Diego: IDW Publishing.
Cornell, Paul, Ryan Kelly, and Adam Guzowski. 2017d. *Saucer State*, no. 4, August. San Diego: IDW Publishing.
Creed, Barbara. 1990. "*Alien* and the Monstrous-Feminine." In *Alien Zone: Cultural Theory and Contemporary Science Fiction Cinema*, edited by Annette Kuhn, 128–44. New York: Verso.
Creed, Barbara. 1993. *The Monstrous-Feminine: Film, Feminism, Psychoanalysis*. New York: Routledge.
Crossley, Robert. 1988. Introduction to *Kindred*, by Octavia E. Butler, ix–xxvii. Boston: Beacon Press.
DC Entertainment. 2012. "*Saucer Country #1*." Available at https://www.dccomics.com/comics/saucer-country-2012/saucer-country-1.
Douglas, Mary. 1966. *Purity and Danger: An Analysis of Concepts of Pollution and Taboo*. London: Routledge.
Duca, Lauren. 2016. "Donald Trump Is Gaslighting America." *Teen Vogue*, December 10. Available at https://www.teenvogue.com/story/donald-trump-is-gaslighting-america.
Falk, Erika. 2008. *Women for President: Media Bias in Eight Campaigns*. Urbana: University of Illinois Press.
Foss, Sonja K. 2009. *Rhetorical Criticism: Exploration and Practice*. 4th ed. Long Grove, IL: Waveland.
Graham, David A. 2017. "The Many Scandals of Donald Trump: A Cheat Sheet." *Atlantic*, January 23. Available at https://www.theatlantic.com/politics/archive/2017/01/donald-trump-scandals/474726/.
Ivie, Robert L. 1987. "Metaphor and the Rhetorical Invention of Cold War 'Idealists.'" *Communication Monographs* 54, no. 2: 165–82.
Iyengar, Shanto, and Jennifer A. McGrady. 2007. *Media Politics: A Citizen's Guide*. New York: W. W. Norton.
Kimmel, Michael. 2011. *Manhood in America: A Cultural History*. 3rd ed. New York: Oxford University Press.
Lakoff, George, and Mark Johnson. 1980. *Metaphors We Live By*. Chicago: University of Chicago Press.
Larbalestier, Justine. 2002. *The Battle of the Sexes in Science Fiction*. Middletown, CT: Wesleyan University Press.
Mair, Jan. 2002. "Rewriting the 'American Dream': Postmodernism and Otherness in *Independence Day*." In *Aliens R Us: The Other in Science Fiction Cinema*, edited by Ziauddin Sardar and Sean Cubitt, 34–50. London: Pluto Press.
Marks-Tarlow, Terry. 2008. *Psyche's Veil: Psychotherapy, Fractals and Complexity*. New York: Routledge.
Marvin, Carolyn, and David W. Ingle. 1999. *Blood Sacrifice and the Nation: Totem Rituals and the American Flag*. Cambridge: Cambridge University Press.

McMillan, Graeme. 2017. "'Saucer State' Comic Explores Connection between Aliens and White House (Exclusive Preview)." *Hollywood Reporter*, February 20. Available at http://www.hollywoodreporter.com/heat-vision/saucer-state-comic-explores-connection-between-aliens-white-house-preview-977765.

Moody, Nickianne. 2002. "Displacements of Gender and Race in *Space: Above and Beyond*." In *Aliens R Us: The Other in Science Fiction Cinema*, edited by Ziauddin Sardar and Sean Cubitt, 51–73. London: Pluto Press.

Osherow, Michelle. 2000. "The Dawn of a New Lilith: Revisionary Mythmaking in Women's Science Fiction." *NWSA Journal* 12, no. 1 (Spring): 68–83.

Rieder, John. 2017. *Science Fiction and the Mass Cultural Genre System*. Middletown, CT: Wesleyan University Press.

Robertson, Kate. 2015. "Ladies Who Lunch: Man-Eating Femmes Fatales in Contemporary Visual Culture." *Australasian Journal of Popular Culture* 4, nos. 2–3: 161–75.

Russ, Joanna. 1972. "The Image of Women in Science Fiction." In *Images of Women in Fiction: Feminist Perspectives*, edited by Susan Koppelman Cornillon, 79–94. Bowling Green, OH: Bowling Green State University Popular Press.

Sanders, Scott. 1977. "Invisible Men and Women: The Disappearance of Character in Science Fiction." *Science Fiction Studies* 4, no. 1 (March): 14–24.

Sardar, Ziauddin. 2002. Introduction to *Aliens R Us: The Other in Science Fiction Cinema*, edited by Ziauddin Sardar and Sean Cubitt, 1–17. London: Pluto Press.

Stäheli, Urs. 2003. "The Popular in the Political System." *Cultural Studies* 17, no. 2: 275–99.

Wertheim, Christine. 2002. "*Star Trek: First Contact*: The Hybrid, the Whore and the Machine." In *Aliens R Us: The Other in Science Fiction Cinema*, edited by Ziauddin Sardar and Sean Cubitt, 74–93. London: Pluto Press.

Witt, Linda, Karen M. Paget, and Glenna Matthews. 1995. *Running as a Woman: Gender and Power in American Politics*. New York: Free Press.

Young, Bryan. 2012. "Paul Cornell Talks about His New Comic Book, Saucer Country." *Huffington Post*, March 13. Available at http://www.huffingtonpost.com/bryan-young/paul-cornell-saucer-country_b_1339009.html.

About the Contributors

Samantha Langsdale, editor, holds a PhD in feminist philosophy and the study of religions from the School of Oriental and African Studies, University of London. Her research interests include feminist philosophy, contemporary critical theory, visual culture, monster studies, and religions. She has published feminist analyses of various types of visual culture including animation, film, and comic books. She is a senior lecturer in philosophy and religion at the University of North Texas and teaches a range of classes in Western philosophy, feminism, gender studies, and cultural studies.

Elizabeth Rae Coody, editor, is an assistant professor of religious studies at Morningside College in Sioux City, Iowa. As a biblical scholar whose PhD is in religious and theological studies with a concentration in biblical interpretation, she values the contributions to biblical interpretation that popular culture can make. Her work in comics began in studying the way comics can help interpreters imagine the scandal of Jesus's death on the Cross, which is often domesticated by modern Christian sensibilities. Her work continues and expands themes of how popular culture can give insight into the Bible and religion, and how knowledge of the Bible and religion can return the favor.

Novia Shih-Shan Chen is a PhD candidate in the Department of Gender, Sexuality and Women's Studies at Simon Fraser University, Burnaby, British Columbia. Her dissertation examines the positionality of contemporary female documentary filmmakers, the historical fluctuation associated with the production of their documentary films, and the implications of independent filmmaking in the context of Sinophone cinema. Aside from writing, she also teaches in the Asian Studies Program at Kwantlen Polytechnic University, British Columbia, and serves on the programming committee for the Vancouver Queer Film Festival.

Keri Crist-Wagner is the program coordinator for the Department of English and a doctoral student in learning sciences at Clemson University. Her research interests include the use of comic books and graphic novels in college classrooms, intersectional and critical pedagogy, and curricular infusion of popular culture.

Sara Durazo-DeMoss is an administrator in higher education and serves as the director of student success and equity programs at California State University, San Bernardino. She is also an EdD candidate at the University of Redlands, and her dissertation explores representations of college life by vlog influencers on YouTube.

Charlotte Johanne Fabricius is a PhD candidate at the University of Southern Denmark. Her work investigates manifestations of superheroic girlhood in contemporary superhero comics through intersectional critique of comics aesthetics.

Ayanni C. H. Cooper is currently pursuing a PhD in English at the University of Florida, where she specializes in comics and animation studies. She received her BA in English from Cornell University and completed her MA in English literature at Brooklyn College. Her research interests include feminist critique, monster theory, independent and mainstream comics, science fiction, fantasy, and robots (big or small). When she's not working or reading, Ayanni likes playing video games with her family and taking pictures of her cat.

Christina M. Knopf is currently an assistant professor in the Communication Studies and Media Studies Department at the State University of New York College Cortland. She earned a PhD in political communication/cultural sociology at the University at Albany in 2005. She is the author of *The Comic Art of War: A Critical Study of Military Cartoons, 1805–2014, with a Guide to Artists* (McFarland, 2015).

Dr. Knopf's studies of gender and comics include "'Hey, Soldier! Your Slip Is Showing!' Militarism vs. Femininity in WWII Comic Pages and Books" in *10 Cent War: Comic Books, Propaganda, and World War II* (University Press of Mississippi, 2017); "PTXD: Gendered Narratives of Combat, Trauma, and the Civil-Military Divide," with Christine Doran, in *The X-Men Films: A Cultural Analysis* (Rowman and Littlefield, 2016); "Sinne Fianna Fáil: Women, Irish Rebellions, and the Graphic Novels of Gerry Hunt" in *Cultures of War in Graphic Novels* (Rutgers University Press, 2018); "Queen of Burlesque: The Subtle (as a Hammer) Satire of *Bomb Queen*" in *Gender and the Superhero*

Narrative (University Press of Mississippi, 2018); and "Marvel's Shamrock: Haunted Heroine, Working Woman, Guardian of the Galaxy" in *Working Class Comic Book Heroes* (University Press of Mississippi, 2018).

Her studies of horror and monstrosity include "Zany Zombies, Grinning Ghosts, Silly Scientists, and Nasty Nazis: Comedy-Horror at the Threshold of World War II" in *The Laughing Dead: The Comedy-Horror Film from "Bride of Frankenstein" to "Zombieland"* (Rowman and Littlefield, 2016); "The U.N. Dead: Cold War Ghosts in *Carol for Another Christmas*" in *Horrors of War: The Undead on the Battlefield* (Rowman and Littlefield, 2015); and "War Is Hell: The (Super)nature of War in the Works of Mike Mignola" in *The Mignolaverse: Critical Essays on Hellboy and the Comics Art of Mike Mignola* (Sequart Organization, 2019).

Tomoko Kuribayashi received her BA and MA from the University of Tokyo and then earned an MA and PhD (with a feminist studies minor) from the Universities of Alberta and Minnesota, respectively. She has published articles on such writers as Margaret Atwood and Sandra Cisneros. Her most recent work, on a short narrative by Moto Hagio titled "Iguana Daughter," appears as a chapter in the volume *Unveiling Desire: Fallen Women in Literature, Culture, and Films of the East*, edited by Devaleena Das and Colette Morrow (Rutgers University Press, 2018). Tomoko is retired from the University of Wisconsin Stevens Point.

Jeannie Ludlow is a professor of English and women's, gender, and sexuality studies at Eastern Illinois University who has worked as a patient advocate at abortion clinics. Her research interests include representations of abortion and reproduction in contemporary literature and writing. Recent publications include "Graphic Abortion: The Grotesque in Diane Noomin's 1990s Abortion Comics" in *Feminist Formations* and "Love and Goodness: Toward a New Abortion Politics" in *Feminist Studies*.

Marcela Murillo grew up and studied law in her hometown of La Paz, Bolivia. In 2012, she completed a master's degree in Spanish literature at Bowling Green State University, Bowling Green, Ohio. Currently, she is working on her doctoral degree in Latin American literature at the University of Florida. At the same time, she is pursuing a master's degree in women's studies. Her dissertation focuses on the contemporary representation of Bolivian indigenous women in literature and visual arts. She is an assistant professor of Spanish at Santa Fe College in Gainesville, Florida.

Sho Ogawa is a lecturer on Asian cinema at Kwantlen Polytechnic University, British Columbia. He obtained his PhD from the Film and Media Studies

Department at the University of Kansas. His research is on sexuality in Japanese media, but recently he is also looking into authenticity and nostalgia in contemporary food culture.

Pauline J. Reynolds is associate professor and department chair of leadership and higher education in the School of Education at the University of Redlands in Redlands, California. Pauline's research examines higher education in popular culture, taking into consideration movies, TV, and, more recently, comics. Publications include her monograph "Representing 'U': Popular Culture, Media, and Higher Education" and a coedited book *Anti-Intellectual Representations of American Colleges and Universities: Fictional Higher Education*.

Stefanie Snider is an assistant professor of art history at Kendall College of Art and Design in Grand Rapids, Michigan. Her research focuses on marginalized communities engaged with contemporary visual culture and fine art; more specifically, she works on the ways in which LGBTQ people, women, disabled people, and/or fat people are represented visually and how they represent themselves in multiple media. These include, but are not limited to, performance, photography, and journals and zines.

J. Richard Stevens is an associate professor of media studies at the University of Colorado Boulder. In his research, he delves into the intersection of ideological formation and media message dissemination. This work comprises studies such as how cultural messages are formed and passed through popular culture, how technology infrastructure affects the delivery of media messages, communication technology policy, and related studies in how media and technology platforms are changing American public discourse. Particular interests include the relationship between technology diffusion patterns and American privacy norms, the communication of science in American culture through both news and popular media, conflicts of cultural values regarding digital texts and copyright law, the role of software interface in communicating social norms, and the framing of nationalist ideology in comic books and children's cartoons.

Justin Wigard is earning his PhD in English at Michigan State University, where he was awarded a University Distinguished Fellowship. His most recent academic work, "Harlequin, Nurse, Street Tough: The Visual Evolution from Non-Traditional Harlequin to Sexualized Villain to Subversive Antihero," examines the visual semiotics at play in the evolution of DC Comics' Harley

Quinn's supercostumes as they shift from cartoon to video game to film, in order to reveal how these supercostumes reflect changes in Harley's identity.

Daniel F. Yezbick is professor of English and media studies at Wildwood College in St. Louis, Missouri, where he teaches comics, film studies, interdisciplinary humanities, and writing courses. His essays on world comics have appeared in a variety of anthologies including *The Blacker the Ink: Constructions of Black Identity in Comics and Sequential Art*; *Icons of the American Comic-Book*; *Comics through Time: A History of Icons, Idols, and Ideas*; *The Rise and Reason of Comics and Graphic Literature: Essays on the Form*; and *The Critical Survey of Graphic Novels: History, Theme, and Technique*. He has presented on comics and culture at numerous conferences and public forums and wrote a critical history of animal and animetaphor comics for an anthology edited by David Herman from Bloomsbury in 2017 entitled *Animal Comics: Multispecies Storyworlds in Graphic Narratives*. He is the author of *Perfect Nonsense: The Chaotic Comics and Goofy Games of George Carlson*, from Fantagraphics Press, and he also contributes to Fantagraphics' archival series of classic Walt Disney comics, *The Carl Barks Library*.

Jing Zhang is an assistant professor in the School of Art at the University of Texas Rio Grande Valley (UTRGV). Before joining UTRGV, she also worked as an assistant professor in the Faculty of Humanities and Arts at Macau University of Science and Technology. Dr. Zhang earned her PhD in creative media and MFA in media design and technology from the City University of Hong Kong. She became an Adobe China certificated designer and Macromedia (now Adobe) qualified web designer in 2001. Dr. Zhang also got her expressive art therapy (EAT) training from Prescott College (Arizona). She coined the term and has been teaching "Healing Graphics" to social science students in higher education by US-Mexico border. She has been conducting EAT workshops for acute and forensic patients at the Rio Grande State Center, a state hospital, since 2017.

Index

abjection, 4, 7–9, 12, 52–55, 59–65, 82, 94, 137, 150, 162, 172–74, 180, 182, 184–89, 192, 198, 204–5, 227, 233, 238, 240, 257
able-bodiedness, 8, 85, 87, 90, 95, 96
abortion, 8, 38, 40, 115–21, 131–34, 160, 206, 277
adaptation, 25, 143, 179, 189, 196, 217, 223–24, 227–30, 233, 236–38
adolescence, 9–10, 69, 72, 191–205
Alien, 265
aliens, 257–73. *See also* extraterrestrials
androgyny, 155, 160–62, 166
anxiety, 17, 47, 120, 124, 126–27, 148, 153, 173, 180–81, 191–93, 196, 198, 206, 267, 269
appearance, 5, 22, 25, 46, 56, 62, 71, 107, 160, 164, 172, 178–79, 186, 201–2, 205, 208, 210, 231, 236–37, 247
Arcadia Alvarado, 257–73
artifactuality, 120, 126–27
Asma, Stephen, 129, 132

Baby Talk, 120–22, 133
Barbara Gordon (Batgirl). *See* Batgirl
Barks, Carl, 10, 171–90
Batgirl (Barbara Gordon), 8, 30, 84–98, 100
Batgirl: The Darkest Reflection, 8, 84–98
Batman: Harley Quinn, 23, 30
Bendis, Brian Michael, 126–28, 132
Bennett, Marguerite, 8, 44, 47, 99, 102, 110–12
Beowulf, 223, 229–37
Beowulf: Dragon Slayer, 223, 229, 238
Beowulf: The Graphic Novel, 11, 223–24, 227, 229–33, 235, 237–38
Beowulf (Gummere translation), 223, 228, 238
Beowulf (Old English epic), 223–33, 238

Bible, the, 27–28, 30, 275
bioengineering, 9, 152, 154, 158, 163–64, 167
birth, 8, 9, 18, 21, 22, 24, 48, 54–55, 62–63, 115, 118, 126, 128–29, 130, 134, 158, 160, 265; birthrate, 198, 200, 204
blood, 7, 8, 18, 23, 25, 33, 49, 52, 54–56, 60–64, 66, 100, 110, 143, 155, 162, 196, 209–11, 251, 266, 272
body, 4, 7, 9, 11, 12, 21, 37, 38, 42, 47, 52–53, 59, 62–63, 65, 67, 69–77, 79–83, 85–86, 88, 90, 92–97, 99, 110, 115–16, 120, 124–26, 137, 141, 154, 156–58, 160, 166–67, 173, 181, 187, 192, 194, 198–99, 201–6, 213, 216, 226–27, 234–37, 247, 250–52, 255, 264–67; body horror, 99–100
Bolivia, 9, 12, 135–51
Bolz-Weber, Nadia, 28–29
borders, 8, 11, 15, 52, 86, 119, 129, 148, 186, 231, 260–61
boundaries, 3, 17, 29, 37, 52, 56, 60–61, 70, 73, 85, 104, 158, 181–82, 194, 199, 203, 260, 266
Braidotti, Rosi, 115, 126, 132, 153, 167
Brown, Jeffrey A., 120–21, 128, 133, 135, 150, 266, 271
Bukatman, Scott, 5, 12
Butler, Judith, 125, 133

Calabash Brothers, 212–18
Calabash Brothers, 10, 207–20
capitalism, 71, 80, 191–92, 202, 205
childhood, 6, 9, 63, 152, 169, 249, 259, 264
Chinese snake culture, 218
cholas, 9, 135–51
Christianity, 15, 17, 26–28, 30

Chute, Hillary, 119, 124, 132–33
class (socio-economic), 10, 64, 65, 70, 95, 131, 136–37, 139, 141, 146, 151, 199. *See also* economy
Cocca, Carolyn, 84, 92, 97
Cohen, Jeffrey Jerome, 3–6, 12, 45, 47, 85, 93–94, 97, 120, 128, 133, 135, 148–50, 173, 188, 224, 226–27, 229, 234–35, 238; *Monster Theory*, 3, 12, 47, 93, 97, 133, 150, 188, 238
college, 11, 144, 188, 219–20, 239–56
colonialism, 155, 163–64; colonization, 157, 163–64, 167, 267–69
commodification, 61, 191, 198–99, 203–4, 239
Creed, Barbara, 6, 8, 12, 17, 19, 29, 51–52, 54, 57, 60, 62–65, 85, 92, 94, 97, 173, 180–81, 186, 188, 192, 205, 227, 230, 233–38, 257, 265, 272; *The Monstrous-Feminine*, 12, 29, 52, 63, 65, 97, 206, 238, 272. *See also* monstrous-feminine
cyborgs, 132, 154, 168, 247, 252, 254

DC Comics, 17–24, 26, 29–30, 40, 84, 89, 91, 97–99, 108, 112, 257, 272, 278
DeConnick, Kelly Sue, 7, 51–57, 60–61, 64–66, 111
Deer Woman, 4–5, 11
Deer Woman, x, 4–5, 12
desire, 3, 11, 34–35, 37, 40, 51, 63, 75, 86, 111, 115, 117, 120–21, 126, 128, 140–41, 144, 149, 156, 160, 173–75, 179–82, 189, 192, 196, 198–99, 202–5, 235, 244, 248–50, 264, 269–70
diffracted choice, 120–21
disability, 4–5, 8, 64, 82, 84–85, 87, 89–91, 93–98; disability studies, 5, 70, 85
discourse, 6, 7, 9, 31–33, 35–39, 41, 43, 45–47, 49, 54, 74, 82, 115, 117–18, 125, 127, 136, 146, 148–50, 154, 157, 161, 194, 199, 200, 202, 264, 268, 278
Disney comics, 10, 171, 176, 187, 279
duality, 192, 244–45, 247, 249, 252–53

economy, 9, 10, 71, 137, 191–92, 194, 198, 200, 204–5, 227, 248, 254, 258. *See also* class
environment, 9, 40, 115, 155–56, 158, 161–63, 166, 216, 263
Estrella y el Zorro, La, 136, 140, 143, 150
extraterrestrials, 259, 270. *See also* aliens

Faith, 7, 69, 70–83
Faith Herbert (Zephyr), 8, 69–83
fatness, 7–8, 69–83; fat studies, 70, 81, 82
female, 3, 6–11, 21, 22, 26, 29, 31–37, 41–42, 44, 46, 51–53, 55, 57, 59, 61–63, 65, 69, 70, 72, 74, 79, 83–84, 90, 92, 94, 100, 105, 120, 138, 149, 152–53, 155–64, 166–67, 171–73, 175–79, 182, 184, 185–86, 191–94, 196, 198–203, 205, 210, 215, 217, 224, 226–27, 236–37, 240–44, 252–55, 257–73
femininity, 3, 6, 8, 31, 40, 46–48, 55–57, 65, 72, 74, 120, 142–43, 146, 148–149, 151, 162, 172, 178, 186, 192, 195, 202–3, 205, 215, 267. *See also* monstrous-feminine
feminism, 5, 7, 12, 17, 19, 21, 29, 30–50, 65–66, 71, 79, 82, 97, 112, 124, 127, 129, 132–33, 151, 172–73, 193, 196, 198–99, 238, 241, 244, 254–55, 258, 261, 264, 269–73
fertility, 153, 155, 158, 160–64, 166–67, 200

gender, 3–6, 8–12, 15, 17, 21, 32–33, 35, 37, 44, 46–47, 49–50, 52, 57, 65, 69, 73, 80, 82, 95, 97, 99–101, 103–5, 107–12, 125–26, 128, 132, 138, 146, 151–56, 161, 166–67, 171–73, 175–76, 178–79, 181–82, 185–86, 188, 192–94, 204, 224, 227, 233–35, 241, 243–45, 249, 252–57, 260–61, 263, 271, 273; gender roles, 8, 17, 32, 52, 57, 99–100, 104, 110, 155, 204, 224, 234
genres, 85–87, 90, 93–94, 96, 100–101, 117, 153, 187, 193–94, 199, 258, 263–64, 273
goddesses, 18, 21, 57, 62, 132, 154, 158, 161–62, 167, 208
government, 9, 42, 135, 138, 149, 156, 200, 207, 209, 259, 263, 268
Grendel's mother, 11, 223–31, 233–38
grotesque, 9, 51, 74–75, 79, 115, 136, 144, 172, 174, 185, 187
Gummere, Francis Barton, 223–24, 226, 228–29, 231, 238

Halberstam, Jack (Judith), 125, 133
Haraway, Donna, 7, 12, 99, 112, 115, 120, 124–27, 129, 131, 133, 154, 174, 187, 189–90, 240, 254. *See also* cyborg; promising monsters
Harley Quinn, 6, 15, 17, 19, 21–25, 27, 29–30, 174
Helter Skelter, 191–92, 194, 196–98, 201, 204–6

horror, 3, 5, 9–10, 12, 51–52, 61, 64, 79, 82, 99–101, 112, 137, 144, 150, 174, 178–79, 187–93, 195, 197, 199, 201–3, 205–6, 236–38, 258
hybrids, 5, 45, 64, 92, 127, 148, 155, 167, 172, 186–87, 229, 247, 257, 273; hybridity, 65, 92, 95, 115, 168, 234, 245, 247, 252–53

immigrants, 148, 248, 260, 267–68, 270; immigration, 44, 258, 265, 267, 269
imperialism, 112, 189
Indigenous women, 4–5, 9, 135–36, 138–39, 143; Indigenous people, 146–48, 150, 174
InSEXts, 8, 99–112
international college students, 239, 243, 252
invasion, 234, 252, 258–60, 267–70

Jaguar, The, 11, 239–47, 249, 251–55
Jaguar, the (Maria de Guzman), 11, 239–55
Jen Walters (She-Hulk). *See* She-Hulk
Jessica Drew (Spider-Woman). *See* Spider-Woman
Jessica Jones, 72, 126–28

Kristeva, Julia, 6, 8, 12, 52, 73, 79, 82, 137, 150, 173, 180, 182, 184, 185, 189, 192; *Powers of Horror*, 12, 52, 82, 150, 189, 192

Lady White Snake, 211
liminality, 7, 51–53, 55–57, 59–65, 247, 260–61, 263
Liu, Marjorie, 7, 51–53, 55–66, 111

Madrid, Mike, 32–33, 49, 239, 255
Magica DeSpell, 10, 171–90
manga, 5, 9–10, 12, 140, 144, 152, 154, 164, 191, 193–94, 196, 205, 210, 215, 238
Marginal, 9, 152–67
marginalization, 4, 8, 11, 42, 72, 79, 95, 100, 129, 135–36, 143–44, 149, 187, 202–3, 240–41, 248, 252, 261, 266, 268, 270–71; margins, 3, 11, 12, 94, 118, 141, 143, 157, 189, 227, 260–61
Maria de Guzman (the Jaguar). *See* Jaguar, the
Mars Attacks, 270
Marston, William Moulton, 21, 30
Martians, 270

Marvel Comics, 7, 30, 31–33, 35–36, 39, 41, 43–45, 47–49, 72, 99–100, 108, 111–12, 121, 126, 133, 277
Mary Magdalene, 6, 15, 17, 19, 21, 23, 25–30
masculinity, 7, 31, 34, 41–42, 44, 46, 53, 73, 125, 158, 181, 187, 231, 234–37, 254, 258, 260, 263, 265–66, 269
maternity, 8–9, 19, 115–16, 120–21, 125–26, 129, 132–33, 135–51, 162, 215, 267, 271
McCloud, Scott, 122, 133, 224, 230–31, 234, 238
mestizaje, 136, 143–44, 146–49, 151
methodology, 5, 50, 85, 99, 101–2, 124, 173–74, 184, 226, 231, 254, 260
Mittman, Asa, 240, 255
Monstress, 7, 51–66, 270
monstrosity, 3–9, 11–12, 26, 31, 44, 52, 55–56, 64, 70, 73–74, 79, 84–85, 87, 89, 91, 93–95, 97, 110, 115, 120, 124, 129, 134, 141, 143, 146, 148–50, 153, 156, 158, 163–64, 166–67, 175, 179, 182, 192–93, 196, 198, 201–3, 205, 226–29, 237, 239–44, 247, 249, 251–52, 255, 257–58, 260–61, 270–71
monstrous-feminine, 19, 120, 133, 150, 192, 200–203, 205, 227, 230, 233, 237, 265–66, 271–72. *See also* Creed, Barbara
Morrison, Grant, 18, 30
mothers, 9–11, 21, 34, 53–54, 61–63, 128, 135–51, 152–53, 155, 156–57, 160–66, 179, 195, 198–201, 204, 223–38, 265–66; motherhood, 8, 115, 120, 123, 131, 133, 135–51, 152–53, 162, 200, 206, 267
multiplicity, 79, 124, 156–58

"New 52, The," 19, 21, 23, 25, 30, 84
Nina cholita Andina, 136, 140–43, 151
Noche de Mercado, 136, 139, 143, 145, 151
normativity, 3–4, 6–11, 15, 18, 70, 74–75, 80, 85–87, 92–97, 99–101, 107–9, 120, 125, 131, 146, 173, 181, 196, 201–2, 235, 240
Not Funny Ha-Ha: A Handbook for Something Hard, 116–18, 129, 131–33

obscenity, 57, 64
Old English, 223–24, 226–28, 233
oppression, 4, 42, 44–45, 70, 73, 80, 157, 163, 237, 258, 269–71
orientation, 85–87, 90, 92–93, 96–97, 127

origin story, 6–7, 15–18, 21–22, 26–28
otherness, 7, 11–12, 59, 61, 85–87, 94–97, 99, 101, 105, 112, 120, 126–29, 131, 133, 135–37, 149, 158, 189, 204, 227, 229, 234, 245, 247, 249, 252–53, 257–63, 265–73

patriarchy, 3, 5, 8–11, 15, 17, 19, 22, 26–27, 34–35, 41, 44, 53–54, 75, 99–100, 108, 110, 115, 119, 126, 128, 153, 157, 162, 166–67, 172–73, 176, 178, 182, 184–86, 192–93, 195–96, 198–201, 203–4, 224, 227, 237, 261, 263, 265, 269
phallic symbols, 19, 22, 223–24, 233–36
Pink, 191–92, 194, 196, 200, 202, 204–6
politics, 11, 12, 32, 38, 48–50, 80, 82–83, 97, 112, 115–16, 118, 133, 138, 148, 150–51, 173, 189, 254, 257–61, 263, 265, 267–68, 270–73; politicians, 10, 263, 266, 270; campaigns, 261
pollution, 155, 157–58, 214, 218, 272
postfeminism, 7, 31–33, 35–41, 43, 45–47, 49–50, 271
posthumanism, 9, 152–58, 161, 163–64, 166–67, 271
power, 5–8, 10–12, 15, 17, 19, 21, 23–29, 33–34, 38, 41, 45–46, 48, 52–55, 59–65, 69–73, 75, 79–82, 84, 86–88, 90, 94–95, 97, 99–103, 105, 107–10, 112, 115–16, 119, 121, 124–26, 129, 132, 141, 149–50, 154, 156, 158, 161, 163–64, 166–67, 171–73, 175–76, 178, 180–82, 184–89, 192, 198, 207, 209–14, 217, 224, 226, 234, 237, 239–41, 244, 247, 249–50, 252–53, 258–60, 263, 269–71, 273; empowerment, 4, 6, 9, 32, 34–35, 37, 41–42, 44–47, 52, 61, 70, 74, 102, 118, 131, 149, 161, 179, 182, 236–37, 241, 258
pregnancy, 9, 19, 63, 115–34, 157–58, 160, 192, 196, 266
Pregnant Butch: Nine Long Months Spent in Drag, 124, 126, 128, 130, 133
Pretty Deadly, 7, 51–57, 59–61, 63–66, 270
promising monsters, 12, 112, 115, 119, 132–33, 189, 190. *See also* Haraway, Donna
Pulse, The, 126–28, 132

queerness, 8, 15, 70, 80, 82, 94, 97–98, 99–102, 104–5, 107–12, 125–26, 128–30, 133, 180; queer theory, 70, 85–86, 133, 172

race, 4–5, 11–12, 53, 61–62, 64–66, 69, 82, 151, 190, 239, 242, 248, 253, 256, 257, 260, 271, 273; racism, 61, 80, 128, 138; critical race theory, 5, 72
religion, 27, 29, 148, 150, 163, 192, 204, 209, 210, 217, 248–50
representation, 4–5, 8–9, 11, 26, 32, 46, 69–71, 73–75, 79–81, 83, 86, 97, 104, 111, 116, 120, 124, 127, 135–36, 139–40, 143–44, 146, 149, 167, 188–90, 192, 194–95, 198–99, 201, 224, 229–31, 237, 239–45, 253–56, 265, 268–69
reproduction, 9, 19, 21, 115, 118, 120–21, 125–27, 134, 148, 153–54, 166, 185, 191, 196, 198–200, 202–5; reproductivity, 9, 115, 120, 148, 152–58, 160, 162–63, 166, 193–94, 198, 201, 203, 206, 209, 227, 233, 265
River's Edge, 191–92, 194–96, 198, 201–2, 204–6

Saucer Country/State, 11, 257–73
Savage She-Hulk, The, 32–33, 35, 37–38, 41, 48, 244
science fiction, 11, 152–53, 157, 161, 167–68, 215, 257–58, 271–73
Scrooge McDuck (Uncle), 10, 171–90
Sensational She-Hulk, The, 32, 36–40, 44, 46–50
sexism, 32, 34–35, 80, 116, 153, 171, 175–76, 203, 227, 243, 255, 264
sexuality, 4, 8, 10–11, 36–37, 46, 87, 94–95, 99–100, 110, 125, 131, 151, 162, 172, 174–75, 179, 188, 191–94, 196, 198–200, 204–6, 224, 227, 233, 236–37, 250, 265, 267
She-Hulk, 40–44, 47–50
She-Hulk (Jen Walters), 7, 31–50
Shildrick, Margrit, 6–7, 12, 73, 79, 83, 99, 112; *Embodying the Monster*, 12, 83
shōjo (adolescent women), 191, 193–94, 196
Simone, Gail, 8, 84–97, 110, 112
SF (science fiction), 153–54, 258, 261, 263–65, 267–70
snake woman, 10, 207–20. *See also* Chinese snake culture
speculative fiction, 153–55
Spider-Woman (Jessica Drew), 120–22, 133
superhero, 7–8, 12, 17–18, 26, 30–32, 34, 36–37, 40, 44–49, 69–76, 79–83, 84–88, 90, 92–97,

100, 110, 117, 121, 125, 132–33, 150, 239, 243–44, 253, 271

teratology, 132, 224
Trump, Donald, 263–65, 267–68, 271–72

UFOs, 11, 257, 259–61, 263, 265–67, 269, 271, 273
ugliness, 70, 74, 79, 80, 82–83, 184
Unbeatable Squirrel Girl, The, 16, 30

vagina dentata, 233, 236, 269
violence, 4–5, 8, 11–12, 24–26, 44, 51–55, 59, 62, 64, 80, 95, 100–12, 178, 192, 194, 201, 206, 215, 239, 242, 253, 263–65
visual rhetoric, 11, 101, 223–25, 227–31, 233–37

Wonder Woman, 18–20, 29–30, 243, 253
Wonder Woman (Diana Prince), 6, 15–30, 48, 72, 112, 243, 253

X-Files, The, 257, 264, 271

yaoguai (monster), 208

Zephyr (Faith Herbert), 8, 69, 75–76, 81–82. See also *Faith*; Faith Herbert

www.ingramcontent.com/pod-product-compliance
Lightning Source LLC
Chambersburg PA
CBHW082103250426
43661CB00079B/2618